THE NEW FOLGER LIBRARY SHAKESPEARE

Designed to make Shakespeare's plays and poems available to all readers, the New Folger Library edition of Shakespeare provides accurate texts in modern spelling and punctuation, as well as full explanatory notes, many pictures clarifying Shakespeare's language, and notes recording all significant departures from the early printed versions. Each play or collection of poems is prefaced by a brief introduction and by a guide to reading Shakespeare's language. Each is followed by an annotated list of further readings and by a "Modern Perspective" written by an expert on that particular work.

Barbara A. Mowat is Director of Academic Programs at the Folger Shakespeare Library, Executive Editor of *Shakespeare Quarterly,* Chair of the Folger Institute, and author of *The Dramaturgy of Shakespeare's Romances* and of essays on Shakespeare's plays and on the editing of Shakespeare.

Paul Werstine is Professor of English at the Graduate School and at King's University College at the University of Western Ontario. He is general editor of the New Variorum Shakespeare and author of many papers and articles on the printing and editing of Shakespeare's plays.

The Folger Shakespeare Library

The Folger Shakespeare Library in Washington, D.C., a privately funded research library dedicated to Shakespeare and the civilization of early modern Europe, was founded in 1932 by Henry Clay and Emily Jordan Folger. In addition to its role as the world's preeminent Shakespeare collection and its emergence as a leading center for Renaissance studies, the Folger Library offers a wide array of cultural and educational programs and services for the general public.

EDITORS

BARBARA A. MOWAT
Director of Academic Programs
Folger Shakespeare Library

PAUL WERSTINE
Professor of English
King's University College at the University of
Western Ontario, Canada

FOLGER SHAKESPEARE LIBRARY

Shakespeare's Sonnets and Poems

EDITED BY BARBARA A. MOWAT
AND PAUL WERSTINE

WASHINGTON SQUARE PRESS
New York   London   Toronto   Sydney

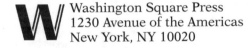 Washington Square Press
1230 Avenue of the Americas
New York, NY 10020

ISBN-13: 978-0-7432-7328-2
ISBN-10:   0-7432-7328-1

Washington Square Press New Folger Library Trade Paperback
Edition July 2006

10   9   8   7   6   5   4   3   2   1

WASHINGTON SQUARE PRESS and colophon are registered
trademarks of Simon & Schuster, Inc.

Manufactured in the United States of America

For information regarding special discounts for bulk purchases,
please contact Simon & Schuster Special Sales at 1-800-456-6798
or business@simonandschuster.com.

From the Director of the Library

Shakespeare has never been more alive as author, playwright, and poet than he is today, with productions being staged all over the world, new film versions appearing on screen every year, and millions of students in classrooms at all levels absorbed in the human drama and verbal richness of his works.

The New Folger Library Shakespeare editions welcome the interested reader with newly edited texts, commentary in a friendly facing-page format, and illustrations, drawn from the Folger archives, that wonderfully illuminate references and images in the plays and poems.

In these editions, students, teachers, actors, and thousands of other readers will find the best of modern textual scholarship and up-to-date critical essays, written especially for these volumes, that offer original and often surprising interpretations of Shakespeare's characters, action, and language.

I thank editors Barbara Mowat and Paul Werstine for undertaking this ambitious project, which is nothing less than an entirely new look at the texts from the earliest printed versions. Lovers of Shakespeare everywhere must be grateful for the breadth of their learning, the liveliness of their imaginations, and the scholarly rigor that they bring to the challenge of re-editing the plays and poems.

Gail Kern Paster, Director
The Folger Shakespeare Library

Contents

Editors' Preface

In recent years, ways of dealing with Shakespeare's texts and with the interpretation of his plays and poems have been undergoing significant change. This edition, while retaining many of the features that have always made the Folger Shakespeare so attractive to the general reader, at the same time reflects these current ways of thinking about Shakespeare. For example, modern readers, actors, and teachers have become interested in the differences between, on the one hand, the early forms in which Shakespeare's plays and poems were first published and, on the other hand, the forms in which editors through the centuries have presented them. In response to this interest, we have based our edition on what we consider the best early printed version of a particular play, poem, or collection of poems (explaining our rationale in a section called "An Introduction to This Text") and have marked our changes in the text—unobtrusively, we hope, but in such a way that the curious reader can be aware that a change has been made and can consult the "Textual Notes" to discover what appeared in the early printed version.

Current ways of looking at the plays and poems are reflected in our brief prefaces, in many of the commentary notes, in the annotated lists of "Further Reading," and especially in each edition's "Modern Perspective," an essay written by an outstanding scholar who brings to the reader his or her fresh assessment of the play, poem, or collection of poems in the light of today's interests and concerns.

As in the Folger Library General Reader's Shakespeare, which this edition replaces, we include explanatory notes designed to help make Shakespeare's language clearer to a modern reader, and we place the notes on the page facing the text that they explain. We also follow the earlier edition in including illustrations—of objects, of clothing, of mythological figures—from books and manuscripts in the Folger Library collection. We provide a brief account of the life of Shakespeare and an introduction to the text of the *Sonnets* and one to the texts of the poems. We also include essays on "Reading Shakespeare's Language" in the *Sonnets* and in the poems. In both we try to help readers learn to "break the code" of Elizabethan poetic language.

For each section of each volume, we are indebted to a host of generous experts and fellow scholars. The "Reading Shakespeare's Language" sections, for example, could not have been written had not Arthur King, of Brigham Young University, and Randall Robinson, author of *Unlocking Shakespeare's Language,* led the way in untangling Shakespearean language puzzles and shared their insights and methodologies generously with us. "Shakespeare's Life" profited by the careful reading given it by the late S. Schoenbaum. Our commentary notes in this volume were enormously improved through consultation of several of the more recent scholarly editions of the *Sonnets.* These editions are listed in our "Introduction to This Text," page 15. We, as editors, take sole responsibility for any errors in our editions.

We are grateful to the authors of the "Modern Perspectives"; to Peter Hawkins, Steven May, and Marion Trousdale for helpful conversations about the *Sonnets;* to the Huntington and Newberry Libraries for fellowship support; to King's University College for the grants it has provided to Paul Werstine; to the Social Sciences and Humanities Research Council of Canada, which provided him with a Research Time Stipend for 1990–91; to R. J. Shroyer of the University of Western Ontario for essential computer support; to the Folger Institute's Center for Shakespeare Studies for its sponsorship of a workshop on "Shakespeare's Texts for Students and Teachers" (funded by the National Endowment for the Humanities and led by Richard Knowles of the University of Wisconsin), a workshop from which we learned an enormous amount about what is wanted by college and high-school teachers of Shakespeare today; to Alice Falk for her expert copyediting; and especially to Stephen Llano, our production editor at Washington Square Press, whose expertise and attention to detail are essential to this project.

Our biggest debt is to the Folger Shakespeare Library—to Gail Kern Paster, Director of the Library, whose interest and support are unfailing, and to Werner Gundersheimer, the Library's Director from 1984 to 2002, who made possible our edition; to Deborah

Curren-Aquino, who provides extensive editorial and production support; to Jean Miller, the Library's former Art Curator, who combs the Library holdings for illustrations, and to Julie Ainsworth, Head of the Photography Department, who carefully photographs them; to Peggy O'Brien, former Director of Education at the Folger and now Director of Education Programs at the Corporation for Public Broadcasting, who gave us expert advice about the needs being expressed by Shakespeare teachers and students (and to Martha Christian and other "master teachers" who used our texts in manuscripts in their classrooms); to Allan Shnerson and Mary Bloodworth for their expert computer support; to the staff of the Academic Programs Division, especially Solvei Robertson (whose help is crucial), Mary Tonkinson, Mimi Godfrey, Kathleen Lynch, Carol Brobeck, Liz Pohland, Owen Williams, and Virginia Millington; and, finally, to the generously supportive staff of the Library's Reading Room.

Barbara A. Mowat and Paul Werstine

A stylized representation of the Globe theater.

Shakespeare's Life

Surviving documents that give us glimpses into the life of William Shakespeare show us a playwright, poet, and actor who grew up in the market town of Stratford-upon-Avon, spent his professional life in London, and returned to Stratford a wealthy landowner. He was born in April 1564, died in April 1616, and is buried inside the chancel of Holy Trinity Church in Stratford.

We wish we could know more about the life of the world's greatest dramatist. His plays and poems are testaments to his wide reading—especially to his knowledge of Virgil, Ovid, Plutarch, Holinshed's *Chronicles,* and the Bible—and to his mastery of the English language, but we can only speculate about his education. We know that the King's New School in Stratford-upon-Avon was considered excellent. The school was one of the English "grammar schools" established to educate young men, primarily in Latin grammar and literature. As in other schools of the time, students began their studies at the age of four or five in the attached "petty school," and there learned to read and write in English, studying primarily the catechism from the Book of Common Prayer. After two years in the petty school, students entered the lower form (grade) of the grammar school, where they began the serious study of Latin grammar and Latin texts that would occupy most of the remainder of their school days. (Several Latin texts that Shakespeare used repeatedly in writing his plays and poems were texts that schoolboys memorized and recited.) Latin comedies were introduced early in the lower form; in the upper form, which the boys entered at age ten or eleven, students wrote their own Latin orations and declamations, studied Latin historians and rhetoricians, and began the study of Greek using the Greek New Testament.

Since the records of the Stratford "grammar school" do not survive, we cannot prove that William Shakespeare attended the school; however, every indication (his father's position as an alderman and bailiff of Stratford, the playwright's own knowledge of the Latin classics, scenes in the plays that recall grammar-school experiences—for example, *The Merry Wives of Windsor* 4.1) suggests that he did. We also lack generally accepted documentation about Shakespeare's life after his schooling ended and his professional life in London began. His marriage in 1582 (at age eighteen) to Anne Hathaway and the subsequent births of his daughter Susanna (1583) and the twins Judith and Hamnet (1585) are recorded, but how he supported himself and where he lived are not known. Nor do we know when and why he left Stratford for the London theatrical world, nor how he rose to be the important figure in that world that he had become by the early 1590s.

We do know that by 1592 he had achieved some prominence in London as both an actor and a playwright. In that year was published a book by the playwright Robert Greene attacking an actor who had the audacity to write blank-verse drama and who was "in his own conceit [i.e., opinion] the only Shake-scene in a country." Since Greene's attack includes a parody of a line from one of Shakespeare's early plays, there is little doubt that it is Shakespeare to whom he refers, a "Shake-scene" who had aroused Greene's fury by successfully competing with university-educated dramatists like Greene himself. It was in 1593 that Shakespeare became a published poet. In that year he published his long narrative poem *Venus and Adonis;* in 1594, he followed it with *Lucrece.* Both poems were dedicated to the young earl of Southampton (Henry Wriothesley), who may have become Shakespeare's patron.

It seems no coincidence that Shakespeare wrote these narrative poems at a time when the theaters were closed because of the plague, a contagious epidemic disease that devastated the population of London. When the theaters reopened in 1594, Shakespeare apparently resumed his double career of actor and playwright and began his long (and seemingly profitable) service as an acting-company shareholder. Records for December of 1594 show him to be a leading member of the Lord Chamberlain's Men. It was this company of actors, later named the King's Men, for whom he would be a principal actor, dramatist, and shareholder for the rest of his career.

So far as we can tell, that career spanned about twenty years. In the 1590s, he wrote his plays on English history as well as several comedies and at least two tragedies (*Titus Andronicus* and *Romeo and Juliet*). These histories, comedies, and tragedies are the plays credited to him in 1598 in a work, *Palladis Tamia,* that in one chapter compares English writers with "Greek, Latin, and Italian Poets." There the author, Francis Meres, claims that Shakespeare is comparable to the Latin dramatists Seneca for tragedy and Plautus for comedy, and calls him "the most excellent in both kinds for the stage." He also names him "Mellifluous and honey-tongued Shakespeare": "I say," writes Meres, "that the Muses would speak with Shakespeare's fine filed phrase, if they would speak English." Since Meres also mentions Shakespeare's "sugared sonnets among his private friends," it is assumed that many of Shakespeare's sonnets (not published until 1609) were also written in the 1590s.

In 1599, Shakespeare's company built a theater for themselves across the river from London, naming it the Globe. The plays that are considered by many to be Shakespeare's major tragedies (*Hamlet, Othello, King Lear,* and *Macbeth*) were written while the company was resident in this theater, as were such comedies as *Twelfth Night* and *Measure for Measure.* Many of Shakespeare's plays were performed at court (both for Queen Elizabeth I and, after her death in 1603, for King James I), some were presented at the Inns of Court (the residences of London's legal societies), and some were doubtless performed in other towns, at the universities, and at great houses when the King's Men went on tour; otherwise, his plays from 1599 to 1608 were, so far as we know, performed only at the Globe. Between 1608 and 1612, Shakespeare wrote several plays—among them *The Winter's Tale* and *The Tempest*—presumably for the company's new indoor Blackfriars theater, though the plays seem to have been performed also at the Globe and at court. Surviving documents describe a performance of *The Winter's Tale* in 1611 at the Globe, for example, and performances of *The Tempest* in 1611 and 1613 at the royal palace of Whitehall.

Shakespeare wrote very little after 1612, the year in which he probably wrote *King Henry VIII.* (It was at a performance of *Henry VIII* in 1613 that the Globe caught fire and burned to the ground.) Sometime between 1610 and 1613 he seems to have returned to live in Stratford-upon-Avon, where he owned a large house and considerable property, and where his wife and his two daughters and their husbands lived. (His son Hamnet had died in 1596.) During his professional years in London, Shakespeare had presumably derived in-

come from the acting company's profits as well as from his own career as an actor, from the sale of his play manuscripts to the acting
company, and, after 1599, from his shares as an owner of the Globe.
It was presumably that income, carefully invested in land and other
property, which made him the wealthy man that surviving documents show him to have become. It is also assumed that William
Shakespeare's growing wealth and reputation played some part in
inclining the crown, in 1596, to grant John Shakespeare, William's
father, the coat of arms that he had so long sought. William Shakespeare died in Stratford on April 23, 1616 (according to the epitaph
carved under his bust in Holy Trinity Church) and was buried on
April 25. Seven years after his death, his collected plays were published as *Mr. William Shakespeares Comedies, Histories, & Tragedies*
(the work now known as the First Folio).

The years in which Shakespeare wrote were among the most exciting in English history. Intellectually, the discovery, translation,
and printing of Greek and Roman classics were making available
a set of works and worldviews that interacted complexly with Christian texts and beliefs. The result was a questioning, a vital intellectual ferment, that provided energy for the period's amazing
dramatic and literary output and that fed directly into Shakespeare's plays. The Ghost in *Hamlet*, for example, is wonderfully
complicated in part because he is a figure from Roman tragedy—
the spirit of the dead returning to seek revenge—who at the same
time inhabits a Christian hell (or purgatory); Hamlet's description
of humankind reflects at one moment the Neoplatonic wonderment
at mankind ("What a piece of work is a man!") and, at the next, the
Christian disparagement of human sinners ("And yet, to me, what is
this quintessence of dust?").

As intellectual horizons expanded, so also did geographical and
cosmological horizons. New worlds—both North and South America—were explored, and in them were found human beings who
lived and worshiped in ways radically different from those of Renaissance Europeans and Englishmen. The universe during these
years also seemed to shift and expand. Copernicus had earlier theo-
rized that the earth was not the center of the cosmos but revolved as
a planet around the sun. Galileo's telescope, created in 1609, allowed scientists to see that Copernicus had been correct; the uni-

verse was not organized with the earth at the center, nor was it so nicely circumscribed as people had, until that time, thought. In terms of expanding horizons, the impact of these discoveries on people's beliefs—religious, scientific, and philosophical—cannot be overstated.

London, too, rapidly expanded and changed during the years (from the early 1590s to around 1610) that Shakespeare lived there. London—the center of England's government, its economy, its royal court, its overseas trade—was, during these years, becoming an exciting metropolis, drawing to it thousands of new citizens every year. Troubled by overcrowding, by poverty, by recurring epidemics of the plague, London was also a mecca for the wealthy and the aristocratic, and for those who sought advancement at court, or power in government or finance or trade. One hears in Shakespeare's plays the voices of London—the struggles for power, the fear of venereal disease, the language of buying and selling. One hears as well the voices of Stratford-upon-Avon—references to the nearby Forest of Arden, to sheepherding, to small-town gossip, to village fairs and markets. Part of the richness of Shakespeare's work is the influence felt there of the various worlds in which he lived: the world of metropolitan London, the world of small-town and rural England, the world of the theater, and the worlds of craftsmen and shepherds.

That Shakespeare inhabited such worlds we know from surviving London and Stratford documents, as well as from the evidence of the plays and poems themselves. From such records we can sketch the dramatist's life. We know from his works that he was a voracious reader. We know from legal and business documents that he was a multifaceted theater man who became a wealthy landowner. We know a bit about his family life and a fair amount about his legal and financial dealings. Most scholars today depend upon such evidence as they draw their picture of the world's greatest playwright. Such, however, has not always been the case. Until the late eighteenth century, the William Shakespeare who lived in most biographies was the creation of legend and tradition. This was the Shakespeare who was supposedly caught poaching deer at Charlecote, the estate of Sir Thomas Lucy close by Stratford; this was the Shakespeare who fled from Sir Thomas's vengeance and made his way in London by taking care of horses outside a playhouse; this was the Shakespeare who reportedly could barely read but whose natural gifts were extraordinary, whose father was a butcher who allowed his gifted son sometimes to help in the butcher shop, where William supposedly killed calves "in a high style," making a speech for the occasion. It was this legendary William Shakespeare whose Falstaff (in *1* and *2 Henry IV*) so pleased Queen Elizabeth that she demanded a play about Falstaff in love, and demanded that it be written in fourteen days (hence the existence of *The Merry Wives of Windsor*). It was this legendary Shakespeare who reached the top of his acting career in the roles of the Ghost in *Hamlet* and old Adam in *As You Like It*—and who died of a fever contracted by drinking too hard at "a merry meeting" with the poets Michael Drayton and Ben Jonson. This legendary Shakespeare is a rambunctious, undisciplined man, as attractively "wild" as his plays were seen by earlier generations to be. Unfortunately, there is no trace of evidence to support these wonderful stories.

Perhaps in response to the disreputable Shakespeare of legend—or perhaps in response to the fragmentary and, for some, all-too-

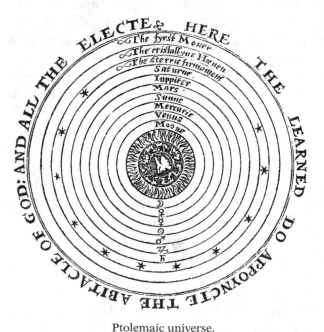

Ptolemaic universe.

ordinary Shakespeare documented by surviving records—some people since the mid–nineteenth century have argued that William Shakespeare could not have written the plays that bear his name. These persons have put forward some dozen names as more likely authors, among them Queen Elizabeth, Sir Francis Bacon, Edward de Vere (earl of Oxford), and Christopher Marlowe. Such attempts to find what for these people is a more believable author of the plays is a tribute to the regard in which the plays are held. Unfortunately for their claims, the documents that exist that provide evidence for the facts of Shakespeare's life tie him inextricably to the body of plays and poems that bear his name. Unlikely as it seems to those who want the works to have been written by an aristocrat, a university graduate, or an "important" person, the plays and poems seem clearly to have been produced by a man from Stratford-upon-Avon with a very good "grammar-school" education and a life of experience in London and in the world of the London theater. How this particular man produced the works that dominate the cultures of much of the world almost four hundred years after his death is one of life's mysteries—and one that will continue to tease our imaginations as we continue to delight in his plays and poems.

SHAKESPEARE'S
SONNETS

Reading Shakespeare's Language: *Sonnets*

The language of Shakespeare's *Sonnets*, like that of poetry in general, is both highly compressed and highly structured. While most often discussed in terms of its images and its metrical and other formal structures, the language of the *Sonnets*, like that of Shakespeare's plays, also repays close attention to such basic linguistic elements as words, word order, and sentence structure.

Shakespeare's Words

Because Shakespeare's sonnets were written four hundred years ago, they inevitably contain words that are unfamiliar today. Some are words that are no longer in general use—words that the dictionaries label *archaic* or *obsolete,* or that have so fallen out of use that dictionaries no longer include them. One surprising feature of the *Sonnets* is how rarely such archaic words appear. Among the more than a thousand words that make up the first ten sonnets, for instance, only eleven are not to be found in current usage: *self-substantial* ("derived from one's own substance"), *niggarding* ("being miserly"), *unfair* ("deprive of beauty"), *leese* ("lose"), *happies* ("makes happy"), *steep-up* ("precipitous"), *highmost* ("highest"), *hap* ("happen"), *unthrift* ("spendthrift"), *unprovident* ("improvident"), and *ruinate* ("reduce to ruins"). Somewhat more common in the *Sonnets* are words that are still in use but that in Shakespeare's day had meanings that are no longer current. In the first three sonnets, for example, we find *only* used where we might say "peerless" or "preeminent," *gaudy* used to mean "brilliantly fine," *weed* where we would say "garment," *glass* where we would say "mirror," and *fond* where we would say "foolish." Words of this kind—that is, words that are no longer used or that are used with unfamiliar meanings—will be defined in our facing-page notes.

The most significant feature of Shakespeare's word choice in the *Sonnets* is his use of words in which multiple meanings function simultaneously. In line 5 of the first sonnet, for example, the word *contracted* means "bound by contract, bethrothed," but it also carries the sense of "limited, shrunken." Its double meaning enables the phrase "contracted to thine own bright eyes" to say succinctly to the young man not only that he has betrothed himself to his own good looks but that he has also thereby become a more limited person. In a later line in the same sonnet ("Within thine own bud buriest thy content" [s. 1.11]), the fact that *thy content* means both (1) "that which is contained within you, specifically, your seed, that with which you should produce a child," and (2) "your happiness" enables the line to say, in a highly compressed fashion, that by refusing to propagate, refusing to have a child, the young man is destroying his own future well-being.

It is in large part through choosing words that carry more than one pertinent meaning that Shakespeare packs into each sonnet almost incalculable richness of thought and imagery. In the opening line of the first sonnet ("From fairest creatures we desire increase"), each of the words *fairest, creatures,* and *increase* carries multiple relevant senses; when these combine with each other, the range of significations in this single line is enormous. In Shakespeare's day, the word *fair* primarily meant "beautiful," but it had recently also picked up the meaning of "blond" and "fair-skinned." In this opening line of Sonnet 1, the meaning "blond" is probably not operative (though it becomes extremely pertinent when the word *fair* is used in later sonnets), but the aristocratic (or upper-class) implications of "fair-skinned" are very much to the point (or so argues Margreta de Grazia; see Further Reading), since upper-class gentlemen and ladies need not work out of doors and expose their skins to wind and sun. (The negative class implications of outdoor labor carried in the sonnets by "dark" or "tanned" are carried today in the label "redneck.") The second word, *creatures,* had several meanings, referring, for example, to everything created by God, including the plant kingdom, while in some contexts referring specifically to human beings. When combined with the third word, *increase* (which meant, among its pertinent definitions, "procreation," "breeding," "offspring," "a child," "crops," and "fruit"), the word *creatures* takes the reader's mind to Genesis 1.28 and God's instructions to humankind to multiply and be fruitful, while the plant-life connotation of all three of the words provides a context for later words in the sonnet, such as *rose, famine, abundance, spring,* and *bud.* The words Shakespeare places in this first line ("From *fairest creatures* we desire *increase*")—with their undoubted link to concerns about upper-class propagation and inheritance—could well have alerted a contemporary reader to the sonnet's place in a familiar rhetorical tradition, that concerned with persuading a young gentleman to marry in order to reproduce and thus secure his family line and its heritable property. (See Erasmus's "Epistle to persuade a young gentleman to marriage," excerpted in the Appendix, pages 619–24.)

While almost every line of the 154 sonnets begs for a comparable unpacking of Shakespeare's words, we will here limit ourselves to two additional examples, these from lines 2 and 4 of the same sonnet (Sonnet 1). First, the word *rose* in the phrase *beauty's rose* (line 2) engages the reader's mind and imagination at many levels. Most simply, it refers simultaneously to the rose blossom and the rosebush; this double signification, as Stephen Booth points out (see Further Reading), enables the sonnet to acknowledge that although the individual person, like the rose blossom, inevitably withers and dies, the family line, like the rosebush, lives on through continual *increase.* But the *rose* signifies as well that which is most beautiful in the natural world. (See, e.g., Isaiah 35.1: "The desert and the wilderness shall rejoice; the waste ground shall be glad and flourish as the rose.") And *beauty's rose* not only meant youthful beauty but also inevitably called up memories of the *Romance of the Rose* (widely published in Chaucer's translation), in which the *rose* stands allegorically for the goal of the lover's quest. (The fact that the lover in the *Romance* desires a specific unopened rosebud, rather than one of the rosebush's opened flowers, may have implications for the word *bud* in line 11.)

The word *rose,* then, gains its multiple resonances by referring to both a flower and its bush and through meanings accumulated in cultural and poetic traditions. In contrast, the particular verbal richness of the word *his* in line 4, "*His* tender heir might bear *his* memory" (and in many of the other sonnets), exists because Shakespeare took advantage of a language change in process at the very time he was writing. Until around 1600 the pronoun *his* served double duty, meaning both *his* and *its.* However, in the late 1590s and early 1600s, the word *its* came into existence as possessive of *it*, and *his* began gradually to be limited to the meaning it has today as the possessive of *he*. Because of the emerging gender implications of *his*, the pronoun as used in line 4, while primarily meaning *its* and thus referring to *beauty's rose*, also serves as a link between the sonnet's first line, where the *fairest* creature is not yet a *rose*, and the young man, first directly addressed in line 5.

Because the diction of the *Sonnets* is so incredibly rich in meanings, and because space for our facing-page notes is limited, we have had to curtail severely our notes on words with multiple meanings. Where the primary meaning of a word is clear and where secondary meanings are readily available or are not essential to an understanding of the poem, we all too often have had to remain silent. When it seems possible that a given word might have more than one relevant meaning, the reader should test out possible additional meanings and decide if they add richness to the line. The only hazard here is that some words have picked up new meanings since Shakespeare's death; careful study of the diction of his *Sonnets* thus compels one to turn to a dictionary based on historical principles, such as the *Oxford English Dictionary*.

Shakespeare's Sentences

When Shakespeare made the decision to compose his *Sonnets* using the English (in contrast to the Italian) sonnet form, he seems at the same time to have settled on the shape of the *Sonnets'* sentences. The two forms are distinguished by rhyme scheme: in the Italian sonnet, the rhyme scheme in effect divides the poem into two sections, the eight-line *octave* followed by the six-line *sestet;* in the English, it sets three four-line quatrains in parallel, followed by the two-line rhyming couplet. While Shakespeare finds almost infinite ways to provide variety within the tightly controlled form of the English sonnet, and while the occasional sonnet is made up of a single sentence (e.g., Sonnet 29), his sentences tend to shape themselves within the bounds set by the quatrain and the couplet—that is, most quatrains and most couplets are each made up of one sentence or question, with occasional quatrains made up of two or more sentences or questions. (Quatrains that, in modern printed editions, end with a semicolon rather than a period or question mark are often so marked only to indicate that the thought continues into the next quatrain; syntactically, the clause is generally independent and could be completed with a period instead.) The reader therefore seldom finds in the *Sonnets* the long, complicated sentences often encountered in Shakespeare's plays. One does, though, find within the sentences the inversions, the interruptions of normal word order, and the postponements of essential sentence elements that are familiar to readers of the plays.

In the *Sonnets* as in the plays, for example, Shakespeare often rearranges subjects and verbs (i.e., instead of "He goes" we find "Goes he"); he frequently places the object before the subject and verb (i.e., instead of "I hit him," we might find "Him I hit"), and he puts adverbs and adverbial phrases before the subject and verb (i.e., "I hit fairly" becomes "Fairly I hit"). The first sonnet in the sequence, in fact, opens with an inversion, with the adverbial phrase "From fairest creatures" moved forward from its ordinary syntactical position after the verb. This transformation of the sentence "We desire increase from fairest creatures" into "From fairest creatures we desire increase" (s. 1.1) has a significant effect on the rhythm of the line and places the emphasis of the sentence immediately on the "fairest" creature who will be the topic of this and many sonnets to follow. In Sonnet 2 the sentence "Thy beauty's use would deserve much more praise" is transformed into "How much more praise deserved thy beauty's use" (s. 2.9), in large part through a double inversion: the transposing of the subject ("thy beauty's use") and the verb ("deserved") and the placing of the object before the inverted subject and verb. Again, the impact on the rhythm of the line is significant, and the bringing of the word *praise* toward the beginning of the line emphasizes the word's echo of and link to the preceding line ("Were an all-eating shame and thriftless praise") through its reiteration of the word *praise* and through repetition of the vowel sound in *shame*.

Occasionally the inversions in the *Sonnets* seem primarily to provide the poet with a needed rhyme word. In Sonnet 3, for example, the difference between *"she calls back / In thee the lovely April of her prime"* and *"she in thee / Calls back the lovely April of her prime"* (s. 3.9–10) seems largely to rest on the poet's choice of "thee" rather than "back" for the sonnet's rhyme scheme. However, Shakespeare's inversions in the *Sonnets* often create a space for ambiguity and thus for increased richness and compression. Sometimes the ambiguity exists only for a moment, until the eye and mind progress further along the line and the reader sees that one of the initially possible meanings cannot be sustained. For example, in Sonnet 5, the line "And that unfair which fairly doth excel" (s. 5.4) seems initially to present "that unfair" as the demonstrative adjective *that* followed by another adjective, *unfair*, until a reading of the whole line reveals that there is no noun for these apparent adjectives to modify, and that "that unfair" is more likely an inversion of the verb *to unfair* and its object, the pronoun *that*. The line thus means simply "deprive that of beauty which fairly excels"—though wordplay on *fairly* as (1) "completely," (2) "properly," and/or (3) "in beauty" makes the line far from simple.

Often the doubleness of meaning created by the inversion remains unresolved. In Sonnet 3, for example, the line "But if thou live remembered not to be" (s. 3.13) clearly contains an inversion in the words "remembered not to be"; however, it is unclear whether "remembered not to be" inverts "to be not remembered" (i.e., "[only] to be forgotten") or "not to be remembered" (i.e., "[in order] to be forgotten"). Thus, while the primary meaning of the line may well be "if you live in such a way that you will not be remembered," the reader cannot dismiss the line's simultaneous suggestion that the young man is living "with the intent of being forgotten" (Booth). The inversion, in other words, allows the line to carry two distinct tones, one of warning and the other of accusation.

Inversions are not the only unusual sentence structures in Shakespeare's language. Often in his *Sonnets* as in his plays, words that would in a normal English sentence appear together are separated from each other, usually in order to create a particular rhythm or to stress a particular word or phrase. In Sonnet 1, for example, in lines 5–6 ("But *thou*, contracted to thine own bright eyes, / *Feed'st* thy light's flame with self-substantial fuel"), the subject *thou* is separated from its verb *feed'st* by a phrase that, because of its placement, focuses sharp attention on the young man's looks and the behavior that the poet sees as defining him. A few lines later in the same sonnet,

Thou that art now the world's fresh ornament
And only herald to the gaudy spring
Within thine own bud *buriest* thy content . . .

(lines 9–11)

the subject *Thou* is separated from its verb *buriest,* first by a clause
that in its extreme praise ("that art now the world's fresh ornament
/ And only herald to the gaudy spring") is in interesting and direct
contrast to the tone of accusation of the basic sentence elements
within which the clause is set ("Thou buriest thy content"); the separation is further extended through the inversion that moves forward a prepositional phrase ("Within thine own bud") that would in
ordinary syntax come after the verb. Line 12 of this same sonnet—
"And, *tender churl,* mak'st waste in niggarding"—exemplifies a familiar kind of interruption in these poems, namely, an interjected
compound vocative. Direct address to the beloved in the form of
compound epithets, especially where one term of the compound
("tender") contradicts the other ("churl"), in meaning or in tone, is a
device that Shakespeare uses frequently in the *Sonnets,* heightening
the emotional tone and creating the kind of puzzle that makes the
poems so intellectually intriguing. (Sonnet 4, for example, contains
three such vocatives: "Unthrifty loveliness," "beauteous niggard,"
and "Profitless usurer.")

Sometimes, rather than separating basic sentence elements,
Shakespeare simply holds back the subject and predicate, delaying
them until other material to which he wants to give particular emphasis has been presented. The first quatrain of Sonnet 2 holds off
until line 3 the presentation of the subject of the sentence, and delays the verb until line 4:

When forty winters shall besiege thy brow
And dig deep trenches in thy beauty's field,
Thy youth's proud *livery,* so gazed on now,
Will be a tattered weed of small worth held.

In this quatrain, the subject and predicate, "thy . . . livery . . . will be
a tattered weed," are held back while for two lines the poet draws a
vivid picture of the young man as he will look in middle age. Son-

net 2 is, in effect, an attempt to persuade, an exhortation to the recipient to change; the powerful description of youth attacked by the
forces of time gains much of its strength from its placement in advance of the basic sentence elements. (One need only reverse the
order of the lines, placing lines 3–4 before lines 1–2, to see how
much power the poem loses with that reversal.)

In addition to the delaying device, the quatrain contains two further Shakespearean sentence strategies—a subject/verb interruption in lines 3–4 followed by a compression in line 4. The phrase "so
gazed on now," which separates the subject and verb ("livery . . .
will be"), stresses both the beauty of the young man and the briefness of the moment for which that beauty will exist. The last line, an
example of the kind of compression that one finds throughout the
Sonnets, would, if fully unpacked and its inversion reversed, read
"[that will be] held [to be] a tattered weed of small worth."

Metaphor and Metrical Effects

This first quatrain of Sonnet 2 can serve as a small example not only
of some of Shakespeare's sentence strategies but also of how his
word choice and word order operate to create the visual and musical effects that distinguish the Sonnets. While this topic is so large
that we can only touch on it here, it seems appropriate to look at
least briefly at two of the Sonnets' most important poetic techniques—metaphor and metrical effects.

The metaphor, a primary device of poetry, can be defined as a
play on words in which one object or idea is expressed as if it were
something else, something with which it is said to share common
features. In the first quatrain of Sonnet 2 (quoted earlier), the young
man's forehead, "so gazed on now," is imaged as a "field" that Time
places under siege, digging "deep trenches" in its now youthful
smoothness. The metaphor fast-forwards the aging process, turning the youth's smooth forehead in imagination into a furrowed,
lined brow. While the word "field" could allude to any kind of open
land or plain, the words "besiege" and "trenches" make it more
specifically a battlefield ravaged by the armies of "forty winters." In
line 3 the metaphor shifts, and the young man's youthful beauty is
imaged as his "livery," a kind of uniform or splendid clothing that

under the onslaught of time will become a "tattered weed" *(weed* having here the meaning "garment"). The quatrain seems, then, divided into two parts, with the metaphor shifting from that of the brow as a field to the brow (and other youthful features) as clothing. But the word *weed* carries its inevitable, though here secondary, meaning of an unwanted plant in a "field" of grass or flowers. This wordplay, which expands the scope of the word *field*, forces the reader to turn from line 4 back to lines 1 and 2, to visualize again the ravaged "field" of the once-smooth brow, and thus to experience with double force the quatrain's final phrase "of small worth held"—a phrase that syntactically belongs only to the tattered clothing but that, in the quatrain's overlapping metaphors, applies more broadly to the young man himself, now "so gazed on" but moving inevitably toward the day when he, no longer beautiful, will be considered "of small worth."

We mentioned at the outset that the language of the *Sonnets* is, like poetic language in general, highly structured. Nowhere is this fact more in evidence than in the rhythm of the *Sonnets'* lines. All of the *Sonnets* (except for Sonnet 145) are written in what is called "iambic pentameter" (that is, each line is composed of five metrical "feet," with each foot containing two syllables, usually with the first syllable unstressed and the second stressed). But within this general pattern, Shakespeare takes advantage of several features that characterize pronunciation in English—for example, the syllable stresses that inhere in all English words of more than one syllable, as well as the stress patterns in normal English sentences—and he arranges his words to create amazing metrical variety within the structure of the iambic pentameter line.

To return to the first quatrain of Sonnet 2: the first line of the sonnet ("When forty winters shall besiege thy brow") contains three two-syllable words; two carry stress on the first syllable ("forty" and "winter") and one is stressed on the second syllable ("besiege"). Shakespeare combines these words with four one-syllable words, three of which are unstressed in normal English sentences—a conjunction ("When"), an auxiliary verb ("shall"), and a possessive pronoun ("thy"). The resulting combination of words produces an almost perfect iambic pentameter (the only departure being the pyrrhic third foot, with its two unstressed syllables—"-ters shall"):

"When *for'*ty *win'*ters shall be*siege'* thy *brow'.*" After thus establishing the meter, the poet can depart radically from the iambic in line 2 without creating confusion about the poem's overall metrical structure. Line 2 ("And dig deep trenches in thy beauty's field") begins with an iamb ("And *dig'*") but then moves to a "spondee," a foot with two stressed syllables (*"deep' trench'-"*); the resulting rhythm for the opening of the line is the very strong series of three stressed syllables of *"dig' deep' trench'-."* The line then moves to the unstressed syllables in the pyrrhic foot ("-es in") before ending in iambic meter ("thy *beau'*ty's *field'*")—a pattern that produces three unstressed syllables in mid-line. Line 3 ("Thy youth's proud livery, so gazed on now") echoes the opening rhythm of line 2—that is, an iamb followed by a spondee to create three stressed syllables ("Thy *youth's' proud' liv'-"*) again followed by three unstressed syllables ("-er-y so"); but then, instead of returning to the iambic, as did line 2, the line concludes with another group of three stressed syllables (*"gazed' on' now'"*). Line 4 seems to return us to the base of iambic pentameter ("Will *be'* a *tat'*tered *weed'* of *small'*") only to end with a spondee (*"worth' held'"*), so that the beat of three stressed syllables (heard once in line 2 and twice in line 3) concludes the quatrain. It is to Shakespeare's skillful use of the unstressed pyrrhic foot that George Wright (see Further Reading, "An Art of Small Differences") credits much of the "softness and musical grace" of the *Sonnets.* "The strong iambs and spondees," he writes, rise from this pyrrhic base, a contrast that allows important spondaic and iambic syllables to gain special emphasis. In the lines we have been examining in Sonnet 2, one can see how the pyrrhics direct attention to such key words and phrases as "besiege" and "gazed on now."

With metaphors and metrics, as with word choice, word order, and sentence structure, every sonnet provides its own richness and its own variations, as well as occasional exceptions to any generalizations we have suggested. (Two of the *Sonnets,* for example, deviate even from the standard fourteen-line length, with Sonnet 99 having 15 lines and Sonnet 126 having only 12.) But each sonnet provides rich language, a wonderfully controlled tone, and an intellectual challenge sufficient to reward the most patient and dedicated reader.

Shakespeare's Sonnets

Few collections of poems—indeed, few literary works in general—
intrigue, challenge, tantalize, and reward as do Shakespeare's *Sonnets*. Almost all of them love poems, the *Sonnets* philosophize,
celebrate, attack, plead, and express pain, longing, and despair, all
in a tone of voice that rarely rises above a reflective murmur, all spoken as if in an inner monologue or dialogue, and all within the tight
structure of the English sonnet form.

Individual sonnets have become such a part of present-day culture that, for example, Sonnet 116 ("Let me not to the marriage of
true minds") is a fixture of wedding ceremonies today, and Sonnet
18 ("Shall I compare thee to a summer's day"), Sonnet 29 ("When in
disgrace with fortune and men's eyes"), and Sonnet 73 ("That time
of year thou mayst in me behold")—to name only a few—are known
and quoted in the same way that famous lines and passages are
quoted from *Hamlet* or *Romeo and Juliet* or *Macbeth*. Yet it is not
just the beauty and power of individual well-known sonnets that
tantalize us, but also the story that the sequence as a whole seems
to tell about Shakespeare's love life. The 154 sonnets were published
in 1609 with an enigmatic dedication, presumably from the publisher Thomas Thorpe: "To The Onlie Begetter Of These Insuing
Sonnets. Mr. W.H." Attempts to identify "Mr. W.H." have become inevitably entangled with the narrative that insists on emerging
whenever one reads the *Sonnets* sequentially as they are ordered in
the 1609 Quarto.

The narrative goes something like this: The poet (i.e., William
Shakespeare) begins with a set of 17 sonnets advising a beautiful
young man (seemingly an aristocrat, perhaps "Mr. W.H." himself) to
marry and produce a child in the interest of preserving the family
name and property but even more in the interest of reproducing the
young man's remarkable beauty in his offspring. These poems of advice modulate into a set of sonnets which urge the poet's love for the
young man and which claim that the young man's beauty will be
preserved in the very poems that we are now reading. This second

set of sonnets (Sonnets 18–126), which in the supposed narrative celebrate the poet's love for the young man, includes clusters of poems that seem to tell of such specific events as the young man's mistreatment of the poet, the young man's theft of the poet's mistress, the appearance of "rival poets" who celebrate the young man and gain his favor, the poet's separation from the young man through travel or through the young man's indifference, and the poet's infidelity to the young man. After this set of 109 poems, the *Sonnets* concludes with a third set of 28 sonnets to or about a woman who is presented as dark and treacherous and with whom the poet is sexually obsessed. Several of these sonnets seem also to involve the beautiful young man, who is, according to the *Sonnets'* narrative, also enthralled by the "dark lady."

The power of the narrative sketched above is so strong that counterevidence putting in doubt its validity seems to matter very little. Most critics and editors agree, for example, that it is only in specific clusters that the sonnets are actually linked, and that close attention to the sequence reveals the collection to be more an anthology of poems written perhaps over many years and perhaps to or about different men and women. Most are also aware that only about 25 of the 154 sonnets specify the sex of the beloved, and that in the century following the *Sonnets'* publication, readers who copied individual sonnets into their manuscript collections gave them titles that show, for example, that sonnets such as Sonnet 2 were seen as *carpe diem* ("seize the day") poems addressed "To one that would die a maid." Such facts, such recognitions, nevertheless, lose out to the narrative pull exerted by the 1609 collection. The complex and intriguing persona of the poet created by the language of the *Sonnets,* the pattern of emotions so powerfully sustained through the sequence, the sense of the presence of the aristocratic young man and the seductive dark lady—all are so strong that few editors can resist describing the *Sonnets* apart from their irresistible story. (Our own introduction to the language of the *Sonnets,* for example, discusses Sonnet 2 as a poem addressed to the beautiful young man, despite the fact that the sex of the poem's recipient is not specified and despite our awareness that in the seventeenth century, this extremely popular poem was represented consistently as being written to a young woman.) Individually and as a sequence, these poems remain more powerful than the mere mortals who read or study or edit them.

For a very helpful exploration of the *Sonnets* as they are read today, we invite you to read "A Modern Perspective" written by Professor Lynne Magnusson of the University of Toronto and printed at the back of this book.

An Introduction to This Text

A complete text of the Sonnets was first published in a 1609 Quarto titled *SHAKE-SPEARES SONNETS. Neuer before Imprinted.* The present edition is based directly on that printing.* The 1609 Quarto prints immediately before its text of the poems a dedication page that reads as follows (each word printed entirely in capitals, except for "Mr.," and followed by a period): "TO. THE. ONLIE. BEGET-TER. OF. I THESE. INSVING. SONNETS. I Mr. W.H. ALL. HAPPI-NESSE. I AND. THAT. ETERNITIE. I PROMISED. I BY. I OVR.EVER-LIVING. POET. I WISHETH. I THE. WELL-WISHING. I ADVENTVRER. IN. I SETTING. I FORTH. I T.T. [i.e., Thomas Thorpe, publisher of the Quarto]." Scholars have long speculated on the identity of "Mr. W.H." without arriving at any widely accepted conclusion. Following the Sonnets in the 1609 Quarto appears a poem of disputed authorship titled "A Louers complaint," which is not included in this edition.

In addition to providing an edited text of the 1609 Quarto version of the Sonnets, we include on pages 330–31 alternative texts of two of the sonnets (Sonnet 138 and Sonnet 144) that were first printed ten years before this quarto in a book titled *The Passionate Pilgrime. By W. Shakespeare.* The 1599 attribution of the entire *Passionate Pilgrime* to Shakespeare is misleading because much of the verse collected in it is not his; however, it does contain the earliest printing of the two sonnets in question, and for this reason those texts deserve

---

* We have also consulted the computerized text of the Quarto provided by the Text Archive of the Oxford University Computing Centre, to which we are grateful.

consideration. There also exist a number of manuscript copies of particular sonnets, none of them thought to be in Shakespeare's own handwriting. Nonetheless, it has recently been argued that among these may lie an alternative Shakespearean version of Sonnet 2, as well as versions of other sonnets (8, 106, 128) that may derive from manuscript sources independent of that from which the 1609 Quarto was printed. We have, however, been persuaded by Katherine Duncan-Jones's argument in her 1997 Arden edition of the *Sonnets*, where she cogently refutes the claims for the authenticity of the Sonnet 2 manuscript version and also puts into serious question the independent authority of the other surviving manuscript texts. We thus have not included any manuscript versions in this edition.

For the convenience of the reader, we have modernized the punctuation and the spelling of the Quarto. Whenever we change the wording of the Quarto or add anything to it, we mark the change by enclosing it in superior half-brackets (⌜ ⌝). We want our readers to be immediately aware when we have intervened. (Only when we correct an obvious typographical error in the Quarto does the change not get marked.) Whenever we change the Quarto's wording or alter its punctuation so that meaning changes, we list the change in the textual notes at the back of the book, even if all we have done is fix an obvious error.

The Explanatory Notes

The notes that appear on the pages facing the text are designed to provide readers with the help that they may need to enjoy the poems. Whenever the primary meaning of a word in the text is not readily accessible in a good contemporary dictionary, we offer the meaning in a note. Sometimes we provide a note even when the relevant meaning is to be found in the dictionary but when the word has acquired since Shakespeare's time other potentially confusing meanings. In our notes, we try to offer modern synonyms for Shakespeare's words. We also try to indicate to the reader the connection between the word in the sonnet and the modern synonym. For example, Shakespeare sometimes uses the word *glass* to mean *mirror*, but, for modern readers, there may be no connection evident between these two words. We provide the connection by explaining Shakespeare's usage as follows: "**glass:** looking glass, mirror." Often in the *Sonnets*, a phrase or clause needs explanation. Then, if space allows, we rephrase in our own words the difficult passage, and add at the end synonyms for individual words in the passage. When scholars have been unable to determine the meaning of a word or phrase, we acknowledge the uncertainty. Biblical quotations are from the Geneva Bible (1560), modernized.

In the centuries since the publication of Shakespeare's *Sonnets*, many editors have worked at understanding and explaining the very condensed language of these poems. When we find the work of a particular editor especially helpful to the reader, we occasionally refer to that editor's notes. The following are editions that provide especially useful commentary:

Booth, Stephen, ed. *Shakespeare's Sonnets* (New Haven, 1977)

Duncan-Jones, Katherine, ed. *Shakespeare's Sonnets* (The Arden Shakespeare, 1997)

Evans, G. Blakemore, ed. *The Sonnets* (The New Cambridge Shakespeare, 1996)

Ingram, W. G., and Theodore Redpath, eds. *Shakespeare's Sonnets* (London, 1964, 1967)

Kerrigan, John, ed. *The Sonnets and A Lover's Complaint* (The New Penguin Shakespeare, 1986)

Orgel, Stephen, ed. *The Sonnets* (The Pelican Shakespeare, 2001)

Vendler, Helen, ed. *The Art of Shakespeare's Sonnets* (Cambridge, Mass., 1997)

When an edition is mentioned in conjunction with a particular poem, the editor's remarks will be found in his or her commentary on that poem.

Illustrations are from the Folger archives. See "Index of Illustrations" (pp. 677–84) for information on the books or manuscripts in which the engravings or prints are found.

SHAKESPEARE'S SONNETS

In this first of many sonnets about the briefness of human life, the poet reminds the young man that time and death will destroy even the fairest of living things. Only if they reproduce themselves will their beauty survive. The young man's refusal to beget a child is therefore self-destructive and wasteful.

---

1. **increase:** reproduction, propagation

4. **tender:** i.e., young; **bear his memory:** i.e., carry its (or his) image as a living memorial

5. **contracted:** bound by contract, betrothed (but also with the sense of "limited, shrunken")

6. **Feed'st . . . fuel:** See longer note, p. 332. **self-substantial:** derived from one's own substance

10. **only:** peerless, preeminent; **herald:** forerunner, precursor; **gaudy:** brilliantly fine

11. **thy content:** (1) that which is contained within you—specifically, your seed, that with which you should produce a child; (2) your happiness

12. **churl:** miser (with wordplay on "lowbred fellow" or "villain"); **mak'st waste in niggarding:** i.e., diminishes or impoverishes through miserliness

13–14. **this glutton . . . thee:** i.e., be the kind of **glutton** who devours **the world's due** (the children one owes the world), first by refusing to reproduce and then by dying (See Erasmus's "Epistle" [B], in Appendix, p. 620.)

1

From fairest creatures we desire increase,
That thereby beauty's rose might never die,
But, as the riper should by time decease,
His tender heir might bear his memory.   4
But thou, contracted to thine own bright eyes,
Feed'st thy light's flame with self-substantial fuel,
Making a famine where abundance lies,
Thyself thy foe, to thy sweet self too cruel.   8
Thou that art now the world's fresh ornament
And only herald to the gaudy spring
Within thine own bud buriest thy content
And, tender churl, mak'st waste in niggarding.   12
    Pity the world, or else this glutton be—
    To eat the world's due, by the grave and thee.

The poet challenges the young man to imagine two different futures, one in which he dies childless, the other in which he leaves behind a son. In the first, the young man will waste the uninvested treasure of his youthful beauty. In the other, though still himself subject to the ravages of time, his child's beauty will witness the father's wise investment of this treasure.

---

2. **field:** i.e., the **brow** (imaged as a battlefield, besieged by Time, which digs **deep trenches**)

3. **proud:** magnificent, splendid; **livery:** distinctive clothing, military uniform

4. **weed:** garment (with possible wordplay on a **weed** in a **field**)

6. **lusty:** strong, vigorous (with possible wordplay on *lustful*)

7. **deep-sunken:** i.e., aged (literally, hollow, fallen in)

8. **all-eating shame:** (1) **shame** at having consumed everything; (2) **shame** that consumes you entirely; **thriftless praise:** (1) **praise** for having lived wastefully; (2) worthless **praise**

9. **use:** the act of holding land or other property so as to derive revenue or profit from it (but also with the sense of "employment for sexual purposes")

11. **sum my count:** i.e., provide a statement of reckoning for what I've received and spent; **make my old excuse:** i.e., justify me in my old age

12. **by succession thine:** i.e., inherited from you by legal right

2

When forty winters shall besiege thy brow
And dig deep trenches in thy beauty's field,
Thy youth's proud livery, so gazed on now,
Will be a tattered weed of small worth held.   4
Then being asked where all thy beauty lies,
Where all the treasure of thy lusty days,
To say within thine own deep-sunken eyes
Were an all-eating shame and thriftless praise.   8
How much more praise deserved thy beauty's use
If thou couldst answer "This fair child of mine
Shall sum my count and make my old excuse,"
Proving his beauty by succession thine.   12
 This were to be new made when thou art old
 And see thy blood warm when thou feel'st it cold.

The poet urges the young man to reflect on his own image in a mirror. Just as the young man's mother sees her own youthful self reflected in the face of her son, so someday the young man should be able to look at his son's face and see reflected his own youth. If the young man decides to die childless, all these faces and images die with him.

---

1. **glass:** looking glass, mirror

3. **fresh repair:** youthful condition

4. **beguile:** disappoint, cheat; **unbless some mother:** i.e., deprive someone of the blessings of motherhood

5. **fair:** beautiful; **uneared:** unplowed (The familiar metaphor that images copulation in agricultural terms continues in l. 6 with **tillage** and with wordplay on *husband* in **husbandry.**) See Erasmus's "Epistle" [D], in Appendix, p. 622.

7. **fond:** foolish

7–8. **be . . . posterity:** i.e., out of his narcissism bury the generations that should succeed him (See Erasmus's "Epistle" [A], in Appendix, p. 615.)

11. **windows . . . age:** i.e., your eyes when you are old

"Swift-footed Time." (s. 19.6)

3

Look in thy glass and tell the face thou viewest
Now is the time that face should form another,
Whose fresh repair if now thou not renewest,
Thou dost beguile the world, unbless some mother.   4
For where is she so fair whose uneared womb
Disdains the tillage of thy husbandry?
Or who is he so fond will be the tomb
Of his self-love, to stop posterity?   8
Thou art thy mother's glass, and she in thee
Calls back the lovely April of her prime;
So thou through windows of thine age shalt see,
Despite of wrinkles, this thy golden time.   12
  But if thou live remembered not to be,
  Die single, and thine image dies with thee.

The poet returns to the idea of beauty as treasure that should be invested for profit. Here, the young man's refusal to beget a child is likened to his spending inherited wealth on himself rather than investing it or sharing it generously.

2. **thy beauty's legacy:** i.e., the beauty you have inherited

4. **frank:** generous; **are free:** i.e., who give freely

7. **Profitless usurer:** i.e., moneylender who makes no profit (The metaphor that links investment with the proper use of one's gifts recalls both the parable of the talents in Matthew 25 and Marlowe's *Hero and Leander.* See Appendix, pp. 617–19 and 624, and see also p. 620 for Erasmus's "Epistle" [B].) **use:** expend, exhaust (with wordplay on "invest for profit") See picture below.

8. **live:** (1) make a living; (2) survive

9. **traffic:** dealings, business

10. **deceive:** cheat, defraud

11–12. See Erasmus's "Epistle" [C], in Appendix, p. 621.

A usurer. (s. 4.7)

4

Unthrifty loveliness, why dost thou spend
Upon thyself thy beauty's legacy?
Nature's bequest gives nothing but doth lend,
And being frank, she lends to those are free.　　　　4
Then, beauteous niggard, why dost thou abuse
The bounteous largess given thee to give?
Profitless usurer, why dost thou use
So great a sum of sums yet canst not live?　　　　8
For, having traffic with thyself alone,
Thou of thyself thy sweet self dost deceive.
Then how, when nature calls thee to be gone,
What acceptable audit canst thou leave?　　　　12
　　Thy unused beauty must be tombed with thee,
　　Which usèd lives th' executor to be.

In this first of two linked sonnets, the poet compares the young man to summer and its flowers, doomed to be destroyed by winter. Even though summer inevitably dies, he argues, its flowers can be distilled into perfume. The beauty of the flowers and thereby the essence of summer are thus preserved.

---

1. **frame:** fashion, form
2. **gaze:** object gazed on
4. **that unfair:** i.e., deprive **that** of beauty; **fairly:** (1) completely; (2) properly; (3) i.e., in beauty
6. **confounds him:** i.e., destroys it, brings it to ruin
7. **lusty:** healthy, vigorous
9. **summer's distillation:** i.e., the essence of summer
10. **A liquid prisoner pent in walls of glass:** See Philip Sidney's *Arcadia:* "Have you ever seen a pure rosewater kept in a crystal glass, how fine it looks, how sweet it smells, while that beautiful glass imprisons it?" (1590 ed., p. 380).
11. **with beauty were bereft:** i.e., would be lost along with **beauty**
12. **Nor it nor no remembrance:** i.e., neither **it nor** any memory of
14. **Leese but:** lose only; **substance:** essence

5

Those hours that with gentle work did frame
The lovely gaze where every eye doth dwell
Will play the tyrants to the very same
And that unfair which fairly doth excel;⁣ 4
For never-resting time leads summer on
To hideous winter and confounds him there,
Sap checked with frost and lusty leaves quite gone,
Beauty o'er-snowed and bareness everywhere. 8
Then, were not summer's distillation left
A liquid prisoner pent in walls of glass,
Beauty's effect with beauty were bereft,
Nor it nor no remembrance what it was. 12
 But flowers distilled, though they with winter meet,
 Leese but their show; their substance still lives sweet.

Continuing the argument from s. 5, the poet urges the young man to produce a child, and thus distill his own summerlike essence. The poet then returns to the beauty-as-treasure metaphor and proposes that the lending of treasure for profit—i.e., usury—is not forbidden by law when the borrower is happy with the bargain. If the young man lends his beauty and gets in return enormous wealth in the form of children, Death will be helpless to destroy him, since he will continue to live in his offspring.

---

1. **ragged:** rough; **deface:** destroy, obliterate

3. **vial:** the "walls of glass" holding the perfume in s. 5 (but here also symbolizing the womb in which the young man's child should grow); **treasure:** enrich

5. **usury:** i.e., lending money for interest (also called **use**), which, while legal, was considered sinful (**forbidden**)

6. **happies:** makes happy; **pay the willing loan:** i.e., willingly **pay** back **the loan**

8–10. **Or ten times . . . thee:** These lines play with the interest rate of "one for ten"—i.e., 10 percent (here converted to "**ten for one,**" or 1000 percent)—and with the young man's prospect of reproducing himself tenfold through having ten children and then a thousandfold through his children's issue. **refigured:** duplicated

11–12. See Erasmus's "Epistle" [G], in Appendix, pp. 623–24.

13. **self-willed:** wordplay on (1) obstinately selfish; (2) bequeathed to one's self

6

Then let not winter's ragged hand deface
In thee thy summer ere thou be distilled.
Make sweet some vial; treasure thou some place
With beauty's treasure ere it be self-killed.   4
That use is not forbidden usury
Which happies those that pay the willing loan;
That's for thyself to breed another thee,
Or ten times happier, be it ten for one.   8
Ten times thyself were happier than thou art
If ten of thine ten times refigured thee;
Then what could death do if thou shouldst depart,
Leaving thee living in posterity?   12
    Be not self-willed, for thou art much too fair
    To be death's conquest and make worms thine heir.

This sonnet traces the path of the sun across the sky, noting that mortals gaze in admiration at the rising and the noonday sun. When the sun begins to set, says the poet, it is no longer an attraction. Such is the path that the young man's life will follow—a blaze of glory followed by descent into obscurity—unless he begets a son.

---

2. **under eye:** (1) **eye** on the earth (and therefore below the sun); (2) subordinate **eye**

4. **with looks:** i.e., by gazing upon

5. **having:** i.e., the sun's **having; steep-up:** precipitous (Here, the sun moves around the earth, as in the Ptolemaic system. There is also an allusion to the sun god driving his chariot up the hill toward its highest point at noon. See pictures, pp. xviii and 86.)

8. **Attending on:** (1) waiting on, serving; (2) paying attention to

9. **highmost pitch:** i.e., highest point, summit; **car:** chariot (See note to l. 5.)

11. **'fore duteous:** i.e, previously obedient or dutiful; **converted are:** are turned

12. **tract:** path

13. **thyself outgoing in thy noon:** (1) excelling yourself in this stage of early manhood; (2) outlasting the prime of your youth; (3) beginning to be extinguished even as the flame burns brightest

14. **get:** beget

7

Lo, in the orient when the gracious light
Lifts up his burning head, each under eye
Doth homage to his new-appearing sight,
Serving with looks his sacred majesty;   4
And having climbed the steep-up heavenly hill,
Resembling strong youth in his middle age,
Yet mortal looks adore his beauty still,
Attending on his golden pilgrimage.   8
But when from highmost pitch with weary car
Like feeble age he reeleth from the day,
The eyes, 'fore duteous, now converted are
From his low tract and look another way.   12
   So thou, thyself outgoing in thy noon,
   Unlooked on diest unless thou get a son.

The poet observes the young man listening to music without pleasure, and suggests that the young man hears in the harmony produced by the instrument's individual but conjoined strings an accusation about his refusing to play his part in the concord of "sire and child and happy mother."

---

1. **Music to hear:** i.e., you whose voice is like **music**

3. **lov'st thou:** perhaps, do you bother with, do you spend time on

4. **receiv'st . . . thine annoy:** i.e., do you enjoy being displeased

6. **unions:** combinations, conjunctions

7–8. **who confounds . . . bear:** i.e., **who,** by remaining single, destroy the potential harmony of marriage (and the **parts** of husband and father that you should play)

9–12. **Mark . . . sing:** Editors have suggested that these lines describe the tuning of lute strings, which are tuned in pairs; one string sets off sympathetic vibrations in its fellow, resulting in an enriched tone. (See picture, p. 96.) **Mark:** notice, pay attention to **mutual ordering:** perhaps, harmony; perhaps, sympathetic tuning

14. **Thou . . . none:** The ancient mathematical dictum that "one is no number" became proverbial. (A *number* is [1] an "integer" and [2] an "aggregate or sum"; *one* is "a number" only in the first sense.)

8

Music to hear, why hear'st thou music sadly?
Sweets with sweets war not, joy delights in joy.
Why lov'st thou that which thou receiv'st not gladly,
Or else receiv'st with pleasure thine annoy?   4
If the true concord of well-tunèd sounds,
By unions married, do offend thine ear,
They do but sweetly chide thee, who confounds
In singleness the parts that thou shouldst bear.   8
Mark how one string, sweet husband to another,
Strikes each in each by mutual ordering,
Resembling sire and child and happy mother
Who, all in one, one pleasing note do sing;   12
    Whose speechless song, being many, seeming one,
    Sings this to thee: "Thou single wilt prove none."

The poet argues that if the young man refuses to marry for fear of someday leaving behind a grieving widow, he is ignoring the worldwide grief that will be caused if he dies single, leaving behind no heir to his beauty.

---

3. **issueless:** childless; **hap:** happen

4. **wail thee:** grieve for you; **makeless:** widowed

5. **still:** unceasingly

6. **form:** image, likeness

7. **private:** ordinary, individual (This odd use of the word **private,** as Booth notes, may suggest its derivation from the Latin *privare,* "to bereave, deprive.")

9. **Look what:** whatever; **unthrift:** spendthrift

10. **Shifts but his:** i.e., merely changes its

12. **user:** i.e., the possessor of the beauty (with wordplay on the meanings of **use** evoked in ss. 2, 4, and 6.)

"To give away yourself. . . ." (s. 16.13)

9

Is it for fear to wet a widow's eye
That thou consum'st thyself in single life?
Ah, if thou issueless shalt hap to die,
The world will wail thee like a makeless wife;   4
The world will be thy widow and still weep
That thou no form of thee hast left behind,
When every private widow well may keep,
By children's eyes, her husband's shape in mind.   8
Look what an unthrift in the world doth spend
Shifts but his place, for still the world enjoys it;
But beauty's waste hath in the world an end,
And, kept unused, the user so destroys it.   12
    No love toward others in that bosom sits
    That on himself such murd'rous shame commits.

This sonnet, expanding the couplet that closes s. 9, accuses the young man of a murderous hatred against himself and his family line and urges him to so transform himself that his inner being corresponds to his outer graciousness and kindness.

2. **unprovident:** improvident, heedless of the future

3. **Grant:** granted; or, I **grant,** I concede; **if thou wilt:** if you insist (Booth)

6. **stick'st not:** do not hesitate, are not reluctant

7. **roof:** i.e., house, family; **ruinate:** reduce to ruins (See Erasmus's "Epistle" [E], in Appendix, pp. 622–23.)

9. **thought:** i.e., way of thinking; **mind:** i.e., opinion (of you)

11. **presence:** bearing or appearance, outward demeanor

"Youth's proud livery." (s. 2.3)

10

For shame deny that thou bear'st love to any,
Who for thyself art so unprovident.
Grant, if thou wilt, thou art beloved of many,
But that thou none lov'st is most evident. 4
For thou art so possessed with murd'rous hate
That 'gainst thyself thou stick'st not to conspire,
Seeking that beauteous roof to ruinate
Which to repair should be thy chief desire. 8
O, change thy thought, that I may change my mind.
Shall hate be fairer lodged than gentle love?
Be as thy presence is, gracious and kind,
Or to thyself at least kind-hearted prove. 12
    Make thee another self for love of me,
    That beauty still may live in thine or thee.

The poet once again urges the young man to choose a future in which his offspring carry his vitality forward instead of one in which his natural gifts will be coldly buried. The very exceptionality of the young man's beauty obliges him to cherish and wisely perpetuate that gift.

---

1. **wane:** decrease in splendor (like the waning moon)
2. **one:** i.e., a child; **departest:** leave, forsake
3. **youngly:** in youth
4. **from youth convertest:** turn aside **from youth**
5. **Herein:** i.e., in the course of action here described
6. **Without this:** i.e., outside of **this** course of action **lives**
7. **minded so:** i.e., inclined (to choose **age and cold decay**); **the times should cease:** i.e., the **world** [l. 8] would end (See Revelation 10.5–6: "And the Angel . . . lift up his hand and sware . . . that time shall be no more.")
8. **threescore year:** i.e., a single lifespan (Psalm 90.10 says that "the time of our life is **threescore** years and ten.")
9. **for store:** (1) for purposes of breeding (normally applied to livestock); (2) to reserve for future use; (3) as something precious or valuable
10. **featureless:** ugly; **rude:** coarse, ill-shaped
11. **Look . . . more:** As in the parable of the talents, to him who has the most gifts will be given yet more (Matthew 25.29; see Appendix, pp. 618–19.)   **Look whom:** whomever
12. **in bounty cherish:** i.e., cultivate or care for by sharing generously
13. **seal:** engraved stamp used to make an impression in wax (As nature's **seal,** the young man shows nature's power and authority.)
14. **copy:** pattern, example (the original from which copies are made)

11

As fast as thou shalt wane, so fast thou grow'st
In one of thine, from that which thou departest;
And that fresh blood which youngly thou bestow'st
Thou mayst call thine when thou from youth convertest.   4
Herein lives wisdom, beauty, and increase;
Without this, folly, age, and cold decay.
If all were minded so, the times should cease,
And threescore year would make the world away.   8
Let those whom nature hath not made for store,
Harsh, featureless, and rude, barrenly perish;
Look whom she best endowed she gave the more,
Which bounteous gift thou shouldst in bounty cherish.   12
    She carved thee for her seal, and meant thereby
    Thou shouldst print more, not let that copy die.

As he observes the motion of the clock and the movement of all living things toward death and decay, the poet faces the fact that the young man's beauty will be destroyed by Time. Nothing besides offspring, he argues, can defy Time's scythe.

---

1. **the clock:** i.e., the hours as struck by **the clock**

2. **brave:** splendid, glorious

6. **erst:** not long ago

7–8. **summer's . . . beard:** i.e., harvested wheat tied **in sheaves** and carried off the field on a cart (The words **bier** [the stand on which a corpse is carried to the grave] and **beard** [the bristly spines on wheat and the facial hair on men] conflate the harvested wheat with the dead body of a man.)

9. **of:** i.e., about; **question make:** (1) speculate; (2) entertain doubts

10. **wastes:** wilderness, deserts, desolate regions

11. **sweets:** pleasures, delights; **beauties:** beautiful things; **themselves forsake:** i.e., cease being **themselves** as they decay

12. **others:** i.e., other sweet and lovely things

13. **Time's scythe:** The familiar image of Time carrying an implement for cutting down grass suggests the biblical link between grass and man. See, e.g., 1 Peter 1.24: "For all flesh is as grass, and all the glory of man is as the flower of grass. The grass withereth and the flower falleth away." (See also, e.g., Psalm 103.15–16 and pictures, pp. 80 and 144.)

14. **breed:** generation; **brave:** defy (Note the conflation here of Time and Death.)

12

When I do count the clock that tells the time
And see the brave day sunk in hideous night,
When I behold the violet past prime
And sable curls ⌜all⌝ silvered o'er with white;   4
When lofty trees I see barren of leaves,
Which erst from heat did canopy the herd,
And summer's green all girded up in sheaves
Borne on the bier with white and bristly beard;   8
Then of thy beauty do I question make
That thou among the wastes of time must go,
Since sweets and beauties do themselves forsake
And die as fast as they see others grow;   12
    And nothing 'gainst Time's scythe can make defense
    Save breed, to brave him when he takes thee hence.

The poet argues that the young man, in refusing to prepare for old age and death by producing a child, is like a spendthrift who fails to care for his family mansion, allowing it to be destroyed by the wind and the cold of winter.

1. **your self:** perhaps, your soul (See longer note, p. 332.)
3. **Against . . . end:** i.e., in anticipation of your death
5. **hold in lease:** possess for the limited period of time specified in a contract
6. **determination:** termination, ending; **were:** i.e., would be
8. **When . . . bear:** See Erasmus's "Epistle" [F], in Appendix, p. 623.
9. **Who:** i.e., what kind of tenant or occupant (See Erasmus's "Epistle" [E], in Appendix, pp. 622–23.)
10. **husbandry:** careful household management (with probable wordplay on the word *husband*)
13. **unthrifts:** spendthrifts

"Methinks I have astronomy." (s. 14.2)

13

O, that you were your self! But, love, you are
No longer yours than you yourself here live;
Against this coming end you should prepare,
And your sweet semblance to some other give.   4
So should that beauty which you hold in lease
Find no determination; then you were
⌐Your⌐ self again after yourself's decease
When your sweet issue your sweet form should bear.   8
Who lets so fair a house fall to decay,
Which husbandry in honor might uphold
Against the stormy gusts of winter's day
And barren rage of death's eternal cold?   12
    O, none but unthrifts, dear my love, you know.
    You had a father; let your son say so.

As astrologers predict the future from the stars, so the poet reads the future in the "constant stars" of the young man's eyes, where he sees that if the young man breeds a son, truth and beauty will survive; if not, they die when the young man dies.

---

1. **judgment:** decision or conclusion about the future (an astrological term)

2. **I have astronomy:** i.e., I know astrology, I can read the future from the stars (See picture, p. 44.)

3–7. **But . . . well:** These lines list the kinds of predictions that astrologers claimed to make. **to brief minutes tell:** i.e., foretell to within the minute **Pointing to each his:** i.e., appointing **to each** minute its **say with:** i.e., **say with** regard to

8. **oft predict:** perhaps, frequent omens (The phrase is so uncommon that editors must simply speculate on its meaning.) **in heaven find:** i.e., read in the stars

10. **constant stars:** perhaps in contrast to the "wandering stars," the name given the planets, the "stars" read by astrologers

10–11. **such art / As:** i.e., learning **such as** that

12. **If . . . convert:** i.e., if you turn (your attention) from yourself to breeding

14. **end:** death; **doom:** final fate, destruction; **date:** end, limit (**End, doom,** and **date** all mean, in effect, death.)

14

Not from the stars do I my judgment pluck,
And yet methinks I have astronomy—
But not to tell of good or evil luck,
Of plagues, of dearths, or seasons' quality;   4
Nor can I fortune to brief minutes tell,
Pointing to each his thunder, rain, and wind,
Or say with princes if it shall go well
By oft predict that I in heaven find.   8
But from thine eyes my knowledge I derive,
And, constant stars, in them I read such art
As truth and beauty shall together thrive
If from thyself to store thou wouldst convert;   12
    Or else of thee this I prognosticate:
    Thy end is truth's and beauty's doom and date.

In the first of two linked sonnets, the poet once again examines the evidence that beauty and splendor exist only for a moment before they are destroyed by Time. Here the poet suggests—through wordplay on *engraft*—that the young man can be kept alive not only through procreation but also in the poet's verse.

---

3. **shows:** stage spectacles, plays (though with the suggestion of "illusions," "appearances")

4. **Whereon . . . comment:** The **stars** (i.e., the planets) are the audience to the **shows,** affecting them through occult **influence.** (See longer note, p. 333.)

5. **increase:** thrive, prosper; grow taller

6. **Cheerèd and checked:** (1) applauded and booed; (2) encouraged and restrained; **sky:** i.e., stars

7. **Vaunt:** i.e., rejoice (literally, swagger, boast)

8. **wear . . . memory:** This line holds in suspension several meanings that play against each other to describe the decline of **men** and **plants.** **wear:** (1) waste; (2) have on (as clothes) **brave state:** (1) splendid moment of **height** or zenith; (2) gorgeous display **out of memory:** (1) forgotten; (2) only in **memory**

9. **conceit:** idea, thought; **stay:** duration (though with overtones of "support" and of "pause")

14. **engraft you new:** i.e., renew your life through my poems (wordplay on **engraft,** with its root in the Greek for "to write" and its links to the creating of new life in plants through grafting) See picture, p. 52.

15

When I consider everything that grows
Holds in perfection but a little moment,
That this huge stage presenteth nought but shows
Whereon the stars in secret influence comment;   4
When I perceive that men as plants increase,
Cheerèd and checked even by the selfsame sky,
Vaunt in their youthful sap, at height decrease,
And wear their brave state out of memory;   8
Then the conceit of this inconstant stay
Sets you most rich in youth before my sight,
Where wasteful Time debateth with Decay
To change your day of youth to sullied night;   12
    And, all in war with Time for love of you,
    As he takes from you, I engraft you new.

Continuing the thought of s. 15, the poet argues that procreation is a "mightier way" than poetry for the young man to stay alive, since the poet's pen cannot present him as a living being.

1. **wherefore:** why
3. **in your decay:** i.e., as you decay
6. **unset:** unplanted
8. **liker:** i.e., more like you; **painted counterfeit:** (1) portrait; (2) feigned copy
9. **lines of life:** i.e., living children (The phrase alludes to various meanings of *line* that summon up such contexts as lineage, offspring, palmistry, and genealogy, along with portraiture and writing.)
10. **this time's pencil:** i.e., portraits drawn by artists of today (A **pencil** was a small artist's brush.) In the 1609 Quarto, l. 10 appears as "Which this (Times pensel or my pupill pen)." If one retains the Quarto's punctuation, **"this"** means "this sonnet" and **"time's pencil"** places the artist's brush in the hand of Time, which would here join the writer of the sonnets in preserving the young man's beauty.
11. **fair:** beauty
13. **give away yourself:** (1) marry; (2) produce children (See picture, p. 36.)

16

But wherefore do not you a mightier way
Make war upon this bloody tyrant Time,
And fortify yourself in your decay
With means more blessèd than my barren rhyme? 4
Now stand you on the top of happy hours,
And many maiden gardens, yet unset,
With virtuous wish would bear your living flowers,
Much liker than your painted counterfeit. 8
So should the lines of life that life repair
Which this time's pencil or my pupil pen
Neither in inward worth nor outward fair
Can make you live yourself in eyes of men. 12
 To give away yourself keeps yourself still,
 And you must live, drawn by your own sweet skill.

As further argument against mere poetic immortality, the poet insists that if his verse displays the young man's qualities in their true splendor, later ages will assume that the poems are lies. However, if the young man leaves behind a child, he will remain doubly alive—in verse and in his offspring.

---

2. **deserts:** excellent qualities

4. **parts:** attributes, gifts

6. **numbers:** lines or verses; **graces:** attractions, charms

11. **your true rights:** i.e., that which justly belongs to you; **poet's rage:** i.e., (the product of an) inspired frenzy (from the classical *furor poeticus*)

12. **stretchèd meter:** (1) i.e., poetic exaggeration; (2) strained **meter; antique song:** i.e., old-fashioned poem—or, perhaps, out-of-date poetic tradition

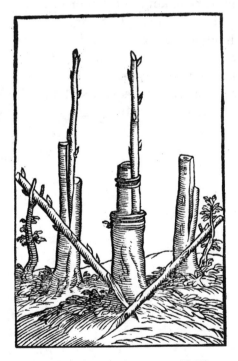

Grafting. (s. 15.14; *Lucrece*, 1062)

17

Who will believe my verse in time to come
If it were filled with your most high deserts?
Though yet, heaven knows, it is but as a tomb
Which hides your life and shows not half your parts.   4
If I could write the beauty of your eyes
And in fresh numbers number all your graces,
The age to come would say "This poet lies;
Such heavenly touches ne'er touched earthly faces."   8
So should my papers, yellowed with their age,
Be scorned, like old men of less truth than tongue,
And your true rights be termed a poet's rage
And stretchèd meter of an antique song.   12
    But were some child of yours alive that time,
    You should live twice—in it and in my rhyme.

In a radical departure from the previous sonnets, the young man's beauty, here more perfect even than a day in summer, is not threatened by Time or Death, since he will live in perfection forever in the poet's verses.

2. **temperate:** wordplay on weather that is **temperate** (i.e., not too hot) and on character that is gentle, not swayed by passion

4. **summer's . . . date:** i.e., summer is here for only a short time (In legal terms, a **lease** is temporary, expiring on a fixed **date.**)

5. **Sometime:** from time to time

6. **his:** i.e., its (the sun's)

7. **every . . . declines:** i.e., **every** thing of beauty will at some point diminish in beauty

8. **untrimmed:** i.e., changed in appearance (literally, stripped of ornament)

10. **Nor lose:** i.e., **nor** will you **lose; thou ow'st:** i.e., you own

11. **shade:** See Psalm 23.4: "though I should walk through the valley of the shadow of death," and see longer note, p. 334.

12. **eternal lines:** immortal verse (though with an echo of the "**lines** of life" of s. 16); **to time thou grow'st:** i.e., you become grafted **to time** and thus will last as long as **time** lasts (Since a graft is bound by cords to the rootstock, **lines** here are also cords. See s. 15.14 and picture, p. 52.)

14. **this:** perhaps this sonnet, or perhaps the collection of sonnets

18

Shall I compare thee to a summer's day?
Thou art more lovely and more temperate.
Rough winds do shake the darling buds of May,
And summer's lease hath all too short a date. 4
Sometime too hot the eye of heaven shines,
And often is his gold complexion dimmed;
And every fair from fair sometime declines,
By chance or nature's changing course untrimmed. 8
But thy eternal summer shall not fade
Nor lose possession of that fair thou ow'st,
Nor shall Death brag thou wand'rest in his shade,
When in eternal lines to time thou grow'st. 12
    So long as men can breathe or eyes can see,
    So long lives this, and this gives life to thee.

The "war with Time" announced in s. 15 is here engaged in earnest as the poet, allowing Time its usual predations, forbids it to attack the young man. Should this command fail to be effective, however, the poet claims that the young man will in any case remain always young in the poet's verse.

---

1. **Devouring Time:** Proverbial: "**Time** devours all things." (See picture below.)

4. **burn . . . blood:** The **phoenix,** according to classical authors, at the end of a given period of time burned itself on a funeral pyre, and from its ashes the new **phoenix** arose. (See pictures, pp. 62 and 536.)

6. **swift-footed Time:** Proverbial: "**Time** flees away without delay." (See picture, p. 24.)

7. **sweets:** pleasures, delights

11. **course:** continuous process (but with wordplay on "running or galloping," "path," and "custom, habitual procedure"); **untainted:** i.e., unblemished

11–12. **allow / For:** i.e., permit (him to remain) as

"Devouring Time." (s. 19.1)

19

Devouring Time, blunt thou the lion's paws
And make the earth devour her own sweet brood;
Pluck the keen teeth from the fierce tiger's ⌜jaws,⌝
And burn the long-lived phoenix in her blood;   4
Make glad and sorry seasons as thou fleet'st
And do whate'er thou wilt, swift-footed Time,
To the wide world and all her fading sweets.
But I forbid thee one most heinous crime: 8
O, carve not with thy hours my love's fair brow,
Nor draw no lines there with thine antique pen;
Him in thy course untainted do allow
For beauty's pattern to succeeding men.   12
    Yet do thy worst, old Time; despite thy wrong,
    My love shall in my verse ever live young.

The poet fantasizes that the young man's beauty is the result of Nature's changing her mind: she began to create a beautiful woman, fell in love with her own creation, and turned it into a man. The poet, thus deprived of a female sexual partner, concedes that it is women who will receive pleasure and progeny from the young man, but the poet will nevertheless have the young man's love.

---

2. **master mistress:** perhaps, supreme **mistress;** or, perhaps, the **mistress** customarily addressed in sonnets, but here a man

5. **rolling:** i.e., wandering, roving

6. **Gilding . . . gazeth:** i.e., turning all that it looks upon to gold, as does the sun (See s. 33.4.)

7. **hue:** appearance, form (With **hues,** the meaning "colors, complexions" is added.) **in his controlling:** i.e., under his control

8. **Which:** perhaps refers to **hue,** but perhaps to his ability to control **all hues; amazeth:** i.e., astounds

9. **for:** i.e., to be, as

10. **wrought:** made; **fell a-doting:** i.e., became foolishly infatuated (but with overtones of "went out of her wits, began to act stupidly") See John Dickenson, *Arisbas* (1594; sig. E2): ". . . Nature in framing him hath wronged her own sex, bereaving it of so great a glory."

11. **by addition:** i.e., by adding a penis (but **addition** also meant something added to a coat of arms as a mark of honor, so that the phrase carries the meaning "by honoring you"); **of thee defeated:** cheated me out of you

12. **to my purpose nothing:** i.e., that is of no use to me (with possible wordplay on **nothing** as a cant term for "vulva")

13. **pricked thee out:** selected you (with wordplay on "supplied you with male genitals")

14. **thy love's use:** wordplay on **use** as meaning "employment," "sexual enjoyment," "interest, profit" (The 1609 Quarto reads "and thy loues vse their treasure." As Orgel notes, if we retain Q's punctuation, the couplet might be understood to mean "since [Nature] selected you to experience pleasure as women do, mine be thy love, and may your lovers use their treasure.")

58

20

A woman's face with Nature's own hand painted
Hast thou, the master mistress of my passion;
A woman's gentle heart, but not acquainted
With shifting change, as is false women's fashion;   4
An eye more bright than theirs, less false in rolling,
Gilding the object whereupon it gazeth;
A man in hue all hues in his controlling,
Which steals men's eyes and women's souls amazeth.   8
And for a woman wert thou first created,
Till Nature as she wrought thee fell a-doting,
And by addition me of thee defeated
By adding one thing to my purpose nothing.   12
    But since she pricked thee out for women's pleasure,
    Mine be thy love, and thy love's use their treasure.

The poet contrasts himself with poets who compare those they love to such rarities as the sun, the stars, or April flowers. His poetry will, he writes, show his beloved as a beautiful mortal instead of using the exaggerated terms of an advertisement.

---

1. **So . . . with:** i.e., I am not like; **muse:** i.e., poet (literally, the inspiring goddess of a poet)

2. **painted beauty:** i.e., one whose beauty is merely painted on

3. **Who . . . use:** i.e., **who** uses (comparisons with) **heaven itself**

4. **fair with his fair:** i.e., beautiful thing with the particular **beauty** he celebrates; **rehearse:** cite, mention (or recite, as an actor would in rehearsing lines written for him)

5. **Making . . . compare:** i.e., coupling (the beloved) proudly in a comparison (**compare**)

7. **rare:** splendid, excellent

8. **rondure:** i.e., sphere (literally, roundness, circle); **hems:** encloses

13. **like of hearsay well:** i.e., enjoy rumors or unsubstantiated reports

14. **that purpose not:** i.e., do not intend to (Proverbial: "He praises who wishes **to sell.**")

21

So is it not with me as with that muse
Stirred by a painted beauty to his verse,
Who heaven itself for ornament doth use
And every fair with his fair doth rehearse,   4
Making a couplement of proud compare
With sun and moon, with earth and sea's rich gems,
With April's firstborn flowers and all things rare
That heaven's air in this huge rondure hems.   8
O, let me, true in love, but truly write,
And then believe me, my love is as fair
As any mother's child, though not so bright
As those gold candles fixed in heaven's air.   12
    Let them say more that like of hearsay well;
    I will not praise that purpose not to sell.

This sonnet plays with the poetic idea of love as an exchange of hearts. The poet urges the young man to take care of himself, since his breast carries the poet's heart; and the poet promises the same care of the young man's heart, which, the poet reminds him, has been given to the poet "not to give back again."

---

1. **glass:** i.e., looking glass, mirror
2. **date:** age
4. **look I:** i.e., I expect; **expiate:** bring to an end
6. **seemly raiment of:** i.e., beautiful clothing that covers
9. **so wary:** as careful
10. **will:** i.e., **will** be careful (of myself)
11. **chary:** carefully (but with strong overtones of "cherished, precious")
12. **faring ill:** i.e., doing badly, not getting on well (though with possible overtones of the more specific "being badly fed")
13. **Presume not on:** i.e., do not count on reclaiming

A phoenix. (s. 19.4; *Lucrece*, 1188; "The Phoenix and Turtle")

22

My glass shall not persuade me I am old
So long as youth and thou are of one date,
But when in thee Time's furrows I behold,
Then look I death my days should expiate.   4
For all that beauty that doth cover thee
Is but the seemly raiment of my heart,
Which in thy breast doth live, as thine in me;
How can I then be elder than thou art?   8
O, therefore, love, be of thyself so wary
As I not for myself but for thee will,
Bearing thy heart, which I will keep so chary
As tender nurse her babe from faring ill.   12
    Presume not on thy heart when mine is slain.
    Thou gav'st me thine not to give back again.

The poet blames his inability to speak his love on his lack of self-confidence and his too-powerful emotions, and he begs his beloved to find that love expressed in his writings.

---

1. **As an unperfect actor:** i.e., like **an actor** who does not know his lines (or, perhaps, like an inexpert or unskilled **actor**)

2. **with:** i.e., by, through; **beside:** i.e., out of (The line can be read as "Whose **fear** makes him forget his lines.")

4. **Whose strength's abundance:** the excess power of which (i.e., the **rage**); **heart:** courage, spirit; purpose

5. **for fear of trust:** perhaps, not trusting myself (This ambiguous phrase links back to the fearful **actor** in l. 2.)

6. **perfect:** i.e., word perfect, exactly memorized (though with overtones of the word's more general meanings); **rite:** (1) ritual; (2) due (While the 1609 Quarto prints "loues right," *rite* was often spelled *right.*)

9. **my books:** perhaps, these poems (The word **books** is sometimes changed by editors to "looks.")

10. **dumb presagers:** perhaps, silent ambassadors (This would be a highly unusual meaning of *presager.*) **speaking breast:** i.e., heart's language

12. **more hath:** i.e., **more** often has

14. **wit:** intelligence

23

As an unperfect actor on the stage
Who with his fear is put beside his part,
Or some fierce thing replete with too much rage,
Whose strength's abundance weakens his own heart;   4
So I for fear of trust forget to say
The perfect ceremony of love's rite,
And in mine own love's strength seem to decay,
O'ercharged with burden of mine own love's might.   8
O, let my books be then the eloquence
And dumb presagers of my speaking breast,
Who plead for love and look for recompense
More than that tongue that more hath more expressed.   12
    O, learn to read what silent love hath writ.
    To hear with eyes belongs to love's fine wit.

This sonnet elaborates the metaphor of carrying the beloved's picture in one's heart. The poet claims that his eyes have painted on his heart a picture of the beloved. The poet's body is both the picture's frame and the shop where it is displayed. His only regret is that eyes paint only what they see, and they cannot see into his beloved's heart.

---

1. **stelled:** portrayed, drawn

2. **table:** a board or other flat surface on which a picture was painted

4. **perspective . . . art:** i.e., seen perspectively (from the right angle or through a perspective glass—or, here, through the eyes of the poet), the lover's image in the poet's heart is the highest **art** (This line can be read in various ways, depending on different usages of **perspective** and of **art,** but the one proposed here seems to work best in context. **Perspective** is accented on the first and third syllables.)

7. **shop:** i.e., workshop

8. **That . . . eyes:** i.e., for which your **eyes** provide the glass for its **windows   his:** its   **glazèd:** fitted with glass

11. **wherethrough:** through which

13. **this cunning want:** i.e., lack this skill or knowledge; **grace:** adorn

24

Mine eye hath played the painter and hath ⌜stelled⌝
Thy beauty's form in table of my heart;
My body is the frame wherein 'tis held,
And perspective it is best painter's art.   4
For through the painter must you see his skill
To find where your true image pictured lies,
Which in my bosom's shop is hanging still,
That hath his windows glazèd with thine eyes.   8
Now see what good turns eyes for eyes have done:
Mine eyes have drawn thy shape, and thine for me
Are windows to my breast, wherethrough the sun
Delights to peep, to gaze therein on thee.   12
  Yet eyes this cunning want to grace their art:
  They draw but what they see, know not the heart.

The poet contrasts himself with those who seem more fortunate than he. Their titles and honors, he says, though great, are subject to whim and accident, while his greatest blessing, his love, will not change.

1. **stars:** In astrological thinking, the wandering **stars** (i.e., planets) govern our good or bad fortune.

4. **Unlooked for:** (1) unexpectedly; (2) unregarded; **joy . . . most:** i.e., rejoice or delight in the person **I most honor** (Booth notes that **joy in** has astrological overtones, in that planets "**joy in**" being in signs of the zodiac where they are most powerful.)

5. **leaves:** i.e., petals

6. **marigold:** a flower described as opening and closing its petals in response to the presence or absence of the sun (See picture below.)

9. **painful:** (1) diligent; (2) suffering; **famousèd:** celebrated

10. **foiled:** overthrown, defeated

11. **razèd:** erased, obliterated

14. **remove . . . removed:** i.e., leave **nor be** forced to leave

"The marigold at the sun's eye." (s. 25.6; *Lucrece*, 397)

25

Let those who are in favor with their stars
Of public honor and proud titles boast,
Whilst I, whom fortune of such triumph bars,
Unlooked for joy in that I honor most.   4
Great princes' favorites their fair leaves spread
But as the marigold at the sun's eye,
And in themselves their pride lies burièd,
For at a frown they in their glory die.   8
The painful warrior famousèd for worth,
After a thousand victories once foiled,
Is from the book of honor razèd quite,
And all the rest forgot for which he toiled.   12
   Then happy I, that love and am beloved
   Where I may not remove nor be removed.

The poet, assuming the role of a vassal owing feudal allegiance, offers his poems as a token of duty, apologizing for their lack of literary worth. He begs his liege lord to protect this expression of his duty until fortune allows him to boast openly of his love.

1. **vassalage:** the state of a devoted servant

2. **duty:** homage, due respect

3. **embassage:** message (of the kind delivered by an ambassador)

4. **wit:** poetic or linguistic facility

5. **wit:** intelligence, skill

6. **bare:** unadorned; paltry; naked; **wanting:** lacking

7. **conceit:** opinion, idea (though with wordplay on "literary conceit," i.e., ingenious language)

8. **bestow:** lodge, place

9. **star:** See note to s. 25.1. **my moving:** i.e., the course of my life or my actions (with possible wordplay on the astrological meaning of **moving** as the name given the course followed by the planets)

10. **Points on:** i.e., directs its rays or influence on; **graciously with fair aspect:** i.e., auspiciously **aspect:** an astrological term meaning the relative position of the planets as observed from the earth

11. **loving:** wordplay on the word's secondary meaning, "expression of devotion"

12. **show me:** i.e., **show me** to be

14. **prove:** test

26

Lord of my love, to whom in vassalage
Thy merit hath my duty strongly knit,
To thee I send this written embassage
To witness duty, not to show my wit;   4
Duty so great, which wit so poor as mine
May make seem bare, in wanting words to show it,
But that I hope some good conceit of thine
In thy soul's thought, all naked, will bestow it;   8
Till whatsoever star that guides my moving
Points on me graciously with fair aspect,
And puts apparel on my tattered loving
To show me worthy of ⌜thy⌝ sweet respect.   12
    Then may I dare to boast how I do love thee;
    Till then, not show my head where thou mayst prove me.

In this first of two linked sonnets, the poet complains that the night, which should be a time of rest, is instead a time of continuing toil as, in his imagination, he struggles to reach his beloved.

2. **travel:** This word means both "**journey**" (l. 3) and "labor, travail." The spellings *travail* and *travel* were used interchangeably.

4. **work:** wordplay on "cause **my mind** to work" and "agitate"

6. **Intend:** set out on

9. **imaginary sight:** i.e., **sight** produced by the imagination

10. **shadow:** image, picture

12. **her old face: Night** is here represented as an **old** woman.

27

Weary with toil, I haste me to my bed,
The dear repose for limbs with travel tired,
But then begins a journey in my head
To work my mind when body's work's expired.   4
For then my thoughts, from far where I abide,
Intend a zealous pilgrimage to thee,
And keep my drooping eyelids open wide,
Looking on darkness which the blind do see;   8
Save that my soul's imaginary sight
Presents ⌜thy⌝ shadow to my sightless view,
Which like a jewel hung in ghastly night
Makes black night beauteous and her old face new.   12
    Lo, thus, by day my limbs, by night my mind,
    For thee and for myself no quiet find.

Continuing the thought of s. 27, the poet claims that day and night conspire to torment him. Though he has flattered both day and night by comparing them to beautiful qualities of his beloved, day continues to exhaust him and night to distress him.

1. **plight**: state, condition (perhaps, specifically, physical and/or mental condition)

7. **to complain:** i.e., to cause me (or give me the opportunity) to lament or bewail

9. **I tell . . . bright:** i.e., I flatter **the day** by saying you are **bright** (like daylight)

10. **dost him grace:** embellish or do honor to **the day**

12. **When:** i.e., by saying that **when; twire:** peep or peer; **even:** evening

"When I consider everything that grows. . . ." (s. 15.1)

74

28

How can I then return in happy plight
That am debarred the benefit of rest,
When day's oppression is not eased by night,
But day by night and night by day oppressed;   4
And each, though enemies to either's reign,
Do in consent shake hands to torture me,
The one by toil, the other to complain
How far I toil, still farther off from thee?   8
I tell the day to please him thou art bright
And dost him grace when clouds do blot the heaven;
So flatter I the swart complexioned night,
When sparkling stars twire not, thou ⌜gild'st⌝ the even.   12
   But day doth daily draw my sorrows longer,
   And night doth nightly make grief's length seem stronger.

The poet, dejected by his low status, remembers his friend's love, and is thereby lifted into joy.

---

2. **beweep:** weep over

6. **Featured like him:** i.e., having one man's (good) looks; **like . . . possessed:** i.e., being **like** another man in having **friends**

7. **art:** learning, skill

10. **Haply:** by chance (with wordplay on *happily*); **state:** i.e., mental or emotional condition

12. **sullen:** dull-colored, gloomy

14. **state:** position in life, status, wealth or possessions (though with wordplay on **state** as used in l. 10)

"Abundant issue." (s. 97.6, 9)

29

When in disgrace with fortune and men's eyes,
I all alone beweep my outcast state,
And trouble deaf heaven with my bootless cries,
And look upon myself and curse my fate,   4
Wishing me like to one more rich in hope,
Featured like him, like him with friends possessed,
Desiring this man's art and that man's scope,
With what I most enjoy contented least;   8
Yet in these thoughts myself almost despising,
Haply I think on thee, and then my state,
Like to the lark at break of day arising
From sullen earth, sings hymns at heaven's gate;   12
    For thy sweet love remembered such wealth brings
    That then I scorn to change my state with kings.

The poet pictures his moments of serious reflection as a court session in which his memories are summoned to appear. As they come forward, he grieves for all that he has lost, but he then thinks of his beloved friend and the grief changes to joy.

---

1. **sessions:** wordplay on (1) judicial trial or investigation (emphasized in the word **summon** [l. 2]); (2) sitting together of a number of persons in conference (See John Dickenson, *Arisbas* [1594; sig. E2]: "Being in these dumps he held a session in his thoughts, whereto he assembled all his powers. . . .") In reading (1), **thought** is the judge; in reading (2), **thought** (regarded as plural) makes up the assembly.

2. **remembrance of things past:** See Wisdom of Solomon, 11.10: ". . . their grief was double with mourning and the **remembrance of things past.**"

6. **dateless:** endless

10. **heavily:** sorrowfully, laboriously

10–11. **tell o'er . . . account:** (1) enumerate the distressing debts (see l. 12); (2) recite the sorrowful story

13. **the while:** i.e., in the meantime

30

When to the sessions of sweet silent thought
I summon up remembrance of things past,
I sigh the lack of many a thing I sought,
And with old woes new wail my dear time's waste;   4
Then can I drown an eye, unused to flow,
For precious friends hid in death's dateless night,
And weep afresh love's long since canceled woe,
And moan th' expense of many a vanished sight.   8
Then can I grieve at grievances foregone,
And heavily from woe to woe tell o'er
The sad account of fore-bemoanèd moan,
Which I new pay as if not paid before.   12
   But if the while I think on thee, dear friend,
   All losses are restored and sorrows end.

The poet sees the many friends now lost to him as contained in his beloved. Thus, the love he once gave to his lost friends is now given wholly to the beloved.

---

1. **endearèd with:** made more precious by

2. **by lacking:** i.e., not having; **dead:** i.e., lost forever "in death's dateless night" (s. 30.6)

5. **obsequious:** mournful (as befitting an obsequy or funeral)

6. **religious:** pious; conscientious

7. **interest of:** i.e., rightful or legal due (with wordplay on tears as coins paid as **interest** on a loan)

8. **removed:** i.e., moved (to another place), absent

9. **doth live:** i.e., (1) resides; (2) survives

10. **Hung . . . gone:** The image is of a mausoleum decorated with memorials to the dead.   **trophies:** memorials, but with the sense of "spoils of victory"   **my lovers:** those who loved me **gone:** dead

11. **their parts of me:** i.e., their shares in my love

12. **due of many:** i.e., debt owed to **many**

"This bloody tyrant Time." (s. 16.2)

31

Thy bosom is endearèd with all hearts
Which I by lacking have supposèd dead,
And there reigns love and all love's loving parts,
And all those friends which I thought burièd.   4
How many a holy and obsequious tear
Hath dear religious love stol'n from mine eye,
As interest of the dead, which now appear
But things removed that hidden in ⌜thee⌝ lie.   8
Thou art the grave where buried love doth live,
Hung with the trophies of my lovers gone,
Who all their parts of me to thee did give;
That due of many now is thine alone.   12
    Their images I loved I view in thee,
    And thou, all they, hast all the all of me.

The poet imagines his poems being read and judged by his beloved after the poet's death, and he asks that the poems, though not as excellent as those written by later writers, be kept and enjoyed because of the love expressed in them.

---

1. **my well-contented day:** i.e., the **day** I am content to see

3. **shalt by fortune:** i.e., you shall perhaps; **resurvey:** reexamine, consider afresh; read again

5. **bett'ring of the time:** (literary) improvement or progress of the age

7. **Reserve:** keep

8. **happier:** more talented, more fortunate

10. **Had . . . age:** i.e., **had** my friend the poet lived to benefit from the superior style of **this age**

11. **dearer birth:** i.e., more worthy offspring; **brought:** i.e., given birth to

12. **march in ranks:** keep in step (as soldiers marching), with wordplay on **ranks** as lines or rows, including lines of poetry or of print; **of better equipage:** i.e. better equipped (another military term)

13. **since he died:** i.e., because **he died** (too soon); **better prove:** i.e., **prove** to be **better** (writers)

32

If thou survive my well-contented day
When that churl Death my bones with dust shall cover,
And shalt by fortune once more resurvey
These poor rude lines of thy deceasèd lover,   4
Compare them with the bett'ring of the time,
And though they be outstripped by every pen,
Reserve them for my love, not for their rhyme,
Exceeded by the height of happier men.   8
O, then vouchsafe me but this loving thought:
"Had my friend's muse grown with this growing age,
A dearer birth than this his love had brought
To march in ranks of better equipage.   12
    But since he died and poets better prove,
    Theirs for their style I'll read, his for his love."

The poet describes the sun first in its glory and then after its being covered with dark clouds; this change resembles his relationship with the beloved, who is now "masked" from him. But if even the sun can be darkened, he writes, it is no wonder that earthly beings sometimes fail to remain bright and unstained. (This is the first of a series of three poems in which the beloved is pictured as having hurt the poet through some unspecified misdeed.)

2. **Flatter:** (1) show honor to; (2) beguile; **sovereign:** superior (though with wordplay on royal flattery of courtiers)

4. **alchemy: Alchemy** sought to turn base metals to gold; the sun's rays make the **streams** appear to be "gilded," or covered with gold.

6. **rack:** mass of **clouds** driven by the wind in the upper air (but with wordplay on *wrack* as damage, ruin, devastation)

10. **all-triumphant:** glorious, magnificent

11. **out alack:** an exclamation of sorrow or anger; **but one hour:** i.e., only a moment

12. **region cloud:** i.e., the **rack** of l. 6 (The atmosphere was supposedly layered in "regions." The beloved is in a **region** above the poet, as are the clouds.)

14. **stain:** (1) lose color or brightness; (2) become discolored or marred; (3) become morally corrupt; **when . . . staineth:** i.e., if even the **sun** can be clouded over

33

Full many a glorious morning have I seen
Flatter the mountain tops with sovereign eye,
Kissing with golden face the meadows green,
Gilding pale streams with heavenly alchemy, 4
Anon permit the basest clouds to ride
With ugly rack on his celestial face,
And from the forlorn world his visage hide,
Stealing unseen to west with this disgrace. 8
Even so my sun one early morn did shine
With all-triumphant splendor on my brow,
But, out alack, he was but one hour mine;
The region cloud hath masked him from me now. 12
    Yet him for this my love no whit disdaineth;
    Suns of the world may stain when heaven's sun staineth.

In this sonnet the sun is again overtaken by clouds, but now the sun/beloved is accused of having betrayed the poet by promising what is not delivered. The poet writes that while the beloved's repentance and shame do not rectify the damage done, the beloved's tears are so precious that they serve as atonement.

3. **base:** dark, dingy; unworthy; **in:** on

4. **brav'ry:** splendor; **smoke:** fume or vapor

8. **heals . . . disgrace:** Proverbial: "Though **the wound** be healed yet the scar remains." **disgrace:** dishonor; disfigurement

9. **physic:** remedy; **grief:** (1) harm or injury; (2) sorrow

12. **cross:** adversity, misfortune

14. **rich:** valuable; powerful; **ill:** evil, bad

The sun god in his chariot. (s. 7.5; *Lucrece*, 775–76)

34

Why didst thou promise such a beauteous day
And make me travel forth without my cloak,
To let base clouds o'ertake me in my way,
Hiding thy brav'ry in their rotten smoke?   4
'Tis not enough that through the cloud thou break
To dry the rain on my storm-beaten face,
For no man well of such a salve can speak
That heals the wound and cures not the disgrace.   8
Nor can thy shame give physic to my grief;
Though thou repent, yet I have still the loss.
Th' offender's sorrow lends but weak relief
To him that bears the strong offense's ⌐cross.⌐   12
    Ah, but those tears are pearl which thy love sheds,
    And they are rich and ransom all ill deeds.

The poet excuses the beloved by citing examples of other naturally beautiful objects associated with things hurtful or ugly. He then accuses himself of being corrupted through excusing his beloved's faults.

---

2. **silver fountains mud:** i.e., silvery springs of water have **mud**

3. **stain:** (1) obscure; (2) blemish

4. **canker:** i.e., cankerworm (Proverbial: "The **canker** soonest eats the fairest rose.") See picture, p. 90.

5. **make faults:** commit wrongs, offend; **this:** i.e., **this** sonnet

6. **Authorizing:** sanctioning (though with possible wordplay on the root word *to author*) The accent falls on the second syllable.   **with compare:** i.e., through comparisons

7. **Myself . . . amiss:** i.e., **corrupting myself** in the process of **salving** your faults   **corrupting:** debasing, defiling; infecting **salving:** smoothing over; healing   **amiss:** error, fault

8. **Excusing . . . are:** There is almost no agreement about the meaning of this debated and variously emended line. See longer note, p. 334.

9. **to:** i.e., to the defense of; **sense:** i.e., reason

10. **advocate:** attorney

12. **civil war:** i.e., **war** within myself (in which **love** [for you] **and hate** [for what you have done] are the combatants)

13. **accessary:** accented on the first syllable

14. **which:** i.e., who

35

No more be grieved at that which thou hast done.
Roses have thorns, and silver fountains mud;
Clouds and eclipses stain both moon and sun,
And loathsome canker lives in sweetest bud.   4
All men make faults, and even I in this,
Authorizing thy trespass with compare,
Myself corrupting salving thy amiss,
Excusing ⌈thy⌉ sins more than ⌈thy⌉ sins are.   8
For to thy sensual fault I bring in sense—
Thy adverse party is thy advocate—
And 'gainst myself a lawful plea commence.
Such civil war is in my love and hate   12
    That I an accessary needs must be
    To that sweet thief which sourly robs from me.

The poet accepts the fact that for the sake of the beloved's honorable name, their lives must be separate and their love unacknowledged.

---

1. **confess:** acknowledge; **twain:** (1) parted; (2) separate (with wordplay on "two")

3. **blots:** faults, blemishes

4. **borne:** (1) carried; (2) endured; **alone:** (1) by myself; (2) in solitude

5. **one respect:** See longer note, p. 334.

6. **separable spite:** (1) injurious or hateful separation; (2) outrage or injury that separates

9. **evermore:** at any future time; **acknowledge thee:** i.e., openly recognize you (as someone close to me)

10. **bewailèd:** i.e., bitter

12. **Unless . . . name:** i.e., without dishonoring yourself

13. **in such sort:** i.e., **in such** a manner

14. **thou . . . report:** i.e., since we are one in our love, your good reputation (**report**) also honors me

A cankerworm. (ss. 35.4, 70.7, and 95.2; *Venus and Adonis*, 656)

36

Let me confess that we two must be twain
Although our undivided loves are one;
So shall those blots that do with me remain,
Without thy help, by me be borne alone.   4
In our two loves there is but one respect,
Though in our lives a separable spite,
Which though it alter not love's sole effect,
Yet doth it steal sweet hours from love's delight.   8
I may not evermore acknowledge thee,
Lest my bewailèd guilt should do thee shame,
Nor thou with public kindness honor me
Unless thou take that honor from thy name.   12
    But do not so. I love thee in such sort
    As, thou being mine, mine is thy good report.

The poet feels crippled by misfortune but takes delight in the blessings heaped by nature and fortune on the beloved.

3. **dearest:** most grievous, direst
4. **of:** from
7. **Entitled . . . sit:** i.e., **sit crowned** among your virtues
Entitled: having a rightful claim or authority
8. **make . . . store:** i.e., attach **my love** to this abundance (**store**)
10. **shadow:** idea, conception
13. **Look what:** i.e., whatever

The nine muses. (s. 38.10)

37

As a decrepit father takes delight
To see his active child do deeds of youth,
So I, made lame by fortune's dearest spite,
Take all my comfort of thy worth and truth.   4
For whether beauty, birth, or wealth, or wit,
Or any of these all, or all, or more,
Entitled in ⌜thy⌝ parts do crownèd sit,
I make my love engrafted to this store.   8
So then I am not lame, poor, nor despised
Whilst that this shadow doth such substance give
That I in thy abundance am sufficed
And by a part of all thy glory live.   12
    Look what is best, that best I wish in thee.
    This wish I have, then ten times happy me.

The poet attributes all that is praiseworthy in his poetry to the beloved, who is his theme and inspiration.

---

1. **muse:** poetic gift or genius (This **muse,** which reappears in l. 13, is different from the **nine** mythological muses of l. 10, who inspire artists in the entire spectrum of human creativity; these are set in contrast to yet another **muse** [l. 9], that represented by the beloved as inspiration.) **want:** lack; **invent:** (1) write about; (2) find (from the Latin *invenio*)

2. **that:** i.e., **thou** who

3. **Thine own sweet argument:** i.e., yourself as the **subject** (l. 1)

4. **vulgar paper:** ordinary or commonplace writing; **rehearse:** repeat; say

6. **stand against thy sight:** i.e., withstand your scrutiny

8. **invention:** the act of poetic composition (See note to **invent,** l. 1.)

10. **nine:** See note to **muse,** l. 1, and picture, p. 92. **invocate:** invoke

12. **Eternal numbers:** immortal verses; **date:** period, duration

13. **muse:** the poetic gift cited in l. 1

38

How can my muse want subject to invent
While thou dost breathe that pour'st into my verse
Thine own sweet argument, too excellent
For every vulgar paper to rehearse? 4
O, give thyself the thanks if aught in me
Worthy perusal stand against thy sight,
For who's so dumb that cannot write to thee
When thou thyself dost give invention light? 8
Be thou the tenth muse, ten times more in worth
Than those old nine which rhymers invocate;
And he that calls on thee, let him bring forth
Eternal numbers to outlive long date. 12
   If my slight muse do please these curious days,
   The pain be mine, but thine shall be the praise.

As in s. 36, the poet finds reasons to excuse the fact that he and the beloved are parted. First, it is easier to praise the beloved if they are not a "single one"; and, second, absence from the beloved gives the poet leisure to contemplate their love.

---

1. **with manners:** politely, with propriety
2. **better:** superior; greater
5. **Even for this:** i.e., precisely **for this** reason
10. **not thy:** i.e., **not** that **thy**
13. **And that:** i.e., **and were it not that** (l. 10); **thou:** addressed to **absence; make one twain:** (1) divide **one** into two; (2) give **one** person an existence in two locations
14. **here:** (1) i.e., where I am; (2) in the poem; **remain:** abide, dwell

A lute. (s. 8.9–12)

39

O, how thy worth with manners may I sing
When thou art all the better part of me?
What can mine own praise to mine own self bring,
And what is 't but mine own when I praise thee?   4
Even for this let us divided live
And our dear love lose name of single one,
That by this separation I may give
That due to thee which thou deserv'st alone.   8
O absence, what a torment wouldst thou prove
Were it not thy sour leisure gave sweet leave
To entertain the time with thoughts of love,
Which time and thoughts so sweetly ⌜doth⌝ deceive,   12
    And that thou teachest how to make one twain
    By praising him here who doth hence remain.

This first of three linked sonnets accuses the young man of having stolen the poet's "love." The poet struggles to justify and forgive the young man's betrayal, but can go no farther than the concluding "we must not be foes." (While the word *love* is elaborately ambiguous in this sonnet, the following two sonnets make it clear that the theft is of the poet's mistress.)

---

6. **for . . . usest:** (1) if you make use of **my love;** (2) because you have intercourse with my mistress

7. **be blamed:** i.e., you are blameworthy

8. **taste:** (1) testing; (2) enjoyment; (3) savoring

10. **steal thee:** i.e., **steal** for yourself; **all my poverty:** i.e., the little bit that I have

11. **grief:** (1) suffering; (2) sorrow

12. **injury:** willful harm

13. **Lascivious grace:** i.e., attractiveness that is both lewd and seductive; **all ill well shows:** everything bad or evil looks good

14. **spites:** insults; **yet:** nevertheless

40

Take all my loves, my love, yea, take them all.
What hast thou then more than thou hadst before?
No love, my love, that thou mayst true love call;
All mine was thine before thou hadst this more. 4
Then, if for my love thou my love receivest,
I cannot blame thee for my love thou usest;
But yet be blamed if thou ⌐thyself¬ deceivest
By willful taste of what thyself refusest. 8
I do forgive thy robb'ry, gentle thief,
Although thou steal thee all my poverty;
And yet love knows it is a greater grief
To bear love's wrong than hate's known injury. 12
    Lascivious grace, in whom all ill well shows,
    Kill me with spites, yet we must not be foes.

The poet again tries to forgive the young man, now on the grounds that the young man could hardly have been expected to refuse the woman's seduction. The attempt to forgive fails because the young man has caused a twofold betrayal: his beauty having first seduced the woman, both he and she have then been faithless to the poet.

---

1. **pretty wrongs:** i.e., little offenses (Proverbial: "Little things are **pretty.**") **liberty:** license

3. **befits:** i.e., befit

4. **still:** always

5–6. **Gentle . . . assailed:** a clever gender inversion of the proverb "All women may be won," which Shakespeare appropriated in *1 Henry VI* 5.3.78–79 as "She's beautiful, and therefore to be wooed; / She is a woman, **therefore to be won.**"   **Gentle:** (1) wellborn; (2) mild in disposition, kind, tender

8. **sourly:** peevishly; **he:** Note the unexpected and witty shift of responsibility here from the woman to the young man.

9. **my seat forbear:** i.e., keep away from a place belonging to me

11. **Who:** i.e., which; **riot:** debauchery

12. **truth:** i.e., troth, constancy, faithfulness

41

Those pretty wrongs that liberty commits
When I am sometime absent from thy heart,
Thy beauty and thy years full well befits,
For still temptation follows where thou art.   4
Gentle thou art, and therefore to be won;
Beauteous thou art, therefore to be assailed;
And when a woman woos, what woman's son
Will sourly leave her till he have prevailed?   8
Ay me, but yet thou mightst my seat forbear,
And chide thy beauty and thy straying youth,
Who lead thee in their riot even there
Where thou art forced to break a twofold truth: 12
    Hers, by thy beauty tempting her to thee,
    Thine, by thy beauty being false to me.

The poet attempts to excuse the two lovers. He first argues that they love each other only because of him; he then argues that since he and the young man are one, in loving the young man, the woman actually loves the poet. The poet acknowledges, though, that all of this is mere "flattery" or self-delusion.

3. **of my wailing chief:** i.e., is the **chief** cause of my sorrow

4. **touches:** (1) affects; (2) injures; **nearly:** (1) closely; (2) particularly

5. **excuse ye:** i.e., find an excuse for you

7. **for my sake:** out of regard for me; **even so:** i.e., in the same way; **abuse:** wrong

8. **Suff'ring:** allowing; **approve her:** wordplay on "commend her" and "try or experience her sexually"

9. **my love's:** i.e., my mistress's

10. **losing:** i.e., I **losing; that loss:** i.e., what I have lost

12. **lay on me this cross:** i.e., put this heavy burden on me

Woman wearing a carcanet. (s. 52.8)

42

That thou hast her, it is not all my grief,
And yet it may be said I loved her dearly;
That she hath thee is of my wailing chief,
A loss in love that touches me more nearly.   4
Loving offenders, thus I will excuse ye:
Thou dost love her because thou know'st I love her,
And for my sake even so doth she abuse me,
Suff'ring my friend for my sake to approve her.   8
If I lose thee, my loss is my love's gain,
And losing her, my friend hath found that loss;
Both find each other, and I lose both twain,
And both for my sake lay on me this cross.   12
    But here's the joy: my friend and I are one;
    Sweet flattery! then she loves but me alone.

The poet, separated from the beloved, reflects on the paradox that because he dreams of the beloved, he sees better with his eyes closed in sleep than he does with them open in daylight. His desire, though, is to see not the dream image but the actual person.

---

1. **wink:** close my eyes

2. **unrespected:** (1) not worth respect; (2) not heeded, not paid attention to

4. **darkly bright:** (1) luminous behind the eyelids' dark shutters; (2) blind but seeing; **are bright:** i.e., are brightly, clearly (See longer note, p. 335.)

5. **shadow:** dream image; **shadows:** dark places; other dream images

6. **thy shadow's form:** i.e., your physical being; **form happy show:** create a joyful spectacle

8. **thy shade:** i.e., your (mere) image

11. **fair imperfect:** i.e., beautiful but deficient (because only a dream image)

12. **stay:** remain, linger, reside

13. **to see:** (1) in appearance; (2) as regards my ability **to see**

14. **show thee me:** i.e., **show** you to **me** (though the syntax insists on the more obvious "**show me** to you")

43

When most I wink, then do mine eyes best see,
For all the day they view things unrespected;
But when I sleep, in dreams they look on thee
And, darkly bright, are bright in dark directed.   4
Then thou whose shadow shadows doth make bright,
How would thy shadow's form form happy show
To the clear day with thy much clearer light
When to unseeing eyes thy shade shines so!   8
How would, I say, mine eyes be blessèd made
By looking on thee in the living day,
When in dead night ⌜thy⌝ fair imperfect shade
Through heavy sleep on sightless eyes doth stay!   12
    All days are nights to see till I see thee,
    And nights bright days when dreams do show thee me.

In this sonnet, which links with s. 45 to form, in effect, a two-part poem, the poet wishes that he were thought rather than flesh so that he could be with the beloved. The poet, being mortal, is instead made up of the four elements—earth, air, fire, and water. The dullest of these elements, earth and water, are dominant in him and force him to remain fixed in place, weeping "heavy tears."

---

1. **dull substance:** heavy material; **thought:** Proverbial: "As swift as **thought.**"

2. **stop my way:** block my path

4. **limits:** regions; **where:** i.e., to **where; stay:** reside, linger

6. **removed:** remote, separated

8. **he would be:** i.e., **thought** wished to **be**

9. **thought kills me:** i.e., reflection makes me despair; **thought:** i.e., (swift) imagination

11. **so . . . wrought:** i.e., composed to such an extent **of earth and water** (In the thinking of the time, all that was material was composed of **earth,** air, fire, and **water,** with air and fire the lighter and freer.)

12. **attend time's leisure:** (1) wait until time passes; (2) wait upon the powerful figure of Time until he is ready to hear me; **moan:** (1) lamentation; (2) expression of grief (in this poem)

14. **badges of either's woe:** Because **tears** are wet (like **water**) and **heavy** (like **earth**), they serve as insignia (**badges**) that tie the poet to the two heavier **elements** and their **woe.**

44

If the dull substance of my flesh were thought,
Injurious distance should not stop my way,
For then, despite of space, I would be brought
From limits far remote, where thou dost stay.   4
No matter then although my foot did stand
Upon the farthest earth removed from thee,
For nimble thought can jump both sea and land
As soon as think the place where he would be.   8
But, ah, thought kills me that I am not thought,
To leap large lengths of miles when thou art gone,
But that, so much of earth and water wrought,
I must attend time's leisure with my moan;   12
    Receiving ⌐nought⌐ by elements so slow
    But heavy tears, badges of either's woe.

This sonnet, the companion to s. 44, imagines the poet's thoughts and desires as the "other two" elements—air and fire—that make up "life's composition." When his thoughts and desires are with the beloved, the poet, reduced to earth and water, sinks into melancholy; when his thoughts and desires return, assuring the poet of the beloved's "fair health," the poet is briefly joyful, until he sends them back to the beloved and again is "sad."

---

1. **two:** i.e., **two** elements; **slight:** i.e., light; **purging:** purifying

4. **These:** i.e., **my thought** and **my desire; with . . . slide:** i.e., move without effort

5. **quicker:** livelier; swifter

6. **In . . . love:** i.e., on an ambassadorial mission (**embassy**) carrying my **love**

7. **four:** i.e., **four** elements

8. **melancholy:** a psychological and physiological condition caused by an excess of black bile, one of the four humors thought to govern man's emotional and physical state (**Melancholy** as a humor is, like **earth** [s. 44.11], considered cold and dry.) For a chart of humors and elements, see picture, p. 112.

9. **recured:** restored

11. **even but now:** i.e., at this very moment

12. **recounting it:** giving a detailed account of it

14. **straight:** immediately

45

The other two, slight air and purging fire,
Are both with thee, wherever I abide;
The first my thought, the other my desire,
These present-absent with swift motion slide.   4
For when these quicker elements are gone
In tender embassy of love to thee,
My life, being made of four, with two alone
Sinks down to death, oppressed with melancholy;   8
Until life's composition be recured
By those swift messengers returned from thee,
Who even but now come back again, assured
Of ⌜thy⌝ fair health, recounting it to me.   12
    This told, I joy; but then, no longer glad,
    I send them back again and straight grow sad.

In this first of another pair of sonnets (perhaps a witty thank-you for the gift of a miniature portrait), the poet's eyes and his heart are in a bitter dispute about which has the legal right to the beloved's picture. The case is brought before a jury made up of the poet's thoughts. This jury determines that the eyes have the right to the picture, since it is the beloved's outer image; the heart, though, has the right to the beloved's love.

---

1. **at a mortal:** i.e., in a deadly

2. **conquest:** (1) booty; (2) property acquired not through inheritance; **thy sight:** i.e., the **sight** of you

3. **my . . . bar:** i.e., **would** forbid **my heart** any glimpse of your picture (On the legal language that fills this sonnet, see longer note, p. 335.)

4. **mine . . . right:** i.e., **would** forbid **mine eye** to exercise its unrestrained **right** (to view the picture)

5. **thou:** i.e., the essential "you"

6. **closet:** either a small private room or a cabinet

7. **defendant:** i.e., the eyes

9. **impanelèd:** constituted

10. **quest:** jury

12. **moiety:** portion; **dear:** loving

46

Mine eye and heart are at a mortal war
How to divide the conquest of thy sight.
Mine eye my heart ⌐thy⌐ picture's sight would bar,
My heart mine eye the freedom of that right.   4
My heart doth plead that thou in him dost lie,
A closet never pierced with crystal eyes;
But the defendant doth that plea deny,
And says in him ⌐thy⌐ fair appearance lies.   8
To ⌐'cide⌐ this title is impanelèd
A quest of thoughts, all tenants to the heart,
And by their verdict is determinèd
The clear eyes' moiety and the dear heart's part,   12
    As thus: mine eyes' due is ⌐thy⌐ outward part,
    And my heart's right, ⌐thy⌐ inward love of heart.

After the verdict is rendered (in s. 46), the poet's eyes and heart become allies, with the eyes sometimes inviting the heart to enjoy the picture, and the heart sometimes inviting the eyes to share in its "thoughts of love." The beloved, though absent, is thus doubly present to the poet through the picture and through the poet's thoughts.

---

1. **league is took:** alliance or compact is made

4. **heart in love:** love-struck **heart; with . . . smother:** i.e., smothers itself **with sighs** (There is a possible allusion to the belief that sighs draw blood from the heart.)

10. **still:** continually

12. **still:** always

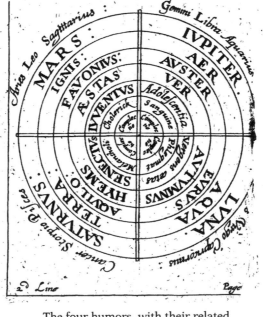

The four humors, with their related
elements, planets, etc. (ss. 44, 45)

47

Betwixt mine eye and heart a league is took,
And each doth good turns now unto the other.
When that mine eye is famished for a look,
Or heart in love with sighs himself doth smother,   4
With my love's picture then my eye doth feast
And to the painted banquet bids my heart.
Another time mine eye is my heart's guest
And in his thoughts of love doth share a part.   8
So, either by thy picture or my love,
Thyself away are present still with me;
For thou ⌜no⌝ farther than my thoughts canst move,
And I am still with them, and they with thee;   12
    Or, if they sleep, thy picture in my sight
    Awakes my heart to heart's and eye's delight.

The poet contrasts the relative ease of locking away valuable material possessions with the impossibility of safeguarding his relationship with the beloved. The beloved can be enclosed only in the poet's heart, which cannot block the beloved's egress nor protect against those who would steal the beloved away.

---

1. **took my way:** set out on my journey

2. **truest:** surest, securest

3. **to:** i.e., for

3–4. **stay / From:** i.e., remain out of

4. **hands of falsehood:** i.e., thieves (literally, treacherous hands); **in . . . trust:** i.e., as in a safely guarded fortress

5. **to whom:** i.e., in comparison **to whom**

6. **Most worthy comfort:** you who are my chief delight (but with the secondary sense "you who most deserve **comfort**"); **grief:** cause of distress

7. **mine only care:** i.e., all that I care about (**Care** could also mean "grief" or "concern.")

8. **vulgar:** common, ordinary

11. **closure:** confines, enclosure

12. **From . . . part:** i.e., which you may enter and leave whenever you please

14. **truth . . . dear:** See *Venus and Adonis* 724: "Rich preys make true men thieves" (p. 411); and *As You Like It* 1.3.116: "Beauty provoketh thieves sooner than gold."   **truth:** honesty **dear:** precious

48

How careful was I, when I took my way,
Each trifle under truest bars to thrust,
That to my use it might unusèd stay
From hands of falsehood, in sure wards of trust!   4
But thou, to whom my jewels trifles are,
Most worthy comfort, now my greatest grief,
Thou best of dearest and mine only care
Art left the prey of every vulgar thief.   8
Thee have I not locked up in any chest,
Save where thou art not, though I feel thou art,
Within the gentle closure of my breast,
From whence at pleasure thou mayst come and part;   12
    And even thence thou wilt be stol'n, I fear,
    For truth proves thievish for a prize so dear.

The poet tries to prepare himself for a future in which the beloved rejects him. When that day comes, he writes, he will shield himself within the knowledge of his own worth, acknowledging that he can cite no reason in support of their love.

---

1. **Against:** in preparation for, in anticipation of

3. **Whenas:** when; **cast his utmost sum:** i.e., made its final reckoning

4. **advised respects:** prudent considerations

5. **strangely:** coldly, distantly

7. **converted:** transformed

8. **of settled gravity:** i.e., for behaving with staid solemnity

9. **ensconce me:** take shelter (A *sconce* is a small fortification or earthwork.)

10. **mine own desert:** i.e., what I deserve, my worth

11. **against:** in front of (Some editors see ll. 11–12 as picturing the poet raising his hand as a witness against himself. In that reading, **against** means "in opposition to," and **guard** [l. 12] means "protect.")

12. **guard:** ward off, parry

14. **allege:** adduce, urge

49

Against that time, if ever that time come,
When I shall see thee frown on my defects,
Whenas thy love hath cast his utmost sum,
Called to that audit by advised respects;   4
Against that time when thou shalt strangely pass
And scarcely greet me with that sun thine eye,
When love, converted from the thing it was,
Shall reasons find of settled gravity;   8
Against that time do I ensconce me here
Within the knowledge of mine own desert,
And this my hand against myself uprear
To guard the lawful reasons on thy part.   12
　　To leave poor me thou hast the strength of laws,
　　Since why to love I can allege no cause.

In this first of two linked sonnets, the poet's unhappiness in traveling away from the beloved seems to him reproduced in the plodding steps and the groans of the horse that carries him.

1. **heavy:** i.e., heavily, sorrowfully

3. **that ease and that repose:** i.e., his **travel's end,** which is what he seeks (l. 2); **say:** remind me

4. **Thus . . . measured:** i.e., you are this many **miles**

6. **to bear that weight:** i.e., bearing **my weight** of **woe** (l. 5)

8. **being made from:** i.e., when that **speed** is **made** away **from**

A jade. (s. 51.12; *Venus and Adonis,* 391; *Lucrece,* 707)

50

How heavy do I journey on the way,
When what I seek, my weary travel's end,
Doth teach that ease and that repose to say
"Thus far the miles are measured from thy friend."   4
The beast that bears me, tired with my woe,
Plods ⌜dully⌝ on, to bear that weight in me,
As if by some instinct the wretch did know
His rider loved not speed, being made from thee.   8
The bloody spur cannot provoke him on
That sometimes anger thrusts into his hide,
Which heavily he answers with a groan,
More sharp to me than spurring to his side;   12
    For that same groan doth put this in my mind:
    My grief lies onward and my joy behind.

The slow-moving horse (of s. 50) will have no excuse for his plodding gait on the return journey, for which even the fastest horse, the poet realizes, will be too slow. Returning to the beloved, desire and love will outrun any horse.

---

1. **slow offense:** i.e., **offense** of moving slowly

4. **Till I return:** i.e., until my return journey; **posting:** riding hard

6. **swift extremity:** i.e., extreme swiftness

8. **no motion shall I know:** perhaps, I will (still) feel as though not moving

11. **Shall neigh no dull flesh in his fiery race:** This puzzling line appears to set up an opposition between the **dull flesh** of the horse and the **fiery** nature of **desire.** (In s. 45, **desire** is said to be composed of the element of fire.)

12. **love for love:** i.e., my **love,** out of compassion (for the horse); **jade:** nag (See picture, p. 118.)

13. **thee:** the beloved; **willful slow:** i.e., deliberately slowly

14. **leave:** permission; **go:** wordplay on "depart" and "walk"

120

51

Thus can my love excuse the slow offense
Of my dull bearer when from thee I speed:
From where thou art, why should I haste me thence?
Till I return, of posting is no need.   4
O, what excuse will my poor beast then find
When swift extremity can seem but slow?
Then should I spur, though mounted on the wind;
In wingèd speed no motion shall I know.   8
Then can no horse with my desire keep pace;
Therefore desire, of ⌐perfect'st¬ love being made,
Shall neigh no dull flesh in his fiery race.
But love for love thus shall excuse my jade: 12
    "Since from thee going he went willful slow,
    Towards thee I'll run, and give him leave to go."

The poet likens himself to a rich man who visits his treasures rarely so that they remain for him a source of pleasure. The poet's infrequent meetings with the beloved, he argues, are, like rare feasts or widely spaced jewels, the more precious for their rarity.

---

1. **So . . . rich:** i.e., **I am** like a wealthy man

3. **will not:** i.e., chooses not to

4. **For blunting:** lest he blunt; **seldom:** rare, infrequent (Proverbial: "A **seldom** use of pleasures maketh the same the more pleasant.")

5. **Therefore:** for that (same) reason; **feasts:** i.e., feast days; **solemn:** ceremonial; **rare:** splendid; exceptional

7. **stones of worth:** valuable gems; **thinly placèd:** i.e., **placed** at wide intervals

8. **captain:** chief; **carcanet:** jeweled collar (See picture, p. 102.)

9–10. **So . . . hide: Time,** which **keeps** the beloved from the poet, serves the function of the rich man's **chest** that holds rarely visited treasure, or the rich man's **wardrobe** (a room where valuable clothes are kept under "ward" or guard), hiding the beloved as if he were a fine **robe** taken out for rare occasions.

12. **new unfolding:** i.e., newly revealing; **his imprisoned pride:** i.e., that among its contents of which it is most proud **his:** its

13–14. **gives scope . . . hope:** i.e., allows **the rich** (l. 1; here, the poet) the range of experience (**scope**) of glorying in your presence, and, in your absence, of entertaining the expectation of seeing you again

52

So am I as the rich whose blessèd key
Can bring him to his sweet up-lockèd treasure,
The which he will not ev'ry hour survey,
For blunting the fine point of seldom pleasure.   4
Therefore are feasts so solemn and so rare,
Since seldom coming in the long year set,
Like stones of worth they thinly placèd are,
Or captain jewels in the carcanet.   8
So is the time that keeps you as my chest,
Or as the wardrobe which the robe doth hide
To make some special instant special blessed
By new unfolding his imprisoned pride.   12
    Blessèd are you whose worthiness gives scope,
    Being had, to triumph, being lacked, to hope.

Using language from Neoplatonism, the poet praises the beloved both as the essence of beauty (its very Idea, which is only imperfectly reflected in lesser beauties) and as the epitome of constancy.

1. **substance:** (1) Platonic essence; (2) matter

2. **strange:** (1) alien (i.e., not yours); (2) unusual; **shadows:** images, reflections; **on you tend:** serve you, follow you

3. **shade:** shadow (wordplay that shifts from the image cast by a body in sunlight to Neoplatonic **shadows** [imperfect reflections of the Idea])

4. **but:** only; **every shadow lend:** perhaps, be the source of (or provide attributes for) **every shadow**

5. **Adonis:** the beautiful mythological youth loved by Venus; **counterfeit:** picture, portrait

7. **On . . . set:** i.e., portray **Helen's cheek** (1) with the highest artistic touch, or (2) with the best cosmetics (The mythological Helen of Troy was the most lovely of women. See picture below.)

8. **Grecian tires:** Greek costume or headdress

9. **spring and foison:** springtime and harvest

10. **shadow:** image

12. **And you:** i.e., **and you** are revealed

13. **external grace:** i.e., outward beauty

14. **you like none, none you:** i.e., **you** are **like none, none** are like **you**

Helen of Troy. (s. 53.7; *Lucrece*, 1369, 1471)

53

What is your substance, whereof are you made,
That millions of strange shadows on you tend?
Since everyone hath, every one, one shade,
And you, but one, can every shadow lend.   4
Describe Adonis, and the counterfeit
Is poorly imitated after you;
On Helen's cheek all art of beauty set,
And you in Grecian tires are painted new.   8
Speak of the spring and foison of the year;
The one doth shadow of your beauty show,
The other as your bounty doth appear,
And you in every blessèd shape we know.   12
    In all external grace you have some part,
    But you like none, none you, for constant heart.

Here the beloved's truth is compared to the fragrance in the rose. As that fragrance is distilled into perfume, so the beloved's truth distills in verse.

---

2. **By:** i.e., through; **truth:** (1) integrity, virtue; (2) constancy (perhaps the "constant heart" of s. 53.14)

3. **fair:** beautiful

4. **For:** because of

5. **canker blooms:** the blossoms of the dog rose, a wild rose that has little fragrance; **dye:** color

6. **tincture:** hue, color

7. **such:** i.e., similar

8. **their maskèd buds discloses:** i.e., opens the **buds** (of the **canker blooms**), the beauty of which is **masked** or concealed until the flowers are open

9. **for their virtue only:** i.e., because **their only virtue; show:** visual appearance

10. **unrespected:** unregarded, unvalued

12. **Of . . . made:** i.e., when **roses** die, their fragrance is distilled into perfume (See s. 5.9–14.)

13. **And so of you:** i.e., **and** thus it is with **you; lovely:** lovable

14. **that:** i.e., beauty and youth; **vade:** (1) depart; (2) fade away; **by verse distils your truth:** i.e., **your truth** will distil itself in (my) **verse**

54

O, how much more doth beauty beauteous seem
By that sweet ornament which truth doth give.
The rose looks fair, but fairer we it deem
For that sweet odor which doth in it live.   4
The canker blooms have full as deep a dye
As the perfumèd tincture of the roses,
Hang on such thorns, and play as wantonly
When summer's breath their maskèd buds discloses;   8
But, for their virtue only is their show,
They live unwooed and unrespected fade,
Die to themselves. Sweet roses do not so;
Of their sweet deaths are sweetest odors made.   12
    And so of you, beauteous and lovely youth,
    When that shall vade, by verse distils your truth.

Continuing the idea of the beloved's distillation into poetry (in the couplet of s. 54), the poet now claims that his verse will be a "living record" in which the beloved will "shine . . . bright" until Doomsday.

1–2. **Not . . . rhyme:** These two lines restate a familiar classical motif. (See, e.g., Ovid, *Metamorphoses* [E], in Appendix, p. 617.) In l. 3, Shakespeare moves away from his models by having the beloved, rather than the poet, immortalized in his verse.

4. **with sluttish:** i.e., by disgustingly dirty

6. **broils:** tumults; **root out:** i.e., destroy

7. **Nor Mars his:** i.e., neither Mars's (**Mars** is the Roman god of war.) **quick:** strongly burning

9. **all oblivious enmity:** i.e., every hostile force that causes forgetfulness (or brings all to oblivion)

10. **your . . . still:** i.e., **praise** of you will always

12. **wear . . . doom:** i.e., survive until the world's end (**Doom** is Doomsday or **Judgment** Day [l. 13].) See picture, p. 194.

13. **that yourself:** i.e., when you **yourself** will

55

Not marble nor the gilded ⌜monuments⌝
Of princes shall outlive this powerful rhyme,
But you shall shine more bright in these contents
Than unswept stone besmeared with sluttish time.   4
When wasteful war shall statues overturn,
And broils root out the work of masonry,
Nor Mars his sword nor war's quick fire shall burn
The living record of your memory.   8
'Gainst death and all oblivious enmity
Shall you pace forth; your praise shall still find room
Even in the eyes of all posterity
That wear this world out to the ending doom.   12
    So, till the judgment that yourself arise,
    You live in this, and dwell in lovers' eyes.

The poet addresses the spirit of love and then the beloved, urging that love be reinvigorated and that the present separation of the lovers serve to renew their love's intensity.

1. **love:** here, the spirit of **love**
4. **his:** its
5. **love:** here addressed to the beloved
6. **wink:** close
8. **dullness:** apathy, lack of interest
9. **Let . . . be:** i.e., **let** us view **this sad** interval of time as if it were an **ocean** (Although ll. 9–12 are difficult, the general image seems to be of two newly betrothed lovers standing **daily** on opposite shores of this **ocean,** awaiting a longed-for reunion.)
13–14. **Or . . . rare:** The **sad int'rim** is now imagined as **winter,** the difficulties of which make the return of summer even more **welcome.**

"The hungry ocean." (s. 64.5–7)

130

56

Sweet love, renew thy force. Be it not said
Thy edge should blunter be than appetite,
Which but today by feeding is allayed,
Tomorrow sharpened in his former might. 4
So, love, be thou. Although today thou fill
Thy hungry eyes even till they wink with fullness,
Tomorrow see again, and do not kill
The spirit of love with a perpetual dullness. 8
Let this sad int'rim like the ocean be
Which parts the shore where two contracted new
Come daily to the banks, that, when they see
Return of love, more blessed may be the view. 12
⌐Or⌐ call it winter, which being full of care
Makes summer's welcome, thrice more wished, more rare.

In this and the following sonnet, the poet presents his relationship with the beloved as that of servant and master. As the beloved's servant, the poet describes himself (with barely suppressed bitterness) as having no life or wishes of his own as he waits like a "sad slave" for the commands of his "sovereign."

1. **slave:** a servant completely divested of freedom and personal rights

1–2. **tend / Upon:** wait for, await (with wordplay on "wait **upon,** serve")

3. **precious time . . . to spend:** i.e., **time to spend** that is **at all precious** or valuable

5. **world-without-end:** seemingly endless

7. **bitterness:** anguish; **sour:** distasteful

8. **bid . . . once adieu:** i.e., **once** said farewell to me   **your servant:** a phrase applied to an attendant, a lover, or a friend

10. **suppose:** imagine, form an idea of

12. **Save . . . those:** i.e., except **how happy you make those** who are **where you are**

13. **So true a fool:** (1) such a complete **fool;** (2) such a faithful, constant **fool**

14. **he:** i.e., **love; ill:** evil

57

Being your slave, what should I do but tend
Upon the hours and times of your desire?
I have no precious time at all to spend
Nor services to do till you require.   4
Nor dare I chide the world-without-end hour
Whilst I, my sovereign, watch the clock for you,
Nor think the bitterness of absence sour
When you have bid your servant once adieu.   8
Nor dare I question with my jealous thought
Where you may be, or your affairs suppose,
But, like a sad slave, stay and think of nought
Save where you are how happy you make those.   12
    So true a fool is love that in your will,
    Though you do anything, he thinks no ill.

This sonnet repeats the ideas and some of the language of s. 57, though the pain of waiting upon (and waiting for) the beloved and asking nothing in return seems even more intense in the present poem.

1–2. **That . . . control:** i.e., may the **god** who **made me your slave** protect me from trying to **control** (wordplay on the phrase **"God forbid** that **I should"**)   **in thought:** i.e., even in my imagination

3. **Or at your hand . . . crave:** i.e., **or should crave** an **account** of how you spend your time

4. **stay your leisure:** wait until you have time for me

5. **suffer:** allow; endure

6. **Th' imprisoned:** i.e., the imprisoning; **of your liberty:** i.e., that results from your freedom (or licentiousness)

7. **patience:** i.e., let **patience; tame to sufferance:** docile under suffering; **bide each check:** endure **each** rebuke or rebuff

9. **where you list:** wherever you please; **charter:** publicly acknowledged right

10. **privilege:** authorize

11. **To what you will:** i.e., **to** do whatever **you** wish

12. **self-doing crime:** offenses done by (or to) you

13. **I am to wait:** As in s. 57.1–2, there is rich wordplay on the concept of the servant who waits upon his master and the lover who waits for an absent beloved.

14. **ill:** bad, evil

58

That god forbid, that made me first your slave,
I should in thought control your times of pleasure,
Or at your hand th' account of hours to crave,
Being your vassal bound to stay your leisure.   4
O, let me suffer, being at your beck,
Th' imprisoned absence of your liberty,
And patience, tame to sufferance, bide each check
Without accusing you of injury.   8
Be where you list, your charter is so strong
That you yourself may privilege your time
To what you will; to you it doth belong
Yourself to pardon of self-doing crime.   12
  I am to wait, though waiting so be hell,
  Not blame your pleasure, be it ill or well.

The poet here plays with the idea of history as cyclical and with the proverb "There is nothing new under the sun." If he could go back in time, he writes, he could see how the beloved's beauty was praised in the distant past and thus judge whether the world had progressed, regressed, or stayed the same.

1–2. **If . . . before:** See Ecclesiastes 1.9–10: "What is it that **hath been**? that that shall be . . . : and there *is* no new thing under the sun. Is there any thing whereof one may say, Behold this, it is **new**? It **hath been** already in the old time that was before us."

2. **beguiled:** deceived, cheated

3. **invention:** a new creation; poetic originality

3–4. **bear . . . child:** i.e., produce a **child** who has lived before **burden:** that which is borne in the womb

5. **record:** memory (accented on the second syllable)

6. **courses of the sun:** i.e., years

8. **at . . . done:** i.e., **was first** expressed in writing

10. **To:** in response to; **composèd . . . frame:** elaborately constructed miracle of your form

11. **mended:** improved; **whe'er better they:** whether **they** were **better** than we

12. **revolution be the same:** i.e., the cycle of history keeps things **the same**

13. **wits:** geniuses, talented writers

14. **To . . . praise:** This faint praise of the beloved is probably ironic understatement.

59

If there be nothing new, but that which is
Hath been before, how are our brains beguiled,
Which, laboring for invention, bear amiss
The second burden of a former child.   4
O, that record could with a backward look,
Even of five hundred courses of the sun,
Show me your image in some antique book,
Since mind at first in character was done,   8
That I might see what the old world could say
To this composèd wonder of your frame;
Whether we are mended, or whe'er better they,
Or whether revolution be the same.   12
   O, sure I am the wits of former days
    To subjects worse have given admiring praise.

The poet meditates on life's inevitable course through maturity to death. Everything, he says, is a victim of Time's scythe. Only his poetry will stand against Time, keeping alive his praise of the beloved.

1–4. **Like . . . contend:** See Ovid, *Metamorphoses* [A], in Appendix, p. 615.   **Like as:** just as   **In sequent toil:** laboring one after another   **contend:** strive

5. **Nativity:** i.e., the newborn (with wordplay on birth considered astrologically); **once:** (1) at one time; (2) when **once; main:** broad expanse (with probable wordplay on **main** as open ocean)

7. **eclipses:** i.e., obscurations (Taken literally, this word calls attention to the metaphor [ll. 5–7] of a human life traced as a rising and then setting sun.)

8. **confound:** destroy (See Ovid, *Metamorphoses* [C], in Appendix, p. 616.)

9. **transfix:** pierce through; **flourish:** bloom

10. **parallels:** i.e., wrinkles (literally, trenches)

11. **Feeds . . . truth:** See Ovid: "Thou time, the eater up of things, . . . / Destroy all things. . . . / You leisurely by ling'ring death consume them every whit" (*Metamorphoses* 15.258–60, Golding translation).

12. **his scythe:** See note to s. 12.13.

13. **to times in hope:** i.e., to ages that exist only in expectation (though with wordplay on "**stand . . . in hope**")

60

Like as the waves make towards the pebbled shore,
So do our minutes hasten to their end,
Each changing place with that which goes before;
In sequent toil all forwards do contend.   4
Nativity, once in the main of light,
Crawls to maturity, wherewith being crowned,
Crookèd eclipses 'gainst his glory fight,
And Time that gave doth now his gift confound.   8
Time doth transfix the flourish set on youth
And delves the parallels in beauty's brow,
Feeds on the rarities of Nature's truth,
And nothing stands but for his scythe to mow.   12
      And yet to times in hope my verse shall stand,
      Praising thy worth, despite his cruel hand.

The poet first wonders if the beloved is deliberately keeping him awake by sending dream images to spy on him, but then admits it is his own devotion and jealousy that will not let him sleep.

---

1. **Is it thy will:** i.e., do you wish that
4. **shadows like to thee:** i.e., dream images that look like you (with possible wordplay on "ghosts")
7. **shames:** shameful acts
8. **scope and tenor of thy jealousy:** i.e., aim and substance of your suspicions
12. **watchman:** one who keeps vigil
13. **watch I:** I stay awake

"Lofty towers . . . down-razed." (s. 64.3)

61

Is it thy will thy image should keep open
My heavy eyelids to the weary night?
Dost thou desire my slumbers should be broken
While shadows like to thee do mock my sight?   4
Is it thy spirit that thou send'st from thee
So far from home into my deeds to pry,
To find out shames and idle hours in me,
The scope and tenor of thy jealousy?   8
O, no. Thy love, though much, is not so great.
It is my love that keeps mine eye awake,
Mine own true love that doth my rest defeat
To play the watchman ever for thy sake.   12
    For thee watch I whilst thou dost wake elsewhere,
    From me far off, with others all too near.

The poet accuses himself of supreme vanity in that he thinks so highly of himself. He then admits that the "self" he holds in such esteem is not his physical self but his "other self," the beloved.

---

4. **inward in:** i.e., in the interior of

5. **Methinks:** it seems to me

8. **As . . . surmount:** i.e., so that I surpass everyone else in every merit or attainment

9. **glass:** looking glass, mirror

10. **Beated:** beaten, battered; **chopped:** chapped; **antiquity:** old age

11. **quite contrary I read:** i.e., I interpret in **quite** the opposite way

12. **Self so self-loving:** i.e., to love such a **self; were iniquity:** i.e., would (indeed) be sinful

13. **myself, that for myself:** i.e., my (real, or other) self, **that** as **myself**

14. **beauty of thy days:** i.e., **thy** youthful **beauty**

62

Sin of self-love possesseth all mine eye
And all my soul and all my every part;
And for this sin there is no remedy,
It is so grounded inward in my heart.   4
Methinks no face so gracious is as mine,
No shape so true, no truth of such account,
And for myself mine own worth do define
As I all other in all worths surmount.   8
But when my glass shows me myself indeed
Beated and chopped with tanned antiquity,
Mine own self-love quite contrary I read;
Self so self-loving were iniquity.   12
    'Tis thee, myself, that for myself I praise,
    Painting my age with beauty of thy days.

By preserving the youthful beauty of the beloved in poetry, the poet makes preparation for the day that the beloved will himself be old.

---

1. **Against:** before; in anticipation of (the time when)
5. **steepy:** precipitous
9. **fortify:** erect fortifications; build defenses
10. **confounding:** destructive, destroying; **age's cruel knife:** Here, age and Time become one destructive enemy, with the scythe blending into the **knife** that cuts wrinkles in the brow and finally kills.
11. **That he:** i.e., so that Time; **memory:** i.e., human **memory**
12. **lover's:** beloved's
14. **still green:** always young

"Time's injurious hand." (s. 63.2)

63

Against my love shall be, as I am now,
With Time's injurious hand crushed and o'erworn;
When hours have drained his blood and filled his brow
With lines and wrinkles; when his youthful morn   4
Hath traveled on to age's steepy night,
And all those beauties whereof now he's king
Are vanishing, or vanished out of sight,
Stealing away the treasure of his spring;   8
For such a time do I now fortify
Against confounding age's cruel knife,
That he shall never cut from memory
My sweet love's beauty, though my lover's life.   12
    His beauty shall in these black lines be seen,
    And they shall live, and he in them still green.

Signs of the destructive power of time and decay—such as fallen towers and eroded beaches—force the poet to admit that the beloved will also be lost to him and to mourn this anticipated loss.

---

1. **fell:** cruel, ruthless
2. **rich . . . age:** (1) ruins of antiquity, remnants of a formerly wealthy city or kingdom; (2) elaborate funeral monuments of once important figures   **proud:** magnificent   **cost:** luxurious objects
3. **sometime:** formerly (See picture, p. 140.)
4. **brass eternal:** (1) (supposedly) indestructible **brass;** (2) **brass** eternally; **mortal rage:** (1) human fury; (2) deadly destruction
6. **Advantage on:** superiority over (The image of the sea and land engaged in an ongoing battle is continued in **win of** [gain from], l. 7.) See Ovid, *Metamorphoses* [D] in Appendix, p. 617, and picture, p. 130.
7. **wat'ry main:** ocean
8. **Increasing . . . store:** i.e., sea and land alternately winning and losing possession of plenty (**store**)
9. **state:** condition; territory
10. **state:** magnificence (with possible wordplay on the meaning "government, ruling power"); **confounded to decay:** utterly destroyed
14. **to have:** i.e., at having

64

When I have seen by Time's fell hand defaced
The rich proud cost of outworn buried age;
When sometime lofty towers I see down-razed
And brass eternal slave to mortal rage;   4
When I have seen the hungry ocean gain
Advantage on the kingdom of the shore,
And the firm soil win of the wat'ry main,
Increasing store with loss and loss with store;   8
When I have seen such interchange of state,
Or state itself confounded to decay,
Ruin hath taught me thus to ruminate,
That Time will come and take my love away.   12
    This thought is as a death, which cannot choose
    But weep to have that which it fears to lose.

In the face of the terrible power of Time, how, the poet asks, can beauty survive? And how can the beloved, most beautiful of all, be protected from Time's injury? The only protection, he decides, lies in the lines of his poetry.

---

1. **Since brass:** i.e., there is neither **brass**

3. **with:** against; **rage:** violence; **hold a plea:** plead its case

4. **action:** wordplay on (1) suit at law; (2) operation; (3) military engagement; **flower:** i.e., flower's

6. **wrackful:** destructive; **batt'ring days:** i.e., **days** that pound like battering rams in a **siege**

7. **stout:** sturdy

9. **fearful:** frightening

9–10. **Where . . . hid:** i.e., **where,** alas, can the beloved hide from **Time,** which would place him in a treasure **chest** or a coffin

11. **his:** i.e., Time's (See note to s. 19.6.)

12. **spoil:** destruction (with wordplay on the *spoils* of war and pillaging)

14. **my love may still: my** beloved **may** always

65

Since brass, nor stone, nor earth, nor boundless sea
But sad mortality o'ersways their power,
How with this rage shall beauty hold a plea,
Whose action is no stronger than a flower?   4
O, how shall summer's honey breath hold out
Against the wrackful siege of batt'ring days,
When rocks impregnable are not so stout
Nor gates of steel so strong, but Time decays?   8
O, fearful meditation! Where, alack,
Shall Time's best jewel from Time's chest lie hid?
Or what strong hand can hold his swift foot back,
Or who his spoil ⌜of⌝ beauty can forbid?   12
    O, none, unless this miracle have might,
    That in black ink my love may still shine bright.

The poet lists examples of the societal wrongs that have made him so weary of life that he would wish to die, except that he would thereby desert the beloved.

---

1. **all these:** i.e., **all** the following
2. **As: as** for instance; **desert:** a deserving person
3. **needy . . . jollity:** (1) perhaps, worthless fops; or, (2) perhaps, beggarly worthlessness dressed in tawdry finery (See longer note, p. 335.)
4. **unhappily forsworn:** (1) regrettably abandoned or betrayed; (2) maliciously perjured
5. **gilded honor:** golden honors or titles; **misplaced:** given to the wrong person
6. **strumpeted:** i.e., accused of being a strumpet
7. **right:** genuine, true
8. **limping sway:** i.e., authority that is slow or ineffectual
9. **art:** scholarship, learning, science (The line could also refer to censored literary works.)
10. **doctor-like:** i.e., in the guise of a learned professor
11. **miscalled simplicity:** maligned as ignorance
12. **attending:** serving, waiting on; **ill:** evil

66

Tired with all these, for restful death I cry:
As, to behold desert a beggar born,
And needy nothing trimmed in jollity,
And purest faith unhappily forsworn,   4
And gilded honor shamefully misplaced,
And maiden virtue rudely strumpeted,
And right perfection wrongfully disgraced,
And strength by limping sway disablèd,   8
And art made tongue-tied by authority,
And folly, doctor-like, controlling skill,
And simple truth miscalled simplicity,
And captive good attending captain ill.   12
   Tired with all these, from these would I be gone,
   Save that, to die, I leave my love alone.

In this first of two linked sonnets, the poet asks why the beautiful young man should live in a society so corrupt, since his very presence gives it legitimacy. He concludes that Nature is keeping the young man alive as a reminder of the world as it used to be.

1. **wherefore:** why; **with infection:** i.e., in a corrupt world
2. **grace:** (1) adorn; (2) countenance
3. **That sin by him:** i.e., so **that sin by** means of **him**
4. **lace itself:** adorn **itself** (with wordplay on "diversify its appearance as with streaks of color," a meaning picked up in l. 5)

5–6. **Why . . . hue:** The allusion is probably to the use of cosmetics, which borrow (**steal**) the mere appearance (**dead seeing**) from **his living hue.** (Editors often change **seeing** to "seeming," and many read the lines as referring to portrait **painting.**)

7. **poor:** inferior; **indirectly:** wrongfully; by means of an intermediary

8. **Roses of shadow:** imitation **roses; his rose:** i.e., the **rose** of **his** complexion

9. **bankrout:** bankrupt
10. **Beggared:** i.e., destitute; **blush:** i.e., show red
11. **For . . . his:** i.e., since **Nature** has **no exchequer** (treasury; source of revenue) **now** except for the beauty of the beloved

12. **many:** perhaps, **many** beauties (Editors sometimes change **proud** to "proved" or "'prived.")

13. **stores:** keeps, preserves

67

Ah, wherefore with infection should he live,
And with his presence grace impiety,
That sin by him advantage should achieve
And lace itself with his society?   4
Why should false painting imitate his cheek
And steal dead seeing of his living hue?
Why should poor beauty indirectly seek
Roses of shadow, since his rose is true?   8
Why should he live, now Nature bankrout is,
Beggared of blood to blush through lively veins,
For she hath no exchequer now but his,
And, proud of many, lives upon his gains?   12
    O, him she stores, to show what wealth she had
    In days long since, before these last so bad.

Continuing the argument of s. 67, the poet sets the natural beauty of the young man against the "false art" of those whose beauty depends on cosmetics and wigs.

---

1. **Thus:** For this reason (the reason given at the conclusion of s. 67); **map:** (1) embodiment; (2) epitome; **days outworn:** a former age

3. **bastard signs of fair:** counterfeit **signs** of beauty; **borne:** worn, displayed, presented

4. **durst inhabit:** dared take up residence

5–8. **Before . . . gay:** i.e., **before** people wore wigs made of hair **shorn** from **the dead** (See *The Merchant of Venice* 3.2.94–98: **"golden** locks . . . often known / To be the dowry of a **second head,** / The skull that bred them in the sepulcher.")   **gay:** lovely; showily attractive

9. **those . . . are:** i.e., that blessed former age is

11. **of another's green:** i.e., from **another's** youth

13. **store:** preserve

68

Thus is his cheek the map of days outworn,
When beauty lived and died as flowers do now,
Before these bastard signs of fair were borne,
Or durst inhabit on a living brow;   4
Before the golden tresses of the dead,
The right of sepulchers, were shorn away
To live a second life on second head,
Ere beauty's dead fleece made another gay.   8
In him those holy antique hours are seen,
Without all ornament, itself and true,
Making no summer of another's green,
Robbing no old to dress his beauty new.   12
    And him as for a map doth Nature store,
    To show false art what beauty was of yore.

The poet tells the young man that while the world praises his outward beauty, those who look into his inner being (as reflected in his deeds) speak of him in quite different terms. They ground their accusations in his having become too "common."

---

1. **Those parts of thee:** i.e., your physical appearance (and, perhaps, your talents, gifts)

2. **Want:** lack; **thought of hearts:** deepest (most heartfelt) **thought; mend:** improve

4. **even so as foes commend:** i.e., giving you grudging praise

6. **give thee so thine own:** i.e., grant you that which clearly belongs to you

7. **In other accents:** i.e., with different language; **confound:** (1) confute; (2) confuse, complicate

9. **look into:** (1) view; (2) investigate

10. **in guess:** by conjecture; **measure:** estimate

13. **But why:** i.e., **but** the reason **why**

14. **soil:** wordplay on (1) earth, ground (so that **soil** becomes "basis, justification"); (2) stain, blemish (The word **soil** is an editorial construction from Q's "solye," a non-word believed to be a typographical error for "soyle," the usual spelling of **soil**. Some editors prefer "solve," "toil," or "sully.") **common:** (1) publicly accessible (like public pasture or prostitutes); (2) ordinary

69

Those parts of thee that the world's eye doth view
Want nothing that the thought of hearts can mend.
All tongues, the voice of souls, give thee that ⌐due,⌐
Utt'ring bare truth, even so as foes commend.   4
⌐Thy⌐ outward thus with outward praise is crowned,
But those same tongues that give thee so thine own
In other accents do this praise confound
By seeing farther than the eye hath shown.   8
They look into the beauty of thy mind,
And that, in guess, they measure by thy deeds;
Then, churls, their thoughts, although their eyes were kind,
To thy fair flower add the rank smell of weeds.   12
    But why thy odor matcheth not thy show,
    The soil is this, that thou dost common grow.

The poet tells the young man that the attacks on his reputation do not mean that he is flawed, since beauty always provokes such attacks. (This sonnet may contradict s. 69, or may simply elaborate on it.)

1. **shall not be:** (1) ought not be attributed to; (2) should not be considered; **thy defect:** a fault or flaw in you
2. **mark:** target; **fair:** beautiful
3. **suspect:** suspicion (accent on second syllable)
4. **crow:** a bird that was associated with malice
5. **So:** provided that; **but approve:** merely prove
6. **wooed of time:** (1) seduced by the present age (but remaining **good**); (2) given Time's gifts
7. **canker vice:** i.e., **vice** like a cankerworm (Proverbial: "The **canker** soonest eats the fairest rose." See picture, p. 90.)
8. **unstainèd prime:** unblemished early manhood
9. **ambush of young days:** i.e., traps laid for youth
10. **charged:** attacked
11. **so:** so much
12. **To tie up envy:** i.e., as to restrain or confine malice; **enlarged:** at large
13. **suspect of ill:** suspicion of evil; **masked not thy show:** i.e., did not mask your **beauty** (l. 3)
14. **owe:** own, possess

70

That thou ⌜art⌝ blamed shall not be thy defect,
For slander's mark was ever yet the fair.
The ornament of beauty is suspect,
A crow that flies in heaven's sweetest air.   4
So thou be good, slander doth but approve
⌜Thy⌝ worth the greater, being wooed of time,
For canker vice the sweetest buds doth love,
And thou present'st a pure unstainèd prime.   8
Thou hast passed by the ambush of young days,
Either not assailed, or victor being charged;
Yet this thy praise cannot be so thy praise
To tie up envy, evermore enlarged.   12
    If some suspect of ill masked not thy show,
    Then thou alone kingdoms of hearts shouldst owe.

In this first of a series of four sonnets in which the poet addresses his own death and its effect on the beloved, he here urges the beloved to forget him once he is gone.

---

2. **surly sullen bell:** i.e., the passing **bell** ("And when any is passing out of this life, a **bell** shall be tolled. . . . And after the party's death, . . . there shall be rung no more than one short peal, and one other before the burial, and one other after the burial." *Constitutions and Canons ecclesiastical . . .* [1603].) **surly:** gloomy, stern **sullen:** solemn

3. **warning:** notice (though also with the sense of "cautionary sign": Kerrigan cites John Donne's "Never send to know for whom the bell tolls; it tolls for thee.")

5. **this line:** i.e., the present sonnet

8. **make you woe:** distress you

10. **compounded am with clay:** am mixed with the dust of the earth

11. **rehearse:** repeat

13–14. **Lest . . . gone:** These lines are expanded and explained in s. 72. **look into your moan:** investigate your grief

71

No longer mourn for me when I am dead
Than you shall hear the surly sullen bell
Give warning to the world that I am fled
From this vile world with vilest worms to dwell.   4
Nay, if you read this line, remember not
The hand that writ it, for I love you so
That I in your sweet thoughts would be forgot,
If thinking on me then should make you woe.   8
O, if, I say, you look upon this verse
When I, perhaps, compounded am with clay,
Do not so much as my poor name rehearse,
But let your love even with my life decay,   12
    Lest the wise world should look into your moan
    And mock you with me after I am gone.

Continuing from s. 71, this sonnet explains that the beloved can defend loving the poet only by speaking falsely, by giving the poet more credit than he deserves. The beloved is urged instead to forget the poet once he is dead.

---

1. **task:** compel, challenge; **recite:** declare

6. **than mine own desert:** (1) than my merits can do; (2) than is warranted by what I deserve

7. **hang . . . I:** The image here is of a tomb hung with trophies. (In *Much Ado About Nothing* 5.3, Claudio hangs an epitaph of praise on Hero's tomb.)   **I:** i.e., me

8. **niggard:** i.e., miserly

9. **your true love:** i.e., **your love,** which is honest

10. **speak . . . untrue:** i.e., say complimentary but **untrue** things about **me**

12. **nor me:** neither me

13. **shamed . . . forth:** The poet may here refer to his verse, or to himself. (The tone can be likened to that of Hamlet's "I could accuse me of such things that it were better my mother had not borne me" [3.1.133–34].) Those who read the sonnets biographically see the line as Shakespeare's admission of shame about writing plays.

14. **should you:** i.e., **should you** be ashamed

72

O, lest the world should task you to recite
What merit lived in me that you should love,
After my death, dear love, forget me quite,
For you in me can nothing worthy prove;   4
Unless you would devise some virtuous lie,
To do more for me than mine own desert,
And hang more praise upon deceasèd I
Than niggard truth would willingly impart.   8
O, lest your true love may seem false in this,
That you for love speak well of me untrue,
My name be buried where my body is
And live no more to shame nor me nor you.   12
    For I am shamed by that which I bring forth,
    And so should you, to love things nothing worth.

The poet describes himself as nearing the end of his life. He imagines the beloved's love for him growing stronger in the face of that death.

1. **time of year:** See Ovid, *Metamorphoses* [B], in Appendix, pp. 615–16.

3. **against the cold:** (1) in **the cold** autumn wind; (2) in anticipation of **the cold** of winter

4. **choirs:** The **boughs,** compared here to the part of the church set apart for choristers, are now **bare,** as if reduced to ruin. One thinks almost inevitably of the monasteries destroyed by Henry VIII, with their **bare ruined choirs** where once there were choristers.   **late:** recently

5. **twilight:** See note to l. 1 (above).

8. **Death's second self:** a description of sleep here applied to **night; seals up:** wordplay on (1) encloses, as in a coffin; (2) seels up (sews shut, as was done to falcons' eyes when the birds were being trained); (3) places a seal on a finished document

10. **his youth:** i.e., its **youth**

12. **with:** (1) by; (2) along with

14. **leave:** part with

73

That time of year thou mayst in me behold
When yellow leaves, or none, or few, do hang
Upon those boughs which shake against the cold,
Bare ruined choirs where late the sweet birds sang.   4
In me thou see'st the twilight of such day
As after sunset fadeth in the west,
Which by and by black night doth take away,
Death's second self, that seals up all in rest.   8
In me thou see'st the glowing of such fire
That on the ashes of his youth doth lie,
As the death-bed whereon it must expire,
Consumed with that which it was nourished by.   12
   This thou perceiv'st, which makes thy love more strong,
   To love that well which thou must leave ere long.

In this sonnet, which continues from s. 73, the poet consoles the beloved by telling him that only the poet's body will die; the spirit of the poet will continue to live in the poetry, which is the beloved's.

1–2. **that fell arrest / Without all bail:** i.e., death **fell:** cruel (Compare Hamlet's reference to "this **fell** sergeant, Death, / [who] Is strict in his **arrest**" [5.2.368–69].)

3. **My . . . interest:** i.e., I have a legal right to (**interest in**) this verse

4. **Which . . . stay:** i.e., **which** will remain with you always as a (1) commemoration; (2) memorandum

5. **thou reviewest:** you reread; **review:** see again

6. **consecrate to:** (1) devoted to; (2) reserved for

7. **his:** its

11. **coward . . . knife:** The **body,** in its subjection to death, is both cowardly and the victim of a cowardly attack by a wretch. (See *Richard II* 3.2.173–75, where Death, having allowed the king to believe his flesh "were brass impregnable," "Comes at the last and with a little pin / Bores through" that flesh, "and farewell, king!")

12. **Too . . . rememberèd:** i.e., too worthless **to be remembered** by you

13. **The worth of that:** i.e., the body's value

74

But be contented when that fell arrest
Without all bail shall carry me away,
My life hath in this line some interest,
Which for memorial still with thee shall stay.   4
When thou reviewest this, thou dost review
The very part was consecrate to thee.
The earth can have but earth, which is his due;
My spirit is thine, the better part of me.   8
So then thou hast but lost the dregs of life,
The prey of worms, my body being dead,
The coward conquest of a wretch's knife,
Too base of thee to be rememberèd.   12
   The worth of that is that which it contains,
   And that is this, and this with thee remains.

The poet compares himself to a miser with his treasure. He finds the beloved so essential to his life that he lives in a constant tension between glorying in that treasure and fearing its loss.

---

1. **So . . . life:** i.e., **you are** (as necessary) **to my thoughts as food** is **to life**

2. **sweet-seasoned:** i.e., springtime

3. **for the peace of you:** i.e., because of **the peace you** bring me (with possible wordplay on *piece*—i.e., piece of money—leading to the **miser and his wealth**); **hold such strife:** i.e., suffer the kind of conflict (This line is subject to any number of readings.)

5. **as an enjoyer: as** one who enjoys (**his wealth**); **anon:** immediately

6. **Doubting:** fearing; **the filching age:** i.e., the pilfering time he lives in

7. **counting:** considering (with wordplay on a **miser counting** his gold)

8. **bettered:** i.e., considering it even better

10. **clean:** completely

12. **is had:** i.e., I already have

13. **pine:** starve; **surfeit:** glut myself

14. **Or:** either; **all away:** possessing nothing

75

So are you to my thoughts as food to life,
Or as sweet-seasoned showers are to the ground;
And for the peace of you I hold such strife
As 'twixt a miser and his wealth is found: 4
Now proud as an enjoyer, and anon
Doubting the filching age will steal his treasure;
Now counting best to be with you alone,
Then bettered that the world may see my pleasure.   8
Sometime all full with feasting on your sight,
And by and by clean starvèd for a look;
Possessing or pursuing no delight
Save what is had or must from you be took.   12
    Thus do I pine and surfeit day by day,
     Or gluttoning on all, or all away.

The poet poses the question of why his poetry never changes but keeps repeating the same language and technique. The answer, he says, is that his theme never changes; he always writes of the beloved and of love.

---

1. **pride:** adornment, ornamentation

2. **variation or quick change:** Since **quick change** is itself synonymous with **variation,** this line is itself an example of **variation** in choice of expression, and thus shows that this **verse** is **far from barren.**

3. **with the time:** i.e., as other poets do today; **glance:** move rapidly

4. **methods:** poetic rules and arrangements; **compounds:** words that combine other words (like the word *compound* itself, which combines the Latin *cum*, meaning "with," and *ponere*, meaning "to put")

5. **still all one:** always the same

6. **invention:** poetic creation; **in a noted weed:** i.e., in familiar clothing (but **noted** also means "famous, celebrated, distinguished")

8. **where:** i.e., from **where**

10. **still my argument:** always my theme

14. **still telling what is:** i.e., always **telling** that which has already been

76

Why is my verse so barren of new pride,
So far from variation or quick change?
Why with the time do I not glance aside
To new-found methods and to compounds strange?   4
Why write I still all one, ever the same,
And keep invention in a noted weed,
That every word doth almost ⌜tell⌝ my name,
Showing their birth and where they did proceed?   8
O, know, sweet love, I always write of you,
And you and love are still my argument;
So all my best is dressing old words new,
Spending again what is already spent.   12
   For as the sun is daily new and old,
   So is my love, still telling what is told.

This sonnet seems to have been written to accompany the gift of a blank notebook. The poet encourages the beloved to write down the thoughts that arise from observing a mirror and a sundial and the lessons they teach about the brevity of life.

---

1. **glass:** mirror; **wear:** waste away (The Quarto uses the variant spelling *were.*)

2. **dial:** sundial (See picture below.) **waste:** dwindle

3. **vacant leaves:** blank pages (of **this book** [l. 4], a notebook in which the beloved is to write)

4. **this learning:** i.e., the **learning** that follows

6. **mouthèd:** gaping; **memory:** a reminder

7. **dial's shady stealth:** i.e., the imperceptible movement of the shadow across the **dial** (with wordplay on **stealth** as "theft," or **thievish progress**)

9. **Look what:** whatever

10. **waste:** unused

11–12. **Those . . . mind:** The image is of thought as a child **delivered from** the **brain,** put out to a wet nurse (i.e., written down), and then later restored to the parent (i.e., reread) for renewed **acquaintance.**

13. **offices:** tasks, functions

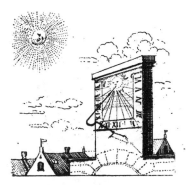

A sundial. (s. 77.2, 7; *Lucrece,* 781)

77

Thy glass will show thee how thy beauties wear,
Thy dial how thy precious minutes waste;
The vacant leaves thy mind's imprint will bear,
And of this book this learning mayst thou taste: 4
The wrinkles which thy glass will truly show,
Of mouthèd graves will give thee memory;
Thou by thy dial's shady stealth mayst know
Time's thievish progress to eternity.   8
Look what thy memory cannot contain
Commit to these waste ⌐blanks,¬ and thou shalt find
Those children nursed, delivered from thy brain,
To take a new acquaintance of thy mind.   12
    These offices, so oft as thou wilt look,
    Shall profit thee and much enrich thy book.

In this first of a series of three sonnets in which the poet expresses his concern that others are writing verses praising the beloved, the other poets are presented as learned and skillful and thus in no need of the beloved, in contrast to the poet speaking here.

---

1. **So . . . muse:** See, e.g., s. 38.

3. **As:** that; **every alien pen:** i.e., pens belonging to other persons; **hath got my use:** has adopted my custom or practice

4. **under thee:** i.e., under your protection

5. **dumb:** mute; **on high:** loudly, aloud

7. **added . . . wing:** In falconry, **feathers** were **added to** a bird's wings to improve its power of flight. Here, the beloved's inspiration has **added feathers to** (i.e., improved the verse of) even the learned.

9. **compile:** compose

10. **Whose . . . thee:** i.e., which is determined by you and is your child (**Influence** is an astrological term. See longer note to s. 15.4, p. 333.)

12. **arts:** learning and poetic skill; **gracèd be:** are adorned

13. **advance:** lift up

78

So oft have I invoked thee for my muse
And found such fair assistance in my verse
As every alien pen hath got my use
And under thee their poesy disperse.   4
Thine eyes, that taught the dumb on high to sing
And heavy ignorance aloft to fly,
Have added feathers to the learnèd's wing
And given grace a double majesty.   8
Yet be most proud of that which I compile,
Whose influence is thine and born of thee.
In others' works thou dost but mend the style,
And arts with thy sweet graces gracèd be.   12
   But thou art all my art and dost advance
   As high as learning my rudc ignorance.

In this sonnet, which follows directly from s. 78, the poet laments the fact that another poet has taken his place. He urges the beloved to recognize that all of the beauty, grace, and virtue found in the rival's praise is taken from the beloved, so that the rival deserves no thanks.

1. **call upon thy aid:** i.e., invoke you as my muse

2. **all . . . grace:** (1) **all** your favor; (2) **all** your charm

3. **gracious numbers:** verses filled with your grace; **are decayed:** have declined

4. **muse:** poetic powers (See note to s. 38.1.) **give another place:** yield to **another**

5. **thy lovely argument:** the **lovely** theme of you

6. **travail:** toil (accent on first syllable)

7. **of thee:** concerning you; **thy poet:** the **poet** writing your praises; **invent:** wordplay on (1) devise; (2) find out (Lines 8–14 show why a third customary meaning of **invent** as "create by original ingenuity" does not apply.)

11. **can afford:** is able to give

79

Whilst I alone did call upon thy aid,
My verse alone had all thy gentle grace;
But now my gracious numbers are decayed,
And my sick muse doth give another place.   4
I grant, sweet love, thy lovely argument
Deserves the travail of a worthier pen;
Yet what of thee thy poet doth invent
He robs thee of and pays it thee again.   8
He lends thee virtue, and he stole that word
From thy behavior; beauty doth he give
And found it in thy cheek. He can afford
No praise to thee but what in thee doth live.   12
    Then thank him not for that which he doth say,
    Since what he owes thee thou thyself dost pay.

The poet admits his inferiority to the one who is now writing about the beloved, portraying the two poets as ships sailing on the ocean of the beloved's worth—the rival poet as large and splendid and himself as a small boat that risks being wrecked by love.

---

1. **faint:** lose heart

2. **better spirit:** i.e., more inspired poet; **use your name:** (1) invoke you as muse; (2) claim your protection as his patron

4. **To make me:** i.e., with the result that I become (though with the implication of deliberate rivalry)

6. **humble as:** i.e., the small (boat) **as** well as

7. **saucy:** rashly venturing, presumptuous

8. **main:** ocean; **willfully:** obstinately; freely

9–10. **Your . . . ride:** Small ships float in shallow water; large ships need the **soundless deep** (water of such depth it cannot be sounded [measured]).

11. **being wracked:** if I should be wrecked

12. **He . . . pride:** i.e., he, in contrast, is a grandly and sturdily constructed ship (and/or a tall-masted ship) of great splendor

14. **my love was my decay:** (1) **my** affection **was my** ruin; (2) **my** beloved (as "**soundless deep**") caused **my** destruction

80

O, how I faint when I of you do write,
Knowing a better spirit doth use your name,
And in the praise thereof spends all his might,
To make me tongue-tied speaking of your fame.   4
But since your worth, wide as the ocean is,
The humble as the proudest sail doth bear,
My saucy bark, inferior far to his,
On your broad main doth willfully appear.   8
Your shallowest help will hold me up afloat
Whilst he upon your soundless deep doth ride,
Or, being wracked, I am a worthless boat,
He of tall building and of goodly pride.   12
    Then, if he thrive and I be cast away,
    The worst was this: my love was my decay.

The poet, imagining a future in which both he and the beloved are dead, sees himself as being completely forgotten while the beloved will be forever remembered because of the poet's verse.

1. **Or:** either
3. **hence:** i.e., the world; **your memory:** i.e., the **memory** of you
   4. **in me each part:** i.e., every **part** of **me**
   5. **from hence:** henceforth
   7. **earth:** world; **common grave:** i.e., burial in the church ground with no marker to record the name
   8. **entombèd in men's eyes:** i.e., buried in a prominent place (as in a sepulcher)
   9. **monument:** wordplay on (1) sepulcher; (2) written document, record
   10. **o'erread:** read over
   11. **rehearse:** speak of
   12. **this world:** i.e., today's **world**
   13. **still:** always, forever; **live:** (1) continue to be alive; (2) dwell; **virtue:** power
   14. **even in the mouths:** i.e., **in the** very **mouths (Breath,** in this line, is not only the air men breathe but also the articulated sounds that will recite the poet's verse and spread the beloved's fame.)

81

Or I shall live your epitaph to make
Or you survive when I in earth am rotten.
From hence your memory death cannot take,
Although in me each part will be forgotten.   4
Your name from hence immortal life shall have,
Though I, once gone, to all the world must die.
The earth can yield me but a common grave,
When you entombèd in men's eyes shall lie.   8
Your monument shall be my gentle verse,
Which eyes not yet created shall o'erread;
And tongues to be your being shall rehearse
When all the breathers of this world are dead.   12
    You still shall live—such virtue hath my pen—
    Where breath most breathes, even in the mouths of men.

In this first of two linked sonnets, the poet again addresses the fact that other poets write in praise of the beloved. The beloved is free to read them, but their poems do not represent the beloved truly.

---

1. **married to my muse:** i.e., under a vow to remain faithful to my poetry alone
2. **attaint:** dishonor; **o'erlook:** read
3. **dedicated words:** wordplay on (1) devoted **words;** (2) **words** of authors' dedications
4. **Of:** about; **blessing every book:** elaborate wordplay that includes (1) (dedications) gracing **every book;** (2) (**words** about the **fair subject**) making **every book** fortunate; and (3) (the beloved) showing favor to **every book**
5. **as fair . . . hue:** i.e., **as** just in comprehension **as** you are lovely in appearance
6. **Finding . . . praise:** i.e., in determining that your merits go beyond my ability to praise   **limit:** region
8. **stamp:** imprint or sign; **time-bettering days:** i.e., this progressive age
10. **What strainèd touches:** i.e., whatever artificial or ornamental details
11. **truly sympathized:** represented in a way that corresponds accurately to you
12. **plain:** unadorned
13. **their gross painting:** i.e., the overelaborate language of other poets   **gross:** flagrant; clumsy; thick   **painting:** description; flattery; application of cosmetics
14. **in thee:** i.e., on your face; **abused:** misused

182

82

I grant thou wert not married to my muse,
And therefore mayst without attaint o'erlook
The dedicated words which writers use
Of their fair subject, blessing every book.   4
Thou art as fair in knowledge as in hue,
Finding thy worth a limit past my praise,
And therefore art enforced to seek anew
Some fresher stamp of the time-bettering days.   8
And do so, love; yet when they have devised
What strainèd touches rhetoric can lend,
Thou, truly fair, wert truly sympathized
In true plain words by thy true-telling friend.   12
    And their gross painting might be better used
    Where cheeks need blood; in thee it is abuscd.

This sonnet continues from s. 82, but the poet has learned to his dismay that his plain speaking (and/or his silence) has offended the beloved. He argues that no words can match the beloved's beauty.

---

1. **painting:** See s. 82.13, and note.
2. **fair . . . set:** i.e., beauty applied **no painting**
3–4. **I . . . debt:** See s. 82.6.   **tender:** offer
5. **slept . . . report:** i.e., stopped writing (or, perhaps, written in an understated way) about you
6. **That:** so **that; extant:** alive
7. **modern:** (1) commonplace, ordinary; (2) up-to-date, present-day
8. **Speaking:** i.e., in **speaking; grow:** flourish
9. **for . . . impute:** i.e., **you** regarded as **my sin**
10. **being dumb:** i.e., I remaining silent
12. **would . . . tomb:** i.e., intending to **give life** instead memorialize
14. **both your poets:** i.e., **both** the poet of the *Sonnets* and the rival poet (or, perhaps, **your** two rival **poets**)

83

I never saw that you did painting need
And therefore to your fair no painting set.
I found, or thought I found, you did exceed
The barren tender of a poet's debt.   4
And therefore have I slept in your report,
That you yourself, being extant, well might show
How far a modern quill doth come too short,
Speaking of worth, what worth in you doth grow.   8
This silence for my sin you did impute,
Which shall be most my glory, being dumb,
For I impair not beauty, being mute,
When others would give life and bring a tomb.   12
    There lives more life in one of your fair eyes
    Than both your poets can in praise devise.

The poet reiterates his claim that poems praising the beloved should reflect the beloved's perfections rather than exaggerate them. He accuses the beloved of caring too much for praise.

1. **Who . . . more:** i.e., **who is it that** in praising you most extravagantly **can say more**

3. **In whose confine:** i.e., within whom; **immurèd is the store:** i.e., is enclosed the entire stock (of beauty and worth)

4. **Which . . . grew:** perhaps, **which** anyone held up as **your equal** would need to possess (The line cannot be paraphrased precisely.)

6. **his subject:** i.e., its **subject** (no matter how ordinary)

8. **so . . . story:** i.e., in this way ennobles his writing

9. **but copy:** only transcribe

10. **making worse:** debasing; **clear:** free of fault

11. **counterpart:** copy; **fame his wit:** make his poetic genius famous

13. **blessings:** gifts of nature, excellent qualities

14. **Being fond on:** (1) having a strong liking for; (2) **being** besotted or dazed by; **your praises:** presumably, "**praises** offered you" (though the more obvious reading of the phrase is "**praises** you give others"); **worse:** perhaps, more blatant

84

Who is it that says most, which can say more
Than this rich praise, that you alone are you,
In whose confine immurèd is the store
Which should example where your equal grew?   4
Lean penury within that pen doth dwell
That to his subject lends not some small glory,
But he that writes of you, if he can tell
That you are you, so dignifies his story.   8
Let him but copy what in you is writ,
Not making worse what nature made so clear,
And such a counterpart shall fame his wit,
Making his style admirèd everywhere.   12
    You to your beauteous blessings add a curse,
    Being fond on praise, which makes your praises worse.

In this first of two linked sonnets, the poet says that his silence in the face of others' extravagant praise of the beloved is only outward muteness. His thoughts are filled with love.

---

1. **in . . . still:** i.e., politely stays quiet

2. **comments of your praise:** i.e., poems praising you (literally, treatises **of praise** of you); **compiled:** composed

3. **Reserve their character:** i.e., keep **their** writings in store (This phrase is often emended.)

4. **phrase:** style, language; **filed:** polished smooth (For the nine muses, see note to s. 38.1, and picture, p. 92.)

5. **other:** others

6–8. **like . . . pen:** The poet, who simply says "yes" when others write in praise of the beloved, compares himself to an illiterate parish **clerk** who answers the priest's prayers with "**amen.**" Evans points out that "**'Tis so, 'tis true**" (l. 9) translates the Hebrew "**amen.**"   **affords:** supplies

10. **most of:** utmost

11. **that is:** i.e., I **add** it

12. **holds . . . before:** i.e., (**my thought**) keeps its position in the front **rank**

13. **respect:** regard well, pay attention to

14. **dumb:** silent; **speaking in effect:** i.e., which in fact speak

85

My tongue-tied muse in manners holds her still
While comments of your praise, richly compiled,
Reserve their character with golden quill
And precious phrase by all the muses filed.   4
I think good thoughts whilst other write good words,
And like unlettered clerk still cry amen
To every hymn that able spirit affords
In polished form of well-refinèd pen.   8
Hearing you praised, I say "'Tis so, 'tis true,"
And to the most of praise add something more;
But that is in my thought, whose love to you,
Though words come hindmost, holds his rank before.   12
    Then others for the breath of words respect,
    Me for my dumb thoughts, speaking in effect.

This final "rival poet" sonnet continues from s. 85 but echoes the imagery of s. 80. The poet explains that his silence is not from fear of his rival, but results from having nothing to write about, now that the rival's verse has appropriated the beloved's favor.

2. **Bound for the prize:** The image is of a privateer sailing off to capture booty. (For the rival poet as a large sailing ship, see s. 80.)

3. **ripe:** ready for birth; **inhearse:** bury

4. **Making . . . womb:** i.e., turning **my brain,** where the **thoughts** were conceived, into **their tomb**

5–11. **Was . . . boast:** See longer note, p. 336.

5. **spirit:** lively intelligence

6. **Above a mortal pitch:** i.e., in a style that transcends the reach of human talent (The **pitch** is the highest point in a falcon's flight.)

7. **compeers:** companions, associates

8. **astonishèd:** struck dumb

9. **He:** neither he

10. **gulls:** deludes; gorges; **intelligence:** reports

11. **cannot:** i.e., can

12. **sick of:** sickened or weakened by

13. **countenance:** face; favor; **line:** verse

14. **matter:** subject matter, something to write about; **that:** i.e., **that** lack; **mine:** my verse

86

Was it the proud full sail of his great verse,
Bound for the prize of all-too-precious you,
That did my ripe thoughts in my brain inhearse,
Making their tomb the womb wherein they grew? 4
Was it his spirit, by spirits taught to write
Above a mortal pitch, that struck me dead?
No, neither he, nor his compeers by night
Giving him aid, my verse astonishèd. 8
He, nor that affable familiar ghost
Which nightly gulls him with intelligence,
As victors of my silence cannot boast;
I was not sick of any fear from thence. 12
But when your countenance filled up his line,
Then lacked I matter; that enfeebled mine.

The poet writes as if his relationship with the beloved has ended—and as if that relationship had been a wonderful dream from which he has now waked.

---

1. **dear:** glorious; expensive (The relationship is here expressed in language that draws on that of economic or property rights but soon becomes legal.)

2. **like enough:** likely, probably; **estimate:** reputation; attributed value

3. **charter of thy worth:** document granting you your value or position; **releasing:** i.e., the right to set (yourself) free or transfer (yourself) to another

4. **My bonds in thee:** legal or emotional covenants binding you to me; **determinate:** no longer in force (a legal term)

5. **hold:** retain possession of; **granting:** bestowal; transfer (of yourself to me) by deed

7. **cause . . . gift:** i.e., reason I should be given **this fair gift; wanting:** lacking, missing

8. **patent:** title to possession; **back again is swerving:** i.e., is returning (to you)

10. **Or me . . . else mistaking:** i.e., **or else** you mistook my **worth** (or mistook **me**) when you gave it

11. **upon misprision growing:** i.e., **growing** out of an error

12. **on . . . making:** i.e., on (your) judging (you or me) more accurately

87

Farewell, thou art too dear for my possessing,
And like enough thou know'st thy estimate.
The charter of thy worth gives thee releasing;
My bonds in thee are all determinate.   4
For how do I hold thee but by thy granting,
And for that riches where is my deserving?
The cause of this fair gift in me is wanting,
And so my patent back again is swerving.   8
Thy self thou gav'st, thy own worth then not knowing,
Or me, to whom thou gav'st it, else mistaking;
So thy great gift, upon misprision growing,
Comes home again, on better judgment making.   12
    Thus have I had thee as a dream doth flatter,
    In sleep a king, but waking no such matter.

In this first of three linked sonnets in which the poet has been (or imagines himself someday to be) repudiated by the beloved, the poet offers to sacrifice himself and his reputation in order to make the now-estranged beloved look better.

1. **set me light:** consider me of small value
2. **place . . . scorn:** i.e., hold **my** merits up to **scorn**
4. **art forsworn:** i.e., have perjured yourself
6. **Upon thy part:** taking your side
7. **attainted:** (1) tainted; (2) accused
8. **losing:** (1) destroying; (2) being deprived of
12. **vantage:** benefit; **double-vantage:** doubly benefit
14. **for:** (1) on behalf of; (2) because of

"Till the judgment that yourself arise. . . ." (s. 55.13)

88

When thou shalt be disposed to set me light
And place my merit in the eye of scorn,
Upon thy side against myself I'll fight
And prove thee virtuous, though thou art forsworn.   4
With mine own weakness being best acquainted,
Upon thy part I can set down a story
Of faults concealed wherein I am attainted,
That thou, in losing me, shall win much glory;   8
And I by this will be a gainer too;
For bending all my loving thoughts on thee,
The injuries that to myself I do,
Doing thee vantage, double-vantage me.   12
    Such is my love, to thee I so belong,
    That, for thy right, myself will bear all wrong.

This sonnet is a detailed extension of the closing line of s. 88. The poet here lists the ways he will make himself look bad in order to make the beloved look good.

1. **Say:** announce, assert; **fault:** transgression
2. **comment upon:** i.e., enlarge on (literally, make remarks about)
3. **straight will halt:** will immediately limp
4. **reasons:** statements, claims
5. **ill:** badly
6. **set . . . change:** make the **change** you wish look more attractive
8. **acquaintance:** i.e., our familiarity; **look strange:** act as if we were strangers
9. **thy walks:** i.e., the places where you walk
11. **too much profane: too** impious or blasphemous
12. **haply:** perhaps
13. **For thee:** on your behalf; **debate:** i.e., combat
14. **For:** because

89

Say that thou didst forsake me for some fault,
And I will comment upon that offense;
Speak of my lameness and I straight will halt,
Against thy reasons making no defense.   4
Thou canst not, love, disgrace me half so ill,
To set a form upon desirèd change,
As I'll myself disgrace, knowing thy will;
I will acquaintance strangle and look strange,   8
Be absent from thy walks, and in my tongue
Thy sweet belovèd name no more shall dwell,
Lest I, too much profane, should do it wrong
And haply of our old acquaintance tell.   12
    For thee, against myself I'll vow debate,
    For I must ne'er love him whom thou dost hate.

Continuing from the final line of s. 89, this sonnet begs the beloved to deliver quickly any terrible blow that awaits the poet. Then the other blows being dealt by the world will seem as nothing.

---

1. **Then:** therefore (The line follows directly from the closing line of s. 89.)

2. **bent . . . cross:** determined to thwart all that I do

3. **the spite of fortune:** fortune's malice; **bow:** submit

4. **drop . . . afterloss:** i.e., fall (on me) after I'm already defeated

5. **'scaped this sorrow:** i.e., recovered from a present **sorrow** (The poem seems to imply that a new, rather devastating blow has struck the poet, something apart from the prospect of the beloved's repudiation.)

6. **in the . . . woe:** i.e., after I've overcome this **woe**

8. **linger out:** prolong; **a purposed overthrow:** an intended defeat

10. **griefs:** (1) injuries; (2) sorrows (**petty** in comparison to the beloved's treachery)

11. **in the onset:** at the beginning of the attack (military language, like **conquered** [l. 6] and **overthrow** [l. 8])

13. **strains:** sorts, kinds

90

Then hate me when thou wilt, if ever, now,
Now, while the world is bent my deeds to cross,
Join with the spite of fortune, make me bow,
And do not drop in for an afterloss. 4
Ah, do not, when my heart hath 'scaped this sorrow,
Come in the rearward of a conquered woe;
Give not a windy night a rainy morrow,
To linger out a purposed overthrow. 8
If thou wilt leave me, do not leave me last,
When other petty griefs have done their spite,
But in the onset come; so ⌐shall⌐ I taste
At first the very worst of fortune's might; 12
    And other strains of woe, which now seem woe,
    Compared with loss of thee will not seem so.

In this first of three linked sonnets, the poet sets the love of the beloved above every other treasure, but then acknowledges that that love can be withdrawn.

1. **birth:** rank, lineage; **skill:** knowledge; cleverness
3. **newfangled ill:** i.e., trendy and badly made
4. **horse:** i.e., horses (See picture below.)
5. **humor:** (1) whim; (2) temperament; **his:** its
7. **not my measure:** i.e., not what satisfy me
10. **prouder:** more splendid
12. **all men's pride:** i.e., (1) what **all** men would be proud to possess; (2) **all** the treasures men possess
13. **Wretched . . . that:** i.e., miserable only in the knowledge **that**

"Hawks, . . . hounds, . . . [and] horse." (s. 91.4)

91

Some glory in their birth, some in their skill,
Some in their wealth, some in their body's force,
Some in their garments, though newfangled ill,
Some in their hawks and hounds, some in their horse;   4
And every humor hath his adjunct pleasure,
Wherein it finds a joy above the rest.
But these particulars are not my measure;
All these I better in one general best.   8
Thy love is ⌜better⌝ than high birth to me,
Richer than wealth, prouder than garments' cost,
Of more delight than hawks or horses be;
And having thee, of all men's pride I boast.   12
    Wretched in this alone, that thou mayst take
    All this away, and me most wretched make.

Continuing the argument from s. 91, the poet, imagining the loss of the beloved, realizes gladly that since even the smallest perceived diminishment of that love would cause him instantly to die, he need not fear living with the pain of loss. But, he asks, what if the beloved is false but gives no sign of defection?

---

1. **But:** nevertheless; **do thy worst:** wordplay on the phrase "**do thy** best"

2. **term of life:** a legal phrase that means "during one's lifetime"; **assurèd:** (1) established securely; (2) pledged

3. **stay:** remain

4. **For it:** i.e., because (my) **life**

5. **worst of wrongs:** i.e., the **worst** the beloved can do (presumably the "stealing away" of l. 1)

6. **When . . . end:** i.e., since **my life** will **end** at the **least** rejection

7. **I see:** i.e., I perceive that

7–8. **a better . . . depend:** i.e., I am in possession of **a state** (of mind) that transcends any condition dependent on your whims or moods

10. **that my . . . lie:** i.e., (the end of) **my life** will be determined by your casting off allegiance to me

11. **happy title:** (1) fortunate legal **title**; (2) **title** to happiness

13. **blessèd-fair:** fortunate and lovely; **blot:** blemish

14. **mayst:** (1) i.e., may someday; (2) may already be; **yet:** (1) nevertheless; (2) as **yet**

92

But do thy worst to steal thyself away,
For term of life thou art assurèd mine,
And life no longer than thy love will stay,
For it depends upon that love of thine.   4
Then need I not to fear the worst of wrongs
When in the least of them my life hath end;
I see a better state to me belongs
Than that which on thy humor doth depend.   8
Thou canst not vex me with inconstant mind,
Since that my life on thy revolt doth lie.
O, what a happy title do I find,
Happy to have thy love, happy to die!   12
    But what's so blessèd-fair that fears no blot?
    Thou mayst be false, and yet I know it not.

The poet explores the implications of the final line of s. 92. It would be easy for the beloved to be secretly false, he realizes, because the beloved is so unfailingly beautiful and (apparently) loving.

1–2. **So . . . husband:** See s. 92.14.   **supposing:** believing, imagining

3. **altered new:** newly **altered**

4. **looks:** glances

6. **in that:** i.e., **in** your **looks, in** your **eye**

7. **looks:** appearances, faces

8. **writ:** written, transcribed

13. **How . . . grow:** i.e., your **beauty** grows seductive but deadly   **Eve's apple:** i.e., the fruit of the tree (described as "pleasant to the eyes") that was forbidden Adam and Eve by God, and that, once eaten, brought death into the world (See Genesis 3 and picture below.)

14. **answer not:** does not correspond to

Eve offering apple to Adam. (s. 93.13)

93

So shall I live, supposing thou art true,
Like a deceivèd husband; so love's face
May still seem love to me, though altered new;
Thy looks with me, thy heart in other place.   4
For there can live no hatred in thine eye;
Therefore in that I cannot know thy change.
In many's looks, the false heart's history
Is writ in moods and frowns and wrinkles strange.   8
But heaven in thy creation did decree
That in thy face sweet love should ever dwell;
Whate'er thy thoughts or thy heart's workings be,
Thy looks should nothing thence but sweetness tell.   12
    How like Eve's apple doth thy beauty grow,
    If thy sweet virtue answer not thy show.

This sonnet describes a category of especially blessed and powerful people who appear to exert complete control over their lives and themselves. These persons are then implicitly compared to flowers and contrasted with weeds, the poem concluding with a warning to such persons in the form of a proverb about lilies.

1. **will do none:** i.e., do not wish **to hurt** (Proverbial: "To be able to do harm and not to do it is noble.")

2. **the thing they most do show:** i.e., what their appearance indicates they will do

3. **moving:** affecting, rousing, stirring

4. **to temptation slow:** i.e., not easily tempted

5. **heaven's graces:** i.e., the blessings of fortune, perhaps the same as **nature's riches** in l. 6

6. **husband:** protect; **expense:** extravagance

7. **faces:** (1) visages, features; (2) appearance; aspect

8. **stewards:** managers, custodians

10. **to . . . die:** (1) it lives and dies alone; (2) it merely lives and dies

12. **outbraves:** surpasses in splendor; **his:** its (One can detect behind ll. 9–12 allusions to Matthew 6.28–29 ["Learn how the **lilies** of the field do grow: they labor not, neither spin; Yet I say unto you, That even Solomon in all his glory was not arrayed like one of these"]. The allusions lead to the word **lilies** in l. 14.)

14. **Lilies . . . weeds:** proverbial

94

They that have power to hurt and will do none,
That do not do the thing they most do show,
Who, moving others, are themselves as stone,
Unmovèd, cold, and to temptation slow,   4
They rightly do inherit heaven's graces
And husband nature's riches from expense;
They are the lords and owners of their faces,
Others but stewards of their excellence.   8
The summer's flower is to the summer sweet,
Though to itself it only live and die;
But if that flower with base infection meet,
The basest weed outbraves his dignity.   12
    For sweetest things turn sourest by their deeds;
    Lilies that fester smell far worse than weeds.

In this first of a pair of related poems, the poet accuses the beloved of using beauty to hide a corrupt moral center.

1. **shame:** morally disgraceful conduct
2. **canker:** i.e., cankerworm (See note to s. 35.4.)
3. **spot . . . name:** i.e., as a cankerworm leaves a small hole on the bud as it enters, so base conduct blemishes the **budding** reputation of the beloved
4. **sweets:** sweet fragrances
6. **on thy sport:** about your pastimes (especially sexual activity)
8. **blesses an ill report:** i.e., converts lewd rumors into something holy (with wordplay on **ill report** as "bad reputation")
9. **mansion:** lordly manor house
11. **beauty's veil:** i.e., beauty, which acts as a **veil**
12. **that eyes can see:** (1) **that** is visible; (2) **that** is mere appearance
13. **of this large privilege:** i.e., **of** (abusing) **this** advantage
14. **hardest:** most hardened, sharpest; **ill used:** badly employed; **his:** its (Booth calls this line "Shakespeare's homemade proverb.")

95

How sweet and lovely dost thou make the shame
Which, like a canker in the fragrant rose,
Doth spot the beauty of thy budding name!
O, in what sweets dost thou thy sins enclose!   4
That tongue that tells the story of thy days,
Making lascivious comments on thy sport,
Cannot dispraise but in a kind of praise;
Naming thy name blesses an ill report.   8
O, what a mansion have those vices got
Which for their habitation chose out thee,
Where beauty's veil doth cover every blot,
And all things turns to fair that eyes can see!   12
    Take heed, dear heart, of this large privilege;
    The hardest knife ill used doth lose his edge.

As in the companion s. 95, the beloved is accused of enjoying the love of many despite his faults, which youth and beauty convert to graces.

1. **wantonness:** lasciviousness; arrogance

2. **grace:** charm; **gentle:** gentlemanly, aristocratic (**Gentle sport** is a kind way of describing **wantonness.**)

3. **more and less:** i.e., higher and lower ranks

4. **mak'st . . . resort:** i.e. turn the **faults that resort to thee** into **graces**

8. **To:** into; **translated:** transformed; **for:** to be

10. **like:** i.e., into the **looks** of (Proverbial: "A wolf in sheep's clothing." See picture below.)

12. **wouldst . . . state:** i.e., chose to exert all your powers

13–14. **But . . . report:** This couplet repeats the couplet of s. 36. See longer note, p. 336.

A wolf disguised as a lamb. (s. 96.9–10)

96

Some say thy fault is youth, some wantonness;
Some say thy grace is youth and gentle sport.
Both grace and faults are loved of more and less;
Thou mak'st faults graces that to thee resort.   4
As on the finger of a thronèd queen
The basest jewel will be well esteemed,
So are those errors that in thee are seen
To truths translated and for true things deemed.   8
How many lambs might the stern wolf betray
If like a lamb he could his looks translate!
How many gazers mightst thou lead away
If thou wouldst use the strength of all thy state!   12
   But do not so. I love thee in such sort
   As, thou being mine, mine is thy good report.

In this first of three sonnets about a period of separation from the beloved, the poet remembers the time as bleak winter, though the actual season was warm and filled with nature's abundance.

---

5. **removed:** i.e., of (our) separation

6. **teeming:** pregnant, prolific (**Autumn** is throughout the poem pictured as a woman giving birth, or about to give birth. Autumn's relationship to **summer's time** is explained by editors in a variety of ways. See longer note, p. 336.) **big:** pregnant; **increase:** abundance (See picture, p. 76.)

7. **wanton:** frolicsome; luxuriant (or lascivious, if modifying **the prime**); **burden of the prime:** i.e., offspring fathered by springtime

8. **widowed wombs:** i.e., the (pregnant) **wombs** of widows

10. **hope . . . fruit:** a bleak image (in that **orphans** and the fatherless [**unfathered**] look to a future with little **hope**)

11. **his:** i.e., its; **wait on thee:** i.e., are in attendance on you, serve you

13. **so dull a cheer:** i.e., such a heavy heart   **cheer:** disposition, mood

14. **pale:** wordplay on (1) no longer bright green; (2) ashen (from dread)

212

97

How like a winter hath my absence been
From thee, the pleasure of the fleeting year!
What freezings have I felt, what dark days seen,
What old December's bareness everywhere!   4
And yet this time removed was summer's time,
The teeming autumn, big with rich increase,
Bearing the wanton burden of the prime,
Like widowed wombs after their lords' decease.   8
Yet this abundant issue seemed to me
But hope of orphans and unfathered fruit;
For summer and his pleasures wait on thee,
And thou away, the very birds are mute;   12
    Or if they sing, 'tis with so dull a cheer
    That leaves look pale, dreading the winter's near.

The poet here remembers an April separation, in which spring-time beauty seemed to him only a pale reflection of the absent beloved.

2. **proud-pied:** gloriously many-colored; **his trim:** i.e., his finery (**April** is here a beautiful youth.)

4. **That:** i.e., so **that** even; **heavy Saturn:** As both the planet in its astrological context and the Roman god, **Saturn** is associated with melancholy, winter, and decrepitude. (See chart, p. 112.) **heavy:** ponderous; sad

5. **nor the lays:** neither the songs

6. **different flowers in:** i.e., **flowers** differing **in**

7. **any summer's story tell:** i.e., narrate a cheerful **story** (See *The Winter's Tale* 2.1.33: "A sad tale's best for winter.")

8. **their proud lap:** (1) the splendid earth; (2) the earth **proud** of their beauty (See *Richard II* 3.3.49: "The fresh green **lap** of fair King Richard's land.")

9. **wonder:** express my astonishment; **white:** i.e., whiteness (Proverbial: "**White** as a lily.")

11. **but sweet:** merely pleasant; **but . . . delight:** i.e., mere representations of essential **delight**

12. **Drawn after:** copied from; **pattern:** model

14. **shadow:** possible wordplay on the Neoplatonic **shadow** (imperfect reflection of the Idea) and the image cast by a body in sunlight (See notes to s. 53.) **these:** perhaps the roses and lilies already mentioned; perhaps the flowers and herbs of s. 99 (Some editors end s. 98.14 with a colon to lead the reader's eye forward to the next poem.)

98

From you have I been absent in the spring,
When proud-pied April, dressed in all his trim,
Hath put a spirit of youth in everything,
That heavy Saturn laughed and leapt with him.   4
Yet nor the lays of birds nor the sweet smell
Of different flowers in odor and in hue
Could make me any summer's story tell,
Or from their proud lap pluck them where they grew.   8
Nor did I wonder at the lily's white,
Nor praise the deep vermilion in the rose;
They were but sweet, but figures of delight,
Drawn after you, you pattern of all those.   12
    Yet seemed it winter still, and, you away,
    As with your shadow I with these did play.

This third poem about the beloved's absence is closely linked to s. 98. In the present sonnet, the poet accuses spring flowers and herbs of stealing color and fragrance from the beloved. The sonnet is unusual in that the first "quatrain" has five lines; the poem therefore has 15 lines, the only such sonnet in the sequence. (See longer note, p. 337.)

1. **forward:** (1) early, precocious; (2) bold, brash

2. **sweet that smells:** i.e., perfume

3. **purple:** a color that at the time included the spectrum from blood-red to deep violet

4. **for complexion:** as color or cosmetic

5. **grossly:** excessively; flagrantly

6. **for thy:** i.e., for stealing its whiteness from your

7. **stol'n thy:** i.e., stolen their fragrance from your

8. **fearfully:** in fear; **on thorns did stand:** i.e., were in a state of anxiety (with wordplay on the **thorns** of the rosebush)

10. **nor red:** i.e., neither **red; of both:** i.e., **both** colors (i.e., the **third** was a pink or damask rose)

11. **annexed:** added (**to his robb'ry** of colors)

12. **for:** because of; **pride . . . growth:** splendor of full bloom

13. **canker:** cankerworm (See note to s. 35.4.)

15. **But . . . thee:** i.e., that had not stolen its fragrance or **color** from you

99

The forward violet thus did I chide:
"Sweet thief, whence didst thou steal thy sweet that smells,
If not from my love's breath? The purple pride
Which on thy soft cheek for complexion dwells   4
In my love's veins thou hast too grossly dyed."
The lily I condemnèd for thy hand,
And buds of marjoram had stol'n thy hair;
The roses fearfully on thorns did stand,   8
⌜One⌝ blushing shame, another white despair;
A third, nor red nor white, had stol'n of both,
And to his robb'ry had annexed thy breath;
But, for his theft, in pride of all his growth   12
A vengeful canker ate him up to death.
   More flowers I noted, yet I none could see
   But sweet or color it had stol'n from thee.

In this first of a group of four sonnets about a period of time in which the poet has failed to write about the beloved, the poet summons his poetic genius to return and compose verse that will immortalize the beloved.

---

1. **muse:** poetic gift or genius (See s. 38.1.)

3. **Spend'st . . . fury:** i.e., do you waste your inspiration (Poetic inspiration was referred to as *furor poeticus,* or "poetic rage.")

4. **lend . . . light:** i.e., make lowly **subjects** luminous

5–6. **straight . . . spent:** i.e., immediately compensate for misspent **time** through noble verses

7. **lays:** songs, poems

8. **argument:** theme

9. **resty:** (1) sluggish, idle; (2) refractory, stubborn

10. **If:** i.e., (to see) whether; **graven:** carved

11. **satire to:** i.e., satirist of

12. **spoils:** acts of destruction (with wordplay on **spoils** as "booty")

13. **wastes:** destroys

14. **So thou prevent'st:** i.e., in that way you forestall

100

Where art thou, muse, that thou forget'st so long
To speak of that which gives thee all thy might?
Spend'st thou thy fury on some worthless song,
Dark'ning thy power to lend base subjects light?   4
Return, forgetful muse, and straight redeem
In gentle numbers time so idly spent;
Sing to the ear that doth thy lays esteem
And gives thy pen both skill and argument.   8
Rise, resty muse; my love's sweet face survey
If Time have any wrinkle graven there.
If any, be a satire to decay
And make Time's spoils despisèd everywhere.   12
    Give my love fame faster than Time wastes life;
    So thou prevent'st his scythe and crookèd knife.

Continuing from s. 100, this poem has the muse tell the poet that the beloved needs no praise. The poet responds that the poems are for the edification of future ages.

---

1. **truant:** lazy; wandering
2. **truth in beauty dyed:** i.e., **truth** steeped **in beauty** (an image of the beloved)
3. **my love:** i.e., the beloved; **depends:** i.e., depend
4. **therein dignified:** i.e., your dependence on my beloved is the source of your dignity and worth
5. **haply:** perhaps
6. **Truth needs no color:** a proverb in which **color** means "rhetorical heightening"; **with . . . fixed:** perhaps, since its complexion is natural and ingrained
7. **Beauty no pencil:** i.e., **Beauty** (needs) **no** artist's brush; **lay:** i.e., paint (literally, arrange colors on canvas)
8. **intermixed:** intermingled, mixed together
9. **he:** the beloved; **dumb:** mute, silent
11. **much:** i.e., long
12. **of ages:** i.e., by **ages**
13. **do thy office:** perform your duty
14. **long hence:** far in the future; **shows:** appears

101

O truant muse, what shall be thy amends
For thy neglect of truth in beauty dyed?
Both truth and beauty on my love depends;
So dost thou too, and therein dignified.   4
Make answer, muse. Wilt thou not haply say
"Truth needs no color with his color fixed,
Beauty no pencil beauty's truth to lay;
But best is best if never intermixed"?   8
Because he needs no praise, wilt thou be dumb?
Excuse not silence so, for 't lies in thee
To make him much outlive a gilded tomb
And to be praised of ages yet to be.   12
    Then do thy office, muse; I teach thee how
    To make him seem long hence as he shows now.

The poet defends his silence, arguing that it is a sign not of lessened love but of his desire, in a world where pleasures have grown common, to avoid wearying the beloved with poems of praise.

1. **love:** affection; **is strengthened:** i.e., has grown in strength; **in seeming:** i.e., to all appearance

2. **show:** i.e., outward manifestation

3. **merchandized:** bought and sold, bartered; **whose rich esteeming:** i.e., the **rich** worth of which

4. **publish:** make public

5. **in the spring:** i.e., in its early days

6. **lays:** songs, poems

7. **Philomel:** i.e., the nightingale (into which, in mythology, a woman named Philomela had been transformed); **in summer's front:** i.e., at the beginning of summer (For the nightingale, see picture, p. 528.)

8. **stops his pipe:** i.e., ceases to sing   **his:** i.e., the nightingale's (Most editors since 1835 have emended the Quarto's **his** to "her" in order to create greater clarity.) **in growth of riper days:** i.e., in the later, more abundant, **days** of summer

10. **her mournful hymns:** i.e., Philomel's sad tunes (Philomela's story was a tragic one.)

11. **But that:** i.e., **but** because; **wild . . . bough:** The image is of hosts of common birds singing in the trees. In conjunction with ll. 12–14, the image may be linked to earlier sonnets about rival poets.

12. **sweets:** pleasures

14. **dull:** i.e., bore (literally, render listless)

102

My love is strengthened, though more weak in seeming;
I love not less, though less the show appear.
That love is merchandized whose rich esteeming
The owner's tongue doth publish everywhere.   4
Our love was new, and then but in the spring,
When I was wont to greet it with my lays,
As Philomel in summer's front doth sing,
And stops his pipe in growth of riper days.   8
Not that the summer is less pleasant now
Than when her mournful hymns did hush the night,
But that wild music burdens every bough,
And sweets grown common lose their dear delight.   12
    Therefore, like her, I sometime hold my tongue,
    Because I would not dull you with my song.

In this fourth poem of apology for his silence, the poet argues that the beloved's own face is so superior to any words of praise that silence is the better way.

1. **poverty:** i.e., poor stuff; **muse:** poetic gift (See note to s. 38.1.)
2. **That:** i.e., in **that; her pride:** (1) her rhetorical splendor; (2) that of which she is proud (the beloved)
3. **argument all bare:** unadorned theme
4. **beside:** as well
6. **glass:** looking glass, mirror
7. **overgoes:** exceeds, excels; overpowers; **blunt invention:** dull creative powers
8. **Dulling:** removing the lustre of; **doing:** i.e., bringing, causing
9-10. **Were . . . well:** See *King Lear* 1.4.369: "Striving to better, oft we **mar** what's **well**" (cited in Kerrigan).   **Were it:** i.e., would it not be
11. **pass:** accomplishment
13. **sit:** have a place or location

103

Alack, what poverty my muse brings forth,
That, having such a scope to show her pride,
The argument all bare is of more worth
Than when it hath my added praise beside.   4
O, blame me not if I no more can write!
Look in your glass, and there appears a face
That overgoes my blunt invention quite,
Dulling my lines and doing me disgrace.   8
Were it not sinful, then, striving to mend,
To mar the subject that before was well?
For to no other pass my verses tend
Than of your graces and your gifts to tell.   12
 And more, much more, than in my verse can sit
 Your own glass shows you when you look in it.

The poet ponders the beloved's seemingly unchanging beauty, realizing that it is doubtless altering even as he watches. He warns that the epitome of beauty will have died before future ages are born.

---

2. **first your eye I eyed:** i.e., **I first** saw you

4. **pride:** splendor

6. **process:** i.e., the progression

8. **fresh, green:** These words may be synonyms, meaning "youthful, blooming"; or **fresh** may be linked to **April** and **green** to **June.** In any case, they mean young and vital, as opposed to **yellow autumn.**

9–10. **like . . . perceived:** Proverbial: "To move as the **dial hand,** which is not seen to move."   **dial:** sundial or clock (See picture, p. 172.)   **Steal from his figure:** wordplay on (1) (**beauty**) departs from its original form; (2) (time, as symbolized by the **dial hand**) steals (**beauty**) from the young man's appearance

11. **hue:** appearance; **still doth stand:** (1) i.e., remains unchanged or **still;** (2) continues to survive

13. **unbred:** unborn

14. **beauty's summer:** i.e., beauty at its peak

104

To me, fair friend, you never can be old,
For as you were when first your eye I eyed,
Such seems your beauty still. Three winters cold
Have from the forests shook three summers' pride,   4
Three beauteous springs to yellow autumn turned
In process of the seasons have I seen,
Three April perfumes in three hot Junes burned,
Since first I saw you fresh, which yet are green.   8
Ah, yet doth beauty, like a dial hand,
Steal from his figure, and no pace perceived;
So your sweet hue, which methinks still doth stand,
Hath motion, and mine eye may be deceived.   12
    For fear of which, hear this, thou age unbred:
    Ere you were born was beauty's summer dead.

Arguing that his poetry is not idolatrous in the sense of "polytheistic," the poet contends that he celebrates only a single person, the beloved, as forever "fair, kind, and true." Yet by locating this trinity of features in a single being, the poet flirts with idolatry in the sense of worshipping his beloved.

---

1. **idolatry:** The wit of the sonnet plays on the poet's pretense that **idolatry** means only polytheistic worship of idols (of which pagans and Roman Catholics alike were accused); the word also means "immoderate attachment to a person or thing."

2. **show:** seem, appear

4. **To . . . one:** i.e., **to** and **of** a single entity (the **belovèd**); **still . . . so:** i.e., **(my songs)** always the same

5. **my love:** i.e., **my belovèd**

6. **Still:** always

8. **difference:** variety, diversity (though with almost inevitable wordplay on "disagreement")

9. **argument:** topic, theme

10. **varying to:** i.e., (though sometimes) expressed in

11. **this change:** i.e., **this** varying of expression; **my invention spent:** i.e., my poetic creativity employed and/or exhausted

12. **Three . . . in one:** This reminder of the Christian Trinity, echoed in l. 14, suggests that the poet, like the Christian, worships a single "god" represented in three "persons" or attributes.

13. **lived alone:** i.e., inhabited separate individuals

14. **kept seat:** resided

105

Let not my love be called idolatry,
Nor my belovèd as an idol show,
Since all alike my songs and praises be
To one, of one, still such, and ever so.   4
Kind is my love today, tomorrow kind,
Still constant in a wondrous excellence;
Therefore my verse, to constancy confined,
One thing expressing, leaves out difference.   8
"Fair, kind, and true" is all my argument,
"Fair, kind, and true," varying to other words;
And in this change is my invention spent,
Three themes in one, which wondrous scope affords.   12
    "Fair," "kind," and "true" have often lived alone,
    Which three till now never kept seat in one.

The poet, in reading descriptions of beautiful knights and ladies in old poetry, realizes that the poets were trying to describe the beauty of the beloved, but, having never seen him, could only approximate it.

---

1. **wasted time: time** gone by (with wordplay on **wasted** as "ravaged")

2. **wights:** men and women (a term already archaic in Shakespeare's day)

3. **beauty:** perhaps the **beauty** of the described **wights,** or perhaps the beautiful poetic style of the **descriptions**

5. **blazon:** description of excellencies (in poetry, a catalogue of the body's beauties, as in l. 6)

6. **brow:** forehead

7. **their antique pen:** i.e., the **pen** of the old poets; **would have expressed:** i.e., were trying to depict

8. **master:** own, possess

9. **their praises:** (1) the **praises** of the beautiful **wights;** or, (2) the poems of praise by the old poets

10. **you prefiguring:** i.e., foreshadowing you (as, in traditional Christianity, events and figures in the earlier scriptures prefigure the life of Jesus Christ)

11. **for:** because; **divining eyes:** i.e., **eyes** of conjecture or prophecy

12. **skill:** understanding (The Quarto reads *still.*)

14. **wonder:** i.e., look on in amazement; **lack tongues:** i.e., **lack** (adequate) language (but with the suggestion of being struck dumb by the beloved's beauty)

106

When in the chronicle of wasted time
I see descriptions of the fairest wights,
And beauty making beautiful old rhyme
In praise of ladies dead and lovely knights,   4
Then in the blazon of sweet beauty's best,
Of hand, of foot, of lip, of eye, of brow,
I see their antique pen would have expressed
Even such a beauty as you master now.   8
So all their praises are but prophecies
Of this our time, all you prefiguring;
And, for they looked but with divining eyes,
They had not ⌐skill⌐ enough your worth to sing.   12
    For we, which now behold these present days,
    Have eyes to wonder, but lack tongues to praise.

This sonnet celebrates an external event that had threatened to be disastrous but that has turned out to be wonderful. The poet's love, in this new time, is also refreshed.

1. **Not:** i.e., neither
1–2. **prophetic . . . come:** i.e., prognostications of **the world** at large
3. **lease . . . control:** i.e., set limits to the length of time that I will love
4. **Supposed as forfeit:** i.e., which had been thought to be subject to; **confined doom:** restricted or limited fate (i.e., fate of being limited)
5. **The mortal . . . endured:** a much-debated reference, accepted by most editors today as referring to the death of Queen Elizabeth, often imaged as Diana or **the moon** (See, e.g., Kerrigan. For Diana, see picture, p. 410.) **endured:** suffered
6. **sad augurs:** solemn or gloomy soothsayers; **presage:** i.e., warnings
7. **Incertainties:** events of which the outcome was uncertain; **assured:** i.e., as certain, safe (perhaps a reference to the peaceful accession of King James)
8. **olives of endless age:** i.e., olive branches that will last forever (The traditional link between the olive tree and **peace** may derive from the olive leaf brought Noah by the dove to signal the end of the flood [Genesis 8.11].)
9. **drops . . . time:** variously interpreted as springtime rain, as oil from the **olives,** and as the balm used in coronations
10. **subscribes:** submits
11. **spite of:** despite; **rhyme:** poem
12. **insults:** triumphs; **dull . . . tribes:** i.e., persons without (poetic) language
13. **this:** i.e., **this** poem
14. **crests:** insignia on coats of arms (perhaps as displayed on **tombs**); **spent:** wasted away

107

Not mine own fears nor the prophetic soul
Of the wide world dreaming on things to come
Can yet the lease of my true love control,
Supposed as forfeit to a confined doom.   4
The mortal moon hath her eclipse endured,
And the sad augurs mock their own presage;
Incertainties now crown themselves assured,
And peace proclaims olives of endless age.   8
Now with the drops of this most balmy time
My love looks fresh, and Death to me subscribes,
Since, spite of him, I'll live in this poor rhyme,
While he insults o'er dull and speechless tribes;   12
    And thou in this shalt find thy monument
    When tyrants' crests and tombs of brass are spent.

The poet explains that his repeated words of love and praise are like daily prayer; though old, they are always new. True love is also always new, though the lover and the beloved may age.

---

1. **character:** write, inscribe
2. **figured:** portrayed, represented
3. **register:** record
5. **prayers divine:** probable allusion to the Anglican matins and evensong (morning and evening prayer) prescribed for daily reciting from the Book of Common Prayer
7. **no old thing old:** i.e., **no** familiar or often-repeated **thing** as worn out or stale
8. **hallowed:** made holy (Scholars link this line with the Lord's Prayer's "**hallowed** be Thy **name**" [Matthew 6.9].)
9. **So that:** i.e., in the same way; **case:** wordplay on (1) condition; (2) covering (as in the **case** of a book, or as in skin or clothing)
10. **Weighs not:** does not take into account
11. **gives . . . place:** i.e., yields to (or pays attention to) inevitable **wrinkles**
12. **for aye his page:** i.e., forever his servant (Several words connected with books—**page, case,** and **dust**—continue in ll. 9–12 the theme of the poet and his writing from ll. 1–8.)
13. **conceit:** understanding, idea; **there bred:** i.e., (still) being **bred there**
14. **would show it:** i.e., try to make it appear

108

What's in the brain that ink may character
Which hath not figured to thee my true spirit?
What's new to speak, what now to register,
That may express my love or thy dear merit?   4
Nothing, sweet boy; but yet, like prayers divine,
I must each day say o'er the very same,
Counting no old thing old, thou mine, I thine,
Even as when first I hallowed thy fair name.   8
So that eternal love in love's fresh case
Weighs not the dust and injury of age,
Nor gives to necessary wrinkles place,
But makes antiquity for aye his page,   12
    Finding the first conceit of love there bred,
    Where time and outward form would show it dead.

The poet defends his infidelities, arguing that his return washes away the blemish of his having left.

---

2. **my flame to qualify:** to diminish my passion

3. **depart:** separate, divide (with wordplay on "go away from")

5. **ranged:** wandered, strayed

7. **Just to the time:** i.e., exactly on **time; with the time exchanged:** i.e., changed by this interval

8. **myself . . . stain:** To "wash a **stain**" meant to remove a moral blemish. (Booth attacks the logic of the poet's excuse: "water can wash away a stain, but the periodic returns of a promiscuous lover do not wash away the crime of his infidelities.")

10. **all . . . blood:** i.e., every sort of temperament

11. **preposterously:** perversely, unnaturally

12. **nothing:** a thing or person not worth considering

14. **Save:** i.e., except for; **it:** i.e., the **universe**

A motley fool. (s. 110.2)

109

O, never say that I was false of heart,
Though absence seemed my flame to qualify;
As easy might I from myself depart
As from my soul, which in thy breast doth lie.   4
That is my home of love. If I have ranged,
Like him that travels I return again,
Just to the time, not with the time exchanged,
So that myself bring water for my stain.   8
Never believe, though in my nature reigned
All frailties that besiege all kinds of blood,
That it could so preposterously be stained
To leave for nothing all thy sum of good.   12
    For nothing this wide universe I call,
    Save thou, my rose; in it thou art my all.

The poet confesses to having been unfaithful to the beloved, but claims that his straying has rejuvenated him and made the beloved seem even more godlike.

---

2. **made . . . view:** i.e., played the fool, made a fool of myself **motley:** i.e., motley fool (one dressed in the parti-colored clothing of the professional or theatrical Fool [See picture, p. 236.]) **to the view:** i.e., in the public eye

3. **Gored:** wounded; made filthy (with wordplay on *to gore* as "to make clothing parti-colored through the use of different colored gores or triangular patches")

4. **Made . . . new:** i.e., turned **new** loves into **old offenses** (perhaps, occasions for customary infidelity)

5. **truth:** constancy, veracity

6. **Askance:** sidewise (in scorn or contempt); **strangely:** coldly (like a stranger)

7. **blenches:** sideways glances; **gave . . . youth:** i.e., rejuvenated **my heart**

8. **worse essays:** i.e., experiments with the inferior

9. **have . . . end:** i.e., accept that which is undying

10. **grind:** sharpen (as in the metaphor "to whet or sharpen the **appetite**")

11. **proof:** experiment, experience; **try:** test; afflict

12. **in love:** i.e., in the capacity to love; **to . . . confined:** i.e., **to whom I** confine myself

13. **next . . . best:** i.e., **the best** (refuge, comfort) short of **heaven**

110

Alas, 'tis true, I have gone here and there
And made myself a motley to the view,
Gored mine own thoughts, sold cheap what is most dear,
Made old offenses of affections new. 4
Most true it is that I have looked on truth
Askance and strangely; but by all above,
These blenches gave my heart another youth,
And worse essays proved thee my best of love. 8
Now all is done, have what shall have no end.
Mine appetite I never more will grind
On newer proof, to try an older friend,
A god in love, to whom I am confined. 12
    Then give me welcome, next my heaven the best,
    Even to thy pure and most most loving breast.

In this first of two linked poems, the poet blames Fortune for putting him in a profession that led to his bad behavior, and he begs the beloved to punish him and to pity him.

1. **for . . . chide:** i.e., **chide** the **goddess Fortune** on my behalf (**Fortune** allotted good and bad luck.) See pictures, pp. 476, 518.

2. **guilty goddess of:** i.e., **goddess** responsible for

4. **public . . . breeds:** Editors generally read this line in terms of Shakespeare's life and suggest that he is here blaming his **public** life in the theater for whatever misdeeds or common behavior he is acknowledging in this group of sonnets.

5. **Thence:** from there; **brand:** mark of disgrace

6–7. **almost . . . To:** i.e., **my nature is almost** overpowered by

7. **like . . . hand:** i.e., as **the dyer's hand** is stained by the dye

8. **renewed:** regenerated, rejuvenated

10. **eisel:** vinegar; **'gainst:** i.e., to fight (This line may refer to the concoction of vinegar sometimes prescribed for the bubonic plague.)

11. **No:** i.e., there is no

12. **Nor:** i.e., **nor** will I consider **bitter** (l. 11); **double penance:** repeated or second punishment

13. **ye:** a form of *you*, here used in the singular

14. **Even that your pity:** i.e., **your pity** alone

111

O, for my sake do you ⌜with⌝ Fortune chide,
The guilty goddess of my harmful deeds,
That did not better for my life provide
Than public means which public manners breeds.   4
Thence comes it that my name receives a brand;
And almost thence my nature is subdued
To what it works in, like the dyer's hand.
Pity me, then, and wish I were renewed,   8
Whilst, like a willing patient, I will drink
Potions of eisel 'gainst my strong infection;
No bitterness that I will bitter think,
Nor double penance, to correct correction.   12
    Pity me, then, dear friend, and I assure ye
    Even that your pity is enough to cure me.

The pity asked for in s. 111 has here been received, and the poet therefore has no interest in others' opinions of his worth or behavior.

---

1. **impression:** indentation

2. **vulgar scandal:** public disgrace; base rumor; **stamped . . . brow:** Disgrace or rumor here becomes a branding iron that marks the poet as a felon.   **brow:** forehead

3. **well or ill:** i.e., good or bad

4. **So you o'ergreen:** perhaps, as long as you cover over; **allow:** commend; grant

7. **to me:** i.e., is **alive to me**

8. **steeled sense:** hardened sensibility; **or changes right or wrong:** i.e., alters either to the good or to the bad (Editors agree that something like this is what these words may mean. See note to l. 14 below.)

9. **so:** such a

9–10. **care / Of:** concern with; consideration of

10. **adder's sense:** i.e., hearing (Proverbial: "Deaf as an adder.")

11. **critic:** faultfinder; **stoppèd are:** i.e., is closed

12. **neglect:** indifference; **dispense:** excuse

14. **besides:** i.e., other than you; **methinks:** it seems to me (This line and ll. 7 and 8 have led Booth to speculate that Shakespeare left this sonnet in an unfinished state. See Booth, pp. 364–70.)

112

Your love and pity doth th' impression fill
Which vulgar scandal stamped upon my brow;
For what care I who calls me well or ill,
So you o'ergreen my bad, my good allow?   4
You are my all the world, and I must strive
To know my shames and praises from your tongue;
None else to me, nor I to none alive,
That my steeled sense or changes right or wrong.   8
In so profound abysm I throw all care
Of others' voices that my adder's sense
To critic and to flatterer stoppèd are.
Mark how with my neglect I do dispense: 12
    You are so strongly in my purpose bred
    That all the world besides methinks ⌜are⌝ dead.

In this first of two linked sonnets, the poet confesses that everything he sees is transformed into an image of the beloved.

---

1. **mine . . . mind:** i.e., I see with **my** mind's **eye** (my imagination)
2. **that which governs:** i.e., the **eye** that guides
3. **Doth part his:** i.e., divides its (As ll. 5ff. explain, the **eye,** while continuing to see that which is exterior, fails to carry that image to the mind.)
4. **seeing:** i.e., to see; **effectually:** in fact; **out:** extinguished (The classical notion that the eye emits rays or beams of light was still generally believed.)
5. **form:** image, representation; **heart:** mind (For a similar use of **heart** to mean "mind," see, e.g., s. 46.10, where thoughts are called "tenants to the **heart.**")
6. **doth latch:** i.e., catches sight of
7. **his quick:** i.e., its (the eye's) quickly fleeting
8. **his . . . holds:** i.e., does its (the eye's) **own vision** retain
9. **rud'st:** roughest, coarsest; **gentlest:** tenderest
10. **sweet favor:** pleasant face (though Q's *sweet-favor* may have been a misprint for *sweet-favored,* in which case the compound would modify **creature**)
12. **shapes . . . feature:** turns them **to your** form
13. **Incapable of:** unable to receive or contain
14. **true:** loyal (though not reliable or truthful)

113

Since I left you, mine eye is in my mind,
And that which governs me to go about
Doth part his function, and is partly blind,
Seems seeing, but effectually is out;   4
For it no form delivers to the heart
Of bird, of flower, or shape which it doth ⌐latch;¬
Of his quick objects hath the mind no part,
Nor his own vision holds what it doth catch.   8
For if it see the rud'st or gentlest sight,
The most sweet favor or deformèd'st creature,
The mountain or the sea, the day or night,
The crow or dove, it shapes them to your feature.   12
    Incapable of more, replete with you,
    My most true mind thus maketh mine ⌐eye¬ untrue.

In a continuation of s. 113, the poet debates whether the lovely images of the beloved are true or are the mind's delusions, and he decides on the latter.

1. **Or whether doth:** The construction that begins with **Or whether** and continues with its repetition in l. 3 is best understood today by (1) taking l. 1 as beginning with **doth** and (2) omitting **whether** from l. 3. (**Doth my mind . . . , Or shall I . . . ?**)

2. **this flattery:** i.e., the gratifying delusions spelled out in s. 113.9–12 (with wordplay on **flattery** as insincere adulation given, e.g., to monarchs)

4. **your love:** i.e., my **love** for you; **alchemy:** power of transforming the base into the golden

5. **of monsters:** i.e., from unnatural creatures; **indigest:** shapeless, crude

6. **cherubins:** one of the second order of angels

7. **Creating:** i.e., making (from)

8. **to his beams assemble:** i.e., come within its (the eye's) gaze **beams:** eyebeams (See note to s. 113.4.)

9. **'tis flattery . . . seeing:** i.e., my eyes are deluding me (See l. 2 and note.)

11. **his gust:** i.e., its (the mind's) taste; **is greeing:** accords or agrees

12. **to his:** i.e., to suit its

13–14. **If . . . begin:** The image is of the eye as the kingly mind's taster; since the **poisoned cup** of flatteringly deceptive images is also loved by the eye/taster, the mind's (or the poet's) **sin** is lessened.

114

Or whether doth my mind, being crowned with you,
Drink up the monarch's plague, this flattery?
Or whether shall I say mine eye saith true,
And that your love taught it this alchemy, 4
To make of monsters and things indigest
Such cherubins as your sweet self resemble,
Creating every bad a perfect best
As fast as objects to his beams assemble? 8
O, 'tis the first: 'tis flattery in my seeing,
And my great mind most kingly drinks it up.
Mine eye well knows what with his gust is greeing,
And to his palate doth prepare the cup. 12
    If it be poisoned, 'tis the lesser sin
    That mine eye loves it and doth first begin.

The poet acknowledges that the very fact that his love has grown makes his earlier poems about the fullness and constancy of his love into lies.

1. **before have writ:** i.e., have written earlier
2. **Even:** precisely
4. **flame:** i.e., of love; **clearer:** more intensely
5. **reckoning time:** i.e., **Time,** which counts, or which settles up accounts (though possibly, instead, "considering what **time** can do"); **millioned:** counted in the millions; **accidents:** events; mishaps
6. **'twixt vows:** i.e., between making a promise and keeping it
7. **Tan:** turn into leather, turn brown; **sacred beauty:** i.e., **beauty** that should be inviolable
8. **course of alt'ring things:** (1) direction that changing **things** take; (2) current of changing situations (Lines 5–8 do not make a sentence. If, as has been suggested, **Divert** is an error for *Diverts*, the resulting sentence would read ". . . time . . . diverts. . . .")
9. **fearing of:** i.e., **fearing**
10. **then:** at that time
11. **o'er incertainty:** over uncertainty, i.e., beyond doubt
12. **Crowning the present:** i.e., making **the present** supreme; **rest:** remainder (of time), future
13. **Love:** i.e., Cupid, represented as **a babe** (See picture, p. 294.) **Then might I not:** i.e., therefore **I might not; say so:** i.e., **say "Now I love you best"**

115

Those lines that I before have writ do lie,
Even those that said I could not love you dearer;
Yet then my judgment knew no reason why
My most full flame should afterwards burn clearer.   4
But reckoning time, whose millioned accidents
Creep in 'twixt vows and change decrees of kings,
Tan sacred beauty, blunt the sharp'st intents,
Divert strong minds to th' course of alt'ring things—   8
Alas, why, fearing of time's tyranny,
Might I not then say "Now I love you best,"
When I was certain o'er incertainty,
Crowning the present, doubting of the rest?   12
    Love is a babe. Then might I not say so,
    To give full growth to that which still doth grow.

The poet here meditates on what he sees as the truest and strongest kind of love, that between minds. He defines such a union as unalterable and eternal.

1. **Let me not:** i.e., may I never

2. **Admit impediments:** wordplay on the **marriage** service in the Book of Common Prayer, where **impediments** to ("obstacles to," "just causes impeding") the legality of the marriage are to be admitted (i.e., "confessed"), while in the sonnet, the word **impediments** (the "millioned accidents" of s. 115.5) suggests instead "impedimenta," things that impede or encumber progress, and **admit** means "concede the existence of" (with additional wordplay on "receive as valid or lawful or compatible with," "allow of the presence of," and "allow to enter")

4. **bends:** turns aside from its true course; **the remover:** i.e., (1) that which separates, takes away; (2) he or she who departs or disappears

5. **mark:** i.e., seamark (a lighthouse or beacon)

7. **the star:** i.e., the polestar or Polaris, used as a fixed point in navigation; **wand'ring bark:** lost ship

8. **worth's unknown:** i.e., value is (1) not mentally apprehended; (2) not attainable through inquiry; **his . . . taken:** i.e., its altitude be measured

11. **his:** i.e., its (**Time's**)

12. **bears it out:** endures; **doom:** i.e., Doomsday

13. **error:** (1) a fault in a legal judgment or the process to that judgment; (2) false belief; **proved:** demonstrated (to be **error**)

116

Let me not to the marriage of true minds
Admit impediments. Love is not love
Which alters when it alteration finds
Or bends with the remover to remove.   4
O, no, it is an ever-fixèd mark
That looks on tempests and is never shaken;
It is the star to every wand'ring bark,
Whose worth's unknown, although his height be taken.   8
Love's not Time's fool, though rosy lips and cheeks
Within his bending sickle's compass come;
Love alters not with his brief hours and weeks,
But bears it out even to the edge of doom.   12
    If this be error, and upon me proved,
    I never writ, nor no man ever loved.

In this first of a group of four sonnets of self-accusation and of attempts at explanation, the poet lists the charges that can be made against him, and then says he was merely testing the beloved's love.

---

1. **Accuse me thus:** i.e., indict me on the following charges (This courtroom language is continued in **Book . . . down, proof,** and **appeal.**)

2. **Wherein:** by which; **your . . . repay:** i.e., recompense **your great** worthiness or excellence

3. **upon . . . to call:** i.e., **to** invoke or appeal to **your dearest love**

4. **Whereto:** to which

5. **frequent been with:** i.e., **been** familiar or often in company **with; unknown minds:** i.e., strangers

6. **given to time:** i.e., wasted

8. **should:** i.e., would

9. **Book . . . down:** i.e., write **down,** record **errors:** wordplay on "mistakes" and "wanderings"

10. **on . . . accumulate:** i.e., **on** top of reliable **proof** (of my misdeeds) pile up conjecture

11. **level:** aim, line of fire

13. **appeal:** i.e., attempt to have the inevitable (negative) decision against me reversed; **did . . . prove:** i.e., was (simply) trying to test

14. **virtue:** goodness; strength

117

Accuse me thus: that I have scanted all
Wherein I should your great deserts repay,
Forgot upon your dearest love to call,
Whereto all bonds do tie me day by day; 4
That I have frequent been with unknown minds,
And given to time your own dear-purchased right;
That I have hoisted sail to all the winds
Which should transport me farthest from your sight. 8
Book both my willfulness and errors down,
And on just proof surmise accumulate;
Bring me within the level of your frown,
But shoot not at me in your wakened hate, 12
    Since my appeal says I did strive to prove
    The constancy and virtue of your love.

In this second sonnet of self-accusation, the poet uses analogies of eating and of purging to excuse his infidelities.

1. **Like as:** in the same way **as; appetites:** (1) craving for food; (2) lusts
2. **eager:** pungent; **urge:** stimulate
3. **As:** i.e., (and) just **as; prevent:** forestall, head off; **unseen:** i.e., not (yet) in evidence
4. **sicken:** i.e., make ourselves sick; **purge:** take drugs to empty the stomach or bowels
5. **Even so:** just **so**
6. **frame my feeding:** i.e., fashion my diet
7. **welfare:** doing (or being) well; **meetness:** appropriateness, suitableness
8. **To be:** i.e., in being; **needing:** need or want
9. **policy:** cunning, craftiness; **anticipate:** forestall
10. **faults assured:** i.e., real illnesses or disorders
12. **rank of:** overfed with; **ill:** badness; sickness
13. **thence:** i.e., from this experience

118

Like as to make our appetites more keen
With eager compounds we our palate urge;
As to prevent our maladies unseen
We sicken to shun sickness when we purge;   4
Even so, being full of your ne'er-cloying sweetness,
To bitter sauces did I frame my feeding;
And, sick of welfare, found a kind of meetness
To be diseased ere that there was true needing.   8
Thus policy in love, t' anticipate
The ills that were not, grew to faults assured,
And brought to medicine a healthful state
Which, rank of goodness, would by ill be cured.   12
    But thence I learn, and find the lesson true:
    Drugs poison him that so fell sick of you.

Filled with self-disgust at having subjected himself to so many evils in the course of his infidelity, the poet nevertheless finds an excuse in discovering that his now reconstructed love is stronger than it was before.

---

1. **siren:** Sirens were fabulous creatures (part woman, part bird, though also often identified with mermaids) whose singing lured sailors to destruction. See longer note, p. 337, and picture, p. 390.

2. **limbecks:** alembics (See picture, p. 258.)

3. **Applying:** administering (as a remedy)

4. **Still:** always, constantly

5. **errors:** sins; mistakes

6. **so blessèd never:** i.e., blessed to an unlimited degree

7. **out . . . fitted:** wordplay on **eyes** (1) convulsed in their sockets by the fits of disease and (2) removed from their proper **spheres** (like stars or planets in the Ptolemaic system, and like men in their proper social **spheres**)

8. **distraction:** temporary madness; **madding:** i.e., delirium-producing

9. **ill:** evil

10. **still made better:** (1) **made** yet **better;** (2) always **made better**

11–12. **ruined . . . greater:** Proverbial: "A broken bone is the stronger when it is well set." **ruined love:** i.e., **love** like a building in ruins

13. **my content:** i.e., that which contents me

14. **ills:** i.e., **wretched errors** (l. 5)

119

What potions have I drunk of siren tears
Distilled from limbecks foul as hell within,
Applying fears to hopes and hopes to fears,
Still losing when I saw myself to win! 4
What wretched errors hath my heart committed,
Whilst it hath thought itself so blessèd never!
How have mine eyes out of their spheres been fitted
In the distraction of this madding fever! 8
O, benefit of ill! Now I find true
That better is by evil still made better;
And ruined love, when it is built anew,
Grows fairer than at first, more strong, far greater. 12
    So I return rebuked to my content,
    And gain by ills thrice more than I have spent.

In this fourth sonnet about his unkindness to the beloved, the poet comforts himself with the memory of the time the beloved was unkind to him.

---

2. **for:** because of, in exchange for

3. **Needs must:** of necessity, necessarily

4. **nerves:** sinews, tendons

7. **leisure:** opportunity

8. **in your crime:** i.e., as a result of your offense

9. **remembered:** reminded

11. **And . . . tendered:** i.e., so that I would quickly have offered (**tendered**) **you as you then** offered **me**

12. **humble salve:** i.e., healing ointment of humility (presumably, an apology); **fits:** befits

13. **that your trespass:** i.e., **that trespass** (i.e., **crime**) of yours; **fee:** payment

14. **ransoms:** pays for; **ransom:** redeem

Alchemy with her alembics. (s. 119.2)

120

That you were once unkind befriends me now,
And for that sorrow which I then did feel
Needs must I under my transgression bow,
Unless my nerves were brass or hammered steel.   4
For if you were by my unkindness shaken
As I by yours, you've passed a hell of time,
And I, a tyrant, have no leisure taken
To weigh how once I suffered in your crime.   8
O, that our night of woe might have remembered
My deepest sense how hard true sorrow hits,
And soon to you as you to me then tendered
The humble salve which wounded bosoms fits!   12
    But that your trespass now becomes a fee;
    Mine ransoms yours, and yours must ransom me.

The poet responds to slurs about his behavior by claiming that he is no worse (and is perhaps better) than his attackers.

---

1. **'Tis . . . esteemed:** This line extends and twists the proverb "There is small difference to the eye of the world in being nought (i.e., **vile**) and in being thought so."

2. **be:** i.e., **be (vile)**

3. **just pleasure:** i.e., (1) the **pleasure** that would have inhered in actually **being vile;** or (2) innocent **pleasure; so deemed:** i.e., **deemed vile**

4. **by others' seeing:** i.e., how others regard it

5. **adulterate:** corrupted; adulterous

6. **Give . . . to:** i.e., greet (as if in fellowship); **sportive blood:** i.e., lively (or amorous) nature

7. **are:** i.e., are there; **frailer:** morally weaker

8. **Which:** who; **in their wills:** i.e., willfully

9. **I . . . am:** i.e., I stand by my own actions and character (When Moses asks God's name, God responds with these words [Exodus 3.14].) **level:** aim; guess

11. **straight:** honest; **bevel:** i.e., dishonest (literally, oblique)

12. **By:** in terms of; **rank:** lustful; corrupt; **shown:** exhibited, displayed

13. **maintain:** assert

121

'Tis better to be vile than vile esteemed,
When not to be receives reproach of being,
And the just pleasure lost, which is so deemed
Not by our feeling but by others' seeing.   4
For why should others' false adulterate eyes
Give salutation to my sportive blood?
Or on my frailties why are frailer spies,
Which in their wills count bad what I think good?   8
No, I am that I am; and they that level
At my abuses reckon up their own.
I may be straight though they themselves be bevel;
By their rank thoughts my deeds must not be shown,   12
    Unless this general evil they maintain:
    All men are bad and in their badness reign.

This sonnet addresses the hard question of why the poet has given away the beloved's gift of a writing tablet. After several stumbling tries, the poet ends by claiming that for him to have kept the tables would have implied that he needed help in remembering the unforgettable beloved.

---

1. **tables:** i.e., writing tablet (probably the kind of tablet described by Peter Stallybrass and Roger Chartier as one or more pieces of coated vellum or paper, folded and stitched and sometimes elegantly bound, the coating allowing the vellum or paper to be written on with a stylus and then erased with a moistened cloth or by scraping)

2. **Full charactered:** fully inscribed or written

3. **idle rank:** perhaps (1) insignificant kind of object (the **tables** themselves); (2) trifling series or list (as were often, in printed form, bound with the **tables**)

6. **faculty:** physical capability, power

7. **razed oblivion:** i.e., **oblivion** that erases, obliterates; **his:** its

8. **record:** memory; writing; **missed:** lost, missing

9. **retention:** capacity for holding something (presumably referring to the **tables**)

10. **tallies:** pieces of wood on which to keep records; **score:** record (by cutting) (Both **tallies** and **score** would support the idea that these **tables** were the kind described in note 1, above, on which records were inscribed and then scraped away.)

11. **give . . . me:** i.e., **give** away the **tables**

13. **adjunct:** something connected but subordinate

14. **Were to import:** i.e., would be to imply

122

Thy gift, thy tables, are within my brain
Full charactered with lasting memory,
Which shall above that idle rank remain
Beyond all date, even to eternity—   4
Or, at the least, so long as brain and heart
Have faculty by nature to subsist;
Till each to razed oblivion yield his part
Of thee, thy record never can be missed.   8
That poor retention could not so much hold,
Nor need I tallies thy dear love to score;
Therefore to give them from me was I bold,
To trust those tables that receive thee more.   12
    To keep an adjunct to remember thee
    Were to import forgetfulness in me.

The poet repeats an idea from s. 59—that there is nothing new under the sun—and accuses Time of tricking us into perceiving things as new only because we live for such a short time. He reasserts his vow to remain constant despite Time's power.

---

2. **pyramids . . . might:** i.e., recently built spires, obelisks, or pinnacles (all of which resemble the great **pyramids** from ancient Egypt)

4. **dressings:** i.e., dressed-up versions; **a former sight:** i.e., something seen before

5. **Our dates are:** i.e., the term of (human) life is

5–6. **admire / . . . old:** i.e., wonder at some **old** thing that you (i.e., **Time**) fraudulently present (as new)

7. **make . . . desire:** i.e., consider these as objects created just for us

8. **before . . . told:** i.e., have heard about **them before**

9. **Thy registers and thee:** i.e., **Time** and its chronicles or records

10. **wond'ring at:** marveling over

11. **For . . . lie:** i.e., because Time's **records** (accented on the second syllable) and perceived experience are both liars

12. **Made more or less:** exaggerated and diminished; **thy . . . haste:** i.e., "swift-footed **Time**" (s. 19.6)

14. **true:** constant, unchanging; **scythe:** See note to s. 12.13.

123

No, Time, thou shalt not boast that I do change.
Thy pyramids built up with newer might
To me are nothing novel, nothing strange;
They are but dressings of a former sight.   4
Our dates are brief, and therefore we admire
What thou dost foist upon us that is old,
And rather make them born to our desire
Than think that we before have heard them told.   8
Thy registers and thee I both defy,
Not wond'ring at the present nor the past;
For thy records and what we see doth lie,
Made more or less by thy continual haste.   12
    This I do vow, and this shall ever be:
    I will be true despite thy scythe and thee.

In this difficult and much-discussed sonnet, the poet declares the permanence and wisdom of his love.

1. **my dear love:** i.e., the precious **love** that I feel; **were . . . state:** i.e., had been produced by circumstances (or by the beloved's privileged status)

2. **for:** i.e., as; **fortune's bastard:** i.e., offspring of whimsical forces; **unfathered:** made illegitimate, deprived of a father (and hence without support)

3. **time's . . . hate:** the favor or disfavor (1) of the present age, or (2) of Time

4. **Weeds . . . gathered:** (1) consigned to live among **weeds** or **gathered** into a bouquet; or (2) subject to a short, uncertain life, either as weed or flower

5. **it was builded:** i.e., **my love was** built; **accident:** i.e., (the forces of) chance or fortune

6. **suffers not in:** i.e., is not affected by

7. **thrallèd:** servile, enslaving

8. **our fashion calls:** i.e., (1) summons that which goes in and out of **fashion;** (2) bids the merely fashionable

9. **policy:** expediency; **heretic:** perhaps, heretical doctrine or practice

10. **on . . . hours:** i.e., as if on short-term contracts

11. **politic:** wise, judicious

12. **That it nor:** i.e., so **that it** neither

13. **I witness call:** i.e., **I call** as witnesses

13–14. **fools . . . crime:** a much-debated reference; perhaps "time-servers who repent at the last minute," or, perhaps "martyrs who **die for** their faith, despising that which is temporal and accused of criminal beliefs"

124

If my dear love were but the child of state,
It might for fortune's bastard be unfathered,
As subject to time's love or to time's hate,
Weeds among weeds, or flowers with flowers gathered.   4
No, it was builded far from accident;
It suffers not in smiling pomp, nor falls
Under the blow of thrallèd discontent,
Whereto th' inviting time our fashion calls.   8
It fears not policy, that heretic
Which works on leases of short-numbered hours,
But all alone stands hugely politic,
That it nor grows with heat nor drowns with showers.   12
    To this I witness call the fools of time,
    Which die for goodness who have lived for crime.

The poet, in apparent response to accusation, claims that his love (and, perhaps, his poetry of praise) is not basely motivated by desire for outward honor.

---

1. **Were 't aught:** i.e., would it matter; **I bore the canopy:** i.e., if I were publicly honored by serving majesty (It was a high honor to hold **the canopy** over the head of the dignitary at a public ceremony.)

2. **extern, outward:** external appearance, exterior

3. **great bases:** massive foundations; **for eternity:** to last forever (with wordplay on "to enshrine **eternity**")

4. **proves:** i.e., prove; **short:** short-lived; **waste:** destruction, decay

5. **dwellers on:** i.e., those who fix their attention on (with wordplay on "inhabitants," continued in l. 6 with **rent**)

7. **compound sweet:** i.e., **sweet** compounds

8. **Pitiful thrivers:** i.e., pathetic successes; **spent:** destroyed; used up

9. **obsequious . . . heart:** i.e., privately attentive

10. **oblation:** offering, gift

11. **seconds:** inferior stuff; **art:** artifice; skill

13. **suborned:** i.e., corrupt (The informant here abjured is apparently someone who claimed that the poet's attachment to [or verse in praise of] the beloved was basely motivated.)

14. **impeached:** discredited; **control:** power

125

Were 't aught to me I bore the canopy,
With my extern the outward honoring,
Or laid great bases for eternity,
Which proves more short than waste or ruining?   4
Have I not seen dwellers on form and favor
Lose all and more by paying too much rent,
For compound sweet forgoing simple savor,
Pitiful thrivers, in their gazing spent?   8
No, let me be obsequious in thy heart,
And take thou my oblation, poor but free,
Which is not mixed with seconds, knows no art
But mutual render, only me for thee.   12
    Hence, thou suborned informer; a true soul
    When most impeached stands least in thy control.

The poet acknowledges that the beloved young man grows love-lier with time, as if Nature has chosen him as her darling, but warns him that her protection cannot last forever—that eventu-ally aging and death will come. (See longer note, p. 338.)

1. **lovely:** lovable; beautiful

2. **glass:** hourglass (with its constantly flowing sand); **his sickle hour:** i.e., the **hour** when **Time's sickle** cuts down the liv-ing (See note to s. 12.13.)

3. **by waning grown:** i.e., become more lovely while aging; **show'st:** serve to exhibit or indicate

4. **Thy lover's:** i.e., the poet's (The 1609 Quarto's *louers* can also be read as "lovers" or "lovers'." In any of these renderings, the word can refer to paramour[s], friend[s], or "he/those who love you.")

5. **mistress over wrack:** ruler over decay

6. **onwards:** i.e., toward death; **still will:** i.e., continues to; **pluck:** pull, draw

7. **keeps:** holds onto; **to this:** i.e., for the following

8. **disgrace:** put to shame by outdoing; **wretched minutes kill:** i.e., destroy even the insignificant units of Time

9. **her:** Nature; **minion:** (1) darling; (2) servant

10. **still:** always, forever

11. **Her audit:** i.e., the accounting that Nature must render (to Time); **answered:** satisfied

12. **quietus:** clearing of accounts (with wordplay on its mean-ing as "death, or that which brings death"); **render:** (1) relin-quish, surrender; (2) give back

126

O thou, my lovely boy, who in thy power
Dost hold Time's fickle glass, his sickle hour;
Who hast by waning grown, and therein show'st
Thy lover's withering as thy sweet self grow'st.   4
If Nature, sovereign mistress over wrack,
As thou goest onwards still will pluck thee back,
She keeps thee to this purpose, that her skill
May Time disgrace, and wretched ⌜minutes⌝ kill.   8
Yet fear her, O thou minion of her pleasure!
She may detain, but not still keep, her treasure.
Her audit, though delayed, answered must be,
And her quietus is to render thee.   12

The poet defends his love of a mistress who does not meet the conventional standard of beauty by claiming that her dark eyes and hair (and, perhaps, dark skin) are the new standard. The old version of beauty—blond hair and light skin—are so readily counterfeited that beauty in that form is no longer trusted.

---

1. **old age:** i.e., past; **black . . . fair:** wordplay on a set of meanings of both **black** and **fair** (**Fair** had long meant "beautiful," and had more recently come also to mean "blond-haired" and/or "light-skinned." **Black,** in reference to a person, meant "dark-skinned" and/or "having dark hair and eyes.")

2. **bore . . . name:** i.e., wasn't called "beauty" (with wordplay on **name** as a sign of legitimate birth)

3. **successive:** legitimate

4. **a bastard shame:** i.e., the **shame** of being (1) illegitimate, or (2) counterfeit, spurious

5. **put on:** assumed (with wordplay on "putting on makeup" or "donning a wig")

6. **Fairing:** beautifying; **art's:** artifice's

7. **hath no name:** i.e., has been bastardized

8. **But is profaned:** i.e., **beauty** has been desecrated, violated (because artificial **beauty** calls all **beauty** into question)

9. **Therefore . . . eyes:** i.e., because of this, (1) I have chosen a mistress whose **eyes;** or (2) my mistress has chosen **eyes** which; **raven black:** Proverbial: "**Black** as a **raven.**"

10. **eyes:** The repetition of **eyes** in ll. 9 and 10 leads many editors to emend to "brows" in l. 9 or 10. While the repetition is arguably a mistake, it is not clear which line is in error. **so suited, and:** i.e., **so** attired that

11. **At such:** i.e., at the behavior of those; **fair:** (1) beautiful; (2) blond and white-skinned; **no beauty lack:** i.e., make themselves beautiful (and white-skinned) artificially

12. **creation:** nature, natural **beauty; with . . . esteem:** i.e., by deeming it artificial

(continued)

127

In the old age, black was not counted fair,
Or, if it were, it bore not beauty's name;
But now is black beauty's successive heir,
And beauty slandered with a bastard shame.   4
For since each hand hath put on nature's power,
Fairing the foul with art's false borrowed face,
Sweet beauty hath no name, no holy bower,
But is profaned, if not lives in disgrace.   8
Therefore my mistress' eyes are raven black,
Her eyes so suited, and they mourners seem
At such who, not born fair, no beauty lack,
Sland'ring creation with a false esteem.   12
  Yet so they mourn, becoming of their woe,
  That every tongue says beauty should look so.

13. **so they mourn:** i.e., the way her eyes **mourn; becoming of:** i.e., so lovely in

The language of this sonnet is remarkably like that of Berowne's speeches in praise of Rosaline in *Love's Labor's Lost.* Having described her (3.1.206–7) as "a whitely [i.e., fair-skinned] wanton with a velvet brow, / With two pitch-balls stuck in her face for eyes," in 4.3 he responds to the King's "thy love is black as ebony" (267) by exclaiming

> Where is a book,
> That I may swear beauty doth beauty lack
> If that she learn not of her eye to look?
> No face is fair that is not full so black. . . .
> O, if in black my lady's brows be decked,
> It mourns that painting and usurping hair
> Should ravish doters with a false aspect:
> And therefore is she born to make black fair.
> Her favor turns the fashion of the days,
> For native blood [i.e., a naturally rosy complexion]
> is counted painting now.
> And therefore red [i.e., rosiness], that would avoid dispraise,
> Paints itself black to imitate her brow.
> (270–73, 278–85)

127

In the old age, black was not counted fair,
Or, if it were, it bore not beauty's name;
But now is black beauty's successive heir,
And beauty slandered with a bastard shame.   4
For since each hand hath put on nature's power,
Fairing the foul with art's false borrowed face,
Sweet beauty hath no name, no holy bower,
But is profaned, if not lives in disgrace.   8
Therefore my mistress' eyes are raven black,
Her eyes so suited, and they mourners seem
At such who, not born fair, no beauty lack,
Sland'ring creation with a false esteem.   12
    Yet so they mourn, becoming of their woe,
    That every tongue says beauty should look so.

This sonnet uses the conventional poetic idea of the poet envying an object being touched by the beloved. Here, the object is the keyboard of an instrument.

---

   1. **oft:** often

   2. **wood:** i.e., the keys of a virginal (a keyboard instrument in which the musician's fingers hitting the keys causes the strings to be plucked); **whose motion:** i.e., the movement of which; **sounds:** resounds; causes to sound (See picture below.)

   3. **thou . . . sway'st:** you . . . control or wield

   4. **concord:** harmony; **confounds:** overcomes

   5. **jacks:** i.e., keys (The **jacks,** in fact, pluck the strings, but here the word is presumably used to mean the entire keyboard mechanism.)

   8. **by:** i.e., beside

   9. **tickled:** *To tickle* is "to play a keyboard instrument" and "to give pleasure or excitement."

   9–10. **state / And situation:** status and location

   13. **saucy jacks:** a phrase that meant "impudent fellows," here with the obvious wordplay; **happy:** fortunate; delighted

A woman playing a virginal. (s. 128)

128

How oft, when thou, my music, music play'st
Upon that blessèd wood whose motion sounds
With thy sweet fingers when thou gently sway'st
The wiry concord that mine ear confounds,　　　　4
Do I envy those jacks that nimble leap
To kiss the tender inward of thy hand,
Whilst my poor lips, which should that harvest reap,
At the wood's boldness by thee blushing stand.　　　8
To be so tickled they would change their state
And situation with those dancing chips,
O'er whom ⌈thy⌉ fingers walk with gentle gait,
Making dead wood more blest than living lips.　　　12
　　Since saucy jacks so happy are in this,
　　Give them ⌈thy⌉ fingers, me thy lips to kiss.

This sonnet describes what Booth calls "the life cycle of lust"—a moment of bliss preceded by madness and followed by despair.

---

1. **expense:** expenditure, using up; **spirit:** vital power; the vital **spirit** (thought to emanate from the heart and transform into clear bodily fluids such as semen), with possible wordplay on spiritual essence; **waste of shame:** i.e., shameful squandering (though with wordplay on **waste** as desert, or as common land, and on **shame** as disgrace, or guilt)

3. **full of blame:** culpable, blameworthy

4. **rude:** violent; **to trust:** i.e., to be trusted

5. **straight:** immediately (See Ben Jonson's translation of a poem by Petronius: "Doing, a filthy pleasure is, and short; / And done, we **straight** repent us of the sport.")

7–8. **as . . . mad:** In *Measure for Measure*, Claudio thus explains his sexual relations with Juliet: "Our natures do pursue, / Like rats that raven down [i.e., devour] their proper bane, / A thirsty evil, and when we drink, we die" (1.2.125–27).

11. **in proof:** i.e., in the experience itself; being tried; **proved:** i.e., having been tried or tested

12. **Before:** in prospect; **behind:** in retrospect; **a dream:** i.e., insubstantial, delusive (Tarquin, the rapist in *Lucrece*, asks himself before the rape "What win I if I gain the thing I seek? / **A dream,** a breath, a froth of fleeting joy. / Who buys a minute's mirth to wail a week / Or sells eternity to get a toy?" [211–14].)

129

Th' expense of spirit in a waste of shame
Is lust in action; and, till action, lust
Is perjured, murd'rous, bloody, full of blame,
Savage, extreme, rude, cruel, not to trust;   4
Enjoyed no sooner but despisèd straight;
Past reason hunted, and no sooner had,
Past reason hated as a swallowed bait
On purpose laid to make the taker mad.   8
⌐Mad⌐ in pursuit and in possession so;
Had, having, and in quest to have, extreme;
A bliss in proof and ⌐proved a⌐ very woe;
Before, a joy proposed; behind, a dream.   12
    All this the world well knows, yet none knows well
    To shun the heaven that leads men to this hell.

This sonnet plays with poetic conventions in which, for example, the mistress's eyes are compared with the sun, her lips with coral, and her cheeks with roses. (See picture below.) His mistress, says the poet, is nothing like this conventional image, but is as lovely as any woman.

---

3. **If snow be white:** Proverbial: "As **white** as **snow**."

4. **wires:** The comparison of golden hair to gold wire (threads of beaten gold, used in embroidery and jewelry) dated back to the thirteenth century.

5. **roses damasked:** Ingram and Redpath note Barnabe Barnes's "Her cheeks to damask roses sweet / In scent and colour were so like, / That honey bees in swarms would meet / To suck!"

8. **reeks:** emanates

11. **go:** walk (In *Venus and Adonis,* when Venus walks "The grass stoops not, she treads on it so light" [l. 1028].)

14. **she:** woman; **belied:** misrepresented, lied about; **false compare:** feigned or mendacious comparisons

Poetic metaphors made literal. (s. 130)

130

My mistress' eyes are nothing like the sun;
Coral is far more red than her lips' red;
If snow be white, why then her breasts are dun;
If hairs be wires, black wires grow on her head.   4
I have seen roses damasked, red and white,
But no such roses see I in her cheeks;
And in some perfumes is there more delight
Than in the breath that from my mistress reeks.   8
I love to hear her speak, yet well I know
That music hath a far more pleasing sound.
I grant I never saw a goddess go;
My mistress, when she walks, treads on the ground.   12
    And yet, by heaven, I think my love as rare
    As any she belied with false compare.

The poet disagrees with those who say that his mistress is not beautiful enough to make a lover miserable. He groans for her as for any beauty. Only her behavior, he says, is ugly.

---

1. **so as thou art:** i.e., just **as** you are

2. **proudly . . . cruel:** Both pride and cruelty were attributes of the beautiful mistress of love poetry.

3. **dear:** wordplay on "loving" and "lovingly"; **doting:** infatuated; foolish

6. **groan:** That the lover should **groan** was a commonplace of the tradition. When surrendering to Cupid in *Love's Labor's Lost*, Berowne says "Well, I will love, write, sigh, pray, sue, **groan**" (3.1.214).

7. **say:** i.e., publicly assert

9. **to be sure:** i.e., as an assurance (that) (Booth: "in order to verify [that]," "to testify [that]"); **that . . . swear:** i.e, **that** what **I swear is not false**

10. **thinking on:** i.e., **thinking** of or about

11. **One on another's neck: one** after another

12. **black, fairest:** See notes to s. 127, esp. lines from *Love's Labor's Lost.*

13–14. **In . . . proceeds:** Booth calls this couplet "a single graceful razor stroke" that cuts the mistress apart. (Berowne, too, accuses Rosaline of being "the worst of all, . . . one that will do the deed / Though Argus were her eunuch and her guard" [*LLL* 3.1.205, 208–9]. The play does not support his accusation.) **black:** foul, iniquitous   **this slander:** i.e., the accusation in l. 6

131

Thou art as tyrannous, so as thou art,
As those whose beauties proudly make them cruel;
For well thou know'st to my dear doting heart
Thou art the fairest and most precious jewel.   4
Yet in good faith some say that thee behold,
Thy face hath not the power to make love groan;
To say they err I dare not be so bold,
Although I swear it to myself alone.   8
And, to be sure that is not false I swear,
A thousand groans, but thinking on thy face,
One on another's neck do witness bear
Thy black is fairest in my judgment's place.   12
    In nothing art thou black save in thy deeds,
    And thence this slander as I think proceeds.

The poet begs the mistress to model her heart after her eyes, which, because they are black as if dressed in mourning, show their pity for his pain as a lover.

---

1. **as:** i.e., **as** if
2. **torment:** i.e., torments (The words **pitying, torment, disdain,** and **pain** [ll. 1–4] recall the medieval love tradition in which the hard-hearted mistress looks with scorn upon the heart-struck lover. In *As You Like It*, the meeting of such a lover and his "proud disdainful" mistress is described as "a pageant truly played / Between the pale complexion of true love / And the red glow of scorn and proud **disdain**" (3.4.48, 51–53).
3. **Have . . . be:** See s. 127.9–10, where the mistress's dark **eyes** are described as dressed in mourning.
4. **ruth:** compassion, pity
6. **Better becomes:** i.e., is more becoming to
7. **that full star:** i.e., Venus, called Hesperus when it ushers in the **even** (i.e., evening)
8. **sober:** solemn; subdued or muted in color
10. **as well:** i.e., just **as** properly; **beseem:** suit, fit (often applied to a person's appearance or clothing)
11. **mourning:** wordplay on (1) grieving; (2) wearing black as a sign of grief
12. **suit:** dress; **like:** i.e., the same way
13–14. **Then . . . lack:** See notes to s. 127.

132

Thine eyes I love, and they, as pitying me,
Knowing thy heart torment me with disdain,
Have put on black, and loving mourners be,
Looking with pretty ruth upon my pain.   4
And truly not the morning sun of heaven
Better becomes the gray cheeks of the east,
Nor that full star that ushers in the even
Doth half that glory to the sober west   8
As those two mourning eyes become thy face.
O, let it then as well beseem thy heart
To mourn for me, since mourning doth thee grace,
And suit thy pity like in every part.   12
    Then will I swear beauty herself is black,
    And all they foul that thy complexion lack.

In this first of two linked sonnets, the pain felt by the poet as lover of the mistress is multiplied by the fact that the beloved friend is also enslaved by her.

1. **Beshrew:** a mild oath (literally, "curse")
2. **my friend and me:** It has been suggested that this sonnet and those linked to it were written at the same time as ss. 40–42, which are addressed to the **friend** seduced by the poet's mistress. (See s. 42.7–8.)
3. **torture:** torment (See note to s. 132.2.)   **me alone:** i.e., just me
4. **to slavery:** i.e., to demeaning servitude (an extreme name for the abject situation of the obsessed lover)
6. **next:** i.e., nearest, closest (For the **friend** as the poet's other **self,** see, e.g., s. 62.13.) **harder:** more cruelly; **engrossed:** monopolized; possessed
7. **Of:** i.e., by
8. **crossed:** thwarted (with wordplay on "barred or precluded [from something desired]")
9. **Prison:** i.e., imprison
10. **bail:** confine (though at first reading the word appears to mean "free by becoming bail or security")
11. **keeps:** holds as prisoner; **guard:** guardroom; protector
12. **rigor:** harshness
13. **pent:** confined, imprisoned
14. **Perforce:** of necessity

286

133

Beshrew that heart that makes my heart to groan
For that deep wound it gives my friend and me.
Is 't not enough to torture me alone,
But slave to slavery my sweet'st friend must be?   4
Me from myself thy cruel eye hath taken,
And my next self thou harder hast engrossed;
Of him, myself, and thee I am forsaken,
A torment thrice threefold thus to be crossed.   8
Prison my heart in thy steel bosom's ward,
But then my friend's heart let my poor heart bail.
Whoe'er keeps me, let my heart be his guard;
Thou canst not then use rigor in my jail.   12
    And yet thou wilt, for I, being pent in thee,
    Perforce am thine, and all that is in me.

The poet continues to rationalize the young man's betrayal, here using language of debt and forfeit.

1. **now:** i.e., **now** that

2. **mortgaged:** pledged (The word picks up the meaning of "bail" as "security" in s. 133.10. For the set of financial/legal terms used in this poem—**forfeit, surety-like, bond, statute, usurer, sue, debtor**—see longer note, p. 338.) **will:** intention; carnal desire

3. **forfeit:** pay as fine or penalty; **so:** in order that; on the condition that; **that other mine:** See s. 133.6 ("my next self") and note.

5. **will not be:** i.e., does not wish to be

7–8. **He . . . bind:** i.e., he signed a **bond** for me merely as my guarantor, but he is now bound as tightly by it as I

9. **statute . . . take:** i.e., you will **take** (everything allowed by) the **statute** your **beauty** enables (As Booth explains, **beauty** is a **bond** in that it is binding; a **bond** is often a **statute;** hence the wordplay: "**statute of thy beauty.**")

10. **put'st . . . use:** wordplay on "lay out for profit **all** your land or money" and "offer **all** of yourself for sexual purposes" **to:** i.e., for **use:** See notes to ss. 2.9, 4.7, and 6.5.

11. **sue:** i.e., **(wilt) sue** (wordplay on "make a legal claim on" and "woo"); **came:** i.e., who became a

12. **my . . . abuse:** (1) my ill-usage (of my friend); (2) your mistreatment of me

14. **the whole:** i.e., the entire (sexual) debt

134

So, now I have confessed that he is thine
And I myself am mortgaged to thy will,
Myself I'll forfeit, so that other mine
Thou wilt restore to be my comfort still.   4
But thou wilt not, nor he will not be free,
For thou art covetous, and he is kind;
He learned but surety-like to write for me
Under that bond that him as fast doth bind.   8
The statute of thy beauty thou wilt take,
Thou usurer that put'st forth all to use,
And sue a friend came debtor for my sake;
So him I lose through my unkind abuse.   12
      Him have I lost; thou hast both him and me.
      He pays the whole, and yet am I not free.

In this first of two linked sonnets, the poet apparently begs his (promiscuous) mistress to allow him back into her bed.

---

1. **Whoever:** i.e., whatever (woman); **will:** Proverbial: "Women will have their wills." Wordplay on **will** dominates this and the following sonnet. For background on that wordplay, and for possible meanings of the word throughout these two sonnets, see longer note, p. 339.

2. **to boot:** in addition; **overplus:** surplus

9. **sea . . . rain:** Proverbial: "**The sea** refuses no river." See also Ecclesiastes 1.7: "All the rivers run into **the sea,** yet **the sea** is not full."

10. **his store:** i.e., its **abundance**

13. **unkind:** perhaps, (1) **unkind** (person), or (2) unkindness; **fair:** handsome, honorable; **beseechers:** suitors, suppliants

14. **all but one:** i.e., **all** (of the **beseechers** and their **wills**) as only **one** lover; **me:** i.e., include me

135

Whoever hath her wish, thou hast thy will,
And will to boot, and will in overplus.
More than enough am I that vex thee still,
To thy sweet will making addition thus.   4
Wilt thou, whose will is large and spacious,
Not once vouchsafe to hide my will in thine?
Shall will in others seem right gracious,
And in my will no fair acceptance shine?   8
The sea, all water, yet receives rain still,
And in abundance addeth to his store;
So thou, being rich in will, add to thy will
One will of mine to make thy large will more.   12
  Let no unkind, no fair beseechers kill.
  Think all but one, and me in that one will.

In this second sonnet built around wordplay on the word *will*, the poet continues to plead for a place among the mistress's lovers.

1–3. **If . . . there:** For the relationship between the **soul** and the **will**, and for meanings of **will** in this sonnet, see longer note to s. 135.1, p. 339.   **check:** rebuke   **come so near:** (1) approach you physically; (2) talk so bluntly   **blind soul:** perhaps a reference to the belief that since the Rational Soul discerns the good through the light of Reason, if Reason is disabled, the **soul** is, in effect, **blind**   **And will:** a specific quibble on (1) the faculty of the **will** as part of the Rational Soul, and (2) the poet's name   **admitted:** (1) acknowledged; (2) allowed entrance

4. **for love:** i.e., out of charity

5. **treasure:** i.e., treasure chest

7. **In . . . receipt:** wordplay on **receipt** as a receptacle, as capacity, as size, and as amount (as of a sum received)   **things:** Like **will,** the word *thing* was a slang term for both the penis and the vagina.

8. **Among . . . none:** i.e., **one** is insignificant when part of a large **number** (with wordplay on the proverb "**One** is no **number**"—see note to s. 8.14)

9. **number:** i.e., crowd (of lovers); **untold:** uncounted (i.e., as if I were **none**)

10. **thy store's account:** i.e., inventory of your accumulated possessions (See s. 135.9–12.)

11. **For:** i.e., as; **hold me:** consider me; **so:** i.e., **so** long as

12. **nothing me:** i.e., **nothing** (which is) **me**

13. **thy love:** i.e., that which you most desire

136

If thy soul check thee that I come so near,
Swear to thy blind soul that I was thy will,
And will, thy soul knows, is admitted there.
Thus far for love my love-suit, sweet, fulfill.   4
Will will fulfill the treasure of thy love,
Ay, fill it full with wills, and my will one.
In things of great receipt with ease we prove
Among a number one is reckoned none.   8
Then in the number let me pass untold,
Though in thy store's account I one must be.
For nothing hold me, so it please thee hold
That nothing me, a something, sweet, to thee.   12
    Make but my name thy love, and love that still,
    And then thou lovest me, for my name is Will.

The poet asks why both his eyes and his heart have fastened on a woman neither beautiful nor chaste.

---

1. **blind . . . Love:** "**Love** looks not with the **eyes** but with the mind; / And therefore is winged Cupid painted **blind**" (*A Midsummer Night's Dream* 1.1.240–41.) See picture below.

3. **lies:** resides

5. **corrupt:** i.e., corrupted; **overpartial:** unduly partial, biased

6. **ride:** (1) lie at anchor; (2) copulate

9. **that:** i.e., **that** place; **a several plot:** i.e., a privately owned piece of land

10. **knows:** i.e., **knows** to be; **common place:** i.e., land held in **common,** open to the community

11. **seeing this:** i.e., recognizing **this** truth (with wordplay on **seeing**)

12. **To put:** i.e., in order **to put**

13–14. **In . . . transferred:** These lines answer the questions posed in ll. 1–12. **false plague:** i.e., affliction of falseness **transferred:** handed over

Blind Cupid. (s. 137.1)

294

137

Thou blind fool, Love, what dost thou to mine eyes
That they behold and see not what they see?
They know what beauty is, see where it lies,
Yet what the best is take the worst to be.   4
If eyes, corrupt by overpartial looks,
Be anchored in the bay where all men ride,
Why of eyes' falsehood hast thou forgèd hooks,
Whereto the judgment of my heart is tied?   8
Why should my heart think that a several plot
Which my heart knows the wide world's common place?
Or mine eyes, seeing this, say this is not,
To put fair truth upon so foul a face?   12
    In things right true my heart and eyes have erred,
    And to this false plague are they now transferred.

The poet describes a relationship built on mutual deception that deceives neither party: the mistress claims constancy and the poet claims youth.

---

1. **love:** lover, mistress
3. **That:** i.e., so **that; untutored:** unsophisticated
4. **Unlearnèd:** unskilled
5. **vainly:** fruitlessly; foolishly; conceitedly
7. **Simply:** i.e., like a simpleton; **credit:** trust
8. **suppressed:** hidden; not expressed
9. **wherefore:** why; **unjust:** faithless, dishonest
11. **habit:** (1) clothing, attire; (2) way of behaving
12. **age in love:** i.e., the infatuated elderly; **told:** (1) counted out; (2) spoken about
13. **lie with:** (1) make love with; (2) **lie** to
14. **in our faults:** i.e., through our failings and offenses; **flattered:** gratified; beguiled

138

When my love swears that she is made of truth
I do believe her though I know she lies,
That she might think me some untutored youth,
Unlearnèd in the world's false subtleties. 4
Thus vainly thinking that she thinks me young,
Although she knows my days are past the best,
Simply I credit her false-speaking tongue;
On both sides thus is simple truth suppressed. 8
But wherefore says she not she is unjust?
And wherefore say not I that I am old?
O, love's best habit is in seeming trust,
And age in love loves not to have years told. 12
   Therefore I lie with her and she with me,
   And in our faults by lies we flattered be.

The poet, after refusing to make excuses for the mistress's wrongs, begs her not to flirt with others in his presence. He then excuses that wrong, only to ask her to direct her eyes against him as if they were mortal weapons.

---

1. **call not me:** i.e., do not ask me

4. **power with power:** i.e., your **power** strongly; **art:** cunning, artfulness

5. **elsewhere:** i.e., someone else

6. **glance thine eye:** turn your gaze

7. **What:** i.e., why; **might:** strength, **power** (l. 4)

8. **o'erpressed:** too burdened, overwhelmed; **bide:** withstand

9. **excuse thee:** i.e., **justify the wrong** (l. 1)

10. **looks:** glances

11. **my foes:** i.e., her eyes

13. **near:** almost

14. **Kill . . . looks:** a cliché in love poetry (Spenser's *Amoretti* 10 speaks of "the huge massacres which her eyes do make," and 49 asks "Is it because your eyes have power to kill?"); also, an allusion to mythological creatures (like the basilisk) whose looks could kill (See picture below.) **rid:** remove

A basilisk. (s. 139.14)

139

O, call not me to justify the wrong
That thy unkindness lays upon my heart;
Wound me not with thine eye but with thy tongue;
Use power with power, and slay me not by art.   4
Tell me thou lov'st elsewhere; but in my sight,
Dear heart, forbear to glance thine eye aside.
What need'st thou wound with cunning when thy might
Is more than my o'erpressed defense can bide?   8
Let me excuse thee: ah, my love well knows
Her pretty looks have been mine enemies;
And therefore from my face she turns my foes,
That they elsewhere might dart their injuries.   12
    Yet do not so; but since I am near slain,
    Kill me outright with looks, and rid my pain.

The poet warns the mistress that she would be wiser to pretend to love him and thus avoid driving him into a despair that would no longer hold its tongue.

---

1. **wise as:** i.e., as **wise as**

1–2. **press . . . patience:** i.e., put too much pressure on my patient silence (with an allusion to the method of torture in which the body of a prisoner who refused to speak was crushed under a mass of stone until he or she spoke or died [See picture below.])

4. **manner:** state of the case; **pity-wanting:** i.e., (1) unpitied; (2) pity-desiring

5. **wit:** i.e., the prudent way to proceed

6. **not to love:** i.e., you don't love me; **so:** i.e., that you do (love me)

7. **As:** i.e., just **as**

10. **speak ill of:** i.e., say ugly things about

11. **ill-wresting:** i.e., twisting (words) adversely

13. **so:** slanderous; **belied:** (1) slandered; (2) called false

14. **go wide:** i.e., go astray (a term from archery)

Torture by pressing. (s. 140.1–2)

140

Be wise as thou art cruel; do not press
My tongue-tied patience with too much disdain,
Lest sorrow lend me words, and words express
The manner of my pity-wanting pain.   4
If I might teach thee wit, better it were,
Though not to love, yet, love, to tell me so,
As testy sick men, when their deaths be near,
No news but health from their physicians know.   8
For if I should despair, I should grow mad,
And in my madness might speak ill of thee.
Now this ill-wresting world is grown so bad,
Mad slanderers by mad ears believèd be.   12
    That I may not be so, nor thou belied,
     Bear thine eyes straight, though thy proud heart go wide.

The poet describes his heart as going against his senses and his mind in its determination to love.

1. **In faith:** i.e., truly
2. **errors:** wordplay on (1) flaws; (2) wrongdoings
4. **Who . . . view:** i.e., which in spite of what the eyes see; **is pleased:** chooses; deigns; is happy; **dote:** (1) love excessively; (2) be deranged
5. **Nor:** neither
6. **tender feeling:** In *Love's Labor's Lost* 4.3.331–32, Berowne, describing the senses of the lover, says of the sense of touch: "Love's **feeling** is more soft and sensible / Than are the **tender** horns of cockled snails." **base:** degrading, low
7. **Nor:** i.e., **nor** does
8. **sensual feast:** i.e., **feast** of the senses; **alone:** exclusively
9. **But my:** i.e., **But** neither **my; five wits:** i.e., the imagination, common wit (i.e., common sense), fantasy, estimation, memory (Burton reduces such **wits** to three and describes them, along with the **five** [outward] **senses,** as part of the Sensible Soul, which is seated in the brain [*Anatomy of Melancholy,* 1.1.2.6–7].)
11. **Who . . . unswayed:** i.e., which **leaves** without a ruler or governor
12. **Thy:** i.e., in order thy
13. **my plague:** (1) the sickness of love; (2) the mistress; **count:** consider
14. **awards me pain:** (1) legally determines my punishment; (2) i.e., puts me in hell

141

In faith, I do not love thee with mine eyes,
For they in thee a thousand errors note;
But 'tis my heart that loves what they despise,
Who in despite of view is pleased to dote.   4
Nor are mine ears with thy tongue's tune delighted,
Nor tender feeling to base touches prone,
Nor taste, nor smell, desire to be invited
To any sensual feast with thee alone.   8
But my five wits nor my five senses can
Dissuade one foolish heart from serving thee,
Who leaves unswayed the likeness of a man,
Thy proud heart's slave and vassal wretch to be.   12
   Only my plague thus far I count my gain,
   That she that makes me sin awards me pain.

The poet accuses the woman of scorning his love not out of virtue but because she is busy making adulterous love elsewhere.

---

1. **Love:** i.e., **love** of you; **sin:** See s. 141.14. **virtue:** i.e., (1) chastity; (2) essential nature

2. **sinful loving:** perhaps, (1) my **sinful** love for you; or, perhaps, (2) your **sinful loving** (ll. 5–8)

3. **but:** only, merely

4. **it:** i.e., my **own state**

6. **profaned their scarlet ornaments:** Her **lips** are here treated as if somehow holy in their redness.

7. **sealed . . . love:** i.e., kissed others illicitly

8. **Robbed:** i.e., and **robbed; others' . . . rents:** i.e., the **beds** of other women of the pleasures and offspring that marriage grants them **revenues:** profits (accent on second syllable) **rents:** i.e., sexual dues (literally, fees paid by tenants)

9. **Be . . . I:** i.e., let it **be lawful** for me to; **as:** (1) in the same way that; (2) while

11. **Root pity:** i.e., implant **pity** deeply (**Pity** in the medieval love tradition referred to the lady's granting the lover her favors.)

12. **Thy pity:** i.e., your pitiable condition

13. **to have . . . hide:** i.e., to receive **pity** when you yourself refuse to **pity** (continuing the wordplay on **pity** as sexual favors and as compassion)

14. **By . . . be:** i.e., (I hope that) your own example will cause you to be

142

Love is my sin, and thy dear virtue hate,
Hate of my sin, grounded on sinful loving.
O, but with mine compare thou thine own state,
And thou shalt find it merits not reproving.   4
Or if it do, not from those lips of thine,
That have profaned their scarlet ornaments
And sealed false bonds of love as oft as mine,
Robbed others' beds' revenues of their rents.   8
Be it lawful I love thee as thou lov'st those
Whom thine eyes woo as mine importune thee;
Root pity in thy heart, that, when it grows,
Thy pity may deserve to pitied be.   12
    If thou dost seek to have what thou dost hide,
    By self-example mayst thou be denied.

The poet expands on s. 142.9–10 (where he pursues a mistress who pursues others) by presenting a picture of a woman who chases a barnyard fowl while her infant chases after her.

---

1. **careful:** heedful, attentive; anxious, distressed; **huswife:** housewife (pronounced "hussif")

2. **broke:** i.e., that has broken

3. **swift dispatch:** i.e., haste, speed

4. **pursuit:** accent on first syllable

5. **holds her in chase:** i.e., chases her

6–7. **bent / To follow:** i.e., intent on following

7. **flies:** flees (with wordplay on the fowl's attempts at flight)

11. **thy hope:** i.e., what you hope for

12. **be kind:** wordplay on showing maternal kindness and granting sexual favors

13. **will:** See longer note to s. 135.1, p. 339. (This line has led some commentators to believe that "the young man" was also named William.)

14. **still:** soothe, pacify

143

Lo, as a careful huswife runs to catch
One of her feathered creatures broke away,
Sets down her babe, and makes all swift dispatch
In pursuit of the thing she would have stay,   4
Whilst her neglected child holds her in chase,
Cries to catch her whose busy care is bent
To follow that which flies before her face,
Not prizing her poor infant's discontent;   8
So runn'st thou after that which flies from thee,
Whilst I, thy babe, chase thee afar behind.
But if thou catch thy hope, turn back to me
And play the mother's part: kiss me, be kind.   12
   So will I pray that thou mayst have thy will,
   If thou turn back and my loud crying still.

The poet's three-way relationship with the mistress and the young man is here presented as an allegory of a person tempted by a good and a bad angel.

---

1. **loves:** objects of love; beloveds; **comfort:** support; delight; solace

2. **suggest me still:** i.e., constantly prompt me

3. **better angel:** This phrase suggests that the **spirits** are "good" and "bad" angels such as those in Marlowe's *Doctor Faustus*, where the good **angel** continually urges the hero toward a virtuous life and the bad **angel** encourages choices that lead to hell.

4. **colored ill:** i.e., dark (See notes to s. 127.)

5–8. **To . . . pride:** This version of the temptation has the "bad angel" proceeding only indirectly against the "hero" by tempting his "good angel" to desert him and become evil.   **foul pride:** evil allure

9. **whether:** i.e., **whether** it is the case

10. **directly:** rightly; immediately

11. **being . . . me:** i.e., since **both** are away **from me; to each friend:** i.e., (**both**) friends **to each** other

12. **hell:** Editors propose a reference to a couples' game called "barley break," which includes an area called "**hell,**" but the allegorical/theological language of the poem and the links to such scenes as those in *Doctor Faustus* make it more likely that the term refers to more than a party game.

14. **fire . . . out:** i.e., drive **my good one out** with flames, with probable allusion to (1) infection with venereal disease and (2) the flames of **hell**

144

Two loves I have, of comfort and despair,
Which like two spirits do suggest me still.
The better angel is a man right fair,
The worser spirit a woman colored ill.   4
To win me soon to hell my female evil
Tempteth my better angel from my ⌐side,⌐
And would corrupt my saint to be a devil,
Wooing his purity with her foul pride.   8
And whether that my angel be turned fiend
Suspect I may, yet not directly tell;
But being both from me, both to each friend,
I guess one angel in another's hell.   12
    Yet this shall I ne'er know, but live in doubt,
    Till my bad angel fire my good one out.

In this sonnet, perhaps written when Shakespeare was very young, the poet plays with the difference between the words "I hate" and "I hate not you." (Note that the lines of the sonnet are in tetrameter instead of pentameter.)

---

1. **Love's:** The reference could be to Venus, goddess of love, or to Cupid, her son.

3. **her:** i.e., the woman whose **lips** said **"I hate"**

5. **Straight in:** wordplay on "directly into" and "immediately into"

7. **used in:** (1) employed in; (2) accustomed to; **doom:** sentence, judgment

11. **who:** i.e., which

13. **from hate:** i.e., from hatred (i.e., she separated the words **"I hate"** from any intention of hating) See longer note on **hate away,** p. 340.

14. **saying:** i.e., adding the words

Cupid torturing a lover.

145

Those lips that Love's own hand did make
Breathed forth the sound that said "I hate"
To me that languished for her sake;
But when she saw my woeful state,   4
Straight in her heart did mercy come,
Chiding that tongue that ever sweet
Was used in giving gentle doom,
And taught it thus anew to greet: 8
"I hate" she altered with an end
That followed it as gentle day
Doth follow night, who, like a fiend,
From heaven to hell is flown away.   12
    "I hate" from hate away she threw,
    And saved my life, saying "not you."

The poet here meditates on the soul and its relation to the body, in life and in death.

---

1. **Poor:** wordplay on (1) unfortunate; (2) ill-fed; (3) poverty-stricken; **earth:** i.e., body (See Genesis 2.7: "And the Lord God formed man of the dust of the ground, and breathed into his nostrils the breath of life; and man became a living **soul.**")

2. **Pressed with:** i.e., assailed by, beset by (See longer note, p. 341, and also note to s. 140.1–2.) **rebel powers:** i.e., the body and the passions, which refuse to be governed by the **soul; array:** (1) afflict, trouble; (2) clothe; (3) defile

4. **outward walls:** i.e., body; **costly:** sumptuously; **gay:** outwardly attractive, showy

5. **so . . . cost:** i.e., such a **large** outlay; **having:** i.e., since you have

6. **thy fading mansion:** The word **mansion** was often used for the body as the enclosure for the **soul.**

7. **excess:** wordplay on (1) extravagance; (2) intemperance in eating and drinking

8. **Eat up thy charge:** wordplay on literal and figurative meanings of **eat up** (i.e., consume) and on **thy charge** as (1) your outlay; (2) that which has been entrusted to you; (3) that which burdens you; **end:** fate; purpose; termination

9. **live thou upon:** (1) subsist on; (2) gain eternal life through; **servant's:** i.e., body's

10. **that:** i.e., the servant; **aggravate:** increase

11. **terms divine:** i.e., eternity (literally, **divine** portions of time)

146

Poor soul, the center of my sinful earth,
⌜Pressed with⌝ these rebel powers that thee array,
Why dost thou pine within and suffer dearth,
Painting thy outward walls so costly gay?   4
Why so large cost, having so short a lease,
Dost thou upon thy fading mansion spend?
Shall worms, inheritors of this excess,
Eat up thy charge? Is this thy body's end?   8
Then, soul, live thou upon thy servant's loss,
And let that pine to aggravate thy store.
Buy terms divine in selling hours of dross;
Within be fed, without be rich no more.   12
   So shalt thou feed on Death, that feeds on men,
   And Death once dead, there's no more dying then.

The poet describes his love for the lady as a desperate sickness.

1. **still:** constantly, incessantly
2. **longer nurseth:** i.e., prolongs
3. **ill:** sickness, **disease;** disaster, calamity
4. **uncertain:** unreliable; **sickly appetite:** wordplay on (1) wish for food by someone in ill-health; (2) unhealthy (sexual) will or **desire** (l. 8) (For "will" and "**reason**" [l. 5], see longer note to s. 135.1, p. 339.)
6. **prescriptions:** instructions; restrictions
7. **desperate:** (1) in despair; (2) given up as hopeless; **approve:** (1) demonstrate (that); (2) find through experience (that)
8. **physic:** i.e., (reason's) medicine; **except:** protest against, object to (The phrase **which physic did except** describes reason's opposition to **desire,** with possible wordplay that allows **which** to refer to **death,** so that the phrase would also describe medicine's operation against **death.**)
9. **past care:** i.e., (1) **past** caring (about my condition); (2) no longer taking **care** of me
10. **evermore:** i.e., constant
11. **discourse:** speech
12. **At random:** i.e., (varying) haphazardly; **vainly:** i.e., (and) senselessly, thoughtlessly
13–14. **fair, black, dark:** See notes to s. 127 and s. 131.13–14. **bright:** beautiful, splendid (a word often associated with Lucifer, brightest of the angels, who, when cast from heaven, became Satan)

147

My love is as a fever, longing still
For that which longer nurseth the disease,
Feeding on that which doth preserve the ill,
Th' uncertain sickly appetite to please.   4
My reason, the physician to my love,
Angry that his prescriptions are not kept,
Hath left me, and I desperate now approve
Desire is death, which physic did except.   8
Past cure I am, now reason is past care,
And, frantic-mad with evermore unrest,
My thoughts and my discourse as madmen's are,
At random from the truth vainly expressed.   12
    For I have sworn thee fair, and thought thee bright,
    Who art as black as hell, as dark as night.

The poet once again (as in ss. 113, 114, 137, and 141) questions his own eyesight. Here, he describes his eyes' image of his mistress as in conflict with his judgment and with the views of the world in general.

---

1. **eyes:** i.e., kind of **eyes; love:** Here, as throughout the sonnet, there is wordplay on **love** as (1) desire, affection; (2) Cupid or Venus; and, in l. 13, (3) the mistress.

4. **censures:** estimates, judges

5. **false:** deceitful, treacherous; **dote:** bestow excessive love

7. **denote:** indicate (that)

8. **eye:** with a pun on "ay" (Q's punctuation ["all mens: no,"] gives a reading of the line in which "no" means "no, it is not" and in which the pun almost disappears. Some editors retain Q's colon.)

10. **vexed with watching:** distressed by wakefulness

11. **though:** if; **mistake my view:** (1) i.e., see wrongly; (2) misinterpret what I see

12. **heaven clears:** i.e., the sky is free of clouds

148

O me, what eyes hath love put in my head,
Which have no correspondence with true sight!
Or if they have, where is my judgment fled,
That censures falsely what they see aright?   4
If that be fair whereon my false eyes dote,
What means the world to say it is not so?
If it be not, then love doth well denote
Love's eye is not so true as all men's "no."   8
How can it? O, how can love's eye be true,
That is so vexed with watching and with tears?
No marvel then though I mistake my view;
The sun itself sees not till heaven clears.   12
   O cunning love, with tears thou keep'st me blind,
   Lest eyes well-seeing thy foul faults should find.

The poet argues that he has proved his love for the lady by turning against himself when she turns against him.

2. **with thee partake:** i.e., take your side

3. **on:** i.e., about

3–4. **forgot . . . of:** i.e., have forgotten

7. **thou lour'st on:** i.e., you scowl at; **spend:** i.e., mete out, take (literally, expend, employ)

8. **present moan:** immediate suffering

10. **so proud . . . despise:** i.e., **so** arrogant or presumptuous as to **despise** being in your **service** (i.e., being the "servant" of Love or of the lady)

11. **defect:** insufficiency, imperfection

12. **Commanded:** controlled, dominated; **motion:** prompting, bidding

14. **blind:** i.e., blinded to the lady's faults (and, Evans suggests, hence of less interest to the lady than **those** who **can see,** and are thus more of a challenge)

149

Canst thou, O cruel, say I love thee not
When I against myself with thee partake?
Do I not think on thee when I forgot
Am of myself, all, tyrant, for thy sake? 4
Who hateth thee that I do call my friend?
On whom frown'st thou that I do fawn upon?
Nay, if thou lour'st on me, do I not spend
Revenge upon myself with present moan? 8
What merit do I in myself respect
That is so proud thy service to despise,
When all my best doth worship thy defect,
Commanded by the motion of thine eyes? 12
    But, love, hate on, for now I know thy mind;
    Those that can see thou lov'st, and I am blind.

The sonnet begins with the poet's questioning why he should love what he knows he should hate; it ends with his claim that this love of her unworthiness should cause the lady to love him.

---

2. **With insufficiency:** See s. 149.11.

3. **give . . . sight:** i.e., accuse **my true sight** of lying

4. **grace:** add splendor to, adorn

5. **becoming . . . things:** i.e., power of beautifying evil **things**

6. **refuse . . . deeds:** i.e., worst actions   **refuse:** scum, dregs, rubbish

7. **warrantise:** guarantee, assurance

12. **With . . . abhor:** i.e., you should not join **others** in loathing (Booth suggests, in **abhor,** wordplay on *whore* in both ll. 11 and 12.) **state:** condition (mental and emotional)

14. **worthy:** wordplay on (1) deserving of esteem (since I am magnanimous enough to love an unworthy person); (2) merited, fitting (since my love for an unworthy person shows my unworthiness)

150

O, from what power hast thou this powerful might
With insufficiency my heart to sway?
To make me give the lie to my true sight,
And swear that brightness doth not grace the day?   4
Whence hast thou this becoming of things ill,
That in the very refuse of thy deeds
There is such strength and warrantise of skill
That in my mind thy worst all best exceeds?   8
Who taught thee how to make me love thee more,
The more I hear and see just cause of hate?
O, though I love what others do abhor,
With others thou shouldst not abhor my state.   12
    If thy unworthiness raised love in me,
    More worthy I to be beloved of thee.

The poet displays the sexually obsessive nature of his love.

1–2. **Love . . . love:** wordplay on **love** as (1) the boy-god Cupid; (2) sexual passion; and on **conscience** as (1) the knowledge of right and wrong; (2) inward consciousness (Also at play are the Latin tag "Penis erectus non habet conscientiam" [i.e., "an erection has no **conscience**"] and the platitude that love ennobles the lover.)

3. **cheater:** (1) deceiver; (2) escheator, or assessor, demanding forfeits from those who have defaulted from their obligations (Evans); **urge . . . amiss:** (1) i.e., do not charge me with misdeeds; (2) do not provoke me to commit misdeeds

5. **betraying me:** (1) revealing my faults; (2) seducing me

6. **nobler part:** i.e., mind or **soul** (l. 7); **gross:** sensual (though also "unrefined, coarse")

7. **he:** i.e., it

8. **stays:** i.e., awaits, waits for

9. **rising at thy name:** As Booth notes, the overt reference is to sexual erection, but the metaphor is that of conjuring spirits— i.e., compelling the spirit to rise through the repetition of names.

10. **his:** i.e., its; **Proud, pride:** Both **proud** and **pride** were used in relation to tumescence and lust.

11. **He:** i.e., it

12. **To . . . side:** The overt reference is sexual, but, as Booth notes, the metaphor is of the knight or soldier who stands beside his king or comrade and is ready to fight to the death (i.e., **fall by the side**) of the one he is protecting.

13. **want:** lack

151

Love is too young to know what conscience is;
Yet who knows not conscience is born of love?
Then, gentle cheater, urge not my amiss,
Lest guilty of my faults thy sweet self prove.   4
For, thou betraying me, I do betray
My nobler part to my gross body's treason.
My soul doth tell my body that he may
Triumph in love; flesh stays no farther reason,   8
But, rising at thy name, doth point out thee
As his triumphant prize. Proud of this pride,
He is contented thy poor drudge to be,
To stand in thy affairs, fall by thy side.   12
   No want of conscience hold it that I call
   Her "love," for whose dear love I rise and fall.

The poet turns his accusations against the woman's inconstancy and oath-breaking against himself, accusing himself of deliberate blindness and perjury.

---

1. **I am forsworn:** I have broken an oath

3. **In act:** through action (specifically, sexual activity, as often in Shakespeare); **thy bed-vow broke:** i.e., having broken your marriage vow; **new faith torn:** i.e., having breached a **new** pledge or promise

4. **bearing:** entertaining, cherishing

6. **perjured:** forsworn, guilty of oath-breaking

7. **misuse:** This word could mean, among other things, "revile," "deceive," and "misrepresent." Lines 9–14 suggest that "misrepresent" is the primary meaning here.

8. **honest faith:** i.e., integrity; **in thee:** i.e., in (loving) you; because of you

9. **oaths of:** i.e., **oaths** asserting, affirming (as also in l. 10)

11. **enlighten thee:** i.e., to make you luminous (with wordplay on *light* as "fair" [and therefore as "beautiful"]); **eyes:** i.e., my **eyes**

12. **against the thing:** i.e., contrary to that which

13. **For . . . fair:** This repeats from s. 147.13, which goes on to attack the lady; here, the poet instead attacks himself. **eye:** probable wordplay on *I* and *ay*

152

In loving thee thou know'st I am forsworn,
But thou art twice forsworn, to me love swearing;
In act thy bed-vow broke, and new faith torn
In vowing new hate after new love bearing.   4
But why of two oaths' breach do I accuse thee
When I break twenty? I am perjured most,
For all my vows are oaths but to misuse thee,
And all my honest faith in thee is lost.   8
For I have sworn deep oaths of thy deep kindness,
Oaths of thy love, thy truth, thy constancy;
And to enlighten thee gave eyes to blindness,
Or made them swear against the thing they see.   12
    For I have sworn thee fair; more perjured eye,
    To swear against the truth so foul a lie.

This sonnet uses an ancient parable to demonstrate that love's fire is unquenchable. It goes on to argue that only the mistress's eyes can cure the poet.

1–7. Cupid . . . bath: These lines retell a story (one that dates back to an ancient Greek poem) in which Diana's nymphs try to quench Cupid's torch in water but instead set the water on fire, turning the pool into a hot bath. The story is told again in s. 154.1–12.

   1. **laid by his brand:** i.e., put down his torch

   2. **maid of Dian's:** i.e., one of the virgin nymphs who serve Diana, the goddess of chastity (See picture, p. 410.) **advantage:** opportunity

   4. **of that ground:** i.e., nearby

   5. **Which:** i.e., the fountain; **Love:** i.e., Cupid

   6. **dateless:** eternal; **still:** always

   7. **grew:** i.e., became; **seething bath:** wordplay on (1) boiling spring or tub of water; (2) spring or tub of water suitable for soaking

   7–8. **yet . . . cure:** i.e., **men** continue to show to be a potent remedy **against** extreme or unusual diseases (The **bath** may have a double reference to [1] hot mineral springs used for medicinal purposes and [2] sweating tubs used to treat venereal disease.)

   9. **new fired:** i.e., ignited once again (For the **eye** as a source of rays, see note to s. 113.4.)

   10. **for trial:** i.e., to test it; **needs would:** i.e., must

   11. **withal:** i.e., with the touch of the **brand**

   12. **hied:** hurried; **distempered:** disturbed; diseased

153

Cupid laid by his brand and fell asleep.
A maid of Dian's this advantage found,
And his love-kindling fire did quickly steep
In a cold valley-fountain of that ground,   4
Which borrowed from this holy fire of Love
A dateless lively heat, still to endure,
And grew a seething bath which yet men prove
Against strange maladies a sovereign cure.   8
But at my mistress' eye Love's brand new fired,
The boy for trial needs would touch my breast;
I, sick withal, the help of bath desired
And thither hied, a sad distempered guest,   12
    But found no cure. The bath for my help lies
    Where Cupid got new fire—my mistress' ⌜eyes.⌝

This sonnet, like s. 153, retells the parable of Cupid's torch turning a fountain into a hot bath, this time to argue that the poet's disease of love is incurable.

1–12. **The . . . diseased:** See note to s. 153.1–7.

2. **brand:** torch (See picture below.)

5. **fairest votary:** i.e., most beautiful of the **nymphs** who had **vowed chaste life to keep** (l. 3)

7. **general:** (military) commander

9. **by:** nearby

11. **Growing:** i.e., becoming; **bath:** spring or tub of water (here, for medicinal purposes, as in note to s. 153.7–8)

Cupid with his torch. (ss. 153, 154)

154

The little love-god, lying once asleep,
Laid by his side his heart-inflaming brand,
Whilst many nymphs that vowed chaste life to keep
Came tripping by; but in her maiden hand   4
The fairest votary took up that fire,
Which many legions of true hearts had warmed;
And so the general of hot desire
Was, sleeping, by a virgin hand disarmed.   8
This brand she quenchèd in a cool well by,
Which from Love's fire took heat perpetual,
Growing a bath and healthful remedy
For men diseased; but I, my mistress' thrall,   12
    Came there for cure, and this by that I prove:
    Love's fire heats water; water cools not love.

Two Sonnets from
The Passionate Pilgrim

The Passionate Pilgrime.
By W. Shakespeare.
London: for W. Iaggard, 1599.

These are the first versions of these two sonnets to be printed.
See "An Introduction to This Text," page 15.

[138]

When my love swears that she is made of truth,
I do believe her, though I know she lies,
That she might think me some untutored youth,
Unskillful in the world's false forgeries.
Thus vainly thinking that she thinks me young,
Although I know my years be past the best,
I, smiling, credit her false-speaking tongue,
Outfacing faults in love with love's ill rest.
But wherefore says my love that she is young?
And wherefore say not I that I am old?
O, love's best habit is a soothing tongue,
And age in love loves not to have years told.
    Therefore I'll lie with love, and love with me,
    Since that our faults in love thus smothered be.
[sig. A 3]

[144]

Two loves I have, of comfort and despair,
That like two spirits do suggest me still.
My better angel is a man right fair,
My worser spirit a woman colored ill.
To win me soon to hell my female evil
Tempteth my better angel from my side,
And would corrupt my saint to be a devil,
Wooing his purity with her fair pride.
And whether that my angel be turned fiend
Suspect I may, yet not directly tell;
For being both to me, both to each friend,
I guess one angel in another's hell.
    The truth I shall not know, but live in doubt,
    Till my bad angel fire my good one out.
                              [sig. A 4]

Shakespeare's Sonnets
Longer Notes

Sonnet 1.6 **Feed'st thy light's flame with self-substantial fuel:**
While the image in this line is of a candle or other flame that lives by burning its own substance, it may also allude to the mythological story of Narcissus, the beautiful youth who destroys himself by falling in love with his own image. Ovid says of Narcissus, "He is the flame that sets on fire, and thing that burneth too" (*Metamorphoses* 3.356; trans. Arthur Golding, 1567).

Sonnet 13.1 **your self:** In the 1609 Quarto the words "your selfe" appear in ll. 1, 2, and 7 of s. 13; in l. 7, "your selfes" also appears. It was as rare for these words to be joined together as a single word in Shakespeare's day as it is for them to be separated today. Ordinarily, then, in this edition we print "yourself" and "yourself's." However, in ll. 1 and 7 of this sonnet, we follow some previous editors in retaining the Quarto's separation of "your" and "self" in order to call attention to the unusual use of the word *self* in these two instances. There is much wordplay in ll. 1 and 7; both lines are parts of apparent contradictions. The sonnet's opening lines, "O, that you were your self! But, love, you are / No longer yours than you yourself here live" (1–2), appear to tell the young man "you yourself are not your self." Similarly, ll. 6–7, "then you were / Your self again after yourself's decease," suggest to the young man "you can continue to be your self after you yourself are dead." These passages can be understood as paradoxes rather than contradictions only if we can find special meanings of the word *self* that allow a difference between "your self" and "yourself."

The sonnet suggests that the special sense of *self* must be associated with the young man's "sweet semblance" (4) and his "sweet form" (8), which he can pass on to his offspring in such a way that a *self* continues to endure even after he himself has died. Usually editors give the term *soul* for this special sense of *self*. There is evidence for the aptness of thinking of *self* as *soul* in a passage from *The Anatomy of Melancholy* (1621), a work by Shakespeare's near-con-

332

temporary Robert Burton. Discussing "the Rationall Soule," Burton presents an understanding of it that he identifies as deriving ultimately from the classical world and revived by recent writers. According to this view, sexual reproduction is reproduction of both body and soul, the body regarded as matter and the soul as form: "one man begets another, body and soule: or as a candle from a candle, to be produced from the seed: otherwise, they say, a man begets but halfe a man, and is worse then a beast that begets both matter and forme" (1.1.2.9). Another text that may bear on the sonnet's possible use of *self* in the special sense of *soul* or *form* is Aristotle's *Metaphysics*. There Aristotle provides the causes of "a man," including the "formal cause," usually explained by scholars as the "design" but called "the essence" by Aristotle, "essence" being another meaning of *soul:* "So whenever we inquire what the cause is, since there are causes in several senses, we must state all the possible causes. E.g., what is the material cause of a man? The menses. What is the moving cause? The semen. What is the formal cause? The essence. What is the final cause? The end" (1044a33–37).

But there are also difficulties with associating *self* in this sonnet with *soul* and *soul* with *form*. Burton, in the same subsection cited above, notes the contrary opinion of the great fathers of the church Jerome and Augustine that the soul is not conceived with the body: "The *Soule* is created of nothing, and so infused in the Childe or *Embrio* in his Mothers wombe, six moneths after the conception." Another difficulty in equating *self* with *soul* arises from the sonnet's strong implication that the *self* is mortal. If the self is to be thought of as the *soul*, then the sonnet implies that the *soul*, too, is mortal. While Burton records that there was in his time ongoing debate about the soul's immortality, he makes clear that any suggestion that the soul is not immortal is for him atheistic. In light of his repugnance toward this view, an attitude that may have been general at that time, it is hard to be sure that the sonnet should be read in terms of an equation of *self* and *soul*.

Sonnet 15.4. **Whereon . . . comment:** *Comment on* usually means "To make comments or remarks (*on, upon*). (Often implying unfavorable remarks)" (*Oxford English Dictionary*). In this instance, because the **influence** of the **stars** is in question, *comment on* may also have the unusual meaning of "control" or "make critical decisions about." Through the combination of these meanings, the stars may be represented as an audience observing and criticizing the human performance while secretly affecting the show's action through astrological influence. *Influence* is defined as "The supposed flowing or streaming from the stars or heavens of an etherial fluid acting upon the character and destiny of humans, and affecting sublunary things generally."

Sonnet 18.11. **shade:** The clearest reference in this line ("Nor shall Death brag thou wand'rest in his shade") is to walking through "the valley of the shadow of death" in Psalm 23. (The phrase **"shade** of death" was used interchangeably with "shadow of death.") In addition to this biblical allusion, however, the line also contains classical allusions, since "the shades," in classical mythology, is another name for Hades, the world of ghosts and disembodied spirits, and is also a way of referring to the darkness of that world; further, a **shade,** in classical mythology, is the ghost of a dead person, a disembodied spirit, or indeed any inhabitant of Hades.

Sonnet 35.8 **Excusing . . . are:** Among the meanings for this line suggested by editors are the following: (1) "Excusing your sins to a greater extent than is warranted by the size of your sins"; (2) "(By) giving excessive exculpation for his friend's misconduct by reducing it, through his analogies (ll. 1–4), from a moral to a natural fault, his excuse for his friend's offense would be stretched so much wider than the offense itself that it would, if valid (which the poet knows it is not), exculpate all sins whatever"; (3) "(By) pleading excuses not only sufficient to cover your actual sins, but to cover them even if they were more (= greater)." The first is Booth's, the second Ingram and Redpath's; the third is quoted by Evans from an earlier editor.

Sonnet 36.5. **one respect:** This phrase is almost impossible to gloss; although **respect** has meanings that are vaguely appropriate, none is exactly right, and the meanings of the word that best fit the context are found only when the word appears as part of such phrases as "in respect to," "in respect of," "with respect to" or "to have respect to." (Booth, acknowledging the impossibility of adequately glossing this line, summarizes ll. 5–6 loosely as "In respect to our loves we are one, but in respect to our lives we are separate.") The word **respect** could mean "rank, standing, station in life," "consideration," "end, aim," "regard," "relationship," "reference," and "aspect"; any of these senses are worth considering in understanding ll. 5 and 6 of this sonnet.

Sonnet 43.4. **darkly bright:** This sonnet is filled with intricate wordplay, often involving paradox and oxymoron. As Booth notes, "The recurring themes of this sonnet—things that are the opposite of what they would normally be expected to be, and the distinction between images or shadows of objects and the objects themselves—are played out stylistically in an intense display of antithesis and a range of rhetorical devices of repetition that make the language of the poem suggest mirror images."

Sonnet 46.3. **Mine eye my heart thy picture's sight would bar:** With the word **bar,** this sonnet begins introducing words with specific legal meanings as the sonnet brings the debate between the heart and the eyes into a court setting. The eyes would **bar** (i.e., arrest or stop [the heart] by ground of legal objection from enforcing its claim); the heart, in turn, **doth plead** (i.e., prosecutes its suit or action), presenting a **plea** (an argument or reason urged by a litigant in support of his case) that is in turn denied by the **defendant** (the eyes). A **quest** (a body of persons appointed to hold an inquiry, a jury) is **impaneled** (enrolled as jurors) to decide the **title** (i.e., who holds legal right to the possession of the property), and **their verdict** determines the **eyes' due** (i.e., that to which the eyes have a legal right) and the **heart's right** (i.e., its legal claim to the possession of property). This **verdict** leads, in s. 47, to a peaceful alliance between the eyes and the heart.

Sonnet 66.3: **needy nothing trimmed in jollity:** The literal meaning of these words would suggest that the poet is alluding to the poverty-stricken who use the money they beg to buy cheap finery. Most editors argue that Shakespeare is instead using "needy nothing" to mean (unusually) "worthless persons in need of nothing."

There is no sure way to determine which meaning applies here. For an extensive argument for the more widely accepted editorial reading (i.e., "wealthy fops"), see Booth; for an answer to this argument, see Kerrigan.

Sonnet 86.5–11. **Was . . . boast:** These lines continue to intrigue scholars because they seem to suggest—through such words as "by spirits taught to write," "his compeers by night / Giving him aid," and "that affable familiar ghost / Which nightly gulls him with intelligence"—that the rival poet has dealings with supernatural spirits. Scholars and editors have pointed out that the lines can be read more innocently as alluding to books ("the spirits of dead writers as they appear in their writings") or to friends ("the lively spirits of companions"), but the hint of the occult continues to fascinate. Further, when taken together with certain hints in the poem's opening lines, ll. 5–11 also seem to give clues as to the identity of the rival poet. The lofty style, the appearance of learning, and the connection to night and to the helping presence of a ghostly forebear seem to many scholars to point most clearly to George Chapman, the first seven books of whose translation of *The Iliad* were published in 1598. For helpful discussions, see especially those in Ingram and Redpath, and in Evans.

Sonnet 96.13–14. **But . . . report:** When this couplet is used at the end of s. 36, the **do not so** urges the beloved to retain his honor, since he and the poet are one in their love and thus the beloved's good reputation (**report**) also honors the poet. In s. 96, the **do not so** instead urges the beloved not to lead others astray, since, the poet's love being so deep, any **report** (rumor or reputation) of the beloved will reflect on the poet. The repetition of the couplet may be authorial or may be a printing-house construction or error.

Sonnet 97.5–6. **summer's time, / The teeming autumn:** It is possible to see the relationship between **summer's time** and **autumn** in this poem in a variety of ways, any one of which is acceptable. Ingram and Redpath suggest that we are to imagine the poem written in autumn as the poet looks back on summer. Booth suggests instead that the transition from summer to autumn in the poem is "fluid, like changes of season themselves." Evans sees the poet writing in summer and looking ahead to the "fecund *promise* of autumn." And Duncan-Jones explains the time of absence as the "whole period presided over by summer, which extends from spring to harvest."

Sonnet 99. There are many ways of accounting for this unusual fifteen-line sonnet. Some editors point to other sonnet sequences that include sonnets of that length, though they admit that such sonnets usually add the fifteenth line just before the concluding couplet. Other editors argue persuasively that the poem as it appears in the 1609 Quarto was in a draft state. They point to other signs of unfinished work, but note that while either l. 1 or l. 5 could be deleted and leave a quatrain that is complete in its rhyme scheme, both ll. 1 and 5 are necessary for the sense of the poem.

The poem is also unusual in that it comes close to duplicating a poem by Henry Constable published in 1592. (See Appendix, p. 625.) Editors assume that Shakespeare reworked the Constable poem. We know, however, that Shakespeare's sonnets were passed around in manuscript long before their printing in 1609 and that Shakespeare was working on his narrative poetry in the very early 1590s. It therefore seems difficult to determine which way the borrowing and reworking went.

Professor Steven May, editor of the *Bibliography and First-Line Index of English Verse, 1559–1603*, suggests (in private communication) that the very similar Shakespeare and Constable poems might have been written in response to "a poetic competition or challenge such as the one that produced Sir Thomas Heneage's response to Ralegh's 'Farewell false love' or Spenser's *Amoretti* 8," variants of which appear in poems by Dyer and Sidney. However the Shakespeare and Constable poems came to be, it is interesting to note their differences, Constable's being more in keeping with the traditional sonnet conventions.

Sonnet 119.1. **siren:** In classical mythology, the Sirens used their alluring songs to entice sailors to their death on the rocks near their island. In the most famous mythological encounter with the Sirens, Odysseus has himself tied to the mast of his ship (after stopping up the ears of his sailors with wax) so that he can safely hear the Sirens' songs as his ship passes their island (Homer's *Odyssey* 12). Although, as Booth notes, the adjective *siren* did not have to refer to women, Shakespeare's other uses of the word are clearly in reference to females. Further, scholars have also linked the sonnet's **"limbecks foul as hell within"** (l. 2) to female anatomy (with Evans, for example, noting that *alembic* "has a long history as a slang term for the female pudendum") and to the kind of sexual nausea expressed in *King Lear* 4.6.142–46, where the female sexual parts are described as, in effect, "limbecks foul as hell": "beneath is all the fiend's. There's hell, there's darkness, there is the sulphurous pit; burning, scalding, stench, consumption!"

Sonnet 126. The 1609 Quarto prints, after l. 12, two sets of empty parentheses, as if to replace the missing ll. 13 and 14. It is possible that Shakespeare placed empty parentheses in his manuscript at the conclusion of the twelve-line poem; but editors generally agree that they were supplied by the Quarto's publisher or its printer, who, most editors argue, would have expected a full fourteen-line sonnet, and signaled with the parentheses that the lines had not been provided. (It has also been suggested that the publisher or the printer removed the final two lines because they contained information that pointed too directly to the identity of the "lovely boy.") Some editors today reproduce the two sets of empty parentheses.

Sonnet 134.2. **And I myself am mortgaged to thy will:** The word **mortgaged** begins a series of technical terms—**forfeit, surety-like, bond, statute, usurer, sue, debtor**—from property law, contracts, and finance. Vendler's explication of the relationship among these terms is helpful: "The speaker's new metaphor for himself is that he is a mortgaged debtor for whom the young man has stood surety, [the young man then] becoming himself forfeit. No matter how much the speaker wants to reverse the situation and forfeit himself instead, he is powerless. . . . Because the mistress now has two sources of repayment instead of one, she exacts the sexual debt from the young man, who pays." (The technical meaning of **surety** is "one who makes himself liable for the default or miscarriage of another, or for the performance of some act on his part [e.g., payment of a debt. . . " (*OED* 7)]. The person who stands as **surety** is **lost** as **forfeit** when, e.g., the contract is breached. Because the poet could not pay, the young man is lost.) Most editors read into ll. 7–8 and 11 a story in which the young man has wooed or interceded with the mistress on behalf of the poet and has then himself been captivated by her. Vendler's explication instead sees the sonnet as the poet's desperate attempt to construct a narrative that will put all the blame on the mistress. We recall that in s. 42 the poet attempted to excuse both the young man and the mistress, arguing first that they love each other only because of him, and then that since he and the young man are one, in loving the young man the woman actually loves the poet. In s. 134, instead of admitting that his strategies are merely "sweet flattery" (s. 42.14), the poet remains caught in what Vendler calls "this text of tangled anguish."

Sonnet 135.1. **will:** This line introduces the complicated wordplay on the word **will** that constitutes s. 135 and s. 136 (and that reappears in the couplet of s. 143). The wordplay finds its roots in the complexity of the word and the concept itself, which ranges from the biblical (which sets God's **will** above man's) through the psychological (which makes man's **will** a preeminent faculty of the soul) to the bawdily physical (which uses the word **will** as a slang term for both the penis and vagina)—with an additional complication available when the poet's name is William and he is called **Will.** Since the determination of the meanings in play in any particular line of these sonnets is presented by the sonnet as a kind of puzzle to be solved and enjoyed, we will leave such determinations to the reader, giving the following background rather than attaching specific meanings in the notes to the poems.

In the psychology of Shakespeare's day (known as "faculty psychology"), **Will** and Understanding (or Reason), the two faculties of the Rational Soul, are "the two principal fountains of human action" (Richard Hooker, *Laws of Ecclesiastical Polity* [1594–97], 1.7.2). Understanding finds the good, and **Will** chooses that good (or would do so had not man fallen as a consequence of original sin). In theology and in faculty psychology, **will** is supposed to govern man's appetites. According to Hooker, "of one thing we must have special care, as being a matter of no small moment, and that is, how the **will** . . . differeth greatly from that inferior natural desire we call appetite. . . . [A]ppetite is the will's solicitor, and the will is the appetite's controller" (1.7.3). Or, as Iago puts it: "Our bodies are our gardens, to the which our **wills** are gardeners. So that if we will plant nettles or sow lettuce, . . . the power and corrigible authority of this lies in our **wills**" (*Othello* 1.3.362–68).

Because **Will** (along with Reason) was corrupted at the Fall, the **will** is "prone to evil, . . . [is] egged on by our natural concupiscence," and "lust . . . we cannot resist" (Robert Burton, *Anatomy of Melancholy* [1621], 1.1.2.11). "The seat of our affections captivates and enforces our **will**. . . . Lust counsels one thing, reason another," and the "depraved **will**" often yields to passion (1.1.2.11). Again to quote Iago, the "lust of the blood" is often granted "the permission of the **will**" (1.3.377–78).

Sonnets 135 and 136 demonstrate the bawdy register of meanings attached to the word **will,** which in these poems means, variously, carnal desire, lust, intention, the penis, the vagina, the poet's name, perhaps the names of others named William (perhaps the young man, perhaps the woman's husband), and, at one point (s. 136.3), that faculty of the soul that governs volition. Vendler points out interestingly, and persuasively, that s. 136.5–10, taken as a freestanding poem, could be a religious poem addressed to God; in context, such a reading would, of course, be supremely blasphemous.

At several places in ss. 135, 136, and 143, the 1609 Quarto prints **will** in italic and with an uppercase *W.* We have printed all these appearances of *"Will"* (except for the final one in s. 136, where it is specifically the poet's name) in lowercase and in roman type. (*"Will"* is found at s. 135.1, 2 [twice], 11 [twice], 12 [the second instance], and 14 and s. 136.2, 5 [the first instance], and 14.) We agree with Booth that "a modern reader's susceptibility to orthographical signals is so acute that Q's capitals and italics" can make it impossible for the full range of the wordplay to be effective.

Sonnet 145.13. **hate away:** In *Essays in Criticism* 21 (1971): 221–26, Andrew Gurr argued that **hate away** is a pun on the name "Hathaway," supposed to be the name of Shakespeare's wife. This argument has appealed to editors and readers who approach the *Sonnets* with a view to coming closer to the poet Shakespeare. However, in the surviving documents concerning Shakespeare's marriage, the wife's name is given once as "Hathwey" and once as "Whateley"; perhaps, then, Shakespeare's wife's name was "Whateley" and not "Hathaway"; or, perhaps, Elizabethan spelling being so variable, what appear to us to be two different names are just different spellings of a no-longer-determinable name. In light of the indeterminacy surrounding the wife's name, certainty about a pun on it is elusive.

Sonnet 146.2. **Pressed with these rebel powers that thee array:** In the 1609 Quarto, the second line of s. 146 opens with a repetition of the final three words of l. 1. In other words, l. 2 in Q (modernized) reads "My sinful earth these rebel powers that thee array." Some editors retain this line despite the repetition and despite its being an unwieldy twelve syllables long. Most editors, though, either replace "My sinful earth" with an ellipsis to show something missing or substitute some two-syllable word or phrase chosen from among a host that have been proposed over the centuries. Among the more familiar of these are "Fooled by," "Foiled by," "Thrall to," and "Feeding." We were persuaded by Stephen Booth's conjecture: "If I had to offer my own no less arbitrary preference, I would choose 'pressed with,' which participates in the phonetic pattern set in motion by the consonants *Poor soul* and which pertains variously to the ideas of weight, siege, and penalties that run through the whole sonnet."

SHAKESPEARE'S
POEMS

Reading Shakespeare's Language: *Venus and Adonis* and *Lucrece*

Venus and Adonis and *Lucrece* share many features of the language of the *Sonnets*, particularly at the level of the word, the sentence, and the figure of speech. (We therefore encourage you to read, in conjunction with this essay, our "Reading Shakespeare's Language: *The Sonnets*" [pp. 3–12].) However, *Venus and Adonis* and *Lucrece* also use a remarkable quantity of elaborately patterned language, often achieved through word repetition. Such verbal patternings, called rhetorical schemes, are concentrated in the passages in which emotion is most intense. After briefly noting some of the similarities between the *Sonnets* and these poems, we will focus on the poems' rhetorical schemes.

Shakespeare's Words and Sentences

As in the *Sonnets,* Shakespeare occasionally uses words that are no longer used today. Among those we find in *Venus and Adonis* are *sick-thoughted* (lovesick), *forceless* (weak), *fondling* (pet, love), and *limning* (painting). In *Lucrece* we find *entitulèd* (entitled), *parling* (parleying, speaking), *margents* (margins), and *welkin* (sky). Again as in the *Sonnets,* some of the words he uses in the poems are ones that we still use but use with different meanings. In *Venus and Adonis,* for instance, we find *enraged* (ardent), *miss* (offense), and *sprite* (spirit); and in *Lucrece* we find *let* (refrain), *publisher* (public proclaimer), *securely* (unsuspectingly), and *ill* (evil). Meanings of words of this kind—both those no longer in use and those used with different meanings—are provided in our facing-page notes.

In the *Sonnets,* as we pointed out on pages 6–7, Shakespeare fits his sentences to the structure of the sonnet; similarly in *Venus and Adonis* and *Lucrece,* he often adapts his sentences to his choice of stanza for each poem. *Venus and Adonis* is written in sixains. Each stanza contains a quatrain that rhymes abab, followed by a couplet that rhymes cc. Shakespeare's use of this stanza was so successful and influential that it has come to be known as the *"Venus and Ado-*

nis stanza." For *Lucrece*, he chose the rhyme royal or Chaucerian stanza. Such stanzas are seven lines long and rhyme ababbcc. In both poems Shakespeare occasionally overrides the stanza form by using sentences of very different lengths. A few exceed the bounds of a single stanza and run over into the following one. Sometimes he puts a half-dozen or so short sentences into a single stanza. However, on the whole, he tends to match sentence structure to the form of his stanza, writing most stanzas as single sentences or as ‚airs of sentences.

To achieve this match of sentence and stanza, to maintain the iambic rhythm and the rhyme scheme, and to achieve other effects, Shakespeare often modifies normal word order. He inverts subject and verb when he describes Venus leading Adonis's horse and carrying the boy. He writes "Over one arm the lusty courser's rein, / Under her other *was the tender boy,*" instead of ending the line lamely and missing the needed rhyme with "the tender boy was" (lines 31–32). In *Lucrece*, Shakespeare again finds an emphatic conclusion for a line through the same inversion of subject and verb, "Now *stole* upon the time *the dead of night*" (line 162). In *Venus and Adonis*, he reverses the usual order of subject-verb-object and puts the objects first: "*Hunting* he loved, but *love* he laughed to scorn" (line 4). Through such inversion, he can emphasize what Adonis loved and what he scorned by according "hunting" and "love" emphatic initial positions in successive clauses. In *Lucrece*, Shakespeare has Tarquin illustrate how pain pays for the arrival of "each precious thing" (line 334) by giving the example of a merchant whose fortune rides in the ship on which he sails: "*Huge rocks, high winds, strong pirates, shelves* [i.e., sandbanks], *and sands* / The merchant fears ere rich at home he lands" (lines 335–36). By putting the list of dangers, real or imagined, first, Shakespeare can emphasize rather than bury them, as he would have done had he put them in the usual position of the object—after the verb "fears."

Besides inverting customary word order, Shakespeare, in the narrative poems as in the *Sonnets*, often separates words that ordinarily are put together in sentences. *Venus and Adonis* begins with the separation of a subject from its verb: "*the sun* with purple-colored face / *Had ta'en* his last leave of the weeping morn" (lines 1–2). Here Shakespeare provides the color of the sun, bright red or crimson, before he offers the verb "Had ta'en" and thus displaces the verb from its ordinary position immediately after the subject. Early in *Lucrece* as well, Shakespeare separates the subject from its verb, this time when describing Tarquin's motive for seeking to rape Lucrece, a motive that sprang from her husband Collatine's boasting: "For *he* the night before, in Tarquin's tent, / *Unlocked* the treasure of his happy state" (lines 15–16).

Shakespeare, again as in the *Sonnets*, often delays his presentation of the essential elements of his sentences, their subjects and verbs, until he has given us something else. Shakespeare's opening to *Venus and Adonis* is marked by delay as well as by the separation already noted:

> Even as the sun with purple-colored face
> Had ta'en his last leave of the weeping morn,
> *Rose-cheeked Adonis hied* him to the chase.
>
> (lines 1–3)

Here Shakespeare postpones his introduction of his principal male character until after presenting the sunrise, perhaps because it is a convention of the epic elaborately to describe the sunrise and Shakespeare wants to announce immediately that he is writing a minor epic. *Lucrece*, too, begins with a delay in the presentation of subject and verb:

> From the besièged Ardea all in post,
> Borne by the trustless wings of false desire,
> *Lust-breathèd Tarquin leaves* the Roman host[.]
>
> (lines 1–3)

This time the delay serves chiefly to propel us into the poem with violent rapidity by doubly emphasizing Tarquin's speed as "all in post" (in all haste) and "borne by . . . wings."

Figures of Speech

Both *Venus and Adonis* and *Lucrece* are heavy with the explicit comparisons that we call similes and the implicit comparisons called metaphors. However, as critics have noted, similes predominate in *Venus and Adonis* and metaphors in *Lucrece*. In a simile typical of *Venus and Adonis*, we are told that as Adonis lies "[p]anting . . . and breatheth in her face," Venus "feedeth on the steam [i.e., his breath] *as on a prey*" (lines 62–63). The comparison of his breath to a creature that she longs to devour as "prey" is thus made explicit. As Lucrece endeavors to dissuade Tarquin from raping her, she is given a series of metaphors typical of that poem:

> "Mud not the fountain that gave drink to thee.
> Mar not the thing that cannot be amended.
> End thy ill aim before thy shoot be ended;
>   He is no woodman that doth bend his bow
>   To strike a poor unseasonable doe."

(lines 577–81)

First she compares herself to a fountain that has already extended hospitality to Tarquin ("gave drink to thee") and that is vulnerable to pollution. Then she compares herself to something that can be damaged ("marred") and never again repaired ("amended"). Finally she compares herself to a "doe," out of season for hunting, standing as the target of an unsportsmanly hunter ("woodman").

Common to both *Venus and Adonis* and *Lucrece* are their many uses of the colors white and red in similes and metaphors. In his early play *Love's Labor's Lost*, Shakespeare emphasizes the conventionality of this poetic convention in the poem recited by Armado's page (1.2.98–105). Yet Shakespeare himself seizes on this convention throughout *Venus and Adonis*, employing it three times in the poem's first one hundred lines. First Venus praises Adonis's complexion as "More white and red than doves or roses are" (line 10). The next two uses might appear simply descriptive rather than figurative, were it not that each is a reference to a long-standing convention in love poetry and is thus an allusion, a figure of speech that refers to an earlier text, whether historical, biblical, mythological, or, in this case, literary. In the first of these allusions, Venus promises Adonis that her kisses will make his lips "red and pale with fresh variety" (line 21). Then Shakespeare, in the role of the poem's narrator, wittily reduces the embarrassed and petulant Adonis's conflicted emotional state to the same literary convention:

Still is he sullen, still he lours and frets,
'Twixt crimson shame and anger ashy pale;
  Being red, she loves him best, and being white,
  Her best is bettered with a more delight.

(lines 75–78)

The most extensive figurative reference to red and white belongs to the "silent war of lilies and of roses" that is fought out in Lucrece's face when Tarquin first appears at her home, Collatium:

When at Collatium this false lord arrived,
Well was he welcomed by the Roman dame,
Within whose face Beauty and Virtue strived
Which of them both should underprop her fame.
When Virtue bragged, Beauty would blush for shame;
  When Beauty boasted blushes, in despite
  Virtue would stain that o'er with silver white.

But Beauty, in that white entituled
From Venus' doves doth challenge that fair field.
Then Virtue claims from Beauty Beauty's red,
Which Virtue gave the golden age to gild
Their silver cheeks, and called it then their shield,
  Teaching them thus to use it in the fight:
  When shame assailed, the red should fence the white.

This heraldry in Lucrece' face was seen,
Argued by Beauty's red and Virtue's white.
Of either's color was the other queen,
Proving from world's minority their right.
Yet their ambition makes them still to fight,
  The sovereignty of either being so great
  That oft they interchange each other's seat.

(lines 50–70)

In this allusion, red, in the first stanza, is associated with Lucrece's personified Beauty and white with her Virtue. By the second stanza, Lucrece's face has metaphorically become both a battlefield and the surface of a heraldic shield on which colors are displayed. As the metaphor extends across the second and third stanzas, it appears that Beauty and Virtue each enjoy a claim on both red and white (though the claim that Beauty owns white and Virtue red depends on the then-current link between silver and white, on the one hand, and gold and red, on the other). Shakespeare, in these stanzas and elsewhere, is competing in his display of "red and white" with the many poets who used the convention before him and with his contemporaries still using them.

Rhetorical Schemes

Rhetorical schemes include anaphora, antanaclasis, antimetabole, antithesis, epistrophe, polyptoton, repetitio, symploce, and synoeciosis. While these terms may seem forbiddingly challenging, derived as they are from Greek and Latin, their meanings are relatively simple, as we hope will be clear as we list them below. After providing examples of each, we then show how Shakespeare depends on combinations of them in those moments when the feelings of his characters are most intense.

Anaphora is the repetition of a word or words at the beginning of successive verse-lines or at the beginning of successive phrases or clauses in the same verse-line. Shakespeare uses anaphora in describing Adonis's attempts to revive Venus:

> *He* wrings her nose, *he* strikes her on the cheeks,
> *He* bends her fingers, holds her pulses hard,
> *He* chafes her lips[.]
>
> (lines 475–77)

Shakespeare uses the same scheme in a more elaborate form as Lucrece wishes a series of retaliatory evils on Tarquin:

> "*Let him have time* to tear his curlèd hair,
> *Let him have time* against himself to rave,

Let him have time of Time's help to despair,
Let him have time to live a loathèd slave,
Let him have time a beggar's orts to crave[.]"

(lines 981–85)

Antanaclasis is the repetition of a word, but in a different grammatical form or different sense. When Venus tells Adonis to "Speak, *fair,* but speak *fair* words" (line 208), her first *fair* is a noun meaning "beautiful one," her second *fair* an adjective meaning "pleasing" or "flattering." Shakespeare's use of the same scheme with the word *fair* in *Lucrece* is even more dazzling as Tarquin prays that his "thoughts might compass his *fair fair*" (line 346)—that is, "his unblemished beautiful one."

Antimetabole is the repetition of words, but in reverse order. An example from *Venus and Adonis* is *"looks* kill *love,* and *love* by *looks* reviveth" (line 464). *Lucrece* supplies *"one* for *all* or *all* for *one* we gage" (line 144).

Antithesis is the balanced opposition of terms, often through negation and sometimes through repetition. Using antithesis by negation, Shakespeare tells us that Venus is more powerful than Adonis and can control him by force, but that she cannot control him by arousing desire in him:

Backward she pushed him as she would be thrust,
And governed him *in strength* though *not in lust.*

(lines 41–42)

In *Lucrece,* Shakespeare uses antithesis through repetition of "kings"/"king" (more precisely, polyptoton) and through the negation of "nor":

. . . *kings* might be espousèd *to more fame,*
But *king nor peer to such a peerless dame.*

(lines 20–21)

The greater "fame" to which "kings" are figuratively married is balanced against the matchless woman (the "peerless dame" Lucrece) to whom no king and no nobleman is literally married—except the noble Collatine.

Epistrophe is the use of the same word at the end of successive verse-lines or at the end of successive phrases or clauses in the same verse-line. One instance appears early in *Venus and Adonis:*

> Sick-thoughtèd Venus makes amain unto *him*
> And, like a bold-faced suitor, gins to woo *him.*

(lines 5–6)

Again, *Lucrece* uses the scheme in a way that is somewhat more elaborate in one of the threats issued by Tarquin just before the rape:

> "If thou deny, . . .
> . . . some worthless slave of thine I'll slay,
> To kill thine honor with thy life's decay,
>   And in thy dead arms do I mean to place *him,*
>   Swearing I slew *him,* seeing thee embrace *him."*

(lines 513–18)

Polyptoton is repetition, within a short space, of words that have the same root. Shakespeare uses it in *Venus and Adonis* with "She's *Love,* she *loves,* and yet she is not *loved"* (line 610). In *Lucrece,* within a single stanza he employs this scheme in every line, uses it twice in the stanza's fifth line, and adds yet a ninth use within the third and fourth lines with "pitiful" and "pity":

> "Disturb his hours of *rest* with *restless* trances.
> Afflict him in his *bed* with *bedrid* groans.
> Let there *bechance* him *pitiful mischances*
> To make him *moan,* but *pity* not his *moans.*
> *Stone* him with *hard'ned* hearts *harder* than *stones,*
>   And let *mild* women to him lose their *mildness,*
>   *Wilder* to him than tigers in their *wildness."*

(lines 974–80)

Repetitio is simple repetition of a word, such as occurs in *Venus and Adonis* when Adonis uses *love* as a noun three times in the same line to mean approximately "desire" every time: "My *love* to *love* is *love* but to disgrace it" (line 412).

Symploce is repetition of a word at the beginning of successive lines (anaphora) combined with repetition of another word at the end of successive lines (epistrophe). This comparatively rare scheme appears in *Venus and Adonis* in the lines

> "*Give* me my hand," saith he. "Why dost thou feel *it?*"
> "*Give* me my heart," saith she, "and thou shalt have *it.*"
> (lines 373–74)

Synoeciosis is defined by a contemporary of Shakespeare's, George Puttenham, in *The Arte of English Poesie* (1589) as "the cross-couple because it takes . . . two contrary words, and tieth them as it were in a pair of couples, and so makes them agree like good fellows, as I saw once in France a wolf coupled with a mastiff, and a fox with a hound" (Book 3, chap. 19; spelling modernized). Venus uses this scheme repeatedly in illustrating her prophecy that "*Sorrow* on *love* hereafter shall attend" (line 1136):

> "The *strongest* body shall it make most *weak,*
> Strike the *wise* dumb, and teach the *fool* to speak. . . .
> It shall be *raging mad* and *silly mild,*
> Make the *young old,* the *old* become a *child.*"
> (lines 1145–46, 1151–52)

Lucrece, too, displays this scheme repeatedly, most simply when, for example, it brings contraries immediately together in "Against *love's fire fear's frost* hath dissolution" (line 355).

At climactic moments in each poem, Shakespeare presents the extreme thought and feeling of his characters by relying on combinations of the schemes just defined and exemplified. When Venus first speaks after she has viewed her Adonis dead, the stanza is marked by highly patterned language:

> "My tongue cannot express my grief for one
> And yet," quoth she, "behold two Adons dead.
> My sighs are blown away, my salt tears gone;
> Mine eyes are turned to fire, my heart to lead.
> Heavy heart's lead, melt at mine eyes' red fire!
> So shall I die by drops of hot desire."
> (lines 1069–74)

Shakespeare employs anaphora in the repetition at the beginning of successive lines and clauses: "My tongue . . . My sighs . . . my salt tears . . . Mine eyes . . . my heart." He uses repetitio in "Mine eyes . . . mine eyes" and polyptoton in "heart . . . heart's." Finally, he uses antithesis in "one . . . two Adons dead."

When Lucrece, after debating her course of action following the rape, decides upon suicide, her language is even more schematic:

> "Thou, Collatine, shalt oversee this will;
> How was I overseen that thou shalt see it!
> My blood shall wash the slander of mine ill;
> My life's foul deed my life's fair end shall free it.
> Faint not, faint heart, but stoutly say, 'So be it.'
>   Yield to my hand; my hand shall conquer thee.
>   Thou dead, both die, and both shall victors be."
>   (lines 1205–11)

In this stanza there is anaphora with "My blood . . . ; / My life's," and epistrophe with "free it. / . . . 'So be it.' " There is also repetitio in "My life's . . . my life's," as well as in "my hand; my hand." The latter case of repetitio also goes by the name anadiplosis, because words at the end of one clause are immediately repeated at the beginning of the next one. Antanaclasis may be found in "Faint not, faint heart," in which *faint* is first a verb and then an adjective. Polyptoton begins and ends the stanza: "oversee . . . overseen . . . see" and "dead . . . die." Antimetabole too begins the stanza: "Thou . . . shalt . . . oversee . . . overseen . . . thou shalt." Synoeciosis brings the stanza to a close, tying together the conquered dead and the victors by identifying them with each other: "Yield to my hand; my hand shall conquer thee. / Thou dead, both die, and both shall victors be."

Modern critics and readers have sometimes been impatient with the obvious contrivance of these rhetorical schemes. The use of such patterns has sometimes even been blamed on the characters into whose speeches Shakespeare worked these verbal arrangements. Yet it is Shakespeare who is to be credited with the artifice, a display of his talent in bringing language to the limit of intelligibility while still rendering it generally comprehensible. If we are to begin to understand the resources of language that Shakespeare and his contemporaries evidently regarded as the means for presenting the extremity of passion and thought in their fictional creations, we must identify (and, ideally, learn to admire) rhetorical schemes. Along with word choice, rhyme schemes, and figurative language, they provide the poetic richness and complexity that have kept these poems alive when the many works with which they competed have long since disappeared.

An Introduction to This Text

Venus and Adonis was first printed in 1593 and *Lucrece* in 1594. "The Phoenix and Turtle" first appeared in 1601 in Robert Chester's *Loves Martyr: or, Rosalins Complaint.* The present edition is based directly upon these printings.* The only other poem that might have been included in this edition is "A Louers Complaint." It was printed in 1609 at the end of the volume of *Shakespeares Sonnets.* However, when "A Louers Complaint" was tested by Ward E. Y. Elliott and Robert J. Valenza in their "Glass Slippers and Seven-League Boots: C-Prompted Doubts about Ascribing *A Funeral Elegy* and *A Lover's Complaint* to Shakespeare" (*Shakespeare Quarterly* 48 [1997]: 177–207), its attribution to Shakespeare was called seriously into question. MacD. P. Jackson attempted to refute Elliott and Valenza in *"A Lover's Complaint* Revisited" (*Shakespeare Studies* 32 [2004]: 267–94). We do not find Jackson's case to be persuasive and so have not included "A Louers Complaint" in this collection of poems.

We have edited the texts of the poems included in this edition following the same principles used in the *Sonnets.* For these editing principles and for those according to which we have written the facing-page commentary, please see pp. 16–17.

---

* We have also consulted the computerized texts provided by the Text Archive of the Oxford University Computing Centre and those on the website of Michael Best, ed., *Internet Shakespeare Editions,* University of Victoria, Canada. We are grateful to both.

Shakespeare's *Venus and Adonis*

With *Venus and Adonis,* Shakespeare in 1593 launches his career as a poet. The poem is a minor epic, a genre chosen by a large number of poets in the 1590s for their first efforts, each attempt at the genre self-consciously imitating the others. The genre is a marginal one, its characters usually drawn from the periphery of mythology or legendary history. Its interest is not in the matters of state that inform major epics but in eroticism, sophistication, and verbal wit. Among these poems, *Venus and Adonis* was such a notable success that it was, during his lifetime, Shakespeare's most popular published work, going through ten editions by 1616 and quoted in numerous journals, letters, and plays of the period. In 1598 a critic wrote that "the sweet witty soul of Ovid lives in mellifluous and honey-tongued Shakespeare, witness his *Venus and Adonis."*

Shakespeare found the story of the encounter between the Roman goddess of love and the boy hunter in book 10 of Ovid's *Metamorphoses.* In Ovid, the beautiful Adonis is the willing lover of Venus, and his death is an accident of the hunt. Shakespeare transforms the story by having his Adonis reject Venus's advances in a way that, for his early readers, was clearly both ironic and comic. Shakespeare makes his Venus highly verbal, a seemingly endless source of arguments for making love. He makes the boy Adonis capable of only brief and petulant protests against her advances. The immense popularity of the poem in Shakespeare's lifetime shows that his transformation of the myth into a struggle between an overheated goddess and an extremely reluctant boy was seized on eagerly. For readers today who might forget that Venus is a goddess—not a woman, not subject to aging—it is easy to focus on Adonis as the uneasy object of desire on the part of a matron. As Adonis squirms and blushes, some of today's readers may squirm and blush as well, as the poem seems to skate along the edge of mother-son incest or give off a faint whiff of pedophilia. Other readers today may find Adonis's smug coldness as unattractive as Venus's ardor, while yet others may find sympathy for Adonis's powerlessness in the embrace of Venus alternating with sympathy for Venus in her erotic frustration, the goddess of love denied satisfaction in her own realm. In other words, for anyone who reads the poem in terms of the characters' emotions rather than as a display of the wanton made sophisticated and rhetorically eloquent, only when Venus suffers grief at the end of the poem does she become sympathetic. As readers today, then, it is important that we remember that this poem is a retelling of a familiar myth in a form that is deliberately artificial, deliberately playing with the notion of what would happen if the goddess of love were herself stricken with the torments of love—and were refused.

Venus and Adonis is also true to the conventions of the minor epic in featuring an elaborate digression from its main plot, focusing attention instead on Adonis's horse as it escapes to be with a wild mare. In another gesture toward convention, the poem takes a turn toward the assignment of cause to a phenomenon, or what is known as *aetiology*. Venus identifies the death of Adonis and its impact on her, the goddess of love, as the reason why the human experience of love will, from that moment on, be always disruptive, attended by jealousy and sorrow. It has now been some centuries since the minor epic and its conventions fell out of fashion. However, *Venus and Adonis* still commands appreciation for its dazzling verbal surface. It is a fine example of baroque art. Further, the emotions felt by Venus and by Adonis, though deliberately made rather ridiculous in the poem, are much like the emotions explored in Shakespeare's romantic comedies (think, for example, of Helena and Demetrius in *A Midsummer Night's Dream*). This poem, then, lets us see the young Shakespeare stretching his wings as a poet, competing with the other poets of his day, and not only winning the competition but also exploring romantic love in a way that will yield his remarkably enduring romantic comedies.

After you have read this poem, we invite you to turn to the essay printed at the back of this book, "*Venus and Adonis* and *Lucrece:* A Modern Perspective," written by Professor Catherine Belsey of Cardiff University.

VENUS AND ADONIS

Dedication

1–2. **Vilia . . . aqua:** Let the vulgar admire vile things; may Apollo provide me with cups filled from the Castalian spring (Latin; Ovid, *Amores* 1.15.35–36). The spring, which was on Mount Parnassus in Delphi, Greece, was sacred to the muses, the nine sister-goddesses who inspired the arts and learning, especially poetry and music. (See picture of muses, p. 92.)

4. **Henry Wriothesley, Earl of Southampton:** See longer note, p. 442, and picture below.

12. **heir:** offspring; product; **invention:** poetic creativity (The metaphor of the poem as the poet's offspring or child is continued in **deformed** and **godfather.**)

13. **ear:** plow

Earl of Southampton (1573–1624).

360

Vilia miretur vulgus: mihi flavus Apollo
Pocula Castalia plena ministret aqua.

TO THE RIGHT HONORABLE
Henry Wriothesley, Earl of Southampton,
and Baron of Titchfield.

Right Honorable,

I know not how I shall offend in dedicating my unpolished lines to your Lordship, nor how the world will censure me for choosing so strong a prop to support so weak a burden; only if your Honor seem but pleased, I account myself highly praised and vow to take advantage of all idle hours till I have honored you with some graver labor. But if the first heir of my invention prove deformed, I shall be sorry it had so noble a godfather and never after ear so barren a land, for fear it yield me still so bad a harvest. I leave it to your honorable survey, and your Honor to your heart's content, which I wish may always answer your own wish and the world's hopeful expectation.

Your Honor's in all duty,
William Shakespeare.

1. **Even as:** i.e., just when; **purple-colored:** crimson or bright red

2. **ta'en:** taken; **weeping morn:** the Roman goddess Aurora, here imaged as **weeping** because the god of the **sun** has left her

3. **Adonis:** in mythology, a beautiful young man (His story is told in Ovid's *Metamorphoses*, book 10.) **hied him:** hurried; **chase:** hunt

5. **Sick-thoughtèd:** i.e., lovesick; **Venus:** the Roman goddess of love; **makes amain unto:** proceeds with all speed toward

6. **gins:** begins

7. **Thrice fairer:** three times more beautiful

8. **compare:** comparison

9. **Stain to all nymphs:** one who eclipses **all** beautiful young women (A *nymph* might also be a female nature spirit.)

11. **with herself at strife:** i.e., in competition **with herself** (perhaps, to exceed her own limitations in creating Adonis)

13. **Vouchsafe:** deign; **alight:** dismount from

15. **meed:** reward

18. **set:** seated

23. **an hour but short:** only a **short hour**

24. **wasted:** spent

26. **precedent:** indication, sign; **pith:** vigor, strength; **livelihood:** liveliness

27. **it:** i.e., the sweat from his **palm** (l. 25); **balm:** a soothing or healing fragrant oil

28. **sovereign:** most powerful

29. **enraged:** ardent, inflamed

30. **Courageously:** (1) lustily; (2) lustfully; **pluck him:** pull him forcibly

Venus and Adonis

Even as the sun with purple-colored face
Had ta'en his last leave of the weeping morn,
Rose-cheeked Adonis hied him to the chase.
Hunting he loved, but love he laughed to scorn.
    Sick-thoughtèd Venus makes amain unto him   5
    And, like a bold-faced suitor, gins to woo him.

"Thrice fairer than myself," thus she began,
"The field's chief flower, sweet above compare,
Stain to all nymphs, more lovely than a man,
More white and red than doves or roses are,   10
    Nature that made thee, with herself at strife,
    Saith that the world hath ending with thy life.

"Vouchsafe, thou wonder, to alight thy steed,
And rein his proud head to the saddlebow.
If thou wilt deign this favor, for thy meed   15
A thousand honey secrets shalt thou know.
    Here come and sit where never serpent hisses,
    And being set, I'll smother thee with kisses,

"And yet not cloy thy lips with loathed satiety,
But rather famish them amid their plenty,   20
Making them red and pale with fresh variety—
Ten kisses short as one, one long as twenty.
    A summer's day will seem an hour but short,
    Being wasted in such time-beguiling sport."

With this she seizeth on his sweating palm,   25
The precedent of pith and livelihood,
And, trembling in her passion, calls it balm,
Earth's sovereign salve to do a goddess good.
    Being so enraged, desire doth lend her force
    Courageously to pluck him from his horse.   30

31. **lusty:** strong

33. **dull:** listless, gloomy

34. **appetite:** desire; **unapt to toy:** not inclined to lovemaking

37. **ragged:** rough, uneven

38. **quick:** wordplay on (1) rapidly moving; (2) full of energy and life; (3) impatient, hasty

39. **stallèd up:** tied up or confined (as in a stall)

40. **prove:** attempt

41. **would:** i.e., wished to be

42. **governed:** mastered (nonce example in *OED*)

43. **along:** i.e., lying beside him

46. **gins:** begins

47. **broken:** interrupted (by her kisses)

50. **maiden burning:** blushing (The words *maid* and *maiden* could apply to a young man still a virgin.)

53. **miss:** offense, wrongdoing

55. **Even:** just; **empty:** hungry; **sharp:** eager for prey; **by fast:** because of fasting

56. **Tires:** pulls or tears in feeding

58. **gorge:** craw, maw

Bird of prey.

Over one arm the lusty courser's rein,
Under her other was the tender boy,
Who blushed and pouted in a dull disdain,
With leaden appetite, unapt to toy—
    She red and hot as coals of glowing fire,   35
    He red for shame but frosty in desire.

The studded bridle on a ragged bough
Nimbly she fastens. O, how quick is love!
The steed is stallèd up, and even now
To tie the rider she begins to prove.   40
    Backward she pushed him as she would be thrust,
    And governed him in strength though not in lust.

So soon was she along as he was down,
Each leaning on their elbows and their hips.
Now doth she stroke his cheek, now doth he frown   45
And gins to chide, but soon she stops his lips
    And kissing speaks, with lustful language broken,
    "If thou wilt chide, thy lips shall never open."

He burns with bashful shame; she with her tears
Doth quench the maiden burning of his cheeks.   50
Then with her windy sighs and golden hairs
To fan and blow them dry again she seeks.
    He saith she is immodest, blames her miss;
    What follows more she murders with a kiss.

Even as an empty eagle, sharp by fast,   55
Tires with her beak on feathers, flesh, and bone,
Shaking her wings, devouring all in haste
Till either gorge be stuffed or prey be gone,
    Even so she kissed his brow, his cheek, his chin,
    And where she ends she doth anew begin.   60

61. **content:** (1) please, delight (Venus); (2) acquiesce (to what Venus is doing)

66. **So:** provided that; **distilling showers:** i.e., water condensed from mist or vapor

67. **Look how:** i.e., just as

69. **awed:** constrained

71. **rank:** swollen

77. **Being:** i.e., he **being;** when he is

78. **more:** greater

79. **Look . . . can:** i.e., no matter how he looks

80. **fair:** beautiful

81. **remove:** depart

82. **take:** make a

86. **divedapper:** small diving waterfowl

87. **Who:** i.e., which

89. **pay:** payment (to her)

90. **winks:** closes his eyes

Forced to content but never to obey,
Panting he lies and breatheth in her face.
She feedeth on the steam as on a prey
And calls it heavenly moisture, air of grace,
    Wishing her cheeks were gardens full of flowers,   65
    So they were dewed with such distilling showers.

Look how a bird lies tangled in a net,
So fastened in her arms Adonis lies.
Pure shame and awed resistance made him fret,
Which bred more beauty in his angry eyes.   70
    Rain added to a river that is rank
    Perforce will force it overflow the bank.

Still she entreats, and prettily entreats,
For to a pretty ear she tunes her tale.
Still is he sullen, still he lours and frets,   75
'Twixt crimson shame and anger ashy pale;
    Being red, she loves him best, and being white,
    Her best is bettered with a more delight.

Look how he can, she cannot choose but love,
And by her fair immortal hand she swears   80
From his soft bosom never to remove
Till he take truce with her contending tears,
    Which long have rained, making her cheeks all wet,
    And one sweet kiss shall pay this countless debt.

Upon this promise did he raise his chin   85
Like a divedapper peering through a wave,
Who, being looked on, ducks as quickly in;
So offers he to give what she did crave,
    But when her lips were ready for his pay,
    He winks and turns his lips another way.   90

91. **passenger:** traveler

95. **gan she cry:** i.e., she cried

98. **the stern . . . war:** The story of Venus's affair with Mars, the Roman **god of war,** is told in Ovid's *Metamorphoses* 4.171–89.   **stern:** fiercely brave, merciless   **direful:** dreadful, terrible (See picture below.)

100. **jar:** dispute, quarrel

103. **Over:** above

104. **uncontrollèd crest:** i.e., unbowed helmet

106. **toy, wanton, dally:** play lovingly or lewdly

107. **churlish:** rude, harsh-sounding; **ensign red:** blood-stained flag or banner

108. **field:** battlefield; **tent:** dwelling place (literally, soldier's **tent**)

109. **overruled, overswayed:** conquered

113. **nor:** i.e., or

114. **foiled:** overthrew; **fight:** i.e., war

115. **fair:** beautiful

119. **Look . . . lies:** i.e., see your **beauty** reflected in my eyes (Compare John Donne's "My face in thine eye, thine in mine appears" ["The Good Morrow," l. 15].)

Mars, the "stern and direful god of war." (*Venus and Adonis,* 98)

Never did passenger in summer's heat
More thirst for drink than she for this good turn.
Her help she sees, but help she cannot get;
She bathes in water, yet her fire must burn.
    "O, pity," gan she cry, "flint-hearted boy!   95
    'Tis but a kiss I beg. Why art thou coy?

"I have been wooed, as I entreat thee now,
Even by the stern and direful god of war,
Whose sinewy neck in battle ne'er did bow,
Who conquers where he comes in every jar,   100
    Yet hath he been my captive and my slave
    And begged for that which thou unasked shalt have.

"Over my altars hath he hung his lance,
His battered shield, his uncontrollèd crest,
And for my sake hath learned to sport and dance,   105
To toy, to wanton, dally, smile, and jest,
    Scorning his churlish drum and ensign red,
    Making my arms his field, his tent my bed.

"Thus he that overruled I overswayed,
Leading him prisoner in a red-rose chain;   110
Strong-tempered steel his stronger strength obeyed,
Yet was he servile to my coy disdain.
    O, be not proud, nor brag not of thy might
    For mastering her that foiled the god of fight!

"Touch but my lips with those fair lips of thine;   115
Though mine be not so fair, yet are they red.
The kiss shall be thine own as well as mine.
What seest thou in the ground? Hold up thy head.
    Look in mine eyeballs; there thy beauty lies.
    Then why not lips on lips, since eyes in eyes?   120

121. **wink:** close your eyes

123. **Love:** Cupid, Roman god of love (See picture, p. 378.) **keeps his revels:** holds his festivities; **twain:** two

124. **sport:** lovemaking; **in sight:** i.e., overseen by anyone

126. **know not:** i.e., **know; mean:** intend to do

127. **spring:** first appearance (i.e., of facial hair)

129. **advantage:** opportunity

131. **prime:** most flourishing stage

133. **hard-favored, foul:** ugly

134. **Ill-nurtured:** badly brought-up, poorly educated; **crookèd:** deformed, bent with age; **churlish:** vulgar, boorish

135. **O'erworn:** spent with age; **rheumatic:** discharging rheum or mucus (accented on the first syllable)

136. **Thick-sighted:** not seeing clearly; **barren:** past child-bearing; **lacking juice:** i.e., dried out (as with age)

142. **marrow burning:** Love was said to "burn the **marrow**" of the lover.

146. **trip:** dance; **green:** i.e., grass

147. **nymph:** a mythological female nature spirit

148. **footing:** footprint (See longer note, p. 442.)

149. **compact:** composed

150. **gross:** i.e., heavy

1 *Viola nigra sue purpurea.*
The purple garden Violet.

"Blue-veined violets." (*Venus and Adonis*, 125)

"Art thou ashamed to kiss? Then wink again,
And I will wink; so shall the day seem night.
Love keeps his revels where there are but twain;
Be bold to play, our sport is not in sight.
    These blue-veined violets whereon we lean   125
    Never can blab, nor know not what we mean.

"The tender spring upon thy tempting lip
Shows thee unripe, yet mayst thou well be tasted.
Make use of time, let not advantage slip;
Beauty within itself should not be wasted.   130
    Fair flowers that are not gathered in their prime
    Rot and consume themselves in little time.

"Were I hard-favored, foul, or wrinkled old,
Ill-nurtured, crookèd, churlish, harsh in voice,
O'erworn, despisèd, rheumatic, and cold,   135
Thick-sighted, barren, lean, and lacking juice,
    Then mightst thou pause, for then I were not for thee,
    But having no defects, why dost abhor me?

"Thou canst not see one wrinkle in my brow;
Mine eyes are gray, and bright, and quick in turning;   140
My beauty as the spring doth yearly grow,
My flesh is soft and plump, my marrow burning;
    My smooth, moist hand, were it with thy hand felt,
    Would in thy palm dissolve or seem to melt.

"Bid me discourse, I will enchant thine ear,   145
Or like a fairy trip upon the green,
Or like a nymph, with long disheveled hair,
Dance on the sands, and yet no footing seen.
    Love is a spirit all compact of fire,
    Not gross to sink, but light, and will aspire.   150

152. **forceless:** weak

154. **even where:** wherever; **list:** desire, like; **sport me:** amuse myself (For Venus and her dove-drawn chariot, see picture, p. 440.)

155. **Is love so light:** Here, Venus equates herself with **love,** playing on the word **light** as weightless. (**Light** could also mean "unchaste, lewd.") In other places in the poem, **Love** refers not to Venus but to Cupid, Venus's son. (See, e.g., ll. 123 and 243, and picture, p. 378.)

156. **heavy:** oppressive, distressful

157. **to . . . affected:** in love with **thine own face**

160. **on:** i.e., of

161. **Narcissus . . . forsook:** i.e., in the same way **Narcissus himself** renounced or abandoned **himself   Narcissus:** a beautiful boy in mythology who drowned when he attempted to embrace his reflection (**shadow**) in a **brook** (See longer note, p. 442, and picture, p. 374.)

164. **fresh beauty for the use:** Proverbial: **Beauty** is made **for use.**

165. **sappy plants to bear:** i.e., **plants** full of sap **are made** [l. 163] **to bear** fruit

166. **to themselves:** i.e., only for **themselves,** without producing any fruit

168. **to get, it is:** i.e., to beget is

169. **increase:** crops

170. **increase:** offspring

175. **By this:** i.e., **by this** time

177. **Titan:** the sun god; **tired:** (1) attired; (2) fatigued, weary

178. **overlook:** look down on

179. **his team:** The sun god is often pictured crossing the sky in a chariot drawn by **his team** of horses. (See picture, p. 86.)

180. **So he:** i.e., provided that **Titan** (l. 177)

"Witness this primrose bank whereon I lie;
These forceless flowers like sturdy trees support me;
Two strengthless doves will draw me through the sky
From morn till night, even where I list to sport me.
    Is love so light, sweet boy, and may it be 155
    That thou should think it heavy unto thee?

"Is thine own heart to thine own face affected?
Can thy right hand seize love upon thy left?
Then woo thyself, be of thyself rejected;
Steal thine own freedom, and complain on theft. 160
    Narcissus so himself himself forsook
    And died to kiss his shadow in the brook.

"Torches are made to light, jewels to wear,
Dainties to taste, fresh beauty for the use,
Herbs for their smell, and sappy plants to bear. 165
Things growing to themselves are growth's abuse;
    Seeds spring from seeds, and beauty breedeth beauty;
    Thou wast begot; to get, it is thy duty.

"Upon the earth's increase why shouldst thou feed,
Unless the earth with thy increase be fed? 170
By law of nature thou art bound to breed,
That thine may live when thou thyself art dead;
    And so in spite of death thou dost survive,
    In that thy likeness still is left alive."

By this the lovesick queen began to sweat, 175
For where they lay the shadow had forsook them,
And Titan, tired in the midday heat,
With burning eye did hotly overlook them,
    Wishing Adonis had his team to guide,
    So he were like him and by Venus' side. 180

181. **sprite:** spirit
182. **heavy:** weary
183. **o'erwhelming:** overhanging (so as almost to cover); **sight:** eyes
186. **remove:** leave
187. **unkind:** (1) unnatural; (2) cruel
197. **done:** finished, ended
199. **obdurate:** accented on the second syllable
200. **relenteth:** dissolves (i.e., is worn away)
202. **want:** lack
203. **hard:** cruel; obstinate
204. **unkind:** See note to l. 187.
205. **this:** like this, thus
206. **dwells . . . suit:** inhabits (i.e., lives in) my wooing
207. **What:** i.e., how
208. **Speak, fair:** i.e., **speak,** beautiful one; **speak fair words:** i.e., **speak** pleasing or flattering **words**

Narcissus. (*Venus and Adonis*, 161; *Lucrece*, 265)

And now Adonis, with a lazy sprite
And with a heavy, dark, disliking eye,
His louring brows o'erwhelming his fair sight,
Like misty vapors when they blot the sky,
 Souring his cheeks, cries, "Fie, no more of love!   185
 The sun doth burn my face; I must remove."

"Ay, me," quoth Venus, "young and so unkind,
What bare excuses mak'st thou to be gone!
I'll sigh celestial breath, whose gentle wind
Shall cool the heat of this descending sun.   190
 I'll make a shadow for thee of my hairs;
 If they burn too, I'll quench them with my tears.

"The sun that shines from heaven shines but warm,
And, lo, I lie between that sun and thee.
The heat I have from thence doth little harm;   195
Thine eye darts forth the fire that burneth me,
 And were I not immortal, life were done
 Between this heavenly and earthly sun.

"Art thou obdurate, flinty, hard as steel?
Nay, more than flint, for stone at rain relenteth.   200
Art thou a woman's son and canst not feel
What 'tis to love, how want of love tormenteth?
 O, had thy mother borne so hard a mind,
 She had not brought forth thee, but died unkind.

"What am I that thou shouldst contemn me this?   205
Or what great danger dwells upon my suit?
What were thy lips the worse for one poor kiss?
Speak, fair, but speak fair words, or else be mute.
 Give me one kiss, I'll give it thee again,
 And one for interest if thou wilt have twain.   210

211. **liveless:** lifeless

215. **complexion:** external appearance

219. **blaze:** (1) flame; (2) proclaim; **her wrong:** i.e., the **wrong** she suffers

220. **Being . . . love:** i.e., although she adjudicates all disputes regarding **love; right:** i.e., set right

221. **fain would:** i.e., is eager to

222. **her intendments break:** i.e., interrupt what she intends to say

226. **would:** i.e., wishes (to bind him)

229. **Fondling:** pet, love

230. **pale:** fence

231. **park:** enclosed expanse of land holding animals to be hunted

235. **this limit:** i.e., these bounds; **relief:** (1) feeding, pasturing; (2) sport, entertainment

236. **bottom-grass:** grass growing in a valley; **plain:** flat meadow land

240. **rouse thee:** cause you to rise from cover

Lighted torches. (*Venus and Adonis*, 163)

"Fie, liveless picture, cold and senseless stone,
Well-painted idol, image dull and dead,
Statue contenting but the eye alone,
Thing like a man, but of no woman bred!
    Thou art no man, though of a man's complexion,   215
    For men will kiss even by their own direction."

This said, impatience chokes her pleading tongue,
And swelling passion doth provoke a pause.
Red cheeks and fiery eyes blaze forth her wrong.
Being judge in love, she cannot right her cause.   220
    And now she weeps, and now she fain would speak,
    And now her sobs do her intendments break.

Sometimes she shakes her head, and then his hand.
Now gazeth she on him, now on the ground;
Sometimes her arms enfold him like a band.   225
She would, he will not in her arms be bound.
    And when from thence he struggles to be gone,
    She locks her lily fingers one in one.

"Fondling," she saith, "since I have hemmed thee here
Within the circuit of this ivory pale,   230
I'll be a park, and thou shalt be my deer.
Feed where thou wilt, on mountain or in dale;
    Graze on my lips, and if those hills be dry,
    Stray lower, where the pleasant fountains lie.

"Within this limit is relief enough,   235
Sweet bottom-grass and high delightful plain,
Round rising hillocks, brakes obscure and rough,
To shelter thee from tempest and from rain.
    Then be my deer, since I am such a park;
    No dog shall rouse thee, though a thousand bark."   240

242. **That:** i.e., so that

243. **Love:** Cupid, god of love (See picture below.) **if himself:** i.e., in case he **himself**

248. **liking:** desire

251. **in thine own law forlorn:** desolate in the very matter in which you hold absolute power

255. **her object:** i.e., Adonis; **will away:** i.e., wants to leave

257. **favor:** kindness; **remorse:** compassion

261. **trampling:** stamping (See picture of **courser,** p. 380.)

264. **straight:** straightaway, immediately

267. **bearing:** fertile, productive

Cupid, the god of love. (*Venus and Adonis,* 243)

At this Adonis smiles as in disdain,
That in each cheek appears a pretty dimple;
Love made those hollows, if himself were slain,
He might be buried in a tomb so simple,
    Foreknowing well if there he came to lie,   245
    Why, there Love lived, and there he could not die.

These lovely caves, these round enchanting pits,
Opened their mouths to swallow Venus' liking.
Being mad before, how doth she now for wits?
Struck dead at first, what needs a second striking?   250
    Poor queen of love, in thine own law forlorn,
    To love a cheek that smiles at thee in scorn!

Now which way shall she turn? What shall she say?
Her words are done, her woes the more increasing;
The time is spent; her object will away   255
And from her twining arms doth urge releasing.
    "Pity," she cries, "some favor, some remorse!"
    Away he springs and hasteth to his horse.

But, lo, from forth a copse that neighbors by,
A breeding jennet, lusty, young, and proud,   260
Adonis' trampling courser doth espy,
And forth she rushes, snorts, and neighs aloud.
    The strong-necked steed, being tied unto a tree,
    Breaketh his rein, and to her straight goes he.

Imperiously he leaps, he neighs, he bounds,   265
And now his woven girths he breaks asunder.
The bearing earth with his hard hoof he wounds,
Whose hollow womb resounds like heaven's thunder.
    The iron bit he crusheth 'tween his teeth,
    Controlling what he was controllèd with.   270

272. **compassed:** arched; **stand:** i.e., stands

275. **glisters:** sparkles (See picture below.)

276. **courage:** lust

277. **told:** counted

280. **who should:** i.e., one who would; **tried:** proved

283. **recketh he:** i.e., does he care about; **stir:** agitation

284. **Stand:** a command that means "halt"

286. **caparisons:** ornamented coverings spread over the horse's saddle or harness; **gay:** brilliant, showy

289. **Look when:** whenever; **life:** living form

290. **limning out:** painting

294. **bone:** bodily frame

295. **shag:** rough, shaggy

296. **full:** protuberant

297. **passing:** surpassingly

299. **Look what:** whatever

300. **Save:** except

"Adonis' trampling courser." (*Venus and Adonis*, 261)

His ears up-pricked, his braided hanging mane
Upon his compassed crest now stand on end.
His nostrils drink the air, and forth again,
As from a furnace, vapors doth he send.
   His eye, which scornfully glisters like fire,   275
   Shows his hot courage and his high desire.

Sometimes he trots, as if he told the steps,
With gentle majesty and modest pride.
Anon he rears upright, curvets, and leaps,
As who should say, "Lo, thus my strength is tried,   280
   And this I do to captivate the eye
   Of the fair breeder that is standing by."

What recketh he his rider's angry stir,
His flattering "Holla," or his "Stand, I say"?
What cares he now for curb or pricking spur,   285
For rich caparisons or trappings gay?
   He sees his love, and nothing else he sees,
   For nothing else with his proud sight agrees.

Look when a painter would surpass the life
In limning out a well-proportioned steed,   290
His art with Nature's workmanship at strife,
As if the dead the living should exceed,
   So did this horse excel a common one
   In shape, in courage, color, pace, and bone.

Round-hoofed, short-jointed, fetlocks shag and long,   295
Broad breast, full eye, small head, and nostril wide,
High crest, short ears, straight legs and passing strong,
Thin mane, thick tail, broad buttock, tender hide—
   Look what a horse should have he did not lack,
   Save a proud rider on so proud a back.   300

301. **scuds:** runs

303. **To bid the wind a base:** to challenge **the wind**

304. **whe'er:** whether; **whether:** which of the two

306. **who:** which

310. **strangeness:** coldness, aloofness

311–12. **scorns . . . heels:** echoes the proverbial "I scorn it with my **heels.**"

314. **vails:** lowers

316. **fume:** fit of anger

319. **goeth about:** sets to work

320. **unbacked:** never broken in to the saddle

321. **Jealous:** fearful; **catching:** i.e., being caught

322. **With . . . horse:** i.e., **the horse** went **with her**

323. **As:** i.e., **as** if; **hie them:** speed

324. **overfly them:** fly faster than they run

325. **chafing:** being angry

326. **Banning:** cursing

327. **happy:** favorable, fortunate; **season:** occasion; **fits:** is suitable

330. **aidance:** aid, help

Sometimes he scuds far off, and there he stares.
Anon he starts at stirring of a feather.
To bid the wind a base he now prepares,
And whe'er he run or fly, they know not whether,
    For through his mane and tail the high wind sings,   305
    Fanning the hairs, who wave like feathered wings.

He looks upon his love and neighs unto her.
She answers him as if she knew his mind.
Being proud, as females are, to see him woo her,
She puts on outward strangeness, seems unkind,   310
    Spurns at his love, and scorns the heat he feels,
    Beating his kind embracements with her heels.

Then like a melancholy malcontent,
He vails his tail that like a falling plume
Cool shadow to his melting buttock lent.   315
He stamps and bites the poor flies in his fume.
    His love, perceiving how he was enraged,
    Grew kinder, and his fury was assuaged.

His testy master goeth about to take him
When, lo, the unbacked breeder, full of fear,   320
Jealous of catching, swiftly doth forsake him,
With her the horse, and left Adonis there.
    As they were mad unto the wood they hie them,
    Outstripping crows that strive to overfly them.

All swollen with chafing, down Adonis sits,   325
Banning his boisterous and unruly beast;
And now the happy season once more fits
That lovesick Love by pleading may be blessed;
    For lovers say the heart hath treble wrong
    When it is barred the aidance of the tongue.   330

331. **stopped:** closed up; **stayed:** i.e., blocked

334. **vent:** utterance

335. **heart's attorney:** i.e., tongue

336. **breaks:** goes into bankruptcy; **suit:** wordplay on (1) legal **suit;** (2) wooing

337. **glow:** grow heated

339. **bonnet:** cap

343. **wistly:** intently

344. **wayward:** perverse, intractable

345. **note:** observe

347. **But now:** only this moment; **by and by:** immediately

351. **heaveth:** lifts (not necessarily with exertion)

354. **apt:** i.e., aptly, readily

356. **suing:** appealing

357. **as:** i.e., **as** if

359. **dumb play: dumb** show (i.e., stage action presented without speech); **his:** i.e., its; **acts:** actions (with wordplay on the **acts** into which a play is divided)

360. **choruslike:** like the chorus in a play, which makes **plain** to the audience through commentary the meaning of the action

An oven that is stopped, or river stayed,
Burneth more hotly, swelleth with more rage;
So of concealèd sorrow may be said,
Free vent of words love's fire doth assuage,
　　But when the heart's attorney once is mute, 335
　　The client breaks, as desperate in his suit.

He sees her coming and begins to glow,
Even as a dying coal revives with wind,
And with his bonnet hides his angry brow,
Looks on the dull earth with disturbèd mind, 340
　　Taking no notice that she is so nigh,
　　For all askance he holds her in his eye.

O, what a sight it was wistly to view
How she came stealing to the wayward boy,
To note the fighting conflict of her hue, 345
How white and red each other did destroy!
　　But now her cheek was pale, and by and by
　　It flashed forth fire as lightning from the sky.

Now was she just before him as he sat,
And like a lowly lover down she kneels. 350
With one fair hand she heaveth up his hat;
Her other tender hand his fair cheek feels.
　　His tend'rer cheek receives her soft hand's print
　　As apt as new-fall'n snow takes any dint.

O, what a war of looks was then between them! 355
Her eyes petitioners to his eyes suing,
His eyes saw her eyes as they had not seen them;
Her eyes wooed still, his eyes disdained the wooing;
　　And all this dumb play had his acts made plain
　　With tears which, choruslike, her eyes did rain. 360

361. **Full:** very

366. **Showed:** looked; **a-billing:** caressing, making love

367. **the engine . . . thoughts:** i.e., her tongue

368. **mover:** person who moves; **this mortal round:** the Earth

369. **Would:** i.e., I wish

370. **my wound:** i.e., with **my wound;** or, perhaps, one large **wound,** as mine is

371. **For:** i.e., in return for

372. **bane:** death, destruction

375. **steel it:** make it hard as steel

376. **grave:** engrave

377. **regard:** pay attention to, take notice of

381. **bereft:** i.e., deprived

382. **hence:** i.e., go **hence,** go away

383. **care:** pains; trouble; concern

387. **Affection:** passion, lust

388. **Else:** otherwise; **suffered:** allowed (to burn)

Full gently now she takes him by the hand,
A lily prisoned in a jail of snow,
Or ivory in an alabaster band,
So white a friend engirts so white a foe.
   This beauteous combat, willful and unwilling,   365
   Showed like two silver doves that sit a-billing.

Once more the engine of her thoughts began:
"O, fairest mover on this mortal round,
Would thou wert as I am and I a man,
My heart all whole as thine, thy heart my wound!   370
   For one sweet look thy help I would assure thee,
   Though nothing but my body's bane would cure thee."

"Give me my hand," saith he. "Why dost thou feel it?"
"Give me my heart," saith she, "and thou shalt have it.
O, give it me, lest thy hard heart do steel it,   375
And being steeled, soft sighs can never grave it.
   Then love's deep groans I never shall regard
   Because Adonis' heart hath made mine hard."

"For shame," he cries, "let go, and let me go.
My day's delight is past, my horse is gone,   380
And 'tis your fault I am bereft him so.
I pray you hence, and leave me here alone,
   For all my mind, my thought, my busy care,
   Is how to get my palfrey from the mare."

Thus she replies: "Thy palfrey, as he should,   385
Welcomes the warm approach of sweet desire.
Affection is a coal that must be cooled;
Else, suffered, it will set the heart on fire.
   The sea hath bounds, but deep desire hath none;
   Therefore no marvel though thy horse be gone.   390

391. **jade:** worthless horse (See picture, p. 118.)
392. **leathern:** leather
393. **fee:** spoil, tribute, reward
400. **agents:** organs; **like:** similar
401. **faint:** cowardly, timid
404. **of him:** i.e., from him
405. **advantage on:** i.e., **advantage** of
406. **dumb:** silent, mute; **proceedings:** actions, behavior
408. **made perfect:** i.e., thoroughly learned
411. **owe it:** (1) acknowledge it as a debt; (2) own it
414. **with a breath:** i.e., in the same **breath**
417. **springing things:** i.e., **things** just beginning to grow; **jot:** bit
419. **backed:** broken in to the saddle
420. **pride:** mettle, spirit

"How like a jade he stood tied to the tree,
Servilely mastered with a leathern rein;
But when he saw his love, his youth's fair fee,
He held such petty bondage in disdain,
    Throwing the base thong from his bending crest,   395
    Enfranchising his mouth, his back, his breast.

"Who sees his truelove in her naked bed,
Teaching the sheets a whiter hue than white,
But when his glutton eye so full hath fed,
His other agents aim at like delight?   400
    Who is so faint that dares not be so bold
    To touch the fire, the weather being cold?

"Let me excuse thy courser, gentle boy,
And learn of him, I heartily beseech thee,
To take advantage on presented joy;   405
Though I were dumb, yet his proceedings teach thee.
    O, learn to love; the lesson is but plain
    And, once made perfect, never lost again."

"I know not love," quoth he, "nor will not know it,
Unless it be a boar, and then I chase it.   410
'Tis much to borrow, and I will not owe it.
My love to love is love but to disgrace it,
    For I have heard it is a life in death
    That laughs and weeps, and all but with a breath.

"Who wears a garment shapeless and unfinished?   415
Who plucks the bud before one leaf put forth?
If springing things be any jot diminished,
They wither in their prime, prove nothing worth.
    The colt that's backed and burdened being young
    Loseth his pride and never waxeth strong.   420

422. **idle:** silly, worthless; **bootless:** unprofitable

424. **alarms:** sudden or unexpected attacks; or, perhaps, signals for parley; **ope:** open

426. **batt'ry:** mark of beating, wound or bruise

428. **would:** i.e., I wish

429. **mermaid's:** i.e., seductive, alluring (See longer note, p. 443, and picture below.) **double wrong:** perhaps, the **wrong** of seducing through his enchanted voice while committing the **wrong** of speaking harsh words

430. **pressed with bearing:** i.e., **pressed** down with carrying the **load**

435. **outward parts:** i.e., body

436. **sensible:** capable of sensing

443. **stillatory:** alembic, still, apparatus for distillation

444. **by smelling:** i.e., by being smelled

446. **nurse:** i.e., wet **nurse,** source of nourishment; **four:** i.e., **four** senses

Mermaids as sirens.
(s. 119; *Venus and Adonis*, 429 and 777; *Lucrece*, 1411)

"You hurt my hand with wringing. Let us part,
And leave this idle theme, this bootless chat.
Remove your siege from my unyielding heart;
To love's alarms it will not ope the gate.
    Dismiss your vows, your feignèd tears, your flatt'ry,   425
    For where a heart is hard, they make no batt'ry."

"What, canst thou talk?" quoth she. "Hast thou a tongue?
O, would thou hadst not, or I had no hearing!
Thy mermaid's voice hath done me double wrong;
I had my load before, now pressed with bearing: 430
    Melodious discord, heavenly tune harsh sounding,
    Ears' deep sweet music, and heart's deep sore wounding.

"Had I no eyes but ears, my ears would love
That inward beauty and invisible.
Or were I deaf, thy outward parts would move   435
Each part in me that were but sensible.
    Though neither eyes, nor ears, to hear nor see,
    Yet should I be in love by touching thee.

"Say that the sense of feeling were bereft me,
And that I could not see, nor hear, nor touch,   440
And nothing but the very smell were left me,
Yet would my love to thee be still as much,
    For from the stillatory of thy face excelling
    Comes breath perfumed that breedeth love by smelling.

"But, O, what banquet wert thou to the taste,   445
Being nurse and feeder of the other four!
Would they not wish the feast might ever last,
And bid Suspicion double-lock the door,
    Lest Jealousy, that sour unwelcome guest,
    Should by his stealing in disturb the feast?"   450

453. **red morn:** Proverbial: "A **red** morning foretells a stormy day."

454. **Wrack:** shipwreck

456. **foul:** stormy; **flaws:** sudden bursts of wind

457. **ill presage:** i.e., threatening portent; **advisedly:** carefully, warily; **marketh:** takes note of

459. **grin:** show its teeth

461. **of:** out of, from

463. **flatly falleth down:** i.e., falls flat (*Flatly* could also mean "unhesitatingly" or "decisively.")

465. **recures:** heals

466. **bankrout:** bankrupt person (This line's "**by love**" is often changed to "by loss" in order to make the meaning clearer [i.e., that Venus is fortunate in profiting from her fainting fit] and to continue the wordplay on such economic terms as **bankrout** and **thriveth.**)

467. **silly:** foolish

468. **Claps:** slaps

469. **amazed:** terrified; bewildered; **brake:** broke

470. **did think:** i.e., had thought, had intended

471. **wittily:** cleverly

472. **Fair fall:** may good fortune befall; **wit:** quick intelligence, ingenuity; **her:** herself

473. **as:** as if

478. **To mend . . . marred:** a mixing of two expressions: (1) **to mend the hurt that his unkindness** caused; (2) **to mend** what was **marred** by **his unkindness**

479. **by her good will:** willingly

480. **so:** **so** long as; or, **so** that

Once more the ruby-colored portal opened,
Which to his speech did honey passage yield,
Like a red morn, that ever yet betokened
Wrack to the seaman, tempest to the field,
　　Sorrow to shepherds, woe unto the birds,   455
　　Gusts and foul flaws to herdmen and to herds.

This ill presage advisedly she marketh.
Even as the wind is hushed before it raineth,
Or as the wolf doth grin before he barketh,
Or as the berry breaks before it staineth,   460
　　Or like the deadly bullet of a gun,
　　His meaning struck her ere his words begun.

And at his look she flatly falleth down,
For looks kill love, and love by looks reviveth;
A smile recures the wounding of a frown.   465
But blessèd bankrout, that by love so thriveth!
　　The silly boy, believing she is dead,
　　Claps her pale cheek till clapping makes it red,

And, all amazed, brake off his late intent;
For sharply he did think to reprehend her,   470
Which cunning Love did wittily prevent.
Fair fall the wit that can so well defend her!
　　For on the grass she lies as she were slain,
　　Till his breath breatheth life in her again.

He wrings her nose, he strikes her on the cheeks,   475
He bends her fingers, holds her pulses hard,
He chafes her lips—a thousand ways he seeks
To mend the hurt that his unkindness marred.
　　He kisses her, and she, by her good will,
　　Will never rise, so he will kiss her still.   480

482. **windows:** eyes; or, possibly, eyelids; **upheaveth:** lifts up

490. **repine:** discontent

494. **drenched:** drowned

495. **Or . . . or:** i.e., either . . . or; **even:** evening

497. **death's annoy:** i.e., **life was** as distressing as death **annoy:** vexation, distress

498. **lively joy:** i.e., as joyful as life (because of Adonis's attentions) **lively:** possessed of life

500. **shrewd:** wicked, malicious

504. **piteous:** compassionate

505. **they:** i.e., **thy . . . lips** (l. 504); **for:** i.e., in recompense for

506. **wear:** i.e., **wear** out

507. **they:** the lips; **verdure:** freshness; fragrance, odor; **still:** always

508. **To . . . year:** Strong-smelling herbs were used as a preventive against disease.

509. **star-gazers:** astrologers (See picture below.) **writ on death:** i.e., published a prediction of **the plague** (l. 510)

Astrologers. (*Venus and Adonis,* 509)

The night of sorrow now is turned to day.
Her two blue windows faintly she upheaveth
Like the fair sun when in his fresh array
He cheers the morn and all the earth relieveth;
　　And as the bright sun glorifies the sky,　　485
　　So is her face illumined with her eye,

Whose beams upon his hairless face are fixed
As if from thence they borrowed all their shine.
Were never four such lamps together mixed,
Had not his clouded with his brow's repine.　　490
　　But hers, which through the crystal tears gave light,
　　Shone like the moon in water seen by night.

"O, where am I?" quoth she. "In earth or heaven,
Or in the ocean drenched, or in the fire?
What hour is this? Or morn or weary even?　　495
Do I delight to die or life desire?
　　But now I lived, and life was death's annoy;
　　But now I died, and death was lively joy.

"O, thou didst kill me; kill me once again.
Thy eyes' shrewd tutor, that hard heart of thine,　　500
Hath taught them scornful tricks and such disdain
That they have murdered this poor heart of mine,
　　And these mine eyes, true leaders to their queen,
　　But for thy piteous lips no more had seen.

"Long may they kiss each other for this cure!　　505
O, never let their crimson liveries wear,
And, as they last, their verdure still endure
To drive infection from the dangerous year,
　　That the star-gazers, having writ on death,
　　May say the plague is banished by thy breath!　　510

511. **seals:** impressions or designs, like those **imprinted** on wax affixed to documents, including financial documents (See longer note, p. 443.)

512. **still to be sealing:** i.e., in order to continue imprinting such impressions

514. **So:** provided that; **good:** i.e., fair

515. **slips:** mistakes that might render invalid a deed recording the **purchase** (with wordplay on **slips** as counterfeit coins)

516. **thy seal manual:** i.e., your personal **seal**

517. **buys:** i.e., buy

520. **told:** counted

521. **Say . . . double:** If a conditional bond became forfeit, the creditor could seek at law double the amount lent.

523. **owe:** bear

524. **strangeness:** coldness, aloofness

525. **to know me:** to have sexual intercourse with me

526. **No . . . forbears:** i.e., all fishermen spare the young fish

529. **Look the world's comforter:** i.e., see how the sun

"Sheep . . . gone to fold." (*Venus and Adonis*, 532)

"Pure lips, sweet seals in my soft lips imprinted,
What bargains may I make, still to be sealing?
To sell myself I can be well contented,
So thou wilt buy, and pay, and use good dealing;
   Which purchase if thou make, for fear of slips,   515
   Set thy seal manual on my wax-red lips.

"A thousand kisses buys my heart from me,
And pay them at thy leisure, one by one.
What is ten hundred touches unto thee?
Are they not quickly told and quickly gone?   520
   Say for non-payment that the debt should double,
   Is twenty hundred kisses such a trouble?"

"Fair queen," quoth he, "if any love you owe me,
Measure my strangeness with my unripe years.
Before I know myself, seek not to know me.   525
No fisher but the ungrown fry forbears.
   The mellow plum doth fall; the green sticks fast
   Or, being early plucked, is sour to taste.

"Look the world's comforter with weary gait
His day's hot task hath ended in the west.   530
The owl, night's herald, shrieks; 'tis very late.
The sheep are gone to fold, birds to their nest,
   And coal-black clouds that shadow heaven's light
   Do summon us to part and bid good night.

"Now let me say goodnight, and so say you.   535
If you will say so, you shall have a kiss."
"Good night," quoth she, and ere he says "Adieu,"
The honey fee of parting tendered is.
   Her arms do lend his neck a sweet embrace;
   Incorporate then they seem; face grows to face,   540

544. **on drouth:** of thirst

545. **pressed: pressed** down

547. **yielding prey:** The image of Adonis as **prey** and Venus ("**quick desire**") as a bird of prey dominates this and the following stanza. (See picture, p. 364.)

550. **insulter:** one who triumphs

551. **price:** i.e., **fee of parting** (l. 538)

553. **the spoil:** the prey; or, perhaps, the act of preying

554. **blindfold:** heedless, reckless; **forage:** glut herself

557. **Planting oblivion:** i.e., causing **oblivion** to take root and grow; setting up **oblivion** (as the ruler)

558. **wrack:** wreck

562. **froward:** unmanageable

564. **listeth:** desires

565. **temp'ring:** softening through heating

566. **impression:** See longer note to **seals** (l. 511), p. 443.

567. **compassed:** achieved; **vent'ring:** i.e., venturing, risking peril or loss

568. **whose leave:** i.e., the permission (love grants itself); **commission:** i.e., behavior prescribed (by the beloved)

570. **his choice:** i.e., the object of its **choice; froward:** perverse, hard to please

Till, breathless, he disjoined and backward drew
The heavenly moisture, that sweet coral mouth,
Whose precious taste her thirsty lips well knew,
Whereon they surfeit, yet complain on drouth.
  He with her plenty pressed, she faint with dearth, 545
  Their lips together glued, fall to the earth.

Now quick desire hath caught the yielding prey,
And gluttonlike she feeds yet never filleth.
Her lips are conquerors, his lips obey,
Paying what ransom the insulter willeth, 550
  Whose vulture thought doth pitch the price so high
  That she will draw his lips' rich treasure dry.

And having felt the sweetness of the spoil,
With blindfold fury she begins to forage.
Her face doth reek and smoke, her blood doth boil, 555
And careless lust stirs up a desperate courage,
  Planting oblivion, beating reason back,
  Forgetting shame's pure blush and honor's wrack.

Hot, faint, and weary with her hard embracing,
Like a wild bird being tamed with too much handling, 560
Or as the fleet-foot roe that's tired with chasing,
Or like the froward infant stilled with dandling,
  He now obeys and now no more resisteth,
  While she takes all she can, not all she listeth.

What wax so frozen but dissolves with temp'ring 565
And yields at last to every light impression?
Things out of hope are compassed oft with vent'ring,
Chiefly in love, whose leave exceeds commission.
  Affection faints not like a pale-faced coward
  But then woos best when most his choice is froward. 570

571. **gave over:** i.e., given over, desisted

578. **fool:** term of endearment and pity; **prays:** petitions, begs

580. **and look well to:** i.e., and **bids him** take good care of

581. **Cupid's bow:** See picture, p. 378.

583. **waste:** spend

584. **watch:** stay awake

586. **match:** agreement, bargain (The phrase **make the match** usually referred to arranging a marriage.)

589. **pale:** paleness, pallor

590. **lawn:** fine, almost transparent, cloth

595. **lists:** enclosures in which combats are fought

597. **All . . . prove:** i.e., **all she** experiences **is** only **imaginary**

598. **manage her:** put her through her paces (a term from horse training)

599. **That:** i.e., so that; **Tantalus':** In mythology, **Tantalus'** torment was hunger and thirst while he was surrounded by water and fruit he could never touch. (See picture below.) **annoy:** i.e., pain

600. **clip:** embrace; **Elysium:** in mythology, the place of the blessed after death

Tantalus. (*Venus and Adonis*, 599; *Lucrece*, 858)

When he did frown, O, had she then gave over,
Such nectar from his lips she had not sucked.
Foul words and frowns must not repel a lover.
What though the rose have prickles, yet 'tis plucked.
　　Were beauty under twenty locks kept fast,　　　　575
　　Yet love breaks through and picks them all at last.

For pity now she can no more detain him.
The poor fool prays her that he may depart.
She is resolved no longer to restrain him,
Bids him farewell, and look well to her heart,　　　580
　　The which, by Cupid's bow she doth protest,
　　He carries thence encagèd in his breast.

"Sweet boy," she says, "this night I'll waste in sorrow,
For my sick heart commands mine eyes to watch.
Tell me, Love's master, shall we meet tomorrow?　　585
Say, shall we, shall we? Wilt thou make the match?"
　　He tells her no, tomorrow he intends
　　To hunt the boar with certain of his friends.

"The boar!" quoth she, whereat a sudden pale,
Like lawn being spread upon the blushing rose,　　590
Usurps her cheek. She trembles at his tale,
And on his neck her yoking arms she throws.
　　She sinketh down, still hanging by his neck;
　　He on her belly falls, she on her back.

Now is she in the very lists of love,　　　　　　595
Her champion mounted for the hot encounter.
All is imaginary she doth prove;
He will not manage her, although he mount her,
　　That worse than Tantalus' is her annoy,
　　To clip Elysium and to lack her joy.　　　　　600

601–4. **Even . . . saw:** Venus is here compared to the **birds** tricked by Zeuxis's **painted grapes.** (See longer note, p. 443.) **pine:** starve **maw:** stomach **helpless:** providing no help

605. **warm effects:** i.e., signs of warmth, sexual response

608. **assayed . . . proved:** i.e., tried everything that could be tried

609. **fee:** reward

612. **withhold me:** keep me in bondage

615. **be advised:** be careful; be warned; consider

616. **churlish:** violent

617. **tushes:** tusks; **still:** continually

618. **mortal:** deadly

619. **bow-back:** i.e., arched **back; battle:** an army drawn up in formation

621. **fret:** become vexed

622. **sepulchers:** i.e., graves

623. **moved:** provoked

626. **proof:** i.e., proof armor, impenetrable armor

628. **venter:** i.e., venture

630. **whom:** which

Even so poor birds, deceived with painted grapes,
Do surfeit by the eye, and pine the maw;
Even so she languisheth in her mishaps
As those poor birds that helpless berries saw.
    The warm effects which she in him finds missing   605
    She seeks to kindle with continual kissing.

But all in vain; good queen, it will not be.
She hath assayed as much as may be proved.
Her pleading hath deserved a greater fee.
She's Love, she loves, and yet she is not loved.   610
    "Fie, fie," he says, "you crush me. Let me go.
    You have no reason to withhold me so."

"Thou hadst been gone," quoth she, "sweet boy, ere this,
But that thou toldst me thou wouldst hunt the boar.
O, be advised! Thou know'st not what it is   615
With javelin's point a churlish swine to gore,
    Whose tushes, never sheathed, he whetteth still
    Like to a mortal butcher bent to kill.

"On his bow-back he hath a battle set
Of bristly pikes that ever threat his foes.   620
His eyes like glowworms shine when he doth fret.
His snout digs sepulchers where'er he goes.
    Being moved, he strikes whate'er is in his way,
    And whom he strikes his crookèd tushes slay.

"His brawny sides, with hairy bristles armed,   625
Are better proof than thy spear's point can enter.
His short thick neck cannot be easily harmed.
Being ireful, on the lion he will venter.
    The thorny brambles and embracing bushes,
    As fearful of him, part, through whom he rushes.   630

631. **naught:** i.e., as nothing

632. **pays:** i.e., pay; **tributary gazes:** i.e., **gazes** offered as tribute

633. **eyne:** eyes

634. **amazes:** infatuates

635. **thee at vantage:** the advantage over you

636. **mead:** meadow

637. **keep:** remain in; **cabin:** den; **still:** always

639. **danger:** power

642. **feared: feared** for

643. **mark:** observe

645. **downright:** straight down

647. **boding:** foreboding

649. **Jealousy:** anxiety, fear of loss, vigilance in guarding against damage

651. **suggesteth:** prompts

652. **Kill, kill:** the word given an English army for a general assault on the enemy

653. **Distemp'ring:** vexing, upsetting; or, perhaps, weakening, quenching; **his:** i.e., its

655. **bate-breeding:** strife-causing

656. **canker:** cankerworm (See picture, p. 90.) **spring:** shoot, sprout

657. **carry-tale:** talebearer, tattletale

"Alas, he naught esteems that face of thine,
To which Love's eyes pays tributary gazes,
Nor thy soft hands, sweet lips, and crystal eyne,
Whose full perfection all the world amazes;
    But having thee at vantage—wondrous dread!—   635
    Would root these beauties as he roots the mead.

"O, let him keep his loathsome cabin still!
Beauty hath naught to do with such foul fiends.
Come not within his danger by thy will.
They that thrive well take counsel of their friends.   640
    When thou didst name the boar, not to dissemble,
    I feared thy fortune, and my joints did tremble.

"Didst thou not mark my face? Was it not white?
Sawest thou not signs of fear lurk in mine eye?
Grew I not faint, and fell I not downright?   645
Within my bosom, whereon thou dost lie,
    My boding heart pants, beats, and takes no rest,
    But, like an earthquake, shakes thee on my breast.

"For where Love reigns, disturbing Jealousy
Doth call himself Affection's sentinel,   650
Gives false alarms, suggesteth mutiny,
And in a peaceful hour doth cry 'Kill, kill!'
    Distemp'ring gentle Love in his desire
    As air and water do abate the fire.

"This sour informer, this bate-breeding spy,   655
This canker that eats up Love's tender spring,
This carry-tale, dissentious Jealousy,
That sometimes true news, sometimes false doth bring,
    Knocks at my heart and whispers in mine ear
    That if I love thee, I thy death should fear;   660

662. **chafing:** raging

673. **needs wilt:** i.e., must; **ruled:** guided

674. **Uncouple:** set loose your dogs

678. **well-breathed:** strong of wind

679. **on foot:** in motion, stirring

680. **Mark:** observe; **overshoot:** run beyond

682. **cranks:** zigzags; **doubles:** sharp turns

683. **musets:** hiding places; gaps in fences or thickets (See longer note, p. 443.)

684. **amaze:** bewilder

686. **cunning:** sly, crafty; **smell:** scent

687. **earth-delving conies:** rabbits that make burrows (See picture below.) **keep:** dwell

688. **yell:** loud outcry

689. **sorteth with:** consorts with, accompanies

690. **shifts:** evasive strategies; **waits on:** serves, is a servant of

OF THE CONY.

Cony. (*Venus and Adonis*, 687)

"And more than so, presenteth to mine eye
The picture of an angry chafing boar,
Under whose sharp fangs on his back doth lie
An image like thyself, all stained with gore,
    Whose blood upon the fresh flowers being shed   665
    Doth make them droop with grief and hang the head.

"What should I do, seeing thee so indeed,
That tremble at th' imagination?
The thought of it doth make my faint heart bleed,
And fear doth teach it divination.   670
    I prophesy thy death, my living sorrow,
    If thou encounter with the boar tomorrow.

"But if thou needs wilt hunt, be ruled by me.
Uncouple at the timorous flying hare,
Or at the fox, which lives by subtlety,   675
Or at the roe, which no encounter dare.
    Pursue these fearful creatures o'er the downs,
    And on thy well-breathed horse keep with thy hounds,

"And when thou hast on foot the purblind hare,
Mark the poor wretch, to overshoot his troubles   680
How he outruns the wind and with what care
He cranks and crosses with a thousand doubles.
    The many musets through the which he goes
    Are like a labyrinth to amaze his foes.

"Sometimes he runs among a flock of sheep   685
To make the cunning hounds mistake their smell,
And sometimes where earth-delving conies keep
To stop the loud pursuers in their yell,
    And sometimes sorteth with a herd of deer.
    Danger deviseth shifts; wit waits on fear.   690

692. **doubt:** undecidedness

693–94. **singled . . . out:** entirely distinguished, with much difficulty, the **cold** or lost scent

695. **spend their mouths:** give cry, bay

696. **chase:** hunt

697. **By this:** i.e., by **this** time; **Wat:** a familiar term for a hare (See picture below.)

700. **Anon:** soon; **alarums:** cries (literally, calls to arms)

702. **sore:** grievously; **passing bell: bell** tolling as someone dies

703. **dew-bedabbled:** wet with dew

704. **indenting:** zigzagging

705. **envious:** malicious

715. **leave: leave** off

718. **expected of:** i.e., **expected** by

Of the Hare.

A hare. (*Venus and Adonis,* 679)

"For there his smell with others being mingled,
The hot scent-snuffing hounds are driven to doubt,
Ceasing their clamorous cry till they have singled
With much ado the cold fault cleanly out.
    Then do they spend their mouths; echo replies   695
    As if another chase were in the skies.

"By this, poor Wat, far off upon a hill,
Stands on his hinder legs with list'ning ear
To hearken if his foes pursue him still.
Anon their loud alarums he doth hear,   700
    And now his grief may be comparèd well
    To one sore sick that hears the passing bell.

"Then shalt thou see the dew-bedabbled wretch
Turn and return, indenting with the way.
Each envious brier his weary legs do scratch;   705
Each shadow makes him stop, each murmur stay,
    For misery is trodden on by many
    And, being low, never relieved by any.

"Lie quietly, and hear a little more.
Nay, do not struggle, for thou shalt not rise.   710
To make thee hate the hunting of the boar,
Unlike myself thou hear'st me moralize,
    Applying this to that, and so to so,
    For love can comment upon every woe.

"Where did I leave?" "No matter where," quoth he;   715
"Leave me, and then the story aptly ends.
The night is spent." "Why, what of that?" quoth she.
"I am," quoth he, "expected of my friends,
    And now 'tis dark, and going I shall fall."
    "In night," quoth she, "desire sees best of all.   720

722. **footing:** step

724. **true:** honest

725. **Dian:** Diana, goddess of chastity and of the moon (See picture below.) **cloudy:** (1) obscured by clouds; (2) gloomy

726. **forsworn:** i.e., having, through the **kiss,** broken her vow of chastity

727. **Now . . . reason:** i.e., **I now** know why this **night** is **dark**

728. **Cynthia:** i.e., the moon (**Cynthia** is another name for Diana.)

729. **forging:** counterfeiting

732. **her:** i.e., **Cynthia**

733. **Destinies:** Fates, the three goddesses who determine the course of human life (See picture, p. 414.)

734. **cross:** thwart; **curious:** expert

736. **defeature:** disfigurement

739. **pale and faint:** i.e., that make one **pale and faint**

740. **wood:** mad

741. **attaint:** infection

743. **Surfeits:** morbid conditions caused by excessive eating or drinking; **impostumes:** abscesses

747. **favor:** appearance; face; **savor:** tastiness

749. **done:** worn out

Diana. (ss. 107, 153; *Venus and Adonis,* 725)

"But if thou fall, O, then imagine this:
The earth, in love with thee, thy footing trips,
And all is but to rob thee of a kiss.
Rich preys make true men thieves; so do thy lips
   Make modest Dian cloudy and forlorn,   725
   Lest she should steal a kiss and die forsworn.

"Now of this dark night I perceive the reason:
Cynthia for shame obscures her silver shine
Till forging Nature be condemned of treason
For stealing moulds from heaven that were divine,   730
   Wherein she framed thee, in high heaven's despite,
   To shame the sun by day and her by night.

"And therefore hath she bribed the Destinies
To cross the curious workmanship of Nature,
To mingle beauty with infirmities,   735
And pure perfection with impure defeature,
   Making it subject to the tyranny
   Of mad mischances and much misery,

"As burning fevers, agues pale and faint,
Life-poisoning pestilence and frenzies wood,   740
The marrow-eating sickness, whose attaint
Disorder breeds by heating of the blood;
   Surfeits, impostumes, grief, and damned despair
   Swear Nature's death for framing thee so fair.

"And not the least of all these maladies   745
But in one minute's fight brings beauty under.
Both favor, savor, hew, and qualities,
Whereat th' impartial gazer late did wonder,
   Are on the sudden wasted, thawed, and done,
   As mountain snow melts with the midday sun.   750

751. **despite of:** i.e., in scorn of

752. **vestals:** i.e., vestal virgins (See longer note, p. 444, and picture below.)

756. **his:** i.e., its

759. **needs:** necessarily

762. **Sith:** since

763. **made away:** destroyed

764. **mischief:** evil

766. **reaves:** robs

767. **frets:** wears away

769. **you will:** you are determined to

773. **nurse:** nourisher

774. **treatise:** discussion

776. **moving:** persuasive

777. **mermaids' songs:** See longer note to l. 429, p. 443, and picture, p. 390.

A vestal virgin. (*Venus and Adonis*, 752; *Lucrece*, 883)

"Therefore, despite of fruitless chastity,
Love-lacking vestals and self-loving nuns,
That on the earth would breed a scarcity
And barren dearth of daughters and of sons,
    Be prodigal. The lamp that burns by night   755
    Dries up his oil to lend the world his light.

"What is thy body but a swallowing grave
Seeming to bury that posterity
Which by the rights of time thou needs must have
If thou destroy them not in dark obscurity?   760
    If so, the world will hold thee in disdain
    Sith in thy pride so fair a hope is slain.

"So in thyself thyself art made away,
A mischief worse than civil homebred strife,
Or theirs whose desperate hands themselves do slay,   765
Or butcher sire that reaves his son of life.
    Foul cank'ring rust the hidden treasure frets,
    But gold that's put to use more gold begets."

"Nay, then," quoth Adon, "you will fall again
Into your idle over-handled theme.   770
The kiss I gave you is bestowed in vain,
And all in vain you strive against the stream,
    For, by this black-faced night, desire's foul nurse,
    Your treatise makes me like you worse and worse.

"If love have lent you twenty thousand tongues,   775
And every tongue more moving than your own,
Bewitching like the wanton mermaids' songs,
Yet from mine ear the tempting tune is blown;
    For know my heart stands armèd in mine ear
    And will not let a false sound enter there,   780

782. **closure:** enclosure

783. **undone:** destroyed

784. **his:** its

787. **reprove:** disprove

789. **device:** i.e., advice, counsel

791. **do it for increase:** i.e., counsel (me) in terms of procreation

793. **Love:** In this stanza, **Love** is apparently Cupid, not Venus.

795. **simple:** innocent, plain; **he:** i.e., Lust

797. **hot tyrant:** i.e., Lust (The word **hot** itself means lustful.) **bereaves:** plunders, despoils

806. **text:** theme; **green:** young, inexperienced

807. **in sadness:** seriously

808. **teen:** grief, rage

809. **attended:** listened

The Destinies. (*Venus and Adonis*, 733, 945)

"Lest the deceiving harmony should run
Into the quiet closure of my breast,
And then my little heart were quite undone,
In his bed-chamber to be barred of rest.
　　No, lady, no, my heart longs not to groan　　785
　　But soundly sleeps while now it sleeps alone.

"What have you urged that I cannot reprove?
The path is smooth that leadeth on to danger.
I hate not love, but your device in love,
That lends embracements unto every stranger.　　790
　　You do it for increase. O strange excuse,
　　When reason is the bawd to lust's abuse!

"Call it not love, for Love to heaven is fled
Since sweating Lust on earth usurped his name,
Under whose simple semblance he hath fed　　795
Upon fresh beauty, blotting it with blame,
　　Which the hot tyrant stains and soon bereaves,
　　As caterpillars do the tender leaves.

"Love comforteth like sunshine after rain,
But Lust's effect is tempest after sun.　　800
Love's gentle spring doth always fresh remain;
Lust's winter comes ere summer half be done.
　　Love surfeits not, Lust like a glutton dies.
　　Love is all truth, Lust full of forgèd lies.

"More I could tell, but more I dare not say;　　805
The text is old, the orator too green.
Therefore in sadness now I will away.
My face is full of shame, my heart of teen.
　　Mine ears, that to your wanton talk attended,
　　Do burn themselves for having so offended."　　810

813. **laund:** pasture

815. **Look how:** i.e., in the same way that

820. **Whose:** i.e., **the wild waves** (l. 819)

823. **Whereat:** at which; **amazed:** bewildered

824. **flood:** flowing water, rising tide

825. **stonished:** stunned

826. **mistrustful:** causing mistrust or suspicion

827. **confounded:** thrown into mental confusion

828. **discovery:** revelation (**Fair discovery** seems to refer to Adonis.)

832. **Passion:** violent sorrow

835. **marking:** noticing

837. **thrall:** slavelike

838. **foolish witty:** i.e., foolishly wise

839. **heavy:** sorrowful; **anthem:** song; **still:** continually

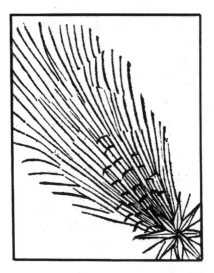

A shooting star. (*Venus and Adonis,* 815; *Lucrece,* 1525)

With this he breaketh from the sweet embrace
Of those fair arms which bound him to her breast
And homeward through the dark laund runs apace,
Leaves Love upon her back deeply distressed.
    Look how a bright star shooteth from the sky,   815
    So glides he in the night from Venus' eye,

Which after him she darts, as one on shore
Gazing upon a late-embarkèd friend
Till the wild waves will have him seen no more,
Whose ridges with the meeting clouds contend;   820
    So did the merciless and pitchy night
    Fold in the object that did feed her sight;

Whereat amazed, as one that unaware
Hath dropped a precious jewel in the flood,
Or stonished, as night wand'rers often are,   825
Their light blown out in some mistrustful wood,
    Even so confounded in the dark she lay,
    Having lost the fair discovery of her way.

And now she beats her heart, whereat it groans,
That all the neighbor caves, as seeming troubled,   830
Make verbal repetition of her moans.
Passion on passion deeply is redoubled.
    "Ay me!" she cries, and twenty times, "Woe, woe!"
    And twenty echoes twenty times cry so.

She marking them begins a wailing note   835
And sings extemporally a woeful ditty
How love makes young men thrall and old men dote,
How love is wise in folly, foolish witty.
    Her heavy anthem still concludes in woe,
    And still the choir of echoes answer so.   840

841. **outwore:** outlasted

844. **sport:** diversion, recreation; amorous play

847. **withal:** with

848. **idle:** meaningless; **parasits:** parasites, flatterers

849. **tapsters:** tavern keepers

850. **humor:** mood, temper; **fantastic wits:** capricious, odd people

854. **cabinet:** dwelling, i.e., nest (presumably **moist** with dew)

859. **morrow:** morning

860. **clear:** brightly shining

861. **lamp:** heavenly body

862. **influence:** influx (See longer note, p. 444.)

863. **son:** wordplay on **sun/son; sucked . . . mother:** a variation on traditional mythology about Adonis (See longer note, p. 444.)

866. **Musing:** marveling that; **o'erworn:** spent

868. **horn:** hunting **horn** (See picture below.)

869. **chant it:** i.e., make music (The baying of hounds was described as musical.)

870. **coasteth:** makes her way; **cry:** baying of the hounds

A hunting horn. (*Venus and Adonis*, 868)

Her song was tedious and outwore the night,
For lovers' hours are long, though seeming short.
If pleased themselves, others they think delight
In suchlike circumstance with suchlike sport.
   Their copious stories, oftentimes begun,   845
   End without audience and are never done.

For who hath she to spend the night withal
But idle sounds resembling parasites,
Like shrill-tongued tapsters answering every call,
Soothing the humor of fantastic wits?   850
   She says, "'Tis so," they answer all, "'Tis so,"
   And would say after her if she said "No."

Lo, here the gentle lark, weary of rest,
From his moist cabinet mounts up on high
And wakes the morning, from whose silver breast   855
The sun ariseth in his majesty,
   Who doth the world so gloriously behold
   That cedar tops and hills seem burnished gold.

Venus salutes him with this fair good morrow:
"O thou clear god and patron of all light,   860
From whom each lamp and shining star doth borrow
The beauteous influence that makes him bright,
   There lives a son that sucked an earthly mother
   May lend thee light, as thou dost lend to other."

This said, she hasteth to a myrtle grove,   865
Musing the morning is so much o'erworn,
And yet she hears no tidings of her love;
She hearkens for his hounds and for his horn.
   Anon she hears them chant it lustily,
   And all in haste she coasteth to the cry.   870

874. **strict:** tight

875. **milch doe:** lactating **doe**

877. **By this:** i.e., **by this** time; **at a bay:** i.e., being faced by the hunted animal that, unable to flee farther, has turned to defend itself

883. **chase:** hunted animal

884. **blunt:** harsh, unsparing

887. **curst:** savage

888. **They . . . first:** i.e., each urges the others to precede him in attacking **their enemy** (l. 887)   **cope:** i.e., fight with

890. **surprise:** overpower

891. **Who:** i.e., which

894. **stay the field:** sustain the battle

895. **ecstasy:** frenzy

897. **fantasy:** figment of imagination

A lurking adder. (*Venus and Adonis*, 878; *Lucrece*, 871)

And as she runs, the bushes in the way
Some catch her by the neck, some kiss her face,
Some twined about her thigh to make her stay.
She wildly breaketh from their strict embrace,
    Like a milch doe whose swelling dugs do ache,   875
    Hasting to feed her fawn hid in some brake.

By this she hears the hounds are at a bay,
Whereat she starts like one that spies an adder
Wreathed up in fatal folds just in his way,
The fear whereof doth make him shake and shudder;   880
    Even so the timorous yelping of the hounds
    Appalls her senses and her spirit confounds.

For now she knows it is no gentle chase,
But the blunt boar, rough bear, or lion proud,
Because the cry remaineth in one place,   885
Where fearfully the dogs exclaim aloud.
    Finding their enemy to be so curst,
    They all strain court'sy who shall cope him first.

This dismal cry rings sadly in her ear,
Through which it enters to surprise her heart,   890
Who, overcome by doubt and bloodless fear,
With cold-pale weakness numbs each feeling part.
    Like soldiers when their captain once doth yield,
    They basely fly and dare not stay the field.

Thus stands she in a trembling ecstasy,   895
Till, cheering up her senses all dismayed,
She tells them 'tis a causeless fantasy
And childish error that they are afraid,
    Bids them leave quaking, bids them fear no more—
    And with that word she spied the hunted boar,   900

903. **sinews:** nerves; **spread:** i.e., spreads

906. **rate:** vehemently reprove

907. **spleens:** impulses, caprices

908. **untreads:** retraces

909. **mated with:** (1) checked or frustrated by; (2) associated or coupled with

911. **respects:** considerations; **naught:** nothing; **respecting:** considering

912. **In hand with:** occupied with

914. **caitiff:** poor wretch

916. **sovereign:** superlatively powerful; **plaster:** medicine

919. **ill-resounding:** harshly or unpleasantly **resounding**

920. **flapmouthed mourner:** i.e., **mourner** with broad hanging lips

921. **welkin:** sky; **volleys out his voice:** i.e., barks rapidly and impetuously

925. **Look how:** i.e., just as; **amazed:** bewildered

928. **Infusing them:** perhaps, filling the **apparitions, signs, and prodigies;** perhaps, filling themselves

930. **exclaims on:** cries out against; apostrophizes, addresses

A hound. (*Venus and Adonis,* 913)

Whose frothy mouth bepainted all with red,
Like milk and blood being mingled both together,
A second fear through all her sinews spread,
Which madly hurries her she knows not whither;
    This way she runs, and now she will no further   905
    But back retires to rate the boar for murder.

A thousand spleens bear her a thousand ways;
She treads the path that she untreads again;
Her more than haste is mated with delays,
Like the proceedings of a drunken brain,   910
    Full of respects, yet naught at all respecting,
    In hand with all things, naught at all effecting.

Here kenneled in a brake she finds a hound
And asks the weary caitiff for his master,
And there another licking of his wound,   915
'Gainst venomed sores the only sovereign plaster,
    And here she meets another, sadly scowling,
    To whom she speaks, and he replies with howling.

When he hath ceased his ill-resounding noise,
Another flapmouthed mourner, black and grim,   920
Against the welkin volleys out his voice;
Another and another answer him,
    Clapping their proud tails to the ground below,
    Shaking their scratched ears, bleeding as they go.

Look how the world's poor people are amazed   925
At apparitions, signs, and prodigies,
Whereon with fearful eyes they long have gazed,
Infusing them with dreadful prophecies;
    So she at these sad signs draws up her breath
    And, sighing it again, exclaims on Death.   930

931. **Hard-favored:** ugly

939. **no eyes: Death** is often pictured as an eyeless skull. (See picture below.)

941. **mark:** target; **false:** treacherous

944. **his:** i.e., its

945. **Destinies:** See note to l. 733, and picture, p. 414.

947–48. **Love's . . . dead:** possibly an allusion to a fable in which Love (Cupid) and Death stay at the same inn overnight and in the morning go off with each other's arrows   **ebon:** black; or, made of ebony

950. **heavy:** woeful, sorrowful; **advantage:** profit

953. **mortal vigor:** deadly strength

956. **vailed:** lowered; **who:** i.e., which

960. **his:** i.e., its

A skull. (*Venus and Adonis,* 939)

"Hard-favored tyrant, ugly, meager, lean,
Hateful divorce of love!"—thus chides she Death—
"Grim-grinning ghost, earth's worm, what dost thou mean
To stifle beauty and to steal his breath,
    Who, when he lived, his breath and beauty set   935
    Gloss on the rose, smell to the violet?

"If he be dead—O no, it cannot be,
Seeing his beauty, thou shouldst strike at it!
O yes, it may; thou hast no eyes to see,
But hatefully at random dost thou hit.   940
    Thy mark is feeble age, but thy false dart
    Mistakes that aim and cleaves an infant's heart.

"Hadst thou but bid beware, then he had spoke,
And hearing him, thy power had lost his power.
The Destinies will curse thee for this stroke;   945
They bid thee crop a weed, thou pluck'st a flower.
    Love's golden arrow at him should have fled,
    And not Death's ebon dart to strike him dead.

"Dost thou drink tears, that thou provok'st such weeping?
What may a heavy groan advantage thee?   950
Why hast thou cast into eternal sleeping
Those eyes that taught all other eyes to see?
    Now Nature cares not for thy mortal vigor
    Since her best work is ruined with thy rigor."

Here overcome as one full of despair,   955
She vailed her eyelids, who, like sluices, stopped
The crystal tide that from her two cheeks fair
In the sweet channel of her bosom dropped;
    But through the flood-gates breaks the silver rain,
    And with his strong course opens them again.   960

964. **still:** continually
968. **who:** i.e., which; **become:** suit
969. **entertained:** received
972. **consulting for:** deliberating about
973. **By this:** i.e., **by this** time; **hallow:** shout (to urge the dogs to hunt)
974. **nurse's:** wet **nurse's**
975. **imagination:** i.e., action of imagining; **follow:** pursue
979. **turn their tide:** i.e., ebb
984. **Who:** i.e., which; **she:** i.e., Venus
985. **hard-believing:** i.e., skeptical
987. **weal:** happiness
988. **Despair and hope:** i.e., the alternation of **despair and hope**

Death, the "hard-favored tyrant." (*Venus and Adonis*, 931)

O, how her eyes and tears did lend and borrow!
Her eye seen in the tears, tears in her eye,
Both crystals, where they viewed each other's sorrow,
Sorrow that friendly sighs sought still to dry;
    But, like a stormy day, now wind, now rain,   965
    Sighs dry her cheeks, tears make them wet again.

Variable passions throng her constant woe
As striving who should best become her grief;
All entertained, each passion labors so
That every present sorrow seemeth chief,   970
    But none is best; then join they all together
    Like many clouds consulting for foul weather.

By this, far off she hears some huntsman hallow;
A nurse's song ne'er pleased her babe so well.
The dire imagination she did follow   975
This sound of hope doth labor to expel,
    For now reviving joy bids her rejoice
    And flatters her it is Adonis' voice,

Whereat her tears began to turn their tide,
Being prisoned in her eye like pearls in glass,   980
Yet sometimes falls an orient drop beside,
Which her cheek melts as scorning it should pass
    To wash the foul face of the sluttish ground,
    Who is but drunken when she seemeth drowned.

O hard-believing Love, how strange it seems   985
Not to believe and yet too credulous!
Thy weal and woe are both of them extremes.
Despair and hope makes thee ridiculous:
    The one doth flatter thee in thoughts unlikely;
    In likely thoughts the other kills thee quickly.   990

991. **web:** literally, fabric; **wrought:** woven
992. **to blame:** blameworthy
993. **called him all to naught:** abused Death vehemently
995. **clepes:** names
996. **Imperious:** majestic; **supreme:** ruler
999. **Whenas:** when
1000. **still:** always; **severe:** unsparing
1001. **shadow:** specter
1004. **wreaked:** avenged
1006. **act:** as an actor, deliver lines written by another; **author:** i.e., dramatist; originator
1008. **rule them:** an allusion to the commonplace that women cannot control their **tongues** (where the word means speech, flow of words); **wit:** intelligence
1010. **rash:** hasty, ill-considered; **suspect:** suspicion; **extenuate:** disparage, make light of
1012. **insinuate:** ingratiate herself
1015. **Jove:** a poetic name for Jupiter, the king of the Roman gods (See picture, p. 492.)
1016. **silly:** foolish
1018. **mutual:** i.e., general; **mortal kind:** i.e., humankind; or, perhaps, all living things

Now she unweaves the web that she hath wrought;
Adonis lives, and Death is not to blame;
It was not she that called him all to naught;
Now she adds honors to his hateful name.
   She clepes him king of graves and grave for kings,   995
   Imperious supreme of all mortal things.

"No, no," quoth she, "sweet Death, I did but jest.
Yet pardon me, I felt a kind of fear
Whenas I met the boar, that bloody beast,
Which knows no pity but is still severe.   1000
   Then, gentle shadow—truth I must confess—
   I railed on thee, fearing my love's decease.

"'Tis not my fault; the boar provoked my tongue.
Be wreaked on him, invisible commander.
'Tis he, foul creature, that hath done thee wrong;   1005
I did but act, he's author of thy slander.
   Grief hath two tongues, and never woman yet
   Could rule them both without ten women's wit."

Thus hoping that Adonis is alive,
Her rash suspect she doth extenuate,   1010
And that his beauty may the better thrive,
With Death she humbly doth insinuate,
   Tells him of trophies, statues, tombs, and stories,
   His victories, his triumphs, and his glories.

"O Jove," quoth she, "how much a fool was I   1015
To be of such a weak and silly mind
To wail his death who lives and must not die
Till mutual overthrow of mortal kind!
   For, he being dead, with him is beauty slain,
   And, beauty dead, black chaos comes again.   1020

1021. **fond:** foolish

1022. **hemmed:** i.e., **hemmed** in

1024. **bethinking:** thinking; **grieves:** i.e., grieve, oppress

1026. **but late:** i.e., only lately, only a moment ago

1029. **unfortunately:** unhappily

1031. **as:** i.e., **as** if

1032. **ashamed of:** i.e., shamed by

1033. **tender:** sensitive

1037. **his bloody view:** i.e., the sight of Adonis's **bloody** body

1038. **cabins:** cells, i.e., eye sockets

1039. **office:** function; **light:** an allusion to the belief that **light** was emitted from the eyes in the act of seeing

1042. **looks:** i.e., looking, seeing

1043. **Who:** i.e., which; **perplexèd:** bewildered, troubled

1044. **their suggestion:** i.e., the eyes' prompting

1045. **tributary subject:** i.e., a **subject** who pays tribute to the **king**

1046–47. **As when . . . shakes:** Earthquakes were believed to be produced by wind trapped in the earth.

1049. **mutiny:** contention, discord; **surprise:** overcome by sudden attack

A snail. (*Venus and Adonis,* 1033)

"Fie, fie, fond Love, thou art as full of fear
As one with treasure laden, hemmed with thieves;
Trifles unwitnessèd with eye or ear
Thy coward heart with false bethinking grieves."
    Even at this word she hears a merry horn,   1025
    Whereat she leaps, that was but late forlorn.

As falcons to the lure, away she flies—
The grass stoops not, she treads on it so light—
And in her haste unfortunately spies
The foul boar's conquest on her fair delight,   1030
    Which seen, her eyes, ⌐as¬ murdered with the view,
    Like stars ashamed of day, themselves withdrew;

Or as the snail, whose tender horns being hit,
Shrinks backward in his shelly cave with pain
And there, all smothered up, in shade doth sit,   1035
Long after fearing to creep forth again;
    So at his bloody view her eyes are fled
    Into the deep-dark cabins of her head,

Where they resign their office and their light
To the disposing of her troubled brain,   1040
Who bids them still consort with ugly night
And never wound the heart with looks again—
    Who, like a king perplexèd in his throne,
    By their suggestion gives a deadly groan,

Whereat each tributary subject quakes,   1045
As when the wind imprisoned in the ground,
Struggling for passage, earth's foundation shakes,
Which with cold terror doth men's minds confound.
    This mutiny each part doth so surprise
    That from their dark beds once more leap her eyes   1050

1057. **solemn:** gloomy
1059. **passions:** sorrows; **doteth:** goes out of her wits
1061. **stopped:** blocked, choked
1062. **till now:** i.e., before this moment (of true horror)
1064. **dazzling:** blurring
1067. **several:** individual
1078. **long since:** i.e., from the past
1079. **trim:** beautiful

"The foul boar's conquest." (*Venus and Adonis*, 1030)

And, being opened, threw unwilling light
Upon the wide wound that the boar had trenched
In his soft flank, whose wonted lily white
With purple tears, that his wound wept, had drenched.
    No flower was nigh, no grass, herb, leaf, or weed,   1055
    But stole his blood and seemed with him to bleed.

This solemn sympathy poor Venus noteth.
Over one shoulder doth she hang her head.
Dumbly she passions, frantically she doteth.
She thinks he could not die, he is not dead.   1060
    Her voice is stopped, her joints forget to bow,
    Her eyes are mad that they have wept till now.

Upon his hurt she looks so steadfastly
That her sight, dazzling, makes the wound seem three,
And then she reprehends her mangling eye,   1065
That makes more gashes where no breach should be.
    His face seems twain, each several limb is doubled,
    For oft the eye mistakes, the brain being troubled.

"My tongue cannot express my grief for one
And yet," quoth she, "behold two Adons dead.   1070
My sighs are blown away, my salt tears gone;
Mine eyes are turned to fire, my heart to lead.
    Heavy heart's lead, melt at mine eyes' red fire!
    So shall I die by drops of hot desire.

"Alas, poor world, what treasure hast thou lost!   1075
What face remains alive that's worth the viewing?
Whose tongue is music now? What canst thou boast
Of things long since, or anything ensuing?
    The flowers are sweet, their colors fresh and trim,
    But true sweet beauty lived and died with him.   1080

1081. **Bonnet:** cap, hat

1082. **Nor:** neither

1083. **fair:** beauty

1087. **bonnet:** cap

1088. **gaudy:** brilliantly fine

1089. **being:** i.e., its **being**

1091. **straight:** straightaway, immediately

1094. **fear:** terrify

1095. **he:** i.e., Adonis

1098. **silly:** defenseless

1099. **shadow:** reflection

1101. **by:** nearby

1104. **his sight:** i.e., the **sight** or view of him

1105. **urchin-snouted:** i.e., with a snout like a hedgehog

1106. **downward:** i.e., downwardly inclining; **still:** continually; **looketh for a grave:** See l. 622, where the boar's rooting in the ground is similarly linked to digging graves.

1107. **the beauteous . . . wore:** i.e., Adonis's beautiful appearance

1108. **entertainment:** reception, treatment

A falcon stooping "to the lure." (*Venus and Adonis,* 1027)

"Bonnet nor veil henceforth no creature wear;
Nor sun nor wind will ever strive to kiss you.
Having no fair to lose, you need not fear;
The sun doth scorn you, and the wind doth hiss you.
   But when Adonis lived, sun and sharp air   1085
   Lurked like two thieves to rob him of his fair.

"And therefore would he put his bonnet on,
Under whose brim the gaudy sun would peep;
The wind would blow it off and, being gone,
Play with his locks. Then would Adonis weep;   1090
   And straight in pity of his tender years,
   They both would strive who first should dry his tears.

"To see his face the lion walked along
Behind some hedge because he would not fear him.
To recreate himself when he hath song,   1095
The tiger would be tame and gently hear him.
   If he had spoke, the wolf would leave his prey
   And never fright the silly lamb that day.

"When he beheld his shadow in the brook,
The fishes spread on it their golden gills.   1100
When he was by, the birds such pleasure took
That some would sing, some other in their bills
   Would bring him mulberries and ripe-red cherries;
   He fed them with his sight, they him with berries.

"But this foul, grim, and urchin-snouted boar,   1105
Whose downward eye still looketh for a grave,
Ne'er saw the beauteous livery that he wore;
Witness the entertainment that he gave.
   If he did see his face, why then I know
   He thought to kiss him and hath killed him so.   1110

1113. **Who:** i.e., which; **again:** in response, in reaction

1125. **heavy:** sorrowful

1128. **lies:** lie

1129. **glasses:** mirrors

1131. **virtue:** power

1132. **his effect:** i.e., the consequence of its power (**virtue**) to reflect beauty; or, perhaps, its appearance

1133. **spite:** vexation

1137. **It:** i.e., **love** (l. 1136); **waited on with:** attended by

1139. **high or low:** i.e., unequal in hereditary rank

1140. **That:** so that; **his:** its

Venus grieves over the slain Adonis. (*Venus and Adonis,* 1121–27)

"'Tis true, 'tis true. Thus was Adonis slain:
He ran upon the boar with his sharp spear,
Who did not whet his teeth at him again,
But by a kiss thought to persuade him there,
   And nuzzling in his flank, the loving swine   1115
   Sheathed unaware the tusk in his soft groin.

"Had I been toothed like him, I must confess,
With kissing him I should have killed him first,
But he is dead, and never did he bless
My youth with his. The more am I accursed!"   1120
   With this, she falleth in the place she stood
   And stains her face with his congealèd blood.

She looks upon his lips, and they are pale.
She takes him by the hand, and that is cold.
She whispers in his ears a heavy tale   1125
As if they heard the woeful words she told.
   She lifts the coffer-lids that close his eyes,
   Where, lo, two lamps, burnt out, in darkness lies.

Two glasses, where herself herself beheld
A thousand times, and now no more reflect,   1130
Their virtue lost, wherein they late excelled,
And every beauty robbed of his effect.
   "Wonder of time," quoth she, "this is my spite,
   That, thou being dead, the day should yet be light.

"Since thou art dead, lo, here I prophesy   1135
Sorrow on love hereafter shall attend;
It shall be waited on with jealousy,
Find sweet beginning but unsavory end,
   Ne'er settled equally, but high or low,
   That all love's pleasure shall not match his woe.   1140

1142. **blasted:** blighted; **breathing while:** space of time in which one takes a breath

1143. **o'erstrawed:** overstrewn

1147. **sparing:** niggardly; **riot:** extravagance

1148. **tread the measures:** i.e., dance (A *measure* referred especially to a grave and solemn dance.)

1149. **staring:** wild

1151. **silly:** humbly

1157. **Perverse:** peevish, stubborn; **toward:** compliant, docile

1163. **Sith:** since

1165. **By this:** i.e., **by this** time

1168. **A purple flower . . . white:** According to Ovid's *Metamorphoses,* the dead Adonis was transformed into an anemone, called *wind-flower* in England because its frail bloom is easily blown away by the wind. (See picture below.)

1 *Anemone tuberofa radice.*
Purple Winde flower.

An anemone. (*Venus and Adonis,* 1168)

"It shall be fickle, false, and full of fraud,
Bud and be blasted in a breathing while,
The bottom poison and the top o'erstrawed
With sweets that shall the truest sight beguile;
    The strongest body shall it make most weak,   1145
    Strike the wise dumb, and teach the fool to speak.

"It shall be sparing and, too, full of riot,
Teaching decrepit age to tread the measures;
The staring ruffian shall it keep in quiet,
Pluck down the rich, enrich the poor with treasures.   1150
    It shall be raging mad and silly mild,
    Make the young old, the old become a child.

"It shall suspect where is no cause of fear;
It shall not fear where it should most mistrust.
It shall be merciful and, too, severe,   1155
And most deceiving when it seems most just.
    Perverse it shall be where it shows most toward,
    Put fear to valor, courage to the coward.

"It shall be cause of war and dire events,
And set dissension 'twixt the son and sire;   1160
Subject and servile to all discontents,
As dry combustious matter is to fire.
    Sith in his prime Death doth my love destroy,
    They that love best their loves shall not enjoy."

By this the boy that by her side lay killed   1165
Was melted like a vapor from her sight,
And in his blood that on the ground lay spilled
A purple flower sprung up, checkered with white,
    Resembling well his pale cheeks and the blood
    Which in round drops upon their whiteness stood.   1170

1177. **guise:** style

1180. **unto himself:** i.e., only for **himself**

1184. **the next of blood:** his nearest relative

1189. **hies:** hurries, speeds

1193. **Paphos:** city on the island of Cyprus, famous for its temple of Venus, the principal seat of her worship in the classical world

1194. **immure herself:** shut **herself** up

Venus with Cupid in her "light chariot." (*Venus and Adonis,* 1192)

She bows her head the new-sprung flower to smell,
Comparing it to her Adonis' breath,
And says within her bosom it shall dwell,
Since he himself is reft from her by death.
    She crops the stalk, and in the breach appears   1175
    Green-dropping sap, which she compares to tears.

"Poor flower," quoth she, "this was thy father's guise—
Sweet issue of a more sweet-smelling sire—
For every little grief to wet his eyes;
To grow unto himself was his desire,   1180
    And so 'tis thine, but know it is as good
    To wither in my breast as in his blood.

"Here was thy father's bed, here in my breast;
Thou art the next of blood, and 'tis thy right.
Lo, in this hollow cradle take thy rest;   1185
My throbbing heart shall rock thee day and night.
    There shall not be one minute in an hour
    Wherein I will not kiss my sweet love's flower."

Thus, weary of the world, away she hies
And yokes her silver doves, by whose swift aid   1190
Their mistress mounted through the empty skies
In her light chariot quickly is conveyed,
    Holding their course to Paphos, where their queen
    Means to immure herself and not be seen.

FINIS

Venus and Adonis
Longer Notes

Dedication 4. **Henry Wriothesley, Earl of Southampton:** Although the purpose of a dedication was to enlist support from a potential patron, Wriothesley's young age—he was only about twenty when *Venus and Adonis* was published—and the limitations placed on him because of it made it unlikely that he was able to provide Shakespeare with significant patronage at that time. Just before he turned eight, Wriothesley had inherited the title of third earl of Southampton. He had also benefited from a fine education at Cecil House provided to him as a royal ward by Queen Elizabeth's powerful lord treasurer and master of wards, Lord Burghley. From there Southampton had gone on to take an MA at St. John's College, Cambridge, and subsequently had been sent to Gray's Inn, where he may still have been in 1593. In his youth, he was extraordinarily attractive, as is indicated by his many portraits. He had already enjoyed the attention of other poets before winning Shakespeare's.

Line 148. **footing:** Here and in the following stanza, Venus draws attention to the qualities that distinguish her from mortal women. Despite her earlier claim that her marrow is burning, she is a spirit, a goddess who can dance on the sand without leaving a footprint and can lie on fragile flowers without crushing them.

Line 161. **Narcissus:** In Ovid's *Metamorphoses*, as translated by Arthur Golding in 1567, Narcissus does not die by drowning but is transformed into the flower that bears his name: "[Narcissus] thinkes the shadow [reflection in the brook] that he sees, to be a liuely boddie. / Astraughted [distraught] . . . he lyes, / There gazing on his shadowe still with fixed staring eyes" (3.522–24). However, the boy is represented as drowning in Christopher Marlowe's *Hero and Leander,* a poem that seems to have influenced ll. 161–62 of *Venus and Adonis:* "[He] leapt into the water for a kiss / Of his own shadow, and despising many, / Died ere he could enjoy the love of any" (1.74–76)

Line 429. **mermaid's voice:** Mermaids are fantasy creatures frequently confused with the mythological beings called Sirens, which, in classical mythology, used their alluring voices to entice sailors to their deaths on the rocks near their island.

Line 511. **seals:** A seal could be (1) an impression imprinted on wax, or (2) the piece of wax that bore the impression, or, finally, (3) the instrument (a signet ring, for example) with which the impression was imprinted in the wax. The impressed wax seal, in turn, had more than one function. It could be (1) attached to a document as evidence of the document's authenticity, or (2) affixed to a folded letter or document so that the document could not be opened without breaking the seal. Shakespeare used the word in most of its available meanings. As in ll. 511 and 516, he often equates seals and kisses. In *Measure for Measure,* for example, we find the lines "But my kisses bring again, bring again, / Seals of love, but sealed in vain, sealed in vain" (4.1.5–6). In *Two Gentlemen of Verona,* we find "And seal the bargain with a holy kiss" (2.2.7), and in *Taming of the Shrew* "And seal the title with a lovely kiss" (3.2.125). In this stanza of *Venus and Adonis,* the **seals** are primarily the impressions "Set . . . on [Venus's] wax-red lips," but in Shakespeare's plays **seals** are often the pieces of impressed wax used to authenticate a legal document (as in *Merchant of Venice,* 4.1.141) or used to prevent a document from being clandestinely opened (as in *Twelfth Night,* 2.5.94–96, and *Two Gentlemen of Verona,* 3.1.141).

Lines 601–4. **Even . . . saw:** The Roman writer Pliny, in his *Natural History* 35.10, tells of the great skill of the painter Zeuxis, whose picture of grapes deceived birds. According to Philemon Holland's 1601 translation of Pliny, "*Zeuxis* for proofe of his cunning [skill], brought upon the scaffold [easel] a table [board on which a picture is painted], wherein were clustres of grapes so lively [vividly] painted that the very birds of the aire flew flocking thither for to bee pecking at the grapes."

Line 683. **musets:** The word **musets,** strictly meaning "dens" or "lairs," is related to *meuses,* another word for "dens," but also a

word for openings in a fence or in a thicket through which a hare
would run to evade pursuit.

Line 752. **vestals:** Vesta, in Roman religion, was the powerful goddess of the hearth. In her temple in Rome, virgin priestesses
(**vestals**) tended the sacred fire. Any vestal who lost her virginity
was punished by being buried alive. The term came to mean a virgin, and especially someone who had taken a vow to remain a
virgin.

Line 862. **influence:** This word, when applied to heavenly bodies, is
usually an astrological term referring to the supposed streaming or
flowing from the stars or heavens of an ethereal fluid acting upon
things beneath the moon, especially upon human beings. Here,
however, the influence is going from the sun to the stars (which are
not sublunary), and, rather than acting upon them, it gives them
light. The image seems also to suggest that the stars and other
lamps (l. 861) are reflections of the sun, borrowing light (l. 862) lent
them by the sun (l. 864).

Line 863. **sucked . . . mother:** This reference to Adonis varies from
the traditional account of Adonis's birth and rearing in classical
mythology, which precluded his having been nursed by his **mother.**
According to Ovid's *Metamorphoses,* his mother was Myrrha, who
was impregnated by her own father, Cinyras, king of Cyprus. Adonis
was born after his mother had been relieved of her torment by being
changed into a myrtle tree. Adonis was raised by naiads, or river
nymphs.

Shakespeare's *Lucrece*

Like his *Venus and Adonis,* Shakespeare's *Lucrece* belongs to the genre of the minor epic; but unlike *Venus, Lucrece* incorporates a second genre, the complaint. As a minor epic, *Lucrece* draws upon the legendary history of a great empire, the moment when Rome ceases to be a kingdom ruled by the Tarquins and becomes a republic governed by elected consuls. Yet, again as a minor epic, *Lucrece* employs as its chief characters figures of seemingly secondary historical or political importance. In place of Rome's last king or her first consuls, the poem gives us instead Sextus Tarquinius, the king's young son, and Lucrece, the wife of one of Rome's first consuls. As in *Venus,* the erotic is made of intense interest as *Lucrece* focuses initially on the young man's overwhelming desire for the beautiful and all-too-naive wife of his kinsman and friend, Collatine. From the moment of the rape through the remainder of the poem, the focus of the poem shifts to the sexual shame felt by Lucrece, a much more disturbing emotion than that felt by Adonis as he is ardently wooed by Venus.

Shakespeare found the incidents for his poem in the accounts of a Roman historian (Livy) and a Roman mythographer (Ovid), as well as in Chaucer and contemporary English writers. He transformed this story of rape and political innovation by introducing into it two extended interior monologues in the form of complaints. Tarquin's complaint presents him as divided against himself, driven by the torment of his lust for Lucrece but aware of his betrayal of Collatine and of the shame her rape will bring upon himself and the honor of his royal family. Until Tarquin commits the rape and feels the bitter disappointment that follows it, Shakespeare writes the poem from the perspective of the rapist-to-be, whose sensitivity to the monstrosity of his projected crime is reminiscent of Macbeth's in his soliloquies contemplating the assassination of his cousin King Duncan.

Almost as soon as the rape is over, Shakespeare drives Tarquin from the poem. Thereafter he appears only in Lucrece's characterizations of him in her own much longer complaint. As she struggles with the shame she feels as Tarquin's victim, she begins with apostrophes to Night, Opportunity, and Time, in which she blames the circumstances attending Tarquin's attack on her. Following these apostrophes comes her long description of a painting of the Trojan War, through which Shakespeare introduces the subject matter of Homer's *Iliad*, a major epic, into his minor epic. Only seemingly a digression, the painting provides Lucrece with a figure whose suffering matches her own—that of Hecuba, the queen of Troy, who has endured the total destruction of her family and her city.

Throughout her complaint Lucrece strives to find a remedy for the defilement she has suffered from Tarquin's attack, deciding finally on suicide. Few acts have proved as enduringly controversial (and as appealing to artists) as Lucrece's self-destruction. While suicide was in Roman culture a hero's death in the face of humiliation or defeat, Christianity has been intolerant of it. The early church fathers Ambrose and Augustine decried Lucrece's chosen death. They argued that if she had indeed been forced by Tarquin, then, no matter the fate of her body, she had kept her soul pure by withholding consent. If she was therefore free of guilt, it was sinful and prideful of her to destroy herself. Although Lucrece briefly argues that she is innocent of what has been done to her, the poem in general concentrates on her overarching view that despite the chastity of her mind, she herself has been rendered unchaste by Tarquin's rape of her body. In other words, mind and body, in her reading of the situation, are not really separable.

After you have read this poem, we invite you to turn to the essay printed at the back of this book, *"Venus and Adonis* and *Lucrece: A Modern Perspective,"* written by Professor Catherine Belsey of Cardiff University.

LUCRECE

2–3. **Henry Wriothesley, Earl of Southampton:** See longer note to *Venus and Adonis*, Dedication 4, p. 442, and picture, p. 360.

6. **pamphlet:** printed poem; **without beginning:** perhaps an allusion to the poem's beginning in the middle of its story (*in medias res* [Latin]); **moiety:** small part

6–8. **warrant . . . acceptance:** Critics have interpreted this sentence to indicate that Wriothesley generously rewarded Shakespeare for dedicating *Venus and Adonis* to him. **warrant:** proof

9. **all I have:** perhaps, **all I have** done or will do

10. **show greater:** i.e., produce something **greater** than the poem that follows

TO THE RIGHT
HONOVRABLE, HENRY
VVriothefley, Earle of Southhampton,
and Baron of Titchfield.

H E loue I dedicate to your Lordſhip is without end:wherof this Pamphlet without beginning is but a ſuperfluous Moity. The warrant I haue of your Honourable diſpoſition, not the worth of my vntutord Lines makes it aſſured of acceptance. VVhat I haue done is yours, what I haue to doe is yours, being part in all I haue, deuoted yours. VVere my worth greater, my duety would ſhew greater, meane time, as it is, it is bound to your Lordſhip; To whom I wiſh long life ſtill lengthned with all happineſſe.

Your Lordſhips in all duety.

William Shakeſpeare.

A 2

Dedication to the 1594 quarto of Shakespeare's *Lucrece*.

TO THE RIGHT
HONORABLE, HENRY
Wriothesley, Earl of Southampton,
and Baron of Titchfield.

The love I dedicate to your Lordship is without end; whereof this pamphlet without beginning is but a superfluous moiety. The warrant I have of your honorable disposition, not the worth of my untutored lines, makes it assured of acceptance. What I have done is yours; what I have to do is yours; being part in all I have, devoted yours. Were my worth greater, my duty would show greater; meantime, as it is, it is bound to your Lordship, to whom I wish long life still lengthened with all happiness.

Your Lordship's in all duty,
William Shakespeare

1. **Lucius Tarquinius:** last legendary king of Rome (534–510 BCE); **surnamed:** given the additional descriptive name; **Superbus:** the proud (Latin)

4. **requiring:** requesting; **suffrages:** votes

5. **the kingdom:** i.e., **the kingdom** of Rome

6. **Ardea:** a wealthy city twenty-four miles south of Rome

9. **Collatinus:** Tarquinius **Collatinus,** great-nephew of Rome's fifth king and later, together with **Junius Brutus** (ll. 25–26), one of Rome's first consuls (See picture below.)

10. **Lucretia:** i.e., Lucrece

11. **posted:** hurried (literally, traveled with relays of horses)

15. **several disports:** various recreations, amusements

19. **privily:** secretly

20. **estate:** rank, status

21. **Collatium:** a city about ten miles east of Rome, properly called *Collatia*

27. **habit:** dress, apparel; **demanded:** asked to know

28. **taking an oath of them for her revenge:** i.e., having **them** take **an oath** to avenge her; **actor:** doer, one who performed the deed

29. **withal:** with that

30. **with one consent:** in complete agreement

34. **moved:** persuaded; roused, stirred, affected with emotion

Collatine. (*Lucrece*, 7, 10)

THE ARGUMENT

Lucius Tarquinius, for his excessive pride surnamed Superbus, after he had caused his own father-in-law Servius Tullius to be cruelly murdered and, contrary to the Roman laws and customs, not requiring or staying for the people's suffrages, had possessed himself of the kingdom, went accompanied with his sons and other no- 5 blemen of Rome to besiege Ardea; during which siege, the principal men of the army meeting one evening at the tent of Sextus Tarquinius, the King's son, in their discourses after supper every one commended the virtues of his own wife; among whom Collatinus extolled the incomparable chastity of his wife Lucretia. In that 10 pleasant humor they all posted to Rome, and intending by their secret and sudden arrival to make trial of that which every one had before avouched, only Collatinus finds his wife, though it were late in the night, spinning amongst her maids; the other ladies were all found dancing and reveling or in several disports; whereupon the 15 noblemen yielded Collatinus the victory and his wife the fame. At that time Sextus Tarquinius, being inflamed with Lucrece' beauty, yet smothering his passions for the present, departed with the rest back to the camp; from whence he shortly after privily withdrew himself and was, according to his estate, royally entertained and 20 lodged by Lucrece at Collatium. The same night he treacherously stealeth into her chamber, violently ravished her, and early in the morning speedeth away. Lucrece, in this lamentable plight, hastily dispatcheth messengers, one to Rome for her father, another to the camp for Collatine. They came—the one accompanied with Junius 25 Brutus, the other with Publius Valerius—and, finding Lucrece attired in mourning habit, demanded the cause of her sorrow. She, first taking an oath of them for her revenge, revealed the actor and whole manner of his dealing, and withal suddenly stabbed herself. Which done, with one consent they all vowed to root out the whole 30 hated family of the Tarquins; and, bearing the dead body to Rome, Brutus acquainted the people with the doer and manner of the vile deed, with a bitter invective against the tyranny of the King, wherewith the people were so moved that with one consent and a general acclamation the Tarquins were all exiled and the state government 35 changed from kings to consuls.

1. **Ardea:** accented on the first syllable; **all in post:** in all haste

2. **trustless:** treacherous; **false:** deceitful, faithless (but also meaning "erroneous, mistaken, not according to correct rule")

3. **Lust-breathèd:** inspired by lust; **host:** army

4. **lightless fire:** i.e., **fire** that gives no light

5. **aspire:** rise up

8. **Haply:** perhaps; **unhapp'ly:** regrettably, unfortunately

9. **bateless:** not to be blunted

10–11. **let / To praise:** i.e., refrain from praising

11. **clear:** bright, brilliant; faultless

12. **triumphed:** prevailed; **sky . . . delight:** i.e., Lucrece's face

13. **mortal stars:** eyes

14. **pure:** chaste; **aspects:** looks (in astrology, the ways in which the heavenly bodies, from their relative positions, look on each other, and look jointly on the earth); **peculiar duties: duties** exclusive to him

16. **happy state:** wordplay on (1) fortunate position in life, wealth, possession; (2) joyful mental or emotional condition

19. **high:** a highly, i.e., a very

22. **of a few:** i.e., by **a few**

23. **done:** used up

24. **Against:** exposed to

26. **expired:** accented on the first syllable; **date:** term, duration

"Lucrece the chaste." (*Lucrece*, 7)

Lucrece

From the besiegèd Ardea all in post,
Borne by the trustless wings of false desire,
Lust-breathèd Tarquin leaves the Roman host
And to Collatium bears the lightless fire
Which, in pale embers hid, lurks to aspire   5
    And girdle with embracing flames the waist
    Of Collatine's fair love, Lucrece the chaste.

Haply that name of "chaste" unhapp'ly set
This bateless edge on his keen appetite
When Collatine unwisely did not let   10
To praise the clear unmatchèd red and white
Which triumphed in that sky of his delight,
    Where mortal stars, as bright as heaven's beauties,
    With pure aspects did him peculiar duties.

For he the night before, in Tarquin's tent,   15
Unlocked the treasure of his happy state,
What priceless wealth the heavens had him lent
In the possession of his beauteous mate,
Reck'ning his fortune at such high proud rate
    That kings might be espousèd to more fame,   20
    But king nor peer to such a peerless dame.

O, happiness enjoyed but of a few,
And, if possessed, as soon decayed and done
As is the morning's silver melting dew
Against the golden splendor of the sun!   25
An expired date, canceled ere well begun.
    Honor and beauty in the owner's arms
    Are weakly fortressed from a world of harms.

30. **orator:** advocate; eloquent public speaker

31. **apology:** formal or legal defense

33. **publisher:** public proclaimer

36. **Lucrece':** accented, as almost invariably in this poem, on the first syllable; **sov'reignty:** supremacy, preeminence

37. **Suggested:** prompted; **issue:** offspring

40. **Braving compare:** defying comparison

41. **meaner:** lower-ranking

42. **hap:** success, prosperity; **want:** lack

44. **timeless:** unseasonable, inappropriate

45. **affairs:** ordinary business; **state:** rank, status

47. **liver:** considered the seat of sexual desire

49. **still blasts:** always is blighted

50. **false:** treacherous

53. **underprop:** maintain, support

55. **despite:** indignation; open defiance

56. **stain that o'er:** i.e., cover Beauty's red **blushes**

L V C R E C E.

LONDON.

Printed by Richard Field, for Iohn Harrifon, and are
to be fold at the figne of the white Greyhound
in Paules Churh yard. 1594.

Title page of the 1594 quarto of Shakespeare's *Lucrece*.

Beauty itself doth of itself persuade
The eyes of men without an orator; 30
What needeth then apology be made
To set forth that which is so singular?
Or why is Collatine the publisher
    Of that rich jewel he should keep unknown
    From thievish ears because it is his own? 35

Perchance his boast of Lucrece' sov'reignty
Suggested this proud issue of a king,
For by our ears our hearts oft tainted be.
Perchance that envy of so rich a thing,
Braving compare, disdainfully did sting 40
    His high-pitched thoughts, that meaner men should
      vaunt
    That golden hap which their superiors want.

But some untimely thought did instigate
His all too timeless speed, if none of those.
His honor, his affairs, his friends, his state 45
Neglected all, with swift intent he goes
To quench the coal which in his liver glows.
    O, rash false heat, wrapped in repentant cold,
    Thy hasty spring still blasts and ne'er grows old!

When at Collatium this false lord arrived, 50
Well was he welcomed by the Roman dame,
Within whose face Beauty and Virtue strived
Which of them both should underprop her fame.
When Virtue bragged, Beauty would blush for shame;
    When Beauty boasted blushes, in despite 55
    Virtue would stain that o'er with silver white.

57–58. entituled / From Venus' doves: having rightful possession of **silver white** by virtue of Venus's association with white **doves** (The **doves** draw the chariot of the goddess of beauty. See picture, p. 440.)

58. challenge: lay claim to; **field:** wordplay on (1) the surface of a heraldic shield or escutcheon on which figures or colors are displayed; (2) battlefield

59–63. Then . . . white: Virtue argues that blushes belong to her, since, in the age of innocence, she gave them to **cheeks** as a **shield.   Beauty's red:** blushes   **golden age:** earliest epoch in legendary human history, the **age** characterized by prosperity, happiness, and innocence   **gild:** (1) adorn, beautify; (2) cover with gold (with wordplay on **red** as a poetic epithet of gold)   **silver:** silvery, having the **white** color of **silver   fence:** (1) shield, protect; (2) fortify

65. Argued: i.e., expressed

67. world's minority: the beginning of time; the **golden age** (l. 60)

68. still: always

70. interchange . . . seat: i.e., exchange thrones

72. fair: beautiful; **field:** battlefield

73. ranks: wordplay on (1) rows (of **lilies and roses** [l. 71]); (2) forces, battalions

76. would: wished to

77. triumph in: prevail over, gain the victory over

81. show: display, exhibit

83. answers: pays

84. still-gazing: continually gazing

But Beauty, in that white entitulèd
From Venus' doves, doth challenge that fair field.
Then Virtue claims from Beauty Beauty's red,
Which Virtue gave the golden age to gild   60
Their silver cheeks, and called it then their shield,
    Teaching them thus to use it in the fight:
    When shame assailed, the red should fence the white.

This heraldry in Lucrece' face was seen,
Argued by Beauty's red and Virtue's white.   65
Of either's color was the other queen,
Proving from world's minority their right.
Yet their ambition makes them still to fight,
    The sovereignty of either being so great
    That oft they interchange each other's seat.   70

This silent war of lilies and of roses,
Which Tarquin viewed in her fair face's field,
In their pure ranks his traitor eye encloses,
Where, lest between them both it should be killed,
The coward captive vanquishèd doth yield   75
    To those two armies that would let him go
    Rather than triumph in so false a foe.

Now thinks he that her husband's shallow tongue,
The niggard prodigal that praised her so,
In that high task hath done her beauty wrong,   80
Which far exceeds his barren skill to show.
Therefore that praise which Collatine doth owe
    Enchanted Tarquin answers with surmise,
    In silent wonder of still-gazing eyes.

88. **limed:** trapped in birdlime spread on **bushes**

89. **securely:** unsuspectingly, trustfully; **good cheer:** entertainment in the form of food and drink

90. **reverend:** i.e., reverent, deeply respectful

91. **ill:** evil

92. **that:** i.e., his **inward ill** (l. 91); **colored:** cloaked; disguised; **estate:** rank, status

93. **pleats:** folds

94. **That:** i.e., so that

97. **so wanteth:** i.e., experiences such deficiency; **his store:** i.e., his great abundance (or, perhaps, its great abundance [since ll. 96–98 may refer to **his eye** (l. 95)])

99. **coped with:** engaged with, contended with; **stranger eyes:** i.e., the **eyes** of a **stranger**

100. **parling:** i.e., parleying, speaking (*To parley* is also to discuss terms with an enemy or opponent.)

102. **margents:** margins (See longer note, p. 586.)

104. **moralize:** interpret the moral significance of; **sight:** look

105. **More than:** i.e., other than that

106. **stories:** narrates, relates

109. **chivalry:** bravery, knightly skill or deeds

110. **bruisèd arms:** battered armor

111. **heaved-up:** raised, lifted

This earthly saint, adorèd by this devil,   85
Little suspecteth the false worshiper,
For unstained thoughts do seldom dream on evil;
Birds never limed no secret bushes fear.
So, guiltless, she securely gives good cheer
　　And reverend welcome to her princely guest,   90
　　Whose inward ill no outward harm expressed.

For that he colored with his high estate,
Hiding base sin in pleats of majesty,
That nothing in him seemed inordinate,
Save sometimes too much wonder of his eye,   95
Which, having all, all could not satisfy,
　　But, poorly rich, so wanteth in his store
　　That, cloyed with much, he pineth still for more.

But she, that never coped with stranger eyes,
Could pick no meaning from their parling looks   100
Nor read the subtle shining secrecies
Writ in the glassy margents of such books.
She touched no unknown baits nor feared no hooks,
　　Nor could she moralize his wanton sight
　　More than his eyes were opened to the light.   105

He stories to her ears her husband's fame,
Won in the fields of fruitful Italy,
And decks with praises Collatine's high name,
Made glorious by his manly chivalry
With bruisèd arms and wreaths of victory.   110
　　Her joy with heaved-up hand she doth express
　　And, wordless, so greets heaven for his success.

116. **welkin:** sky (i.e., face)

118. **display:** unfold, spread out

121. **Intending:** pretending; **heavy:** drowsy; **sprite:** spirit

122. **questionèd:** conversed

125. **betakes:** takes

128. **his will's obtaining:** wordplay on (1) **obtaining his** desire; (2) **his will's** prevailing (For the complex of meanings of the word **will,** see the longer note to Sonnet 135, p. 339.)

129. **ever . . . resolving:** always **resolving to obtain his will**

130. **weak-built hopes:** i.e., the fact that his **hopes** are without ground

131. **Despair to gain:** perhaps, even **despair** of success; **traffic:** bargain, deal

132. **meed:** reward

133. **adjunct:** attendant, consequent

134–37. **Those . . . less:** See longer note, p. 586.   **with . . . fond:** wordplay on (1) **so** eager for profit; (2) made **so** foolish by previous acquisition of wealth   **bond:** i.e., possession   **by hoping more:** i.e., **by hoping** for **more**

138. **profit of excess:** only advantage of having more than enough

140. **bankrout:** bankrupt

A wreath of victory. (*Lucrece,* 110)

460

Far from the purpose of his coming thither
He makes excuses for his being there.
No cloudy show of stormy blust'ring weather   115
Doth yet in his fair welkin once appear,
Till sable Night, mother of dread and fear,
    Upon the world dim darkness doth display
    And in her vaulty prison stows the day.

For then is Tarquin brought unto his bed,   120
Intending weariness with heavy sprite,
For after supper long he questionèd
With modest Lucrece and wore out the night.
Now leaden slumber with life's strength doth fight,
    And everyone to rest himself betakes,   125
    Save thieves and cares and troubled minds that wakes;

As one of which doth Tarquin lie revolving
The sundry dangers of his will's obtaining,
Yet ever to obtain his will resolving,
Though weak-built hopes persuade him to abstaining.   130
Despair to gain doth traffic oft for gaining,
    And when great treasure is the meed proposed,
    Though death be adjunct, there's no death supposed.

Those that much covet are with gain so fond
That what they have not, that which they possess   135
They scatter and unloose it from their bond,
And so, by hoping more, they have but less,
Or, gaining more, the profit of excess
    Is but to surfeit, and such griefs sustain
    That they prove bankrout in this poor-rich gain.   140

141. **nurse:** foster
143. **thwarting:** perverse
144. **gage:** risk
145. **As life:** i.e., **as,** for example, **life; fell:** fierce, terrible
148. **vent'ring:** venturing, taking risks; **ill:** (1) badly, unskill-fully; (2) wickedly; **leave to be:** cease being
151. **defect:** i.e., (the illusion of) the absence
152. **that:** i.e., that which
153. **wit:** good judgment
160. **confounds:** destroys
164. **comfortable:** encouraging, cheering; **his:** i.e., its
166. **season:** opportune time; **surprise:** seize, capture
167. **silly:** helpless, defenseless
168. **wakes:** wake

The aim of all is but to nurse the life
With honor, wealth, and ease in waning age;
And in this aim there is such thwarting strife
That one for all or all for one we gage:
As life for honor in fell battle's rage,   145
   Honor for wealth; and oft that wealth doth cost
   The death of all, and all together lost.

So that, in vent'ring ill, we leave to be
The things we are for that which we expect;
And this ambitious foul infirmity,   150
In having much, torments us with defect
Of that we have. So then we do neglect
   The thing we have and, all for want of wit,
   Make something nothing by augmenting it.

Such hazard now must doting Tarquin make,   155
Pawning his honor to obtain his lust,
And for himself himself he must forsake.
Then where is truth if there be no self-trust?
When shall he think to find a stranger just
   When he himself himself confounds, betrays   160
   To sland'rous tongues and wretched hateful days?

Now stole upon the time the dead of night,
When heavy sleep had closed up mortal eyes.
No comfortable star did lend his light;
No noise but owls' and wolves' death-boding cries   165
Now serves the season that they may surprise
   The silly lambs. Pure thoughts are dead and still,
   While Lust and Murder wakes to stain and kill.

170. **rudely:** inelegantly

173. **honest:** honorable

174. **betake him to retire:** i.e., resorts to withdrawing   **him:** i.e., himself

175. **rude:** harsh, violent

176. **falchion:** sword; **smiteth:** strikes

180. **advisedly:** with deliberation or thought

183. **premeditate:** ponder

188. **naked armor . . . lust:** a much-debated figure of speech (See longer note, p. 586.)

189. **justly:** wordplay on (1) with justice; (2) rationally; (3) properly; (4) accurately

195. **fair:** This word was often used in the general sense of "not foul," as it is here.

196. **weed:** garment

And now this lustful lord leapt from his bed,
Throwing his mantle rudely o'er his arm;   170
Is madly tossed between desire and dread;
Th' one sweetly flatters, th' other feareth harm,
But honest fear, bewitched with lust's foul charm,
    Doth too too oft betake him to retire,
    Beaten away by brainsick rude desire.   175

His falchion on a flint he softly smiteth,
That from the cold stone sparks of fire do fly,
Whereat a waxen torch forthwith he lighteth,
Which must be lodestar to his lustful eye,
And to the flame thus speaks advisedly: 180
    "As from this cold flint I enforced this fire,
    So Lucrece must I force to my desire."

Here pale with fear he doth premeditate
The dangers of his loathsome enterprise,
And in his inward mind he doth debate   185
What following sorrow may on this arise.
Then, looking scornfully, he doth despise
    His naked armor of still-slaughtered lust
    And justly thus controls his thoughts unjust:

"Fair torch, burn out thy light, and lend it not   190
To darken her whose light excelleth thine.
And die, unhallowed thoughts, before you blot
With your uncleanness that which is divine.
Offer pure incense to so pure a shrine.
    Let fair humanity abhor the deed   195
    That spots and stains love's modest snow-white weed.

197. **arms:** armor, weapons

198. **my household's grave:** i.e., the sepulcher of my family

200. **fancy's:** love's, desire's

201. **still:** always; **true respect:** (1) proper consideration (for what is truly courageous); or (2) careful regard (for what is good)

202. **digression:** moral deviation, transgression

205. **coat: coat** of arms (See picture below.)

206. **dash:** bar or stroke (of his pen [in his records], or of color [in the coat of arms]) See longer note, p. 587.

207. **cipher me:** express, show forth (**Me** is the ethical dative, an old form of indirect object.) **fondly:** foolishly

208. **note:** mark or sign (here, the herald's **dash** [l. 206])

214. **toy:** trifle

217. **Would:** i.e., wishes to; **straight:** straightaway, immediately

220. **Post:** ride quickly (as in riding a post-horse)

221. **marriage:** i.e., wife

222. **blur:** moral stain, blemish

224. **ever-during:** everlasting

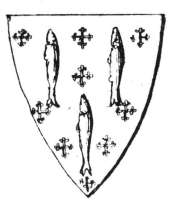

A coat of arms. (*Lucrece*, 205)

"O, shame to knighthood and to shining arms!
O, foul dishonor to my household's grave!
O, impious act including all foul harms!
A martial man to be soft fancy's slave!   200
True valor still a true respect should have.
    Then my digression is so vile, so base,
    That it will live engraven in my face.

"Yea, though I die, the scandal will survive
And be an eyesore in my golden coat;   205
Some loathsome dash the herald will contrive
To cipher me how fondly I did dote,
That my posterity, shamed with the note,
    Shall curse my bones and hold it for no sin
    To wish that I their father had not been.   210

"What win I if I gain the thing I seek?
A dream, a breath, a froth of fleeting joy.
Who buys a minute's mirth to wail a week
Or sells eternity to get a toy?
For one sweet grape who will the vine destroy?   215
    Or what fond beggar, but to touch the crown,
    Would with the scepter straight be strucken down?

"If Collatinus dream of my intent,
Will he not wake and, in a desp'rate rage,
Post hither this vile purpose to prevent—   220
This siege, that hath engirt his marriage,
This blur to youth, this sorrow to the sage,
    This dying virtue, this surviving shame,
    Whose crime will bear an ever-during blame?

225. **can . . . make:** i.e., **can** I find

230. **extreme:** accented on the first syllable

236. **quittal:** requital; retaliation

238. **finds:** find

239. **fact:** deed; crime

243. **will:** See longer note to Sonnet 135, p. 339. **removing:** alteration

244. **Who:** i.e., he who; **sentence, saw:** maxim

245. **painted cloth:** wall hanging onto which pictures (often of classical or biblical subjects), with a motto or proverb included, were painted

248. **makes dispensation:** dispenses, does away

249. **worser:** i.e., (morally) worse; **for vantage:** i.e., to achieve a superior position; **still:** always

251. **effects:** purposes; possibly also, "affects" or feelings

"O, what excuse can my invention make   225
When thou shalt charge me with so black a deed?
Will not my tongue be mute, my frail joints shake,
Mine eyes forgo their light, my false heart bleed?
The guilt being great, the fear doth still exceed,
    And extreme fear can neither fight nor fly   230
    But cowardlike with trembling terror die.

"Had Collatinus killed my son or sire
Or lain in ambush to betray my life,
Or were he not my dear friend, this desire
Might have excuse to work upon his wife,   235
As in revenge or quittal of such strife;
    But as he is my kinsman, my dear friend,
    The shame and fault finds no excuse nor end.

"Shameful it is: ay, if the fact be known,
Hateful it is: there is no hate in loving.   240
I'll beg her love. But she is not her own.
The worst is but denial and reproving;
My will is strong, past reason's weak removing.
    Who fears a sentence or an old man's saw
    Shall by a painted cloth be kept in awe."   245

Thus, graceless, holds he disputation
'Tween frozen conscience and hot-burning will,
And with good thoughts makes dispensation,
Urging the worser sense for vantage still,
Which in a moment doth confound and kill   250
    All pure effects, and doth so far proceed
    That what is vile shows like a virtuous deed.

255. **hard news: news** difficult to endure; **band:** army

258. **lawn:** fine linen

259. **took:** i.e., having been taken

264. **cheer:** face; expression

265. **Narcissus:** See longer note to *Venus and Adonis*, l. 161, p. 442, and picture, p. 374.

266. **flood:** stream, brook

267. **color:** pretext

269. **Poor:** i.e., only inferior, cowardly; **remorse in poor abuses:** i.e., compassion in the course of inflicting paltry injuries

271. **Affection:** desire

272. **gaudy:** fine, showy

273. **The coward:** i.e., even **the coward**

274. **avaunt:** be gone

275. **Respect:** (prudent) consideration; **wait on:** accompany, attend on

276. **countermand:** annul by a contrary command

277. **Sad:** grave; **regard:** consideration; **beseems:** i.e., beseem, are appropriate to

278. **part:** dramatic role

Quoth he, "She took me kindly by the hand
And gazed for tidings in my eager eyes,
Fearing some hard news from the warlike band   255
Where her belovèd Collatinus lies.
O, how her fear did make her color rise!
    First red as roses that on lawn we lay,
    Then white as lawn, the roses took away.

"And how her hand, in my hand being locked,   260
Forced it to tremble with her loyal fear,
Which struck her sad, and then it faster rocked
Until her husband's welfare she did hear,
Whereat she smilèd with so sweet a cheer
    That, had Narcissus seen her as she stood,   265
    Self-love had never drowned him in the flood.

"Why hunt I then for color or excuses?
All orators are dumb when Beauty pleadeth.
Poor wretches have remorse in poor abuses;
Love thrives not in the heart that shadows dreadeth.   270
Affection is my captain, and he leadeth;
    And when his gaudy banner is displayed,
    The coward fights and will not be dismayed.

"Then, childish fear, avaunt! Debating, die!
Respect and Reason, wait on wrinkled Age.   275
My heart shall never countermand mine eye.
Sad pause and deep regard beseems the sage;
My part is youth, and beats these from the stage.
    Desire my pilot is, beauty my prize;
    Then who fears sinking where such treasure lies?"   280

281. **corn:** wheat

284. **fond:** i.e., foolish (from Tarquin's perspective)

285. **servitors:** servants

286. **cross:** contradict; thwart

287. **a league:** alliance (i.e., peace)

289. **the selfsame seat:** i.e., his mind or **thought** (l. 288)

293. **seeks to:** petitions

294. **once:** i.e., having already been

295. **his servile powers:** perhaps, his inferior passions, or his senses (See longer note, p. 587.)

296. **Who:** i.e., which; **jocund show:** cheering display of military strength

297. **Stuff up:** support (as if they were troops filling up an army)

303. **enforced:** forced; **retires:** draws back; **his:** i.e., its

304. **rate:** reproach (by making noise); **ill:** wicked act

305. **regard:** attention (to what he is doing)

306. **grates the door:** rubs against **the door** harshly, producing a jarring sound; **to have him heard:** i.e., in order that he may be **heard**

307. **weasels:** domesticated **weasels** kept to kill vermin (See picture below.)

308. **fright:** frighten; **his fear:** i.e., that which he ought to fear

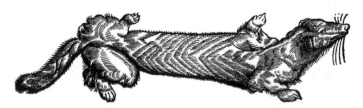

A weasel. (*Lucrece,* 307)

As corn o'ergrown by weeds, so heedful fear
Is almost choked by unresisted lust.
Away he steals with open list'ning ear,
Full of foul hope and full of fond mistrust,
Both which, as servitors to the unjust,   285
    So cross him with their opposite persuasion
    That now he vows a league and now invasion.

Within his thought her heavenly image sits,
And in the selfsame seat sits Collatine.
That eye which looks on her confounds his wits;   290
That eye which him beholds, as more divine,
Unto a view so false will not incline,
    But with a pure appeal seeks to the heart,
    Which once corrupted takes the worser part;

And therein heartens up his servile powers,   295
Who, flattered by their leader's jocund show,
Stuff up his lust, as minutes fill up hours;
And as their captain, so their pride doth grow,
Paying more slavish tribute than they owe.
    By reprobate desire thus madly led,   300
    The Roman lord marcheth to Lucrece' bed.

The locks between her chamber and his will,
Each one by him enforced, retires his ward;
But, as they open, they all rate his ill,
Which drives the creeping thief to some regard.   305
The threshold grates the door to have him heard;
    Night-wand'ring weasels shriek to see him there;
    They fright him, yet he still pursues his fear.

311. **stay:** stop

313. **conduct:** guide

316. **being lighted:** i.e., the torch **being lighted** again

318. **rushes:** Fresh **rushes** were used to strew the floors of dwellings in Shakespeare's time.

320. **who should:** i.e., one who would

324. **consters:** construes, interprets

326. **accidental things of trial:** i.e., inessential **things** that test his resolve

327. **bars:** i.e., marks on the face of a clock (**hourly dial**) dividing the hour into minutes; **stop:** punctuate

328. **Who:** i.e., which (the **bars**); **stay:** delay; **his:** its (the hour's); **let:** impede

329. **his:** its

330. **lets:** impediments; **attend:** go with; **time:** occasion

332. **prime:** spring

333. **sneapèd:** nipped, pinched

334. **pays:** i.e., **pays** for; **income:** arrival

335. **shelves:** sandbanks

As each unwilling portal yields him way,
Through little vents and crannies of the place 310
The wind wars with his torch to make him stay
And blows the smoke of it into his face,
Extinguishing his conduct in this case;
    But his hot heart, which fond desire doth scorch,
    Puffs forth another wind that fires the torch. 315

And being lighted, by the light he spies
Lucretia's glove, wherein her needle sticks.
He takes it from the rushes where it lies,
And gripping it, the needle his finger pricks,
As who should say, "This glove to wanton tricks 320
    Is not inured. Return again in haste.
    Thou seest our mistress' ornaments are chaste."

But all these poor forbiddings could not stay him;
He in the worst sense consters their denial.
The doors, the wind, the glove that did delay him 325
He takes for accidental things of trial,
Or as those bars which stop the hourly dial,
    Who with a ling'ring stay his course doth let
    Till every minute pays the hour his debt.

"So, so," quoth he, "these lets attend the time 330
Like little frosts that sometimes threat the spring,
To add a more rejoicing to the prime
And give the sneapèd birds more cause to sing.
Pain pays the income of each precious thing:
    Huge rocks, high winds, strong pirates, shelves,
      and sands 335
    The merchant fears ere rich at home he lands."

341. **wrought:** worked

342. **for his prey:** i.e., for success in capturing **his prey**

346. **fair fair:** (physically and morally) unblemished beauty

347. **they:** i.e., **the heavens** (l. 343)

349. **fact:** crime, deed

353. **tried:** experienced

355. **hath dissolution:** i.e., dissolves, melts

356. **eye of heaven:** i.e., sun; **out:** no longer alight; extinguished

362. **Who:** i.e., whoever

364. **his:** wordplay on "its" (the serpent's) and **his** (Tarquin's)

"Fortune be . . . my guide." (*Lucrece*, 351; s. 111)

Now is he come unto the chamber door
That shuts him from the heaven of his thought,
Which with a yielding latch, and with no more,
Hath barred him from the blessèd thing he sought. 340
So from himself impiety hath wrought
    That for his prey to pray he doth begin,
    As if the heavens should countenance his sin.

But in the midst of his unfruitful prayer,
Having solicited th' eternal power 345
That his foul thoughts might compass his fair fair,
And they would stand auspicious to the hour,
Even there he starts. Quoth he, "I must deflower.
    The powers to whom I pray abhor this fact;
    How can they then assist me in the act? 350

"Then Love and Fortune be my gods, my guide!
My will is backed with resolution.
Thoughts are but dreams till their effects be tried.
The blackest sin is cleared with absolution.
Against love's fire fear's frost hath dissolution. 355
    The eye of heaven is out, and misty night
    Covers the shame that follows sweet delight."

This said, his guilty hand plucked up the latch,
And with his knee the door he opens wide.
The dove sleeps fast that this night-owl will catch. 360
Thus treason works ere traitors be espied.
Who sees the lurking serpent steps aside,
    But she, sound sleeping, fearing no such thing,
    Lies at the mercy of his mortal sting.

367. **curtains:** bed curtains; **close:** i.e., drawn **close; about:** around

370. **watchword:** signal to begin the attack

372. **Look as:** just **as**

374. **begun:** i.e., began

375. **wink:** close, shut

376. **reflects:** shines

380. **period:** end, conclusion

382. **clear:** unsullied, unspotted

383. **league:** marriage between Collatine and Lucrece

385. **sell:** give up, hand over

387. **Coz'ning:** cozening, cheating

388. **Who:** i.e., which (**the pillow**); **in sunder:** asunder

389. **want his:** i.e., lack its

391. **monument:** effigy on a tomb

Into the chamber wickedly he stalks 365
And gazeth on her yet unstainèd bed.
The curtains being close, about he walks,
Rolling his greedy eyeballs in his head.
By their high treason is his heart misled,
    Which gives the watchword to his hand full soon 370
    To draw the cloud that hides the silver moon.

Look as the fair and fiery-pointed sun,
Rushing from forth a cloud, bereaves our sight;
Even so, the curtain drawn, his eyes begun
To wink, being blinded with a greater light. 375
Whether it is that she reflects so bright
    That dazzleth them, or else some shame supposed,
    But blind they are and keep themselves enclosed.

O, had they in that darksome prison died,
Then had they seen the period of their ill! 380
Then Collatine again by Lucrece' side
In his clear bed might have reposèd still.
But they must ope, this blessèd league to kill,
    And holy-thoughted Lucrece to their sight
    Must sell her joy, her life, her world's delight. 385

Her lily hand her rosy cheek lies under,
Coz'ning the pillow of a lawful kiss,
Who, therefore angry, seems to part in sunder,
Swelling on either side to want his bliss;
Between whose hills her head entombèd is, 390
    Where like a virtuous monument she lies,
    To be admired of lewd unhallowed eyes.

393. **Without the bed:** i.e., outside the covers

394. **whose:** i.e., the hand's

397. **marigolds:** flowers that, according to books of the time, opened and closed their petals in response to the presence or absence of the sun (See picture, p. 68.)

401. **modest . . . modesty:** wordplay on **wanton** as both "lewd" and "playful," first as a plural noun ("lewd and/or playful ones"), then as an adjective

402. **Showing:** displaying; **map of death:** image **of death** (i.e., sleep)

403. **life's mortality:** mortal human life

404. **Each:** both life and death

405. **them twain:** i.e., the two of them

412. **went about:** set to work

417. **tired:** fed greedily, gorged

Without the bed her other fair hand was,
On the green coverlet, whose perfect white
Showed like an April daisy on the grass, 395
With pearly sweat resembling dew of night.
Her eyes, like marigolds, had sheathed their light
    And, canopied in darkness, sweetly lay
    Till they might open to adorn the day.

Her hair, like golden threads, played with her breath— 400
O, modest wantons, wanton modesty!—
Showing life's triumph in the map of death
And death's dim look in life's mortality.
Each in her sleep themselves so beautify
    As if between them twain there were no strife, 405
    But that life lived in death and death in life.

Her breasts like ivory globes circled with blue,
A pair of maiden worlds unconquerèd,
Save of their lord no bearing yoke they knew,
And him by oath they truly honorèd. 410
These worlds in Tarquin new ambition bred,
    Who, like a foul usurper, went about
    From this fair throne to heave the owner out.

What could he see but mightily he noted?
What did he note but strongly he desired? 415
What he beheld, on that he firmly doted,
And in his will his willful eye he tired.
With more than admiration he admired
    Her azure veins, her alabaster skin,
    Her coral lips, her snow-white dimpled chin. 420

424. **qualified:** abated, diminished

425. **Slaked:** moderated, weakened in intensity

426. **late:** recently

428. **slaves:** i.e., baseborn soldiers (Military and war imagery continues through this and the following seven stanzas. See longer note, p. 588.)

431. **Nor:** neither

432. **pride:** wordplay on (1) flourishing state; (2) sexual desire

433. **alarum:** call to arms, signaled by the beating of drums (See longer notes to ll. 295 and 428, pp. 587, 588.)

436. **commends the leading:** i.e., entrusts **the leading** of **the charge** (l. 434)

437. **as:** i.e., **as** if

438. **Smoking:** steaming; **his:** its

440. **scale:** ascend or attack (as if with scaling ladders) (See picture, p. 484.)

442–43. **They . . . lies:** i.e., the blood in the **veins** (l. 440) rushes to assemble in the chamber housing Lucrece's heart

446. **She:** i.e., Lucrece; **amazed:** terrified, alarmed

447. **Who:** i.e., which

448. **controlled:** overpowered

As the grim lion fawneth o'er his prey,
Sharp hunger by the conquest satisfied,
So o'er this sleeping soul doth Tarquin stay,
His rage of lust by gazing qualified—
Slaked, not suppressed; for, standing by her side,   425
   His eye, which late this mutiny restrains,
   Unto a greater uproar tempts his veins.

And they, like straggling slaves for pillage fighting,
Obdurate vassals fell exploits effecting,
In bloody death and ravishment delighting,   430
Nor children's tears nor mothers' groans respecting,
Swell in their pride, the onset still expecting.
   Anon his beating heart, alarum striking,
   Gives the hot charge and bids them do their liking.

His drumming heart cheers up his burning eye;   435
His eye commends the leading to his hand;
His hand, as proud of such a dignity,
Smoking with pride, marched on to make his stand
On her bare breast, the heart of all her land,
   Whose ranks of blue veins, as his hand did scale,   440
   Left their round turrets destitute and pale.

They, must'ring to the quiet cabinet
Where their dear governess and lady lies,
Do tell her she is dreadfully beset,
And fright her with confusion of their cries.   445
She, much amazed, breaks ope her locked-up eyes,
   Who, peeping forth this tumult to behold,
   Are by his flaming torch dimmed and controlled.

450. **dreadful fancy:** i.e., nightmare
451. **sprite:** spirit, ghost
453. **worser taking:** i.e., a worse plight
456. **confounded:** thrown into confusion of mind
458. **winking:** closing her eyes
459. **antics:** grotesque figures
460. **shadows:** delusive images; phantoms
465. **citizen:** i.e., inhabitant of the besieged city
467. **bulk:** trunk, body; **withal:** with it
471. **heartless:** disheartened, spiritless
472. **peers:** shows a little of
473. **alarm:** attack; signal for battle or **parley** (l. 471)
475. **urgeth:** demands
476. **color:** pretext; **ill:** wrong

Scaling ladders. (*Lucrece,* 440)

Imagine her as one in dead of night
From forth dull sleep by dreadful fancy waking,   450
That thinks she hath beheld some ghastly sprite,
Whose grim aspect sets every joint a-shaking.
What terror 'tis! But she, in worser taking,
  From sleep disturbèd, heedfully doth view
  The sight which makes supposèd terror true.   455

Wrapped and confounded in a thousand fears,
Like to a new-killed bird she trembling lies.
She dares not look; yet, winking, there appears
Quick-shifting antics, ugly in her eyes.
Such shadows are the weak brain's forgeries,   460
  Who, angry that the eyes fly from their lights,
  In darkness daunts them with more dreadful sights.

His hand, that yet remains upon her breast,
Rude ram to batter such an ivory wall,
May feel her heart, poor citizen, distressed,   465
Wounding itself to death, rise up and fall,
Beating her bulk, that his hand shakes withal.
  This moves in him more rage and lesser pity
  To make the breach and enter this sweet city.

First, like a trumpet doth his tongue begin   470
To sound a parley to his heartless foe,
Who o'er the white sheet peers her whiter chin
The reason of this rash alarm to know,
Which he by dumb demeanor seeks to show.
  But she with vehement prayers urgeth still   475
  Under what color he commits this ill.

477. **color:** the white and red of her **face,** more lovely than the **lily** and the **red rose**

481. **color:** (1) pretext; (2) flag (See longer note to l. 428, p. 588.)

486. **will:** desire (For probable wordplay, see longer note, p. 588.)

488. **Which:** i.e., **my will** (l. 487)

491. **crosses:** afflictions, misfortunes

494. **counsel:** deliberation

496. **Only he hath:** i.e., **will** has **only**

500. **affection's:** desire's; **control:** hold in check

501. **his:** its

A rose defended by thorns. (*Lucrece,* 492)

Thus he replies: "The color in thy face,
That even for anger makes the lily pale,
And the red rose blush at her own disgrace,
Shall plead for me and tell my loving tale.   480
Under that color am I come to scale
    Thy never-conquered fort; the fault is thine,
    For those thine eyes betray thee unto mine.

"Thus I forestall thee if thou mean to chide:
Thy beauty hath ensnared thee to this night,   485
Where thou with patience must my will abide,
My will that marks thee for my earth's delight,
Which I to conquer sought with all my might.
    But as reproof and reason beat it dead,
    By thy bright beauty was it newly bred.   490

"I see what crosses my attempt will bring;
I know what thorns the growing rose defends;
I think the honey guarded with a sting;
All this beforehand counsel comprehends.
But will is deaf and hears no heedful friends;   495
    Only he hath an eye to gaze on beauty
    And dotes on what he looks, 'gainst law or duty.

"I have debated, even in my soul,
What wrong, what shame, what sorrow I shall breed,
But nothing can affection's course control   500
Or stop the headlong fury of his speed.
I know repentant tears ensue the deed,
    Reproach, disdain, and deadly enmity,
    Yet strive I to embrace mine infamy."

506. **tow'ring:** soaring (See picture below.)

507. **Coucheth:** causes to lie hidden

508. **crookèd:** curved; **threats:** i.e., threatens that

509. **insulting falchion:** triumphing sword

510. **marking:** listening to

516. **decay:** destruction

520. **scornful mark:** object of scorn

522. **issue:** offspring; **blurred:** defiled; **nameless:** In law, a bastard had the right to no one's name.

523. **author of:** one responsible for

524. **cited up:** called to mind, referred to

526. **rest:** remain

528–29. **A little . . . enacted:** See longer note, p. 588.

530. **simple:** medicine composed of only one herb or plant; **compacted:** combined

532. **His:** its

A "falcon tow'ring in the skies." (*Lucrece,* 506)

This said, he shakes aloft his Roman blade,   505
Which, like a falcon tow'ring in the skies,
Coucheth the fowl below with his wings' shade,
Whose crookèd beak threats, if he mount, he dies.
So under his insulting falchion lies
    Harmless Lucretia, marking what he tells   510
    With trembling fear, as fowl hear falcons' bells.

"Lucrece," quoth he, "this night I must enjoy thee.
If thou deny, then force must work my way,
For in thy bed I purpose to destroy thee.
That done, some worthless slave of thine I'll slay,   515
To kill thine honor with thy life's decay,
    And in thy dead arms do I mean to place him,
    Swearing I slew him, seeing thee embrace him.

"So thy surviving husband shall remain
The scornful mark of every open eye,   520
Thy kinsmen hang their heads at this disdain,
Thy issue blurred with nameless bastardy;
And thou, the author of their obloquy,
    Shalt have thy trespass cited up in rhymes
    And sung by children in succeeding times.   525

"But if thou yield, I rest thy secret friend.
The fault unknown is as a thought unacted;
A little harm done to a great good end
For lawful policy remains enacted.
The poisonous simple sometimes is compacted   530
    In a pure compound; being so applied,
    His venom in effect is purified.

534. **Tender:** comply graciously with

537. **slavish wipe:** scar or brand identifying a slave as such; **birth-hour's blot:** congenital blemish, birthmark

540. **cockatrice:** a mythical serpent (with the head, wings, and feet of a cock) whose looks could kill (See picture below.)

543. **gripe's:** A *gripe* could be the mythological griffin or a vulture.

548. **his:** its; **aspiring:** rising, soaring

549. **gust:** For the belief in subterranean air currents, see note to *Venus and Adonis*, ll. 1046–47. **get:** escape

550. **blow:** i.e., blows; **biding:** dwelling

551. **present fall:** immediate **fall** of rain; **dividing:** breaking up

552. **delays:** i.e., delay

553. **Pluto . . . plays:** i.e., the god **Pluto** is charmed by Orpheus's music (See longer note, p. 589.) **winks:** closes his eyes, sleeps

554. **dally:** play, amuse himself

555. **hold-fast:** firmly grasping

556. **vulture folly:** i.e., vulturous or ravenous desire

557. **wanteth:** i.e., has too little

559. **plaining:** complaint, lamentation

A cockatrice. (*Lucrece*, 540)

"Then, for thy husband and thy children's sake,
Tender my suit. Bequeath not to their lot
The shame that from them no device can take,   535
The blemish that will never be forgot,
Worse than a slavish wipe or birth-hour's blot,
    For marks descried in men's nativity
    Are nature's faults, not their own infamy."

Here with a cockatrice' dead-killing eye   540
He rouseth up himself and makes a pause,
While she, the picture of pure piety,
Like a white hind under the gripe's sharp claws,
Pleads, in a wilderness where are no laws,
    To the rough beast that knows no gentle right   545
    Nor aught obeys but his foul appetite.

But when a black-faced cloud the world doth threat,
In his dim mist th' aspiring mountains hiding,
From earth's dark womb some gentle gust doth get,
Which blow these pitchy vapors from their biding,   550
Hind'ring their present fall by this dividing;
    So his unhallowed haste her words delays,
    And moody Pluto winks while Orpheus plays.

Yet, foul night-waking cat, he doth but dally,
While in his hold-fast foot the weak mouse panteth.   555
Her sad behavior feeds his vulture folly,
A swallowing gulf that even in plenty wanteth.
His ear her prayers admits, but his heart granteth
    No penetrable entrance to her plaining;
    Tears harden lust, though marble wear with raining.   560

562. **remorseless:** pitiless; **wrinkles:** frown
565. **his:** i.e., its
566. **accent:** i.e., voice
569. **gentry:** rank by birth; good breeding; courtesy
571. **troth:** truth, good faith
573. **make retire:** return
574. **stoop:** yield, submit
576. **pretended:** intended, planned
579. **ill:** (1) poor; (2) evil; **shoot:** shot
580. **woodman:** hunter
581. **unseasonable:** out of season (for hunting)
584. **a weakling:** one lacking physical strength
587. **moved:** persuaded

"High almighty Jove." (*Lucrece,* 568; *Venus and Adonis,* 1015)

Her pity-pleading eyes are sadly fixed
In the remorseless wrinkles of his face.
Her modest eloquence with sighs is mixed,
Which to her oratory adds more grace.
She puts the period often from his place,   565
    And midst the sentence so her accent breaks
    That twice she doth begin ere once she speaks.

She conjures him by high almighty Jove,
By knighthood, gentry, and sweet friendship's oath,
By her untimely tears, her husband's love,   570
By holy human law, and common troth,
By heaven and earth, and all the power of both,
    That to his borrowed bed he make retire
    And stoop to honor, not to foul desire.

Quoth she, "Reward not hospitality   575
With such black payment as thou hast pretended;
Mud not the fountain that gave drink to thee.
Mar not the thing that cannot be amended.
End thy ill aim before thy shoot be ended;
    He is no woodman that doth bend his bow   580
    To strike a poor unseasonable doe.

"My husband is thy friend; for his sake spare me.
Thyself art mighty; for thine own sake leave me.
Myself a weakling, do not then ensnare me;
Thou look'st not like deceit; do not deceive me.   585
My sighs, like whirlwinds, labor hence to heave thee.
    If ever man were moved with woman's moans,
    Be movèd with my tears, my sighs, my groans,

590. **wrack-threat'ning:** shipwreck-threatening

603. **seeded:** matured

605. **in thy hope:** i.e., before you inherit the full power of kingship

607. **be remembered:** i.e., remember

608. **From vassal actors:** i.e., performed by mere subjects

609. **in clay:** i.e., even in death

611. **happy:** fortunate; **still:** always

613. **like:** same; **prove:** experience

614. **remove:** do away with, put aside

615. **glass:** looking glass, mirror

"All which together, like a troubled ocean,
Beat at thy rocky and wrack-threat'ning heart,   590
To soften it with their continual motion,
For stones dissolved to water do convert.
O, if no harder than a stone thou art,
    Melt at my tears and be compassionate!
    Soft pity enters at an iron gate.   595

"In Tarquin's likeness I did entertain thee.
Hast thou put on his shape to do him shame?
To all the host of heaven I complain me:
Thou wrong'st his honor, wound'st his princely name.
Thou art not what thou seem'st, and if the same,   600
    Thou seem'st not what thou art, a god, a king;
    For kings, like gods, should govern everything.

"How will thy shame be seeded in thine age
When thus thy vices bud before thy spring?
If in thy hope thou dar'st do such outrage,   605
What dar'st thou not when once thou art a king?
O, be remembered, no outrageous thing
    From vassal actors can be wiped away;
    Then king's misdeeds cannot be hid in clay.

"This deed will make thee only loved for fear,   610
But happy monarchs still are feared for love.
With foul offenders thou perforce must bear
When they in thee the like offenses prove.
If but for fear of this, thy will remove,
    For princes are the glass, the school, the book,   615
    Where subjects' eyes do learn, do read, do look.

618. **read lectures:** i.e., receive instructive counsel

627. **all that brood:** i.e., varieties of **iniquity** (l. 626)

629. **patterned by:** i.e., taking as a precedent

634. **partially:** unjustly, in a biased manner

636. **wrapped in:** enveloped

637. **askance:** turn aside

638. **heaved-up:** lifted

639. **thy rash relier:** i.e., one who recklessly relies on you (to continue to set aside your majesty)

640. **sue:** petition; **repeal:** recall

642. **prison:** imprison, confine

643. **doting:** foolish, stupid, imbecile; **eyne:** eyes

644. **state:** wordplay on (1) Tarquin's position as future king, and (2) Lucrece's physical and emotional situation

"And wilt thou be the school where Lust shall learn?
Must he in thee read lectures of such shame?
Wilt thou be glass wherein it shall discern
Authority for sin, warrant for blame,   620
To privilege dishonor in thy name?
    Thou back'st reproach against long-living laud
    And mak'st fair reputation but a bawd.

"Hast thou command? By Him that gave it thee,
From a pure heart command thy rebel will.   625
Draw not thy sword to guard iniquity,
For it was lent thee all that brood to kill.
Thy princely office how canst thou fulfill
    When, patterned by thy fault, foul Sin may say
    He learned to sin, and thou didst teach the way.   630

"Think but how vile a spectacle it were
To view thy present trespass in another.
Men's faults do seldom to themselves appear;
Their own transgressions partially they smother.
This guilt would seem death-worthy in thy brother.   635
    O, how are they wrapped in with infamies
    That from their own misdeeds askance their eyes!

"To thee, to thee, my heaved-up hands appeal,
Not to seducing lust, thy rash relier.
I sue for exiled majesty's repeal;   640
Let him return, and flatt'ring thoughts retire.
His true respect will prison false desire
    And wipe the dim mist from thy doting eyne,
    That thou shalt see thy state and pity mine."

645. **uncontrollèd:** unchecked

646. **let:** impediment

648. **fret:** devour, consume

655. **Who:** i.e., which; **blood:** i.e., nobility, majesty

657. **hearsed:** entombed, enclosed

661. **fair:** desirable

668. **enforcèd hate:** perhaps, force driven by hatred; or, perhaps, hatred employing force

669. **coy:** quiet

670. **despitefully:** spitefully, cruelly

671. **rascal:** wretched, base; **groom:** inferior servant

"Have done," quoth he. "My uncontrollèd tide   645
Turns not, but swells the higher by this let.
Small lights are soon blown out; huge fires abide,
And with the wind in greater fury fret.
The petty streams that pay a daily debt
    To their salt sovereign with their fresh falls' haste   650
    Add to his flow but alter not his taste."

"Thou art," quoth she, "a sea, a sovereign king,
And, lo, there falls into thy boundless flood
Black lust, dishonor, shame, misgoverning,
Who seek to stain the ocean of thy blood.   655
If all these petty ills shall change thy good,
    Thy sea within a puddle's womb is hearsed,
    And not the puddle in thy sea dispersed.

"So shall these slaves be king, and thou their slave;
Thou nobly base, they basely dignified;   660
Thou their fair life, and they thy fouler grave;
Thou loathèd in their shame, they in thy pride.
The lesser thing should not the greater hide;
    The cedar stoops not to the base shrub's foot,
    But low shrubs wither at the cedar's root.   665

"So let thy thoughts, low vassals to thy state—"
"No more," quoth he. "By heaven, I will not hear thee.
Yield to my love. If not, enforcèd hate,
Instead of love's coy touch, shall rudely tear thee.
That done, despitefully I mean to bear thee   670
    Unto the base bed of some rascal groom,
    To be thy partner in this shameful doom."

676. **tyrannize:** act cruelly or oppressively
678. **controlled:** checked
684. **prone:** eager (with wordplay on "lying face downward")
685. **spots:** stigma, disgrace
686. **should:** i.e., would
688. **would:** i.e., wished to
689. **league:** alliance, union
694. **Look as:** just **as**
695. **Unapt:** unfit; **tender smell:** i.e., perceiving subtle odors
696. **balk:** refuse, shun

This said, he sets his foot upon the light,
For light and lust are deadly enemies.
Shame folded up in blind concealing night,   675
When most unseen, then most doth tyrannize.
The wolf hath seized his prey; the poor lamb cries,
    Till, with her own white fleece her voice controlled,
    Entombs her outcry in her lips' sweet fold.

For with the nightly linen that she wears   680
He pens her piteous clamors in her head,
Cooling his hot face in the chastest tears
That ever modest eyes with sorrow shed.
O, that prone lust should stain so pure a bed!
    The spots whereof could weeping purify,   685
    Her tears should drop on them perpetually.

But she hath lost a dearer thing than life,
And he hath won what he would lose again.
This forcèd league doth force a further strife;
This momentary joy breeds months of pain;   690
This hot desire converts to cold disdain.
    Pure Chastity is rifled of her store,
    And Lust, the thief, far poorer than before.

Look as the full-fed hound or gorgèd hawk,
Unapt for tender smell or speedy flight,   695
Make slow pursuit, or altogether balk
The prey wherein by nature they delight;
So surfeit-taking Tarquin fares this night.
    His taste delicious, in digestion souring,
    Devours his will, that lived by foul devouring.   700

701. **conceit:** understanding

702. **still:** silent

703. **his receipt:** what it has received or taken in

705. **in his pride:** flourishing; sexually excited; **exclamation:** loud protest

707. **jade:** worthless horse (See picture, p. 118.)

710. **all:** completely; **recreant:** cowardly, fainthearted

711. **bankrout:** bankrupt; **wails:** laments, bewails

712. **proud:** sexually aroused

713. **there:** i.e., in **the flesh**; **that:** i.e., **the flesh**

714. **guilty rebel:** (1) Desire; (2) the **flesh** (See longer note, p. 589.) **remission:** forgiveness

715. **faultful:** faulty, culpable

716. **accomplishment:** fulfillment

717. **doom:** sentence

721. **the spotted princess:** i.e., his contaminated soul

727–28. **Which . . . will:** i.e., the soul's foreknowledge (**prescience**) had always governed her subjects, the senses and passions, but this knowledge could not prevent their lustful action **Which:** i.e., **her subjects** (l. 722)

O, deeper sin than bottomless conceit
Can comprehend in still imagination!
Drunken Desire must vomit his receipt
Ere he can see his own abomination.
While Lust is in his pride, no exclamation   705
    Can curb his heat or rein his rash desire,
    Till, like a jade, Self-will himself doth tire.

And then with lank and lean discolored cheek,
With heavy eye, knit brow, and strengthless pace,
Feeble Desire, all recreant, poor, and meek,   710
Like to a bankrout beggar wails his case.
The flesh being proud, Desire doth fight with Grace,
    For there it revels; and when that decays,
    The guilty rebel for remission prays.

So fares it with this faultful lord of Rome,   715
Who this accomplishment so hotly chased,
For now against himself he sounds this doom,
That through the length of times he stands disgraced.
Besides, his soul's fair temple is defaced,
    To whose weak ruins muster troops of cares   720
    To ask the spotted princess how she fares.

She says her subjects with foul insurrection
Have battered down her consecrated wall
And, by their mortal fault, brought in subjection
Her immortality, and made her thrall   725
To living death and pain perpetual,
    Which in her prescience she controllèd still,
    But her foresight could not forestall their will.

733. **spoil:** prey, i.e., Lucrece; **perplexed:** bewildered, tormented

740. **faintly:** spiritlessly, like a coward

743. **heavy:** sad; **convertite:** convert to a religious life, i.e., penitent

744. **castaway:** reprobate, outcast

747. **scapes:** transgressions

750. **They:** i.e., her **eyes** (l. 748)

752. **would they:** i.e., they wished that they might

754. **unfold:** reveal

755. **grave:** engrave; **water . . . steel:** i.e., aqua fortis (literally, strong water [Latin]), the acid used to engrave steel plates

E'en in this thought through the dark night he stealeth,
A captive victor that hath lost in gain, 730
Bearing away the wound that nothing healeth,
The scar that will, despite of cure, remain,
Leaving his spoil perplexed in greater pain.
    She bears the load of lust he left behind,
    And he the burden of a guilty mind. 735

He like a thievish dog creeps sadly thence;
She like a wearied lamb lies panting there.
He scowls and hates himself for his offense;
She, desperate, with her nails her flesh doth tear.
He faintly flies, sweating with guilty fear; 740
    She stays, exclaiming on the direful night;
    He runs and chides his vanished, loathed delight.

He thence departs a heavy convertite;
She there remains a hopeless castaway.
He in his speed looks for the morning light; 745
She prays she never may behold the day.
"For day," quoth she, "night's scapes doth open lay,
    And my true eyes have never practiced how
    To cloak offenses with a cunning brow.

"They think not but that every eye can see 750
The same disgrace which they themselves behold,
And therefore would they still in darkness be,
To have their unseen sin remain untold.
For they their guilt with weeping will unfold,
    And grave, like water that doth eat in steel, 755
    Upon my cheeks what helpless shame I feel."

757. **exclaims against:** rails at, protests against

758. **still:** always

761. **chest:** (1) breast; (2) case; **close:** enclose

765. **register:** i.e., keeper of a register; **notary:** clerk, secretary

766. **fell:** cruel, savage

767. **nurse:** nourisher

768. **defame:** dishonor, infamy

770. **close-tongued:** i.e., secretive

772. **crime:** sin, grave offense

774. **proportioned course of time:** i.e., alternation of night and day

776. **wonted:** accustomed (For the sun god in his chariot, see picture, p. 86.)

778. **damps:** noxious mists or fumes; **ravish:** spoil, corrupt

780. **life . . . fair:** essence of **purity** and king of beauty, i.e., the sun

781. **he . . . prick:** i.e., **he, weary, arrive** at the mark of noon on the sundial (See picture, p. 172.)

783. **smoky:** smokelike

Here she exclaims against repose and rest
And bids her eyes hereafter still be blind.
She wakes her heart by beating on her breast,
And bids it leap from thence, where it may find   760
Some purer chest to close so pure a mind.
    Frantic with grief thus breathes she forth her spite
    Against the unseen secrecy of night.

"O, comfort-killing Night, image of hell,
Dim register and notary of shame,   765
Black stage for tragedies and murders fell,
Vast sin-concealing chaos, nurse of blame,
Blind muffled bawd, dark harbor for defame,
    Grim cave of death, whisp'ring conspirator
    With close-tongued treason and the ravisher!   770

"O, hateful, vaporous, and foggy Night,
Since thou art guilty of my cureless crime,
Muster thy mists to meet the eastern light,
Make war against proportioned course of time;
Or, if thou wilt permit the sun to climb   775
    His wonted height, yet ere he go to bed,
    Knit poisonous clouds about his golden head.

"With rotten damps ravish the morning air;
Let their exhaled unwholesome breaths make sick
The life of purity, the supreme fair,   780
Ere he arrive his weary noontide prick,
And let thy musty vapors march so thick
    That in their smoky ranks his smothered light
    May set at noon and make perpetual night.

786. **silver-shining queen:** i.e., moon, associated with Diana, the goddess of chastity; **distain:** defile, dishonor

787. **twinkling handmaids:** i.e., stars

791. **palmers':** i.e., pilgrims' (See picture below.)

792. **Where:** i.e., whereas

793. **To cross . . . heads:** conventional gestures of melancholy

794. **mask their brows:** i.e., pull hats down over their faces

798. **monuments:** mementos

800. **jealous:** watchful

803. **still:** always

806. **object:** a spectacle, a sight; **telltale:** tattletale

807. **charactered:** written in letters, or characters

808. **decay:** destruction

811. **cipher:** decipher, i.e., read

812. **quote:** observe, notice

A palmer. (*Lucrece*, 791)

"Were Tarquin Night, as he is but Night's child,   785
The silver-shining queen he would distain;
Her twinkling handmaids too, by him defiled,
Through Night's black bosom should not peep again.
So should I have copartners in my pain,
      And fellowship in woe doth woe assuage,   790
      As palmers' chat makes short their pilgrimage.

"Where now I have no one to blush with me,
To cross their arms and hang their heads with mine,
To mask their brows and hide their infamy,
But I alone alone must sit and pine,   795
Seasoning the earth with showers of silver brine,
      Mingling my talk with tears, my grief with groans,
      Poor wasting monuments of lasting moans.

"O Night, thou furnace of foul reeking smoke,
Let not the jealous Day behold that face   800
Which underneath thy black all-hiding cloak
Immodestly lies martyred with disgrace!
Keep still possession of thy gloomy place,
      That all the faults which in thy reign are made
      May likewise be sepulchered in thy shade.   805

"Make me not object to the telltale Day.
The light will show charactered in my brow
The story of sweet chastity's decay,
The impious breach of holy wedlock vow.
Yea, the illiterate, that know not how   810
      To cipher what is writ in learnèd books,
      Will quote my loathsome trespass in my looks.

813. **nurse:** wet **nurse**

816. **reproach:** disgrace

817. **tuning:** singing about; **defame:** dishonor

818. **tie:** bind, oblige; **attend:** listen to

820. **senseless:** perhaps, unmoved by sensual desire (as is Lucrece by **reputation**)

825. **attaint:** imputation of dishonor, stain

828. **crest-wounding:** damaging to the family **crest**

830. **mot:** motto, i.e., **reproach** (l. 829)

"The nurse, to still her child, will tell my story
And fright her crying babe with Tarquin's name.
The orator, to deck his oratory,   815
Will couple my reproach to Tarquin's shame.
Feast-finding minstrels, tuning my defame,
    Will tie the hearers to attend each line,
    How Tarquin wrongèd me, I Collatine.

"Let my good name, that senseless reputation,   820
For Collatine's dear love be kept unspotted.
If that be made a theme for disputation,
The branches of another root are rotted
And undeserved reproach to him allotted
    That is as clear from this attaint of mine   825
    As I, ere this, was pure to Collatine.

"O unseen shame, invisible disgrace!
O unfelt sore, crest-wounding private scar!
Reproach is stamped in Collatinus' face,
And Tarquin's eye may read the mot afar,   830
How he in peace is wounded, not in war.
    Alas, how many bear such shameful blows,
    Which not themselves but he that gives them knows!

"If, Collatine, thine honor lay in me,
From me by strong assault it is bereft;   835
My honey lost, and I, a drone-like bee,
Have no perfection of my summer left,
But robbed and ransacked by injurious theft.
    In thy weak hive a wand'ring wasp hath crept
    And sucked the honey which thy chaste bee kept.   840

841. **wrack:** shipwreck

842. **entertain:** hospitably receive

843. **put him back:** reject or refuse him

848. **intrude:** enter forcibly

850. **founts:** fountains; **venom:** venomous

851. **tyrant:** cruelly violent; **folly:** desire; **gentle:** noble

854. **pollute:** i.e., **pollute** it

855. **coffers up:** secures in a coffer

858. **still-pining:** forever deprived; **Tantalus:** See note to *Venus and Adonis*, l. 599, and picture, p. 400.

859. **useless barns:** i.e., futilely stores in barns

863. **mastered:** possessed

864. **presently:** immediately

A cuckoo. (*Lucrece*, 849)

"Yet am I guilty of thy honor's wrack;
Yet for thy honor did I entertain him.
Coming from thee, I could not put him back,
For it had been dishonor to disdain him.
Besides, of weariness he did complain him   845
   And talked of virtue. O, unlooked-for evil,
   When virtue is profaned in such a devil!

"Why should the worm intrude the maiden bud?
Or hateful cuckoos hatch in sparrows' nests?
Or toads infect fair founts with venom mud?   850
Or tyrant folly lurk in gentle breasts?
Or kings be breakers of their own behests?
   But no perfection is so absolute
   That some impurity doth not pollute.

"The agèd man that coffers up his gold   855
Is plagued with cramps and gouts and painful fits
And scarce hath eyes his treasure to behold,
But like still-pining Tantalus he sits,
And useless barns the harvest of his wits,
   Having no other pleasure of his gain   860
   But torment that it cannot cure his pain.

"So then he hath it when he cannot use it
And leaves it to be mastered by his young,
Who in their pride do presently abuse it.
Their father was too weak and they too strong   865
To hold their cursèd-blessèd fortune long.
   The sweets we wish for turn to loathèd sours
   Even in the moment that we call them ours.

869. **blasts:** gusts of wind; **wait on:** accompany

874. **ill-annexèd:** injuriously attached; **Opportunity:** occasion, chance, or circumstance

875. **Or:** i.e., either; **his:** i.e., its; **quality:** nature, character

877. **execut'st:** carries out, performs (by providing the occasion)

879. **thou 'point'st:** you appoint; **season:** favorable occasion

883. **vestal:** See longer note to *Venus and Adonis*, l. 752, p. 444, and picture, p. 412.

885. **troth:** faithfulness, loyalty

892. **smoothing:** flattering; **raggèd:** imperfect, i.e., contemptible

894. **vanities:** worthless activities

"Unruly blasts wait on the tender spring;
Unwholesome weeds take root with precious flowers;   870
The adder hisses where the sweet birds sing;
What Virtue breeds Iniquity devours.
We have no good that we can say is ours
    But ill-annexèd Opportunity
    Or kills his life or else his quality.   875

"O Opportunity, thy guilt is great!
'Tis thou that execut'st the traitor's treason;
Thou sets the wolf where he the lamb may get;
Whoever plots the sin, thou 'point'st the season.
'Tis thou that spurn'st at right, at law, at reason,   880
    And in thy shady cell, where none may spy him,
    Sits Sin, to seize the souls that wander by him.

"Thou makest the vestal violate her oath;
Thou blowest the fire when temperance is thawed;
Thou smother'st honesty, thou murd'rest troth.   885
Thou foul abettor, thou notorious bawd,
Thou plantest scandal and displacest laud.
    Thou ravisher, thou traitor, thou false thief,
    Thy honey turns to gall, thy joy to grief.

"Thy secret pleasure turns to open shame,   890
Thy private feasting to a public fast,
Thy smoothing titles to a raggèd name,
Thy sugared tongue to bitter wormwood taste.
Thy violent vanities can never last.
    How comes it, then, vile Opportunity,   895
    Being so bad, such numbers seek for thee?

898. **suit:** petition

899. **sort:** choose

901. **physic:** medicine

902. **halt:** (1) perhaps, crippled (an adjective used as a noun); (2) perhaps the verb meaning "to limp"

905. **pines:** starves; **feeds:** eats

907. **Advice:** medical or legal counsel; **sporting:** amusing itself

910. **wait on:** accompany; **as:** i.e., **as** if

911. **have to do with: have** dealings or business **with**

912. **crosses:** adversities, obstacles

914. **apaid:** pleased

916. **else:** otherwise

917. **stayed:** detained

920. **shift:** subterfuge

924. **general doom:** doomsday (See picture below.)

"The general doom." (*Lucrece,* 924)

"When wilt thou be the humble suppliant's friend
And bring him where his suit may be obtained?
When wilt thou sort an hour great strifes to end,
Or free that soul which wretchedness hath chained,   900
Give physic to the sick, ease to the pained?
   The poor, lame, blind, halt, creep, cry out for thee,
   But they ne'er meet with Opportunity.

"The patient dies while the physician sleeps;
The orphan pines while the oppressor feeds;   905
Justice is feasting while the widow weeps;
Advice is sporting while infection breeds.
Thou grant'st no time for charitable deeds.
   Wrath, envy, treason, rape, and murder's rages,
   Thy heinous hours wait on them as their pages.   910

"When Truth and Virtue have to do with thee,
A thousand crosses keep them from thy aid.
They buy thy help, but Sin ne'er gives a fee;
He gratis comes, and thou art well apaid
As well to hear as grant what he hath said.   915
   My Collatine would else have come to me
   When Tarquin did, but he was stayed by thee.

"Guilty thou art of murder and of theft,
Guilty of perjury and subornation,
Guilty of treason, forgery, and shift,   920
Guilty of incest, that abomination—
An accessory by thine inclination
   To all sins past and all that are to come,
   From the creation to the general doom.

925. **copesmate:** associate, companion

926. **subtle:** imperceptible, insidious; **post:** fast messenger

928. **Base . . . packhorse:** See longer note, p. 589.   **watch:** perhaps, watchman   **packhorse:** (1) horse used to carry packs or bundles; (2) drudge

929. **nursest:** i.e., nurse, nourish

935. **date:** duration, period

936. **office:** duty, function; **fine:** bring to an end (also, perhaps, refine or purify)

944. **ruinate:** reduce to ruins

950. **cherish springs:** This sudden shift from destroying to creating anticipates the next stanza.   **springs:** saplings

952. **giddy . . . wheel:** Lady **Fortune** is the goddess who presides over apparently senseless changes from one state of affairs to another, and thus is associated in art with a ceaselessly and sometimes wildly turning **wheel.** (See picture below.)

"The giddy round of Fortune's wheel." (*Lucrece*, 952)

"Misshapen Time, copesmate of ugly Night,   925
Swift subtle post, carrier of grisly care,
Eater of youth, false slave to false delight,
Base watch of woes, sin's packhorse, virtue's snare!
Thou nursest all and murd'rest all that are.
    O, hear me, then, injurious, shifting Time!   930
    Be guilty of my death, since of my crime.

"Why hath thy servant Opportunity
Betrayed the hours thou gav'st me to repose,
Canceled my fortunes, and enchainèd me
To endless date of never-ending woes?   935
Time's office is to fine the hate of foes,
    To eat up errors by opinion bred,
    Not spend the dowry of a lawful bed.

"Time's glory is to calm contending kings,
To unmask falsehood and bring truth to light,   940
To stamp the seal of time in agèd things,
To wake the morn and sentinel the night,
To wrong the wronger till he render right,
    To ruinate proud buildings with thy hours
    And smear with dust their glitt'ring golden towers,   945

"To fill with worm-holes stately monuments,
To feed oblivion with decay of things,
To blot old books and alter their contents,
To pluck the quills from ancient ravens' wings,
To dry the old oak's sap and cherish springs,   950
    To spoil antiquities of hammered steel
    And turn the giddy round of Fortune's wheel,

953. **beldam:** grandmother

956. **tame the unicorn:** According to Edward Topsell in *A Historie of Foure-Footed Beastes* (1607), the unicorn "is a beast of vntamable nature[;] . . . except they bee taken before they bee two yeares old they will neuer be tamed" (sig. 3S6).

958. **increaseful:** fruitful, productive

960. **mischief:** misfortune, trouble

962. **retiring:** returning, coming back again

964. **wit:** good judgment

967. **lackey:** running footman

968. **cross:** thwart

970. **crimeful:** criminal, laden with crime

971. **shadows:** delusive images; phantoms

974. **trances:** states of dread

975. **bedrid:** bedridden (a transferred epithet; i.e., an adjective used to modify a noun that it does not logically modify)

976. **bechance:** befall, happen to

A plowman. (*Lucrece*, 958)

"To show the beldam daughters of her daughter,
To make the child a man, the man a child,
To slay the tiger that doth live by slaughter,   955
To tame the unicorn and lion wild,
To mock the subtle in themselves beguiled,
    To cheer the plowman with increaseful crops
    And waste huge stones with little water drops.

"Why work'st thou mischief in thy pilgrimage,   960
Unless thou couldst return to make amends?
One poor retiring minute in an age
Would purchase thee a thousand thousand friends,
Lending him wit that to bad debtors lends.
    O this dread night, wouldst thou one hour come back, 965
    I could prevent this storm and shun thy wrack!

"Thou ceaseless lackey to Eternity,
With some mischance cross Tarquin in his flight.
Devise extremes beyond extremity
To make him curse this cursèd crimeful night.   970
Let ghastly shadows his lewd eyes affright,
    And the dire thought of his committed evil
    Shape every bush a hideous shapeless devil.

"Disturb his hours of rest with restless trances.
Afflict him in his bed with bedrid groans.   975
Let there bechance him pitiful mischances
To make him moan, but pity not his moans.
Stone him with hard'ned hearts harder than stones,
    And let mild women to him lose their mildness,
    Wilder to him than tigers in their wildness.   980

985. **orts:** scraps, leavings

987. **Disdain . . . give:** i.e., think it beneath him **to give disdainèd scraps to** Tarquin

989. **to . . . resort:** i.e., make their way to him in order to **mock him**

990. **mark:** observe

992. **folly:** lewdness

993. **unrecalling:** perhaps, unrecalled or irrevocable (The word is not recorded as occurring elsewhere.)

996. **ill:** evil

997. **the thief:** a reminder that a primary meaning of *rape* is violent theft

1000. **who . . . have:** i.e., who is **so base** that he **would** accept **such** a position

1001. **sland'rous:** disgraceful; **deathsman:** executioner (See picture below.) **slave:** a general term of contempt

1002. **coming:** descending

1003. **hope:** i.e., of succeeding to the kingship

1005. **begets him:** i.e., produces for him

1006. **waits on:** accompanies; **greatest state:** highest rank

1007. **presently:** immediately

1008. **them:** i.e., themselves; **list:** please

An executioner. (*Lucrece,* 1001)

"Let him have time to tear his curlèd hair,
Let him have time against himself to rave,
Let him have time of Time's help to despair,
Let him have time to live a loathèd slave,
Let him have time a beggar's orts to crave   985
    And time to see one that by alms doth live
    Disdain to him disdainèd scraps to give.

"Let him have time to see his friends his foes,
And merry fools to mock at him resort.
Let him have time to mark how slow time goes   990
In time of sorrow, and how swift and short
His time of folly and his time of sport;
    And ever let his unrecalling crime
    Have time to wail th'abusing of his time.

"O Time, thou tutor both to good and bad,   995
Teach me to curse him that thou taught'st this ill!
At his own shadow let the thief run mad,
Himself himself seek every hour to kill.
Such wretched hands such wretched blood should spill,
    For who so base would such an office have   1000
    As sland'rous deathsman to so base a slave?

"The baser is he, coming from a king,
To shame his hope with deeds degenerate.
The mightier man, the mightier is the thing
That makes him honored or begets him hate;   1005
For greatest scandal waits on greatest state.
    The moon being clouded presently is missed,
    But little stars may hide them when they list.

1011. **the like:** i.e., the same kind of thing

1013. **grooms:** lowly servants; **sightless night:** i.e., as if invisible

1016. **Out:** expression of abhorrence

1018. **skill-contending schools:** i.e., university debates that display skill with words

1019. **leisure serves with:** i.e., there is **leisure** for

1021. **force . . . straw:** care **not a straw** for **argument**

1024. **uncheerful:** cheerless

1025. **cavil:** dispute

1026. **despite:** shameful injury

1027. **helpless:** unhelpful

1033. **defame:** infamy

1035. **affeard:** afraid

"The crow may bathe his coal-black wings in mire
And unperceived fly with the filth away,   1010
But if the like the snow-white swan desire,
The stain upon his silver down will stay.
Poor grooms are sightless night, kings glorious day.
    Gnats are unnoted wheresoe'er they fly,
    But eagles gazed upon with every eye.   1015

"Out, idle words, servants to shallow fools,
Unprofitable sounds, weak arbitrators!
Busy yourselves in skill-contending schools;
Debate where leisure serves with dull debaters;
To trembling clients be you mediators.   1020
    For me, I force not argument a straw,
    Since that my case is past the help of law.

"In vain I rail at Opportunity,
At Time, at Tarquin, and uncheerful Night.
In vain I cavil with mine infamy.   1025
In vain I spurn at my confirmed despite.
This helpless smoke of words doth me no right.
    The remedy indeed to do me good
    Is to let forth my foul defilèd blood.

"Poor hand, why quiver'st thou at this decree?   1030
Honor thyself to rid me of this shame,
For if I die, my honor lives in thee,
But if I live, thou liv'st in my defame;
Since thou couldst not defend thy loyal dame
    And wast affeard to scratch her wicked foe,   1035
    Kill both thyself and her for yielding so."

1037. **betumbled:** disordered

1042. **Etna:** volcanic mountain in Sicily (See picture below.) **consumes:** perishes, disappears

1045. **happy:** fortunate; **mean:** means

1050. **type:** distinguishing mark or sign

1054. **badge:** Servants of a noble house wore as a **badge** on their uniforms or **livery** their master's device, crest, or coat of arms.

1062–64. **bastard . . . fruit:** wordplay on reproduction in plants and humans (See longer note, p. 590, and picture, p. 52.)

Mount Etna. (*Lucrece*, 1042)

This said, from her betumbled couch she starteth,
To find some desp'rate instrument of death,
But this, no slaughterhouse, no tool imparteth
To make more vent for passage of her breath,   1040
Which, thronging through her lips, so vanisheth
  As smoke from Etna, that in air consumes,
  Or that which from dischargèd cannon fumes.

"In vain," quoth she, "I live, and seek in vain
Some happy mean to end a hapless life.   1045
I feared by Tarquin's falchion to be slain,
Yet for the selfsame purpose seek a knife.
But when I feared, I was a loyal wife;
  So am I now.—O no, that cannot be!
  Of that true type hath Tarquin rifled me.   1050

"O, that is gone for which I sought to live,
And therefore now I need not fear to die.
To clear this spot by death, at least I give
A badge of fame to slander's livery,
A dying life to living infamy.   1055
  Poor helpless help, the treasure stol'n away,
  To burn the guiltless casket where it lay!

"Well, well, dear Collatine, thou shalt not know
The stainèd taste of violated troth;
I will not wrong thy true affection so   1060
To flatter thee with an infringèd oath.
This bastard graff shall never come to growth;
  He shall not boast who did thy stock pollute
  That thou art doting father of his fruit.

1067. **int'rest:** i.e., property (i.e., Lucrece)

1070. **with . . . dispense:** will never grant a dispensation for or condone my **trespass**

1071. **acquit:** atone, discharge

1072. **attaint:** imputation of dishonor

1073. **fold:** wrap up; **cleanly:** neatly, cleverly; **coined:** fabricated

1074. **sable:** black (in heraldic language); **ground:** surface of the shield in a coat of arms

1079. **this:** this time; **Philomel:** i.e., the nightingale (In mythology Philomela, sister-in-law of King Tereus, was transformed into a nightingale after he raped her and cut out her tongue.) See picture below.

1084. **cloudy:** gloomy; **shames:** is ashamed

1090. **tickling:** annoying, teasing

1092. **do:** i.e., **do** with

A nightingale. (*Lucrece,* 1079; s. 102.7)

"Nor shall he smile at thee in secret thought,   1065
Nor laugh with his companions at thy state,
But thou shalt know thy int'rest was not bought
Basely with gold, but stol'n from forth thy gate.
For me, I am the mistress of my fate
    And with my trespass never will dispense   1070
    Till life to death acquit my forced offense.

"I will not poison thee with my attaint,
Nor fold my fault in cleanly coined excuses;
My sable ground of sin I will not paint
To hide the truth of this false night's abuses.   1075
My tongue shall utter all; mine eyes, like sluices,
    As from a mountain spring that feeds a dale,
    Shall gush pure streams to purge my impure tale."

By this, lamenting Philomel had ended
The well-tuned warble of her nightly sorrow,   1080
And solemn night with slow sad gait descended
To ugly hell, when, lo, the blushing morrow
Lends light to all fair eyes that light will borrow.
    But cloudy Lucrece shames herself to see
    And therefore still in night would cloistered be.   1085

Revealing day through every cranny spies
And seems to point her out where she sits weeping,
To whom she sobbing speaks: "O eye of eyes,
Why pry'st thou through my window? Leave thy peeping.
Mock with thy tickling beams eyes that are sleeping.   1090
    Brand not my forehead with thy piercing light,
    For day hath naught to do what's done by night."

1093. **cavils:** disputes, finds fault

1094. **fond:** foolish, silly; **testy:** peevish

1095. **wayward once:** i.e., **once** it becomes intractable, obstinate

1096. **bear them mild:** i.e., **bear** themselves with moderation

1097. **Continuance:** duration

1098. **still:** continually

1099. **want:** lack

1100. **drenchèd:** overwhelmed, immersed

1103. **No object . . . renews:** i.e., there is nothing she sees that does not renew her grief   **passion's strength:** i.e., grief

1104. **shifts:** slips from observation; **straight ensues:** follows immediately

1107. **tune:** sing

1109. **search . . . annoy:** i.e., probe to the **bottom** of distress (**annoy**) as if probing a wound

1112. **feelingly sufficed:** appropriately satisfied

1113. **like semblance:** appearance identical to its own; **sympathized:** matched

1114. **ken:** sight

1115. **pines:** starves

1117. **that:** i.e., that which

1118. **flood:** body of flowing water

1119. **Who:** i.e., which

1120. **dallied with:** played with mockingly; **nor law:** neither law

Thus cavils she with everything she sees.
True grief is fond and testy as a child,
Who, wayward once, his mood with naught agrees.   1095
Old woes, not infant sorrows, bear them mild:
Continuance tames the one; the other, wild,
    Like an unpracticed swimmer plunging still
    With too much labor drowns for want of skill.

So she, deep drenchèd in a sea of care,   1100
Holds disputation with each thing she views
And to herself all sorrow doth compare;
No object but her passion's strength renews,
And as one shifts, another straight ensues.
    Sometimes her grief is dumb and hath no words;   1105
    Sometimes 'tis mad and too much talk affords.

The little birds that tune their morning's joy
Make her moans mad with their sweet melody,
For mirth doth search the bottom of annoy;
Sad souls are slain in merry company.   1110
Grief best is pleased with grief's society;
    True sorrow then is feelingly sufficed
    When with like semblance it is sympathized.

'Tis double death to drown in ken of shore;
He ten times pines that pines beholding food;   1115
To see the salve doth make the wound ache more;
Great grief grieves most at that would do it good.
Deep woes roll forward like a gentle flood,
    Who, being stopped, the bounding banks o'erflows;
    Grief dallied with nor law nor limit knows.   1120

1121–41. **You . . . languishment:** These stanzas are full of wordplay on musical terms: **tunes, discord, stops, rests, relish, notes, dumps, time, strain, diapason, burden, hum, descants, part, means, frets, instrument, tune, heartstrings.** For the musical meanings of the less common of these terms, see longer note, p. 590.

1124. **stops:** acts of coming to a halt; hesitations; obstacles

1125. **brooks:** tolerates, endures

1126. **Relish:** (1) sing, warble; (2) perhaps, embellish (As a noun, *relish* can mean "ornament, embellishment" and was used in that sense in connection with lute music.) **pleasing ears:** i.e., **ears** likely to be pleased

1131. **sad strain: sad** tune or melody; **will strain:** i.e., **will** squeeze out

1132. **diapason:** bass sounding in exact concord with the melody (an octave below)

1134. **Tereus:** the rapist of Philomela (See note to l. 1079.) **descants:** sing harmoniously; **better skill:** perhaps, with **better skill** (See longer note, p. 590.)

1139. **Who:** i.e., which; **wink:** closes

1140. **means:** (1) methods; (2) complaints

1141. **heartstrings:** tendons and nerves supposed to brace and sustain the heart; **languishment:** distress, sadness

1143. **shaming:** being ashamed that

1144. **desert:** stretch of uninhabited land; **seated . . . way:** i.e., situated away from the road or path

1146. **unfold:** reveal

1147. **creatures stern:** merciless, terrible beasts; **kinds:** natures

"You mocking birds," quoth she, "your tunes entomb
Within your hollow-swelling feathered breasts,
And in my hearing be you mute and dumb;
My restless discord loves no stops nor rests.
A woeful hostess brooks not merry guests.   1125
    Relish your nimble notes to pleasing ears;
    Distress likes dumps when time is kept with tears.

"Come, Philomel, that sing'st of ravishment,
Make thy sad grove in my disheveled hair.
As the dank earth weeps at thy languishment,   1130
So I at each sad strain will strain a tear
And with deep groans the diapason bear;
    For burden-wise I'll hum on Tarquin still,
    While thou on Tereus descants better skill.

"And whiles against a thorn thou bear'st thy part   1135
To keep thy sharp woes waking, wretched I,
To imitate thee well, against my heart
Will fix a sharp knife to affright mine eye,
Who if it wink shall thereon fall and die.
    These means, as frets upon an instrument,   1140
    Shall tune our heartstrings to true languishment.

"And for, poor bird, thou sing'st not in the day,
As shaming any eye should thee behold,
Some dark, deep desert seated from the way,
That knows not parching heat nor freezing cold,   1145
Will we find out, and there we will unfold
    To creatures stern sad tunes to change their kinds.
    Since men prove beasts, let beasts bear gentle minds."

1149. **at gaze:** i.e., in bewilderment or wonder

1155. **death reproach's debtor:** i.e., **death** is in debt to reproach (See longer note, p. 591.)

1157. **with my body:** i.e., add the defilement of **my body** to

1159. **confusion:** destruction

1160. **conclusion:** experiment

1162. **be nurse to:** i.e., feed or nourish

1164. **the one . . . divine:** i.e., the **body,** being **pure, made** the **soul** worthy of salvation

1167. **pilled:** stripped

1168. **His:** its (the pine's)

1172. **spotted:** blemished

As the poor frighted deer that stands at gaze,
Wildly determining which way to fly,   1150
Or one encompassed with a winding maze,
That cannot tread the way out readily,
So with herself is she in mutiny,
  To live or die which of the twain were better
  When life is shamed and death reproach's debtor.   1155

"To kill myself," quoth she, "alack, what were it
But with my body my poor soul's pollution?
They that lose half with greater patience bear it
Than they whose whole is swallowed in confusion.
That mother tries a merciless conclusion   1160
  Who, having two sweet babes, when death takes one,
  Will slay the other and be nurse to none.

"My body or my soul, which was the dearer
When the one pure, the other made divine?
Whose love of either to myself was nearer   1165
When both were kept for heaven and Collatine?
Ay me, the bark pilled from the lofty pine,
  His leaves will wither and his sap decay;
  So must my soul, her bark being pilled away.

"Her house is sacked, her quiet interrupted,   1170
Her mansion battered by the enemy,
Her sacred temple spotted, spoiled, corrupted,
Grossly engirt with daring infamy.
Then let it not be called impiety
  If in this blemished fort I make some hole   1175
  Through which I may convey this troubled soul.

1183. **his due:** i.e., that to which he has a legal right; **writ:** written

1186. **deprive:** remove

1187. **The one:** i.e., **honor**

1188. **of shame's . . . bred: Fame** is compared to the mythical phoenix, which is reborn from the **ashes** of its own death by fire. (See picture below.)

1191. **Dear lord:** i.e., Collatine

1202. **confound:** overthrow

A phoenix. (s. 19.4; *Lucrece*, 1188; "The Phoenix and Turtle")

"Yet die I will not till my Collatine
Have heard the cause of my untimely death,
That he may vow, in that sad hour of mine,
Revenge on him that made me stop my breath.   1180
My stainèd blood to Tarquin I'll bequeath,
   Which, by him tainted, shall for him be spent,
   And as his due writ in my testament.

"My honor I'll bequeath unto the knife
That wounds my body so dishonorèd.   1185
'Tis honor to deprive dishonored life;
The one will live, the other being dead.
So of shame's ashes shall my fame be bred,
   For in my death I murder shameful scorn;
   My shame so dead, mine honor is new born.   1190

"Dear lord of that dear jewel I have lost,
What legacy shall I bequeath to thee?
My resolution, love, shall be thy boast,
By whose example thou revenged mayst be.
How Tarquin must be used, read it in me;   1195
   Myself, thy friend, will kill myself, thy foe,
   And for my sake serve thou false Tarquin so.

"This brief abridgement of my will I make:
My soul and body to the skies and ground;
My resolution, husband, do thou take;   1200
Mine honor be the knife's that makes my wound;
My shame be his that did my fame confound;
   And all my fame that lives disbursèd be
   To those that live and think no shame of me.

1205. **oversee:** i.e., be the one who assists the executor(s) of

1206. **overseen:** deceived, deluded

1207. **ill:** sin, misdeed

1208. **free it:** i.e., clear from blame

1214. **untuned tongue:** i.e., croaking voice

1215. **hies:** hurries

1218. **meads:** meadows

1220. **mark:** sign

1221. **sorts:** adapts

1222. **Forwhy:** because; **livery:** uniform, distinctive suit

1228. **gan wet:** began to **wet**

1229. **circled eyne:** rounded eyes; or, perhaps, eyes rimmed with red

1229–30. **sympathy / Of:** i.e., empathy with

"Thou, Collatine, shalt oversee this will;   1205
How was I overseen that thou shalt see it!
My blood shall wash the slander of mine ill;
My life's foul deed my life's fair end shall free it.
Faint not, faint heart, but stoutly say, 'So be it.'
    Yield to my hand; my hand shall conquer thee.   1210
    Thou dead, both die, and both shall victors be."

This plot of death when sadly she had laid,
And wiped the brinish pearl from her bright eyes,
With untuned tongue she hoarsely calls her maid,
Whose swift obedience to her mistress hies,   1215
For fleet-winged duty with thought's feathers flies.
    Poor Lucrece' cheeks unto her maid seem so
    As winter meads when sun doth melt their snow.

Her mistress she doth give demure good morrow
With soft slow tongue, true mark of modesty,   1220
And sorts a sad look to her lady's sorrow,
Forwhy her face wore sorrow's livery,
But durst not ask of her audaciously
    Why her two suns were cloud-eclipsèd so,
    Nor why her fair cheeks over-washed with woe.   1225

But as the earth doth weep, the sun being set,
Each flower moistened like a melting eye,
Even so the maid with swelling drops gan wet
Her circled eyne, enforced by sympathy
Of those fair suns set in her mistress' sky,   1230
    Who in a salt-waved ocean quench their light,
    Which makes the maid weep like the dewy night.

1233. **pretty while:** fairly long time

1234. **ivory . . . filling:** See longer note, p. 591.

1235–36. **takes . . . spilling:** i.e., **weeps** only to keep Lucrece **company**

1241. **they:** i.e., women's minds; **formed:** shaped; **will:** determines

1242. **impression:** stamp; **strange kinds:** alien natures

1244. **ill:** evil

1247. **champaign plain:** expanse of level, open country

1248. **Lays open:** exposes to view; **worms:** i.e., creatures that **creep** or crawl

1250. **Cave-keeping evils:** i.e., **evils** that remain hidden, as in caves; **obscurely sleep:** i.e., **sleep** in obscurity

1251. **mote:** speck

1254. **No man:** i.e., let **no man**

1256. **Not that:** i.e., **not that** which is

1257. **hild:** i.e., held

1258. **fulfilled:** filled up

1259. **lords:** property owners; **to blame:** i.e., who are blameworthy

A pretty while these pretty creatures stand
Like ivory conduits coral cisterns filling.
One justly weeps; the other takes in hand   1235
No cause but company of her drops' spilling.
Their gentle sex to weep are often willing,
    Grieving themselves to guess at others' smarts,
    And then they drown their eyes or break their hearts.

For men have marble, women waxen, minds,   1240
And therefore are they formed as marble will.
The weak oppressed, th' impression of strange kinds
Is formed in them by force, by fraud, or skill.
Then call them not the authors of their ill
    No more than wax shall be accounted evil   1245
    Wherein is stamped the semblance of a devil.

Their smoothness, like a goodly champaign plain,
Lays open all the little worms that creep;
In men, as in a rough-grown grove, remain
Cave-keeping evils that obscurely sleep.   1250
Through crystal walls each little mote will peep.
    Though men can cover crimes with bold stern looks,
    Poor women's faces are their own faults' books.

No man inveigh against the withered flower,
But chide rough winter that the flower hath killed.   1255
Not that devoured, but that which doth devour,
Is worthy blame. O, let it not be hild
Poor women's faults that they are so fulfilled
    With men's abuses. Those proud lords, to blame,
    Make weak-made women tenants to their shame.   1260

1261. **precedent whereof:** i.e., example or illustration of the above generalization

1263. **present:** imminent

1266–67. **That dying fear . . . dead:** These lines suggest, although ambiguously, that Lucrece may have fainted as Tarquin was about to assault her, as she does in Chaucer's version in *The Legende of Good Women.*

1268. **this:** i.e., this time; **bid:** bade

1269. **poor counterfeit of:** i.e., her maid, who pitifully imitates

1270. **quoth:** says

1272. **of my sustaining:** i.e., that I have suffered

1273. **small:** little; **avails:** helps

1275. **stayed:** stopped

1278. **to blame:** blameworthy

1279. **with . . . dispense:** i.e., I can excuse the shortcoming to this extent

1283. **heaviness:** sorrow

1285. **repetition:** narration

The precedent whereof in Lucrece view,
Assailed by night with circumstances strong
Of present death, and shame that might ensue
By that her death, to do her husband wrong.
Such danger to resistance did belong   1265
   That dying fear through all her body spread,
   And who cannot abuse a body dead?

By this, mild patience bid fair Lucrece speak
To the poor counterfeit of her complaining:
"My girl," quoth she, "on what occasion break   1270
Those tears from thee, that down thy cheeks are raining?
If thou dost weep for grief of my sustaining,
   Know, gentle wench, it small avails my mood.
   If tears could help, mine own would do me good.

"But tell me, girl, when went"—and there she stayed   1275
Till after a deep groan—"Tarquin from hence?"
"Madam, ere I was up," replied the maid,
"The more to blame my sluggard negligence.
Yet with the fault I thus far can dispense:
   Myself was stirring ere the break of day,   1280
   And, ere I rose, was Tarquin gone away.

"But, lady, if your maid may be so bold,
She would request to know your heaviness."
"O, peace!" quoth Lucrece. "If it should be told,
The repetition cannot make it less,   1285
For more it is than I can well express,
   And that deep torture may be called a hell
   When more is felt than one hath power to tell.

1292. **by and by:** soon

1298. **Conceit:** thought

1299. **wit:** mind; **straight:** i.e., immediately

1300. **curious-good:** ingenious; **ill:** unsatisfactory

1301. **press:** crowd

1302. **inventions:** mental creations; **before:** first

1307. **present:** urgent, immediate

1309. **tedious:** (1) painful; (2) wearisome to be told

1310. **tenor:** transcript of the general sense

1311. **certain:** definite, settled; **uncertainly:** ambiguously

1312. **schedule:** note

1314. **thereof make discovery:** i.e., reveal **her grief's true quality**

1316. **her stained excuse:** perhaps, **her** body, **stained** by Tarquin, which in death will be offered to Collatine as an **excuse,** a reason for believing her innocent (For other possible meanings, see longer note, p. 591.)

"Go, get me hither paper, ink, and pen.
Yet save that labor, for I have them here.—   1290
What should I say?—One of my husband's men
Bid thou be ready by and by to bear
A letter to my lord, my love, my dear.
    Bid him with speed prepare to carry it;
    The cause craves haste, and it will soon be writ."   1295

Her maid is gone, and she prepares to write,
First hovering o'er the paper with her quill.
Conceit and grief an eager combat fight;
What wit sets down is blotted straight with will;
This is too curious-good, this blunt and ill.   1300
    Much like a press of people at a door
    Throng her inventions, which shall go before.

At last she thus begins: "Thou worthy lord
Of that unworthy wife that greeteth thee,
Health to thy person. Next, vouchsafe t' afford,   1305
If ever, love, thy Lucrece thou wilt see,
Some present speed to come and visit me.
    So I commend me from our house in grief.
    My woes are tedious, though my words are brief."

Here folds she up the tenor of her woe,   1310
Her certain sorrow writ uncertainly.
By this short schedule Collatine may know
Her grief, but not her grief's true quality.
She dares not thereof make discovery
    Lest he should hold it her own gross abuse   1315
    Ere she with blood had stained her stained excuse.

1318. **by:** nearby

1319. **fashion:** behavior; manner

1324. **moves more:** persuades better

1326. **heavy:** sorrowful; **motion:** agitation

1329. **sounds:** wordplay on (1) sorrows **we hear** and (2) narrow passages of water; straits

1333. **post:** messenger; **attends:** waits

1334. **Charging:** ordering; **hie:** hurry

1335. **lagging:** tardy

1338. **homely villain:** simple villein or servant; **curtsies:** bows

1339. **blushing on her:** looking at her with a blush

1340. **or yea:** i.e., either **yea**

Besides, the life and feeling of her passion
She hoards to spend when he is by to hear her,
When sighs and groans and tears may grace the fashion
Of her disgrace, the better so to clear her   1320
From that suspicion which the world might bear her.
　　To shun this blot, she would not blot the letter
　　With words till action might become them better.

To see sad sights moves more than hear them told,
For then the eye interprets to the ear   1325
The heavy motion that it doth behold
When every part a part of woe doth bear.
'Tis but a part of sorrow that we hear.
　　Deep sounds make lesser noise than shallow fords,
　　And sorrow ebbs, being blown with wind of words.   1330

Her letter now is sealed, and on it writ,
"At Ardea to my lord with more than haste."
The post attends, and she delivers it,
Charging the sour-faced groom to hie as fast
As lagging fowls before the northern blast.   1335
　　Speed more than speed but dull and slow she deems;
　　Extremity still urgeth such extremes.

The homely villain curtsies to her low
And, blushing on her with a steadfast eye,
Receives the scroll without or yea or no,   1340
And forth with bashful innocence doth hie.
But they whose guilt within their bosoms lie
　　Imagine every eye beholds their blame,
　　For Lucrece thought he blushed to see her shame,

1345. **silly:** unsophisticated; **groom:** lowly servant; **wot:** knows

1347. **true respect:** proper concern

1348. **saucily:** presumptuously

1350. **pattern:** exemplar; **worn-out:** bygone

1351. **Pawned:** pledged; **laid no words to gage:** offered **no words** as security

1352. **kindled duty:** i.e., ardent (blushing) respectfulness

1353. **That:** i.e., so that

1355. **wistly:** intently

1356. **amazed:** bewildered

1359. **long she thinks:** i.e., she grows weary with waiting (To "think long" meant "to seem long, to be wearisome [to one].")

1361. **entertain:** while away, occupy

1363. **So woe hath:** i.e., **woe hath so**

1364. **stay:** cease, discontinue

1367. **made for:** i.e., representing; **Priam's Troy:** In mythology, **Troy** was besieged by the Greeks for ten years before they burned it. Priam was the city's aged king. (See pictures, pp. 554 and 562.)

1368. **the which:** i.e., Troy; **drawn:** drawn up or arrayed for battle; **power:** army

1369. **Helen's rape:** the cause for the siege of Troy (Paris, a son of Priam, carried off Helen, wife of the Greek Menelaus, whose fellow rulers joined him in attacking Troy. For Helen, see picture, p. 124.) **rape:** carrying off by force

1370. **Ilion:** Troy; **annoy:** trouble (understatement)

1371. **Which:** i.e., Troy; **conceited:** ingenious, clever

1372. **As:** i.e., that

When, silly groom, God wot, it was defect   1345
Of spirit, life, and bold audacity.
Such harmless creatures have a true respect
To talk in deeds, while others saucily
Promise more speed but do it leisurely.
    Even so this pattern of the worn-out age   1350
    Pawned honest looks, but laid no words to gage.

His kindled duty kindled her mistrust,
That two red fires in both their faces blazed.
She thought he blushed as knowing Tarquin's lust
And, blushing with him, wistly on him gazed.   1355
Her earnest eye did make him more amazed.
    The more she saw the blood his cheeks replenish,
    The more she thought he spied in her some blemish.

But long she thinks till he return again,
And yet the duteous vassal scarce is gone.   1360
The weary time she cannot entertain,
For now 'tis stale to sigh, to weep, and groan;
So woe hath wearied woe, moan tirèd moan,
    That she her plaints a little while doth stay,
    Pausing for means to mourn some newer way.   1365

At last she calls to mind where hangs a piece
Of skillful painting, made for Priam's Troy,
Before the which is drawn the power of Greece,
For Helen's rape the city to destroy,
Threat'ning cloud-kissing Ilion with annoy,   1370
    Which the conceited painter drew so proud
    As heaven, it seemed, to kiss the turrets bowed.

1373. **objects:** spectacles

1377. **reeked:** steamed; **strife:** striving (with **Nature** [l. 1374])

1380. **pioneer:** soldier who precedes an army making way for it, e.g., by digging trenches, undermining walls, building earthwork fortifications

1383. **loop-holes:** narrow vertical openings that widen inward

1384. **lust:** delight, pleasure

1385. **sweet:** delightful; **observance:** observant care, heed

1392. **Which:** i.e., who; **heartless:** dejected

1394. **Ajax:** a powerful Greek warrior, gigantic but slow in thought and speech (See longer note, p. 591.) **Ulysses:** the Greek warrior most famous for his cunning strategy (See picture below.)

1396. **ciphered:** expressed

1398. **blunt:** harsh; stupid; **rigor:** severity, harshness

1400. **regard:** consideration; **government:** (self-)control; discretion; leadership

Ulysses. (*Lucrece*, 1394)

A thousand lamentable objects there,
In scorn of Nature, Art gave lifeless life.
Many a dry drop seemed a weeping tear   1375
Shed for the slaughtered husband by the wife.
The red blood reeked to show the painter's strife,
    And dying eyes gleamed forth their ashy lights
    Like dying coals burnt out in tedious nights.

There might you see the laboring pioneer   1380
Begrimed with sweat and smearèd all with dust,
And from the towers of Troy there would appear
The very eyes of men through loop-holes thrust,
Gazing upon the Greeks with little lust.
    Such sweet observance in this work was had   1385
    That one might see those far-off eyes look sad.

In great commanders grace and majesty
You might behold, triumphing in their faces;
In youth, quick bearing and dexterity;
And here and there the painter interlaces   1390
Pale cowards marching on with trembling paces,
    Which heartless peasants did so well resemble
    That one would swear he saw them quake and tremble.

In Ajax and Ulysses, O, what art
Of physiognomy might one behold!   1395
The face of either ciphered either's heart,
Their face their manners most expressly told.
In Ajax' eyes blunt rage and rigor rolled,
    But the mild glance that sly Ulysses lent
    Showed deep regard and smiling government.   1400

1401. **pleading:** making an earnest appeal; **Nestor:** an old and wise king who joined the Greek expedition against Troy

1404. **beguiled:** won; **sight:** sense of **sight**; eyes

1407. **purled:** whirled

1408. **About:** around; **press:** crowd

1410. **several:** particular; **graces:** attractive movements or actions

1411. **mermaid:** See longer note to *Venus and Adonis*, l. 429, p. 443, and picture, p. 390.

1412. **nice:** precise, accurate

1413. **scalps:** tops of the heads

1414. **mock:** delude (by seeming to move)

1416. **shadowed:** concealed

1417. **thronged:** crowded; **bears:** pushes; **boll'n:** swollen

1418. **smothered:** stifled; **pelt:** throw out angry words

1421. **debate:** fight

1422. **imaginary work:** (1) imaginative **work,** creation of images; (2) **work** for the imagination (of the beholder)

1423. **Conceit:** i.e., trick of the imagination; **compact:** closely packed; **kind:** (apparently) natural

1424. **Achilles':** Achilles was the foremost Greek warrior.

There pleading might you see grave Nestor stand,
As 'twere encouraging the Greeks to fight,
Making such sober action with his hand
That it beguiled attention, charmed the sight.
In speech, it seemed, his beard, all silver white,   1405
   Wagged up and down, and from his lips did fly
   Thin winding breath, which purled up to the sky.

About him were a press of gaping faces,
Which seemed to swallow up his sound advice,
All jointly list'ning, but with several graces,   1410
As if some mermaid did their ears entice;
Some high, some low, the painter was so nice.
   The scalps of many, almost hid behind,
   To jump up higher seemed, to mock the mind.

Here one man's hand leaned on another's head,   1415
His nose being shadowed by his neighbor's ear;
Here one being thronged bears back, all boll'n and red;
Another, smothered, seems to pelt and swear;
And in their rage such signs of rage they bear
   As, but for loss of Nestor's golden words,   1420
   It seemed they would debate with angry swords.

For much imaginary work was there,
Conceit deceitful, so compact, so kind,
That for Achilles' image stood his spear
Gripped in an armèd hand; himself, behind,   1425
Was left unseen, save to the eye of mind.
   A hand, a foot, a face, a leg, a head,
   Stood for the whole to be imaginèd.

1429. **strong-besiegèd:** i.e., heavily besieged

1430. **Hector:** eldest of Priam's fifty sons and foremost Trojan warrior; **field:** the battlefield

1433. **odd:** discrepant, discordant; **action:** gesture, attitude

1434. **light:** cheerful, merry

1435. **stained:** deprived of light; **heavy:** oppressive, distressful

1436–37. **from . . . banks:** i.e., from the shore of Dardania to the **banks** of the Simois river (Troy, on the Simois, was the chief city of Dardania, which stretched to the sea. See picture below.)

1440. **gallèd:** worn away

1444. **stelled:** portrayed; fixed

1447. **Hecuba:** the aged queen of Troy, whose grief for her dead sons and husband was legendary (See picture, p. 558.)

1449. **which:** i.e., the wounds; **Pyrrhus':** Pyrrhus, son of Achilles, avenged his father's death by killing Priam.   **lies:** i.e., lie

1450. **anatomized:** analyzed, exposed minutely

1451. **wrack:** destruction

1452. **chaps:** cracks, fissures

1454. **blue:** refers to the veins as they show through fair skin

1455. **Wanting:** lacking; **shrunk pipes:** i.e., shrunken or contracted veins

Troy. (*Lucrece*, 1367)

And from the walls of strong-besiegèd Troy,
When their brave hope, bold Hector, marched to field,   1430
Stood many Trojan mothers, sharing joy
To see their youthful sons bright weapons wield,
And to their hope they such odd action yield
    That through their light joy seemèd to appear,
    Like bright things stained, a kind of heavy fear.   1435

And from the strand of Dardan, where they fought,
To Simois' reedy banks the red blood ran,
Whose waves to imitate the battle sought
With swelling ridges, and their ranks began
To break upon the gallèd shore, and then   1440
    Retire again till, meeting greater ranks,
    They join and shoot their foam at Simois' banks.

To this well-painted piece is Lucrece come
To find a face where all distress is stelled.
Many she sees where cares have carvèd some,   1445
But none where all distress and dolor dwelled,
Till she despairing Hecuba beheld,
    Staring on Priam's wounds with her old eyes,
    Which bleeding under Pyrrhus' proud foot lies.

In her the painter had anatomized   1450
Time's ruin, beauty's wrack, and grim care's reign.
Her cheeks with chaps and wrinkles were disguised;
Of what she was no semblance did remain.
Her blue blood, changed to black in every vein,
    Wanting the spring that those shrunk pipes had fed,   1455
    Showed life imprisoned in a body dead.

1457. **shadow:** portrait

1458. **beldam's:** A *beldam* was (1) an old, or (2) a furious, woman.

1459. **wants:** lacks

1460. **ban:** curse

1465. **tune:** adapt; sing

1466. **balm:** ointment

1471. **strumpet:** i.e., Helen (See note to l. 1369.) **stir:** tumult, disturbance

1473. **fond:** doting; foolish

1477. **dame:** mother

1479. **moe:** more

"Burning Troy." (*Lucrece*, 1474)

On this sad shadow Lucrece spends her eyes,
And shapes her sorrow to the beldam's woes,
Who nothing wants to answer her but cries
And bitter words to ban her cruel foes.   1460
The painter was no god to lend her those,
    And therefore Lucrece swears he did her wrong
    To give her so much grief and not a tongue.

"Poor instrument," quoth she, "without a sound,
I'll tune thy woes with my lamenting tongue,   1465
And drop sweet balm in Priam's painted wound,
And rail on Pyrrhus, that hath done him wrong,
And with my tears quench Troy, that burns so long,
    And with my knife scratch out the angry eyes
    Of all the Greeks that are thine enemies.   1470

"Show me the strumpet that began this stir,
That with my nails her beauty I may tear.
Thy heat of lust, fond Paris, did incur
This load of wrath that burning Troy doth bear;
Thy eye kindled the fire that burneth here,   1475
    And herc in Troy, for trespass of thine eye,
    The sire, the son, the dame, and daughter die.

"Why should the private pleasure of some one
Become the public plague of many moe?
Let sin, alone committed, light alone   1480
Upon his head that hath transgressèd so;
Let guiltless souls be freed from guilty woe.
    For one's offense why should so many fall,
    To plague a private sin in general?

1486. **Troilus:** a son of Priam and the legendary lover of Criseyde (or Cressida); **swounds:** faints

1487. **channel:** gutter

1488. **unadvisèd:** unintentional

1489. **one man's:** i.e., Paris's; **confounds:** destroys

1490. **checked:** curbed; rebuked

1494. **his:** its

1496. **a-work:** to work

1497. **penciled:** painted

1499. **about the painting round:** i.e., all around **the painting**

1500. **who:** whomever

1501. **bound:** tied up (as a prisoner)

1502. **That . . . lent:** i.e., to whom Trojan **shepherds** gave pitying **looks**

1504. **blunt:** unrefined; **swains:** i.e., **shepherds**

1505. **patience:** i.e., his **patience**

1507. **show:** i.e., painted figure

1509. **unbent:** not frowning

1511. **guilty instance:** example of guilt

Hecuba, Queen of Troy. (*Lucrece*, 1447)

"Lo, here weeps Hecuba, here Priam dies,   1485
Here manly Hector faints, here Troilus swounds,
Here friend by friend in bloody channel lies,
And friend to friend gives unadvisèd wounds,
And one man's lust these many lives confounds.
 Had doting Priam checked his son's desire,   1490
 Troy had been bright with fame and not with fire."

Here feelingly she weeps Troy's painted woes,
For sorrow, like a heavy-hanging bell,
Once set on ringing, with his own weight goes;
Then little strength rings out the doleful knell.   1495
So Lucrece, set a-work, sad tales doth tell
 To penciled pensiveness and colored sorrow;
 She lends them words, and she their looks doth borrow.

She throws her eyes about the painting round,
And who she finds forlorn she doth lament.   1500
At last she sees a wretchèd image bound,
That piteous looks to Phrygian shepherds lent.
His face, though full of cares, yet showed content;
 Onward to Troy with the blunt swains he goes,
 So mild that patience seemed to scorn his woes.   1505

In him the painter labored with his skill
To hide deceit and give the harmless show
An humble gait, calm looks, eyes wailing still,
A brow unbent that seemed to welcome woe,
Cheeks neither red nor pale but mingled so   1510
 That blushing red no guilty instance gave,
 Nor ashy pale the fear that false hearts have.

1514. **entertained:** kept up; **show:** appearance; **seeming:** apparently

1516. **jealousy:** suspicion; **mistrust:** i.e., suspect that

1517. **craft:** guile, deceit

1521. **Sinon:** the Greek whose treachery brought about Troy's defeat (See longer note, p. 591, and picture below.)

1522. **after:** later

1523. **wildfire:** mixture of highly inflammable substances, easy to ignite and hard to extinguish, used in warfare

1525–26. **And . . . faces:** In the Ptolemaic system, the **stars** circle the Earth fixed in a crystalline sphere. (See picture, p. xviii.) The poem images them as reflected in Troy until its fall, when they **shot from** their sphere. (See picture, p. 416.)   **glass:** looking **glass,** mirror

1527. **advisedly:** attentively, judiciously

1529. **some shape:** the appearance of some particular person

1532. **plain:** open, frank

1533. **was belied:** was proved false; lied

1539–40. **It cannot be . . . But:** i.e., it can only be that

Sinon overlooking Troy. (*Lucrece*, 1521)

But, like a constant and confirmèd devil,
He entertained a show so seeming just,
And therein so ensconced his secret evil,   1515
That jealousy itself could not mistrust
False-creeping craft and perjury should thrust
    Into so bright a day such black-faced storms,
    Or blot with hell-born sin such saintlike forms.

The well-skilled workman this mild image drew   1520
For perjured Sinon, whose enchanting story
The credulous old Priam after slew;
Whose words like wildfire burnt the shining glory
Of rich-built Ilion, that the skies were sorry,
    And little stars shot from their fixèd places   1525
    When their glass fell wherein they viewed their faces.

This picture she advisedly perused,
And chid the painter for his wondrous skill,
Saying some shape in Sinon's was abused;
So fair a form lodged not a mind so ill.   1530
And still on him she gazed, and gazing still,
    Such signs of truth in his plain face she spied
    That she concludes the picture was belied.

"It cannot be," quoth she, "that so much guile"—
She would have said "can lurk in such a look,"   1535
But Tarquin's shape came in her mind the while
And from her tongue "can lurk" from "cannot" took.
"It cannot be" she in that sense forsook,
    And turned it thus: "It cannot be, I find,
    But such a face should bear a wicked mind.   1540

1542. **sober sad:** solemn, serious
1543. **travail:** suffering
1544. **beguiled:** disguised
1546. **cherish:** entertain kindly
1549. **borrowed:** counterfeit; **sheeds:** sheds
1551. **falls:** lets fall
1554. **fire:** wildfire (See note to l. 1523.)
1561. **he:** i.e., Sinon; **his:** i.e., Priam's
1564. **senseless:** insensate
1565. **unhappy:** evil
1567. **with this gives o'er:** i.e., ceases with these words

"List'ning Priam." (*Lucrece,* 1548)

"For even as subtle Sinon here is painted
So sober sad, so weary, and so mild,
As if with grief or travail he had fainted,
To me came Tarquin armèd too, beguiled
With outward honesty, but yet defiled   1545
    With inward vice. As Priam him did cherish,
    So did I Tarquin; so my Troy did perish.

"Look, look how list'ning Priam wets his eyes
To see those borrowed tears that Sinon sheeds!
Priam, why art thou old and yet not wise?   1550
For every tear he falls, a Trojan bleeds.
His eye drops fire, no water thence proceeds;
    Those round clear pearls of his, that move thy pity,
    Are balls of quenchless fire to burn thy city.

"Such devils steal effects from lightless hell,   1555
For Sinon in his fire doth quake with cold,
And in that cold hot-burning fire doth dwell.
These contraries such unity do hold
Only to flatter fools and make them bold.
    So Priam's trust false Sinon's tears doth flatter,   1560
    That he finds means to burn his Troy with water."

Here, all enraged, such passion her assails
That patience is quite beaten from her breast.
She tears the senseless Sinon with her nails,
Comparing him to that unhappy guest   1565
Whose deed hath made herself herself detest.
    At last she smilingly with this gives o'er:
    "Fool, fool," quoth she, "his wounds will not be sore."

1573. **in . . . sustaining:** i.e., when it is endured in a state of keen **sorrow**

1574. **heavy:** (1) oppressive, distressful; (2) sleepy

1575. **watch:** stay awake

1576. **Which:** i.e., her **woe** (l. 1574); **overslipped:** slipped away from

1579. **surmise:** imagination

1580. **shows:** unreal appearances, pictures

1586. **tear-distainèd:** i.e., tear-stained

1588. **water-galls:** secondary or imperfectly formed rainbows; **element:** i.e., face (literally, sky)

1589. **to:** i.e., in addition to

1590. **sad-beholding:** i.e., sadly gazing

1592. **sod:** soaked, steeped

1593. **lively:** wordplay on (1) fresh and (2) living

1596. **wond'ring . . . chance:** i.e., conjecturing about (or marveling at) what has befallen **each** other

Thus ebbs and flows the current of her sorrow,
And time doth weary time with her complaining.   1570
She looks for night, and then she longs for morrow,
And both she thinks too long with her remaining.
Short time seems long in sorrow's sharp sustaining;
 Though woe be heavy, yet it seldom sleeps,
 And they that watch see time how slow it creeps;   1575

Which all this time hath overslipped her thought
That she with painted images hath spent,
Being from the feeling of her own grief brought
By deep surmise of others' detriment,
Losing her woes in shows of discontent.   1580
 It easeth some, though none it ever cured,
 To think their dolor others have endured.

But now the mindful messenger, come back,
Brings home his lord and other company,
Who finds his Lucrece clad in mourning black,   1585
And round about her tear-distainèd eye
Blue circles streamed like rainbows in the sky.
 These water-galls in her dim element
 Foretell new storms to those already spent;

Which when her sad-beholding husband saw,   1590
Amazedly in her sad face he stares.
Her eyes, though sod in tears, looked red and raw,
Her lively color killed with deadly cares.
He hath no power to ask her how she fares;
 Both stood like old acquaintance in a trance,   1595
 Met far from home, wond'ring each other's chance.

1598. **uncouth:** unknown, strange; **ill:** evil

1600. **spite:** outrage, injury; **spent:** destroyed

1602. **moody:** gloomy; **heaviness:** sadness; torpor

1604. **gives . . . fire:** i.e., tries to express **her sorrow** (The image is of trying to **discharge** [l. 1605] an early firearm by means of a match.)

1606. **addressed:** ready

1609. **his consorted lords:** the **lords** associated with him

1610. **sad:** grave; constant

1611. **swan:** The **swan** is said to sing sweetly just before it dies.

1614. **give . . . amending:** i.e., mitigate the transgression

1615. **moe:** more; **depending:** waiting for settlement (in a legal sense)

1619. **in the interest of:** i.e., to lay claim to

At last he takes her by the bloodless hand
And thus begins: "What uncouth ill event
Hath thee befall'n that thou dost trembling stand?
Sweet love, what spite hath thy fair color spent?   1600
Why art thou thus attired in discontent?
   Unmask, dear dear, this moody heaviness,
   And tell thy grief, that we may give redress."

Three times with sighs she gives her sorrow fire
Ere once she can discharge one word of woe.   1605
At length addressed to answer his desire,
She modestly prepares to let them know
Her honor is ta'en prisoner by the foe,
   While Collatine and his consorted lords
   With sad attention long to hear her words.   1610

And now this pale swan in her wat'ry nest
Begins the sad dirge of her certain ending:
"Few words," quoth she, "shall fit the trespass best
Where no excuse can give the fault amending.
In me moc woes than words are now depending,   1615
   And my laments would be drawn out too long
   To tell them all with one poor tirèd tongue.

"Then be this all the task it hath to say:
Dear husband, in the interest of thy bed
A stranger came, and on that pillow lay   1620
Where thou wast wont to rest thy weary head;
And what wrong else may be imaginèd
   By foul enforcement might be done to me,
   From that, alas, thy Lucrece is not free.

1629. **else:** otherwise

1631. **contradict:** oppose

1632. **hard-favored:** ugly

1634. **straight:** straightway, immediately

1639. **start:** recoil

1641. **patiently:** calmly

1643. **still:** always, forever

1648. **bloody:** bloodthirsty

1650. **scarlet:** the color of (1) a judge's robe and (2) **lust** as portrayed in the Bible; **evidence:** i.e., as a witness

"Against my heart he set his sword." (*Lucrece,* 1640)

"For in the dreadful dead of dark midnight,   1625
With shining falchion in my chamber came
A creeping creature with a flaming light
And softly cried, 'Awake, thou Roman dame,
And entertain my love, else lasting shame
   On thee and thine this night I will inflict   1630
   If thou my love's desire do contradict.

" 'For some hard-favored groom of thine,' quoth he,
'Unless thou yoke thy liking to my will,
I'll murder straight, and then I'll slaughter thee
And swear I found you where you did fulfill   1635
The loathsome act of lust and so did kill
   The lechers in their deed. This act will be
   My fame and thy perpetual infamy.'

"With this, I did begin to start and cry;
And then against my heart he set his sword,   1640
Swearing, unless I took all patiently,
I should not live to speak another word;
So should my shame still rest upon record,
   And never be forgot in mighty Rome
   Th' adulterate death of Lucrece and her groom.   1645

"Mine enemy was strong, my poor self weak,
And far the weaker with so strong a fear.
My bloody judge forbade my tongue to speak;
No rightful plea might plead for justice there.
His scarlet lust came evidence to swear   1650
   That my poor beauty had purloined his eyes,
   And when the judge is robbed, the prisoner dies.

1654. **refuge:** pretext, excuse

1657. **forced:** raped

1658. **accessory yieldings:** i.e., consent that would make it an accessory

1659. **closet:** small private room

1660. **hopeless . . . loss:** i.e., **merchant hopeless** with respect to his **loss** (Collatine is figured as a **merchant** who has lost his ship and hence his treasure—i.e., Lucrece.)

1662. **sad set eyes:** i.e., **eyes** motionless in sadness; **wreathèd arms across:** See l. 793 and note.

1663. **new-waxen:** i.e., newly grown

1667–70. **As through . . . fast:** These lines describe the current of a river rushing **through** the **arch** of a bridge and forming a turbulent **eddy** in its backward flow.   **his:** its   **pride:** A stream when swollen or high was said to be "proud."   **him:** i.e., it

1672. **make a saw:** i.e., move as if they were **a saw,** back and forth

1674. **attendeth:** regards

1675. **frenzy:** insanity (that has put him in a trance)

1678. **sensible:** sensitive

1679. **feeling-painful:** susceptible to pain

"O, teach me how to make mine own excuse,
Or, at the least, this refuge let me find:
Though my gross blood be stained with this abuse,   1655
Immaculate and spotless is my mind;
That was not forced, that never was inclined
    To accessory yieldings, but still pure
    Doth in her poisoned closet yet endure."

Lo, here the hopeless merchant of this loss,   1660
With head declined and voice dammed up with woe,
With sad set eyes and ⌐wreathèd⌐ arms across,
From lips new-waxen pale begins to blow
The grief away that stops his answer so.
    But, wretched as he is, he strives in vain;   1665
    What he breathes out his breath drinks up again.

As through an arch the violent roaring tide
Outruns the eye that doth behold his haste,
Yet in the eddy boundeth in his pride
Back to the strait that forced him on so fast—   1670
In rage sent out, recalled in rage, being past—
    Even so his sighs, his sorrows, make a saw
    To push grief on, and back the same grief draw,

Which speechless woe of his poor she attendeth,
And his untimely frenzy thus awaketh: 1675
"Dear lord, thy sorrow to my sorrow lendeth
Another power; no flood by raining slaketh.
My woe too sensible thy passion maketh
    More feeling-painful. Let it then suffice
    To drown one woe, one pair of weeping eyes.   1680

1682. **she:** i.e., her; **attend:** pay attention to

1683. **suddenly:** immediately

1691. **venge:** avenge

1697. **her imposition:** i.e., the task that she is imposing on them

1698. **bewrayed:** revealed, exposed

1702. **quality:** nature

1704. **with . . . dispense:** i.e., condone **the foul act**

1706. **chance:** misfortune

"And for my sake when I might charm thee so,
For she that was thy Lucrece, now attend me:
Be suddenly revengèd on my foe,
Thine, mine, his own. Suppose thou dost defend me
From what is past. The help that thou shalt lend me   1685
    Comes all too late, yet let the traitor die,
    For sparing justice feeds iniquity.

"But ere I name him, you fair lords," quoth she,
Speaking to those that came with Collatine,
"Shall plight your honorable faiths to me   1690
With swift pursuit to venge this wrong of mine,
For 'tis a meritorious fair design
    To chase injustice with revengeful arms.
    Knights, by their oaths, should right poor ladies' harms."

At this request, with noble disposition   1695
Each present lord began to promise aid,
As bound in knighthood to her imposition,
Longing to hear the hateful foe bewrayed.
But she, that yet her sad task hath not said,
    The protestation stops: "O, speak," quoth she,   1700
    "How may this forcèd stain be wiped from me?

"What is the quality of my offense,
Being constrained with dreadful circumstance?
May my pure mind with the foul act dispense,
My low-declinèd honor to advance?   1705
May any terms acquit me from this chance?
    The poisoned fountain clears itself again,
    And why not I from this compellèd stain?"

1709. **With this:** i.e., at these words

1712. **map:** image, picture

1714–15. **No . . . giving:** Shakespeare here is close to Livy's *History of Rome* (*Historiarum ab urbe condita*): "no unchaste woman shall henceforth live and plead Lucretia's example" (2.58). For Livy's *History,* see picture, p. 584.　**dame:** lady

1719. **accents:** perhaps, sounds expressing feelings

1720. **assays:** attempts

1723. **Even here:** i.e., just at this point; **harmless:** innocent

1728. **sprite:** spirit

1729. **Life's lasting date:** eternal life; **destiny:** i.e, (her) human lot in life

1730. **astonished:** stupefied

1734. **Brutus:** Lucius Junius **Brutus** (See longer note to ll. 1807–13, p. 592.)

1736. **held it in chase:** pursued it

Lucrece's suicide. (*Lucrece,* 1723–24)

With this they all at once began to say
Her body's stain her mind untainted clears,   1710
While with a joyless smile she turns away
The face, that map which deep impression bears
Of hard misfortune, carved ⌜in it⌝ with tears.
    "No, no," quoth she, "no dame hereafter living
    By my excuse shall claim excuse's giving."   1715

Here with a sigh, as if her heart would break,
She throws forth Tarquin's name: "He, he," she says,
But more than "he" her poor tongue could not speak,
Till after many accents and delays,
Untimely breathings, sick and short assays,   1720
    She utters this: "He, he, fair lords, 'tis he
    That guides this hand to give this wound to me."

Even here she sheathèd in her harmless breast
A harmful knife, that thence her soul unsheathed.
That blow did bail it from the deep unrest   1725
Of that polluted prison where it breathed.
Her contrite sighs unto the clouds bequeathed
    Her wingèd sprite, and through her wounds doth fly
    Life's lasting date from canceled destiny.

Stone-still, astonished with this deadly deed,   1730
Stood Collatine and all his lordly crew,
Till Lucrece' father, that beholds her bleed,
Himself on her self-slaughtered body threw,
And from the purple fountain Brutus drew
    The murd'rous knife, and, as it left the place,   1735
    Her blood, in poor revenge, held it in chase;

1738. **that:** i.e., so that

1740. **Who:** i.e., which; **late-sacked:** recently plundered; **vastly:** in desolation

1745. **rigol:** circle

1747. **as:** i.e., **as** if

1748. **token:** vestige

1752. **deprived:** divested

1754. **unlived:** deprived of life

1758. **glass:** looking glass, mirror

1758–59. **I often . . . born:** See Sonnet 3, ll. 9–14, for the same metaphor.　　**semblance:** likeness, image

1761. **bare-boned death:** i.e., skeleton (*King John* includes a reference to "a bare-ribbed Death" [5.2.180].)

1763. **shivered:** shattered

"Bare-boned death." (*Lucrece*, 1761)

And, bubbling from her breast, it doth divide
In two slow rivers, that the crimson blood
Circles her body in on every side,
Who, like a late-sacked island, vastly stood   1740
Bare and unpeopled in this fearful flood.
    Some of her blood still pure and red remained,
    And some looked black, and that false Tarquin stained.

About the mourning and congealèd face
Of that black blood a wat'ry rigol goes,   1745
Which seems to weep upon the tainted place;
And ever since, as pitying Lucrece' woes,
Corrupted blood some watery token shows,
    And blood untainted still doth red abide,
    Blushing at that which is so putrefied.   1750

"Daughter, dear daughter," old Lucretius cries,
"That life was mine which thou hast here deprived.
If in the child the father's image lies,
Where shall I live now Lucrece is unlived?
Thou wast not to this end from me derived.   1755
    If children predecease progenitors,
    We are their offspring, and they none of ours.

"Poor broken glass, I often did behold
In thy sweet semblance my old age new born,
But now that fair fresh mirror dim and old   1760
Shows me a bare-boned death by time outworn.
O, from thy cheeks my image thou hast torn,
    And shivered all the beauty of my glass,
    That I no more can see what once I was!

1766. **surcease:** cease

1772. **By this:** i.e., by this time; **starts:** awakes suddenly

1773. **give his sorrow place:** i.e., make room for his grieving; **give** Collatine's **sorrow** precedence

1774. **key-cold:** i.e., deathly cold

1776. **counterfeits to die:** perhaps, faints away or lies motionless in grief, as if dead; **space:** period of time

1780. **dumb arrest:** i.e., decree of silence

1781. **Who:** i.e., Collatine; **his:** its

1784. **thick:** rapidly

1789. **more:** greater

1790. **give o'er:** i.e., **give** over, cease

1791. **strife:** exertion of rivalry

"O Time, cease thou thy course and last no longer   1765
If they surcease to be that should survive!
Shall rotten Death make conquest of the stronger
And leave the falt'ring feeble souls alive?
The old bees die, the young possess their hive.
    Then, live, sweet Lucrece, live again and see   1770
    Thy father die, and not thy father thee."

By this starts Collatine as from a dream
And bids Lucretius give his sorrow place,
And then in key-cold Lucrece' bleeding stream
He falls and bathes the pale fear in his face,   1775
And counterfeits to die with her a space,
    Till manly shame bids him possess his breath
    And live to be revengèd on her death.

The deep vexation of his inward soul
Hath served a dumb arrest upon his tongue,   1780
Who, mad that sorrow should his use control
Or keep him from heart-easing words so long,
Begins to talk, but through his lips do throng
    Weak words, so thick come in his poor heart's aid
    That no man could distinguish what he said.   1785

Yet sometimes "Tarquin" was pronouncèd plain,
But through his teeth, as if the name he tore.
This windy tempest, till it blow up rain,
Held back his sorrow's tide, to make it more.
At last it rains, and busy winds give o'er.   1790
    Then son and father weep with equal strife
    Who should weep most, for daughter or for wife.

1797. **interest:** right, title, share

1801. **spilled:** destroyed

1803. **owed:** owned

1805. **who:** i.e., which

1807–13. **Brutus . . . things:** See longer note, p. 592.

1808. **emulation:** rivalry

1809. **wit:** intelligence; **state:** dignity; **pride:** honor

1810. **folly's show:** pretense to foolishness

1811. **esteemèd:** regarded

1812–13. **As . . . things:** i.e., as professional fools are by monarchs   **silly:** poor   **jeering:** mocking   **sportive:** jesting

1814. **habit:** (1) outward form or appearance; (2) pattern of behavior; (3) garment

1815. **policy:** political acumen

1816. **wits:** intelligence; **advisedly:** deliberately

1819. **unsounded:** unexplored

The one doth call her his, the other his,
Yet neither may possess the claim they lay.
The father says, "She's mine." "O, mine she is,"   1795
Replies her husband. "Do not take away
My sorrow's interest. Let no mourner say
　　He weeps for her, for she was only mine
　　And only must be wailed by Collatine."

"O," quoth Lucretius, "I did give that life   1800
Which she too early and too late hath spilled."
"Woe, woe," quoth Collatine, "she was my wife.
I owed her, and 'tis mine that she hath killed."
"My daughter" and "my wife" with clamors filled
　　The dispersed air, who, holding Lucrece' life,   1805
　　Answered their cries, "my daughter" and "my wife."

Brutus, who plucked the knife from Lucrece' side,
Seeing such emulation in their woe,
Began to clothe his wit in state and pride,
Burying in Lucrece' wound his folly's show.   1810
He with the Romans was esteemèd so
　　As silly jeering idiots are with kings,
　　For sportive words and utt'ring foolish things.

But now he throws that shallow habit by
Wherein deep policy did him disguise,   1815
And armed his long-hid wits advisedly
To check the tears in Collatinus' eyes:
"Thou wrongèd lord of Rome," quoth he, "arise!
　　Let my unsounded self, supposed a fool,
　　Now set thy long-experienced wit to school.   1820

1825. **humor:** mood

1829. **relenting:** melting, softening

1832. **suffer:** allow

1834. **chased:** i.e., to be **chased**

1835. **Capitol:** Temple of Jupiter Capitolinus on the Capitoline Hill (Jupiter was king of the Roman gods.) See picture below.

1836. **stained:** defiled

1837. **fat:** fertile; **store:** abundance

1838. **country rights: rights** of our **country**

1839. **complained:** i.e., complained of

1844. **protestation:** solemn resolution

1845. **allow:** approve, praise

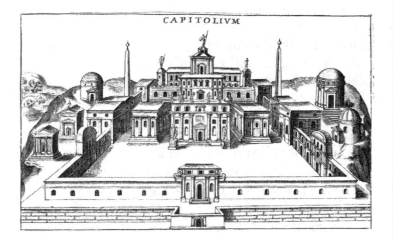

The Roman Capitol. (*Lucrece*, 1835)

"Why, Collatine, is woe the cure for woe?
Do wounds help wounds, or grief help grievous deeds?
Is it revenge to give thyself a blow
For his foul act by whom thy fair wife bleeds?
Such childish humor from weak minds proceeds.   1825
    Thy wretchèd wife mistook the matter so
    To slay herself, that should have slain her foe.

"Courageous Roman, do not steep thy heart
In such relenting dew of lamentations,
But kneel with me and help to bear thy part   1830
To rouse our Roman gods with invocations,
That they will suffer these abominations—
    Since Rome herself in them doth stand disgraced—
    By our strong arms from forth her fair streets chased.

"Now, by the Capitol, that we adore,   1835
And by this chaste blood so unjustly stained,
By heaven's fair sun that breeds the fat earth's store,
By all our country rights in Rome maintained,
And by chaste Lucrece' soul that late complained
    Her wrongs to us, and by this bloody knife,   1840
    We will revenge the death of this true wife."

This said, he struck his hand upon his breast,
And kissed the fatal knife to end his vow,
And to his protestation urged the rest,
Who, wond'ring at him, did his words allow.   1845
Then jointly to the ground their knees they bow,
    And that deep vow which Brutus made before
    He doth again repeat, and that they swore.

1849. **advisèd:** judicious; **doom:** judgment, sentence
1850. **conclude:** decide, resolve
1851. **thorough:** through
1852. **publish:** make publicly known
1854–55. **The Romans . . . banishment:** While the end of the poem itself mentions only the rapist Tarquin's **banishment,** the "Argument" preceding the poem (p. 451) follows Livy's legendary Roman history in narrating the **banishment** of the whole royal family: "the people were so moved that with one consent and a general acclamation the Tarquins were all exiled and the state government changed from kings to consuls." **plausibly:** approvingly, with applause

T. Liulj Patauini,

HISTORIARVM
AB VRBE·CONDITA
LIBRI QVI.EXTANT
X X X V
Cum Vniuerfae Hiftoriae
EPITOMIS

.Additis C A R O L I · S I G O N I I Scholijs,
Quibus ijdem libri , atque epitomae partim emendantur,
partim etiam explanantur,

Ab Auĉĵore multis in partibus POSTREMO *auĉĵis , & emendatis.*
CVM rerum ,& verborum locupletifsimo INDICE,
ET . PRIVILEGIO

VENETIIS . CIↃ IↃ XCII
ApudAldum.

Title page of Livy, . . . *Historiarvm ab vrbe condita.* . . . (1592)

When they had sworn to this advisèd doom,
They did conclude to bear dead Lucrece thence   1850
To show her bleeding body thorough Rome,
And so to publish Tarquin's foul offense;
Which being done with speedy diligence,
    The Romans plausibly did give consent
    To Tarquin's everlasting banishment.   1855

Lucrece
Longer Notes

102. **margents:** Many Renaissance books contain printed marginal comments explaining, summarizing, or clarifying the text's content. In ll. 101–2, the secret matters shining in the "glassy" corners of Tarquin's eyes are like such marginal comments in that, if they were properly read, they would instruct the reader about the message the eyes are sending. *Romeo and Juliet* uses a similar metaphor: "what obscured in this fair volume lies / Find written in the margent of his eyes" (1.3.91–92). In *Lucrece*, the eyes themselves are the books, while in *Romeo*, the lover's body is the book; in both, the commentary appears in the "margins" of the eyes.

134–37. **Those . . . less:** Editors agree that these lines expand a Latin saying taught to Elizabethan schoolboys that in English would read "The miser lacks what he has as much as what he has not." The syntax of ll. 135–36, though, presents a serious problem that editors have tried unsuccessfully to address by emending words or punctuation. The problem has been best described as Shakespeare's having omitted some necessary words: "That what they have not [they are so eager to obtain that] that which they possess / They scatter." The simplest solution is that proposed by David Bevington, who interprets "That what they have not" as "That [for] what they have not."

188. **naked armor . . . lust:** This line contains a violent antithesis of nakedness and **armor,** combined with the paradox of **still-slaughtered lust.** It has been suggested that these represent the intense struggle between **desire and dread** (l. 171) that has just been presented as going on within Tarquin. **Desire** or **lust** sometimes appears to him to have the strength of **armor,** but dread of his exposure to **lust's** consequences in turn renders that **armor** apparently useless, and he seems **naked** and therefore defenseless in it. His

lust itself is thus **still-slaughtered,** or always **slaughtered,** by his dread; but however often **lust** is killed, it is always in need of being **slaughtered** because it is always enlivened as desire. In another sense, **lust** is **still-slaughtered** because it is always slain whenever it is satisfied.

206. **dash:** It has been suggested that this **loathsome dash** is what was known as an "abatement." According to J. Guillim's 1611 *Display of Heraldrie,* "An Abatement is an accidental mark annexed to coat armor denoting some ungentlemanlike, dishonorable, or disloyal demeanor, quality, or stain in the bearer whereby the dignity of the coat armor is greatly abased" (spelling modernized).

295. **his servile powers:** Since the image that dominates ll. 293–99 is that of the heart as the **captain** of the body's passions or affections, it is possible that **his servile powers** might also be read as "its [i.e., the heart's] attendant faculties." In the first 400 or so lines of *Lucrece,* Shakespeare explores the inward action of lust as it drives Tarquin toward rape. In the stanzas here considered, as well as in passages mentioned below, the heart, having been corrupted by the eyes, seems to be the organ most responsible for driving him on.

Burton's *Anatomy of Melancholy* (1621) quotes numerous authorities who agree that beauty is the most common cause of lust, and that it is the faculty of sight which most often "conveys those admirable rays of beauty and pleasing graces to the heart" (Burton, 3.2.2.2 "Other causes of Love-Melancholy, Sight, Beauty from the face, eyes, other parts, and how it pierceth"). But Burton makes it clear that philosophers did not all agree that it was the heart that was responsible for this "mad and beastly passion" of lust. Langius, for example, "will have this passion sited in the liver, and to keep residence in the heart, 'to proceed first from the eyes so carried by our spirits, and kindled with imagination in the liver and heart," while Guianerius, "though many put all the affections in the heart, refers [lust] to the brain." Burton agrees with those who see lust as a disease of the brain, and argues that when the lust is violent, "both imagination and reason are misaffected, first one, then the other" (3.1.2.2 "How Love tyrannizeth over men").

When, at l. 414, Tarquin approaches the actual rape, his eyes, though momentarily sated by the sight of Lucrece's beauty, then function once again to stir up the heart and the veins, which in turn incite the eye to give motion to the hand (ll. 435ff.). See the longer note to l. 428, where the poem's language becomes more specifically the language of a military siege.

428. slaves: The metaphor that dominates ll. 428–83—that of Lucrece as a city under siege and Tarquin as the besieging army—begins here with an image of the city after its fall, with heartless soldiers looting and killing. Such mindless brutality is ascribed to "his veins" as they await the "onset" of the attack. The poem then traces the action of the siege, moving back and forth between images of the marching and attacking army, on the one side, and, on the other, the besieged city, with, for example, its "ranks of blue veins" as soldiers, first guarding the city walls and then rushing to alert the heart, their "governess"—i.e., female governor. Tarquin's hand, which in l. 436 is the soldier leading the charge, becomes in l. 464 the battering ram that will breach the city's defenses. The poem begins to move away from this metaphor in l. 476, with wordplay on the word **color,** which not only means "pretext," as Lucrece uses it, but is also a military word applied to the flag or ensign under which a regiment fights and simultaneously a word describing the beauty of the red and white of Lucrece's face, which Tarquin cites as "the color" under which he besieges her.

486. will: Although this word is used throughout the poem in ways that blur the line between its psychological, theological, and bawdy meanings (as discussed in our longer note to Sonnet 135 [p. 339, above]), its use in this stanza has suggested to critics especially notable wordplay. In these lines, **will** seems to be simultaneously "male erotic desire," "forceful intention," and "male genitalia." It has been suggested that in "thou . . . must my will abide," Tarquin makes a bawdy pun in which Lucrece's vagina is to become the abode of his penis.

528–29. A little . . . enacted: Tarquin's lines might be paraphrased as follows: "The principle that a **good end** justifies somewhat harmful means remains in force as state **policy.**" It is also worthy of note that **policy** was a loaded word, often associated with Machiavellian underhandedness and deceit.

553. **Pluto . . . plays:** In Greek mythology, a celebrated musician, **Orpheus,** married the nymph Eurydice. When she died and descended to Hades, Orpheus followed her and so entranced the god of the underworld, **Pluto,** with his music that Pluto gave him a chance to redeem Eurydice from the land of the dead.

714. **guilty rebel:** Although in this line the words **guilty rebel** seem to refer to **Desire,** it is tempting to see an oblique reference to **the flesh** (l. 712) as well. The idea of the flesh as rebellious is spelled out by St. Augustine in *The City of God against the Pagans,* where he uses human powerlessness over sexual arousal as his primary and most obvious example of humanity's fall from grace. He writes that in Paradise before man's fall, "not yet did lust move those members without the will's consent; not yet did the flesh by its disobedience testify against the disobedience of man . . . [Adam and Eve] had no consciousness of their members warring against their will" (Book XIV, chap. xvii). However, since man's fall, "our flesh . . . torments us by insubordination" (chap. xv). George Herbert, in his poem "The H. Communion" (from *The Temple,* 1633), sees the body itself as the "rebel flesh" to which the soul is "captive." Thus it seems not far-fetched to see **guilty rebel** as referring not only to **Desire** but also, glancingly, to **the flesh.**

928. **Base . . . packhorse:** The phrases **watch of woes** and **sin's packhorse** can, as *synonyms* for **Time** (l. 925), be read in various ways. A **watch** could be, among other things, a period of wakefulness or of careful vigilance, or a man who guards a town and cries the hours during the night. But a **watch** was also the face of a clock or dial or the name of a portable timepiece, meanings clearly linked to Time. With one of these meanings, the phrase would describe Time as no more than a ticking clock measuring out woe. Again, with **sin's packhorse,** the word **packhorse** might refer to the word's literal meaning, in which case Time is compared to a horse on which sin carries its bundles. However, if Shakespeare is using

packhorse to mean a drudge, someone employed in servile or distasteful work (as he does in more than one play), then Time is characterized as the slave of sin. One meaning, of course, does not necessarily drive out others, and the kind of ambiguity we find here may well have been intended.

1062–64. **bastard . . . fruit: Graff, stock,** and **fruit** are words from horticulture. A **graff** is a shoot or scion inserted into another stem or **stock** for purposes of grafting to produce a new kind of **fruit.** The word **stock,** though, could also mean both the progenitor of a family and the descendants of a common ancestor. Thus, when Lucrece describes the illegitimate child that she may be carrying as the **fruit** of the rape, she plays on the several meanings of **stock** and uses figuratively the other horticultural terms. The same combination of terms describes human offspring in *Henry V,* where French noblemen cast scorn on the threatening Englishmen as hybrid descendants of French (Norman) noblemen and barbarous wild Saxon women: "shall a few sprays [i.e., shoots, twigs] of us, / The emptying of our fathers' luxury [i.e., the dregs of our ancestors' lust], / Our scions, put in wild and savage **stock** [i.e., French slips grafted to a wild Saxon plant], / Spurt up so suddenly into the clouds / And overlook their grafters [i.e., look down on the plants from which the slips were taken]?" "Normans, but **bastard** Normans, Norman bastards" (3.5.5–10).

1121–41. **You . . . languishment:** Each of the following terms is used with a double meaning, one having the ordinary sense of the word and one with the musical sense. In musical terminology, **discord** is lack of harmony; **stops** are (among several musical meanings) the closing of finger holes in a wind instrument; **rests** are intervals of silence or pauses; **dumps** are mournful or plaintive songs; **time** is rhythm; a **strain** is a tune or melody; a **burden** is a bass vocal accompaniment; **means** are (1) the middle or intermediate parts in harmonies, or (2) the people who sing or the instruments on which are played those parts; and **frets** are ridges of wood or metal on the fingerboards of stringed instruments.

1134. **better skill:** The only justification we have for interpreting this phrase to mean "with **better skill,**" as many other editors also do, is that such interpretation allows us to make sense of the line.

1155. death reproach's debtor: Editors have debated what it might mean for **death** to owe a debt to **reproach.** Some say that **death** is to pay **reproach** with Lucrece's life. Others say that if **death** takes her life, **death** will be in debt to **reproach;** that is, Lucrece's suicide would be criticized or reproached.

1234. ivory . . . filling: The general sense of this image is that the women, in their paleness, are like **ivory** figures serving as **conduits** through which water flows. However, the image of **coral cisterns** is less clear. Editors have speculated that the **cisterns** might be their eyes, reddened from weeping.

1316. her stained excuse: The line "ere she with blood had stained her stained excuse" is very difficult, and it has been variously explained by editors. The line as a whole has been interpreted to mean "before she had given color to—i.e., vindicated—her explanation of her stain by shedding her own blood," and the phrase **her stained excuse** as "the account she will give of her stain," "the explanation of her shame," and "the excuse contaminated by Tarquin's crime against her." The phrase **had stained** has been read as (1) had discolored and (2) had given color or credence to.

1394. Ajax: The **Ajax** depicted here seems to be the elder one, although he was already dead by the time Troy was sacked, as were, for example, Achilles and Hector—both mentioned below. The painting thus seems to telescope the duration of the Trojan War into a single moment. Among the famous events of the war included in the painting are Hector's marching toward the Greek army, Sinon's entry into Troy as a captive, Priam's pity in response to Sinon's lies, and Hecuba's grief as she sees Pyrrhus slay Priam.

1521. Sinon: Pretending to have been abandoned by his countrymen, who, he said, had sailed away from Troy, **Sinon** persuaded the Trojans to take into their city the gigantic wooden horse the Greeks had built as a "gift" for the Trojans. In stories about the Trojan War (from the point of view of the Trojans) Sinon lived in infamy for his pretended sorrow and his successful treachery. The wooden horse was, of course, full of Greek warriors who came out of it that night to conquer and burn the city.

1807–13. **Brutus . . . things:** According to Livy's *History of Rome* (*Historiarum ab urbe condita*), "L. Junius Brutus, the son of the king's sister, Tarquinia, [was] a young man of a very different character from that which he had assumed. . . . He determined that his intelligence should give the king no cause for alarm nor his fortune any provocation to his avarice, and that as the laws afforded no protection, he would seek safety in obscurity and neglect. Accordingly he carefully kept up the appearance and conduct of an idiot, leaving the king to do what he liked with his person and property, and did not even protest against his nickname of 'Brutus' [dullard]; for under the protection of that nickname the soul which was one day to liberate Rome was awaiting its destined hour. The story runs that when brought to Delphi by the Tarquins, more as a butt for their sport than as a companion, he had with him a golden staff enclosed in a hollow one of cornel wood, which he offered to Apollo as a mystical emblem of his own character" (1.56).

Shakespeare's "The Phoenix and Turtle"

Shakespeare's poem now known as "The Phoenix and Turtle" (or as "The Phoenix and *the* Turtle") appears to be his only occasional poem. It was first printed without any title as one of a handful of additional poems in Robert Chester's 1601 *Loves Martyr or, Rosalins Complaint. Allegorically shadowing the truth of Loue, in the constant Fate of the Phoenix and Turtle.* At the end of Chester's long poem we find Shakespeare's contribution above his name, *"William Shakespeare"*; included with it, besides some anonymous pieces, are poems by three other contemporary dramatists and poets: John Marston, George Chapman, and Ben Jonson. These poems are collected after a title page that reads "Hereafter Follow Diverse Poeticall Essaies on the former Subiect; viz: the *Turtle* and *Phoenix. Done by the best and chiefest of our* moderne writers, with their names subscribed to their particular workes: *neuer before extant.* And (now first) consecrated by them all generally, *to the loue and merite of the true-noble Knight,* Sir Iohn Salisburie."

In the classical tradition, the phoenix is a mythological creature that is unique and that consumes itself in fire from the ashes of which another phoenix is born; because it regenerates in this way, it is not characterized as either male or female (although Shakespeare does make her female in Sonnet 19). Ordinarily, too, the turtledove, the symbol of constancy, is female, as it is in Geoffrey Chaucer's *Parliament of Fowls* and in Shakespeare's *The Winter's Tale.* Shakespeare, in making the phoenix female and giving her a male consort in the turtledove, thus seems to begin with Chester's version of the phoenix myth.

The great beauty of Shakespeare's poem has often been thought to lie in its rigorous economy of expression. However, it is just this feature that also gives rise to the great variety of interpretations to which the poem has been subject. It has not even been clear to all readers that it is a single poem. Some few have read its final five stanzas, titled "Threnos" (a dirge), as an independent poem. There has been widespread disagreement about whether Shakespeare presents his phoenix as dying, together with the turtledove, in a fire from which a new phoenix is born, or he presents the couple dying without necessarily producing offspring. Since the poem refers to them as "leaving no posterity," the latter possibility seems the more persuasive.

Readers have also diverged over the significance of the poem's action. Some have read the poem as a celebration of the physical union in love of the phoenix and turtle. Others prefer a mystical reading in which the phoenix and turtle transcend the material world to become one as they approach a Christian heaven, from which they may or may not return. Others who favor transcendence offer a philosophical, often Neoplatonic, reading of the poem. There are also those who have attempted to link the birds to particular historical personages, Queen Elizabeth and the earl of Essex being particular favorites, though such historical interpretations of the poem no longer command wide assent.

The poem is divided into three principal sections. The first five stanzas may be called the "session," or sitting, a word from the poem itself that describes the assembling of the birds to sing the second section, called the "anthem," or song. This second section, of eight stanzas, celebrates the love of the phoenix and turtle in a series of paradoxes, or apparent contradictions, that sometimes use philosophical and theological language to describe the indescribable—two becoming one through their love. Finally, at the end of the anthem we are introduced to an allegorical figure called Reason who is the author of the third and last part of the poem, the "Threnos." In this beautiful poem, many readers find the last part, written with extreme economy in tercets, the most beautiful.

"THE PHOENIX
AND TURTLE"

1. **the bird . . . lay:** i.e., **the bird** whose song (**lay**) is **loudest** (See longer note, p. 602.)

2. **the sole Arabian tree:** See longer note to l. 1, p. 602.

3. **trumpet:** trumpeter

4. **wings:** i.e., birds (synecdoche)

5. **shrieking harbinger:** i.e., screech owl, whose discordant cry was considered an evil omen

6. **precurrer:** precursor

7. **Augur:** prophet; **fever's end:** i.e., death (See *A Midsummer Night's Dream:* "the screech-owl, screeching loud, / Puts the wretch that lies in woe / In remembrance of a shroud" [5.1.393–95].)

9. **session:** sitting (of the assembly of birds); **interdict:** forbid, prohibit

10. **Every . . . wing:** i.e., all birds of prey   **tyrant:** cruel, violent

12. **obsequy:** rite performed at a grave side; **strict:** rigorously observed; limited in number or kind of participants

14. **defunctive music can:** knows music pertaining to dying

15. **death-divining swan:** See note to *Lucrece,* l. 1611.

16. **requiem:** mass for the dead; **his:** i.e., its (with reference perhaps to the **requiem,** perhaps to the **swan**); **right:** (1) due; (2) rite, religious observance

17. **treble-dated:** i.e., long-lived (See longer note, p. 602.)

18–19. **That thy sable . . . tak'st:** i.e., reproduces by exchanging **breath** with its mate (See longer note, p. 602.)   **sable gender:** black race or kind

21. **anthem:** song

23. **Phoenix:** a mythical bird which, in most accounts, is reborn from the ashes of its own death by fire (See pictures, pp. 62 and 536.)   **turtle:** turtledove, a species of dove which, because of its noted affection for its mate, was the symbol of constancy in love (See picture, p. 600.)

"The Phoenix and Turtle"

Let the bird of loudest lay
On the sole Arabian tree
Herald sad and trumpet be,
To whose sound chaste wings obey.

But thou shrieking harbinger,   5
Foul precurrer of the fiend,
Augur of the fever's end,
To this troop come thou not near.

From this session interdict
Every fowl of tyrant wing,   10
Save the eagle, feathered king;
Keep the obsequy so strict.

Let the priest in surplice white,
That defunctive music can,
Be the death-divining swan,   15
Lest the requiem lack his right.

And thou treble-dated crow,
That thy sable gender mak'st
With the breath thou giv'st and tak'st,
'Mongst our mourners shalt thou go.   20

Here the anthem doth commence:
Love and constancy is dead,
Phoenix and the turtle fled
In a mutual flame from hence.

25. **So . . . as:** i.e., **they loved** in such a way that; **in twain:** in two

26. **essence:** substance (a term from Scholastic theology) See longer note, p. 602.

27. **distincts:** separate persons; **division none:** i.e., with no distinction between them (In logic, **division** is the action of dividing into kinds or classes, or the separation of a genus into species.)

28. **Number . . . slain:** This line plays with the proverb "One is no number." Because the **two distincts** are in **essence one** and "**one** is no **number**," then "**number . . . was slain.**" (But see longer note, p. 603.)

32. **But . . . wonder:** i.e., it (the phenomenon of **hearts remote yet not asunder**) would be cause for **wonder,** were it found anywhere except in these two birds

34. **That:** i.e., in such a way that; **his right:** i.e., what was due to him (i.e., the love returned to him by the phoenix)

35. **sight:** eyes

36. **mine:** (1) i.e., self (through wordplay on the pronoun **mine**); (2) i.e., source of treasure

37. **Property:** (1) the right to possession of something by a single entity with a single name; (2) distinctive quality of a person or thing; (3) proper use of words

38. **the self:** the **same** person or thing

41–44. **Reason . . . compounded:** See longer note, p. 603. **confounded:** confused

45. **twain:** pair, couple

46. **concordant:** harmonious, agreeing

48. **what parts . . . remain:** (1) separates but remains single; (2) departs yet can stay

49. **threne:** threnos (l. 53), dirge, song of lamentation

51. **Co-supremes:** joint rulers

52. **chorus:** In tragedy beginning with the Greeks, the **chorus** represents interested spectators who sympathize with the fortunes of the characters and give expression to the moral and religious sentiments evoked by the action.

So they loved, as love in twain   25
Had the essence but in one,
Two distincts, division none;
Number there in love was slain.

Hearts remote yet not asunder,
Distance and no space was seen   30
'Twixt this turtle and his queen;
But in them it were a wonder.

So between them love did shine
That the turtle saw his right
Flaming in the phoenix' sight;   35
Either was the other's mine.

Property was thus appalled
That the self was not the same;
Single nature's double name
Neither two nor one was called.   40

Reason, in itself confounded,
Saw division grow together,
To themselves yet either neither,
Simple were so well compounded

That it cried, "How true a twain   45
Seemeth this concordant one!
Love hath reason, Reason none,
If what parts can so remain,"

Whereupon it made this threne
To the phoenix and the dove,   50
Co-supremes and stars of love,
As chorus to their tragic scene.

65. **repair:** come frequently or in numbers
66. **true:** constant, faithful; **fair:** beautiful

A turtledove. ("The Phoenix and Turtle")

Threnos

Beauty, truth, and rarity,
Grace in all simplicity,
Here enclosed, in cinders lie.   55

Death is now the phoenix' nest,
And the turtle's loyal breast
To eternity doth rest,

Leaving no posterity;
'Twas not their infirmity,   60
It was married chastity.

Truth may seem, but cannot be;
Beauty brag, but 'tis not she;
Truth and beauty buried be.

To this urn let those repair   65
That are either true or fair;
For these dead birds sigh a prayer.

William Shakespeare

"The Phoenix and Turtle"
Longer Notes

1. **the bird . . . lay:** Because Shakespeare's *The Tempest* includes the lines "in Arabia / There is one tree, the phoenix' throne, one phoenix / At this hour reigning there" (3.3.27–29), it is hard not to see "the bird . . . On the sole Arabian tree" as the phoenix. Critics, though, are divided about whether the bird is the poem's phoenix that is about to die or the phoenix born from the ashes of the poem's previous phoenix and the turtle. Some identify the bird with such other birds as the cock. Many think its identity is left undetermined as simply the bird whose song has proved to be the loudest, and therefore best fitted to be the herald and trumpeter summoning the other birds to the funeral. It has also been suggested that this herald is the phoenix of the original myth, preferred by Shakespeare and restored to preside over the funeral of Chester's female phoenix and male turtledove.

17. **treble-dated:** According to the Roman writer Pliny's *Natural History*, "Hesiodus [the Greek poet and mythographer] . . . saith forsooth, That the crow liveth 9 times as long as we" (Philemon Holland's 1601 translation, 7.48.180).

18–19. **That thy sable . . . tak'st:** According to John Swan's 1635 *Speculum Mundi* (*Mirror of the World*), "Neither (as is thought) doth the raven conceive by conjunction of male and female, but rather by a kind of billing at the mouth, which *Pliny* mentioneth as an opinion of the common people" (p. 397).

26. **essence:** In Scholastic theology, **essence** refers to the respect in which the three persons in the Blessed Trinity are one. Some have suggested that this passage in the poem was influenced by the following language in the Athanasian Creed, found in the Anglican Prayer Book (the Book of Common Prayer) since its first publication in 1549: "For like as we are compelled by the Christian verity to

acknowledge every Person [of the Blessed Trinity] by himself to be God and Lord, so are we forbidden by the Catholic Religion to say, There be three Gods, or three Lords."

28. **Number . . . slain:** Although the accepted reading of this line is reflected in our commentary note, the line can also be read quite differently. As we explain in our note to Sonnet 8, l. 14, the word **number** can mean (1) an "integer" or (2) an "aggregate or sum"; **one** cannot be a sum or an aggregate, and thus can be considered a **number** only in the first sense. If Shakespeare is using **number** in the second sense (i.e., as any integer greater than one or any collection of more than one object), then the line is saying that because there is "no division" in the unity of the phoenix and turtle, they are not "more than one," and therefore, in them, **number is slain.**

41–44. **Reason . . . compounded:** The following useful paraphrases of this stanza have been offered: "A simple is a single element, a compound [is] a mixture of elements changed and broken down in the process. Here the mixture is both simple and compound at the same time, and is thus either both or neither" (Maurice Evans); "Pure reason had seen those unlike and, according to its insight, quite incompatible, unite together. In the union neither had a separate identity, simple, that is, simples or elementary elements, were so perfectly compounded or united" (A. H. R. Fairchild); "Reason . . . saw division grow together, yet saw neither grow to or become absorbed in the other, so well were simple compounded" (R. H. Case).

Shakespeare's Sonnets
Textual Notes

The reading of the present text appears to the left of the square bracket. Unless otherwise noted, the reading to the left of the bracket is from **Q**, the Quarto text (upon which this edition is based). The Sonnets were published again by John Benson in 1640 as *POEMS: WRITTEN BY Wil. Shakespeare. Gent.*, a version that varies widely from Q. **Ed.** indicates an earlier editor of the *Sonnets*, beginning with Gildon, who, in 1710, based his edition on Benson's. Malone, in 1790, was the first to edit Q. No sources are given for emendations of punctuation or for corrections of obvious typographical errors, like turned letters that produce no known word. **Uncorr.** means the first or uncorrected state of the Quarto; **corr.** means the second or corrected state of the Quarto; ~ stands in place of a word already quoted before the square bracket; ʌ indicates the omission of a punctuation mark.

2	4. tattered] Q (totter'd)
	14. cold] O (could)
6	1. ragged] Q (wragged)
	4. beauty's] beautits Q
10	10. lodged] Q (log'd)
11	6. this,] ~ʌ Q; cold] Q (could)
12	4. all] Ed.; or Q
13	1. your self] Q
	7. Your self] Ed.; You selfe Q
15	8. wear] Q (were)
16	10. thisʌ . . . penʌ] ~ (. . . ~) Q
17	12. meter] Q (miter)
19	3. jaws] Ed.; yawes Q
20	2. Hast] Q (Haste)
22	3. furrows] Q (forrwes)
23	2. beside] Q (besides)
	6. rite] Q (right)
	14. with] Q (wit)

14. wit] wiht Q
24   1. stelled] Ed.; steeld Q
      3. 'tis] ti's Q
26   11. tattered] Q (tottered)
      12. thy] Ed.; their Q
27   1. haste] Q (hast)
      2. travel] Q (trauaill)
      6. thee,] Q *corr.;* ~; Q *uncorr.*
      10. thy] Ed.; their Q
28   5. either's] Q (ethers)
      12. gild'st the even] Ed.; guil'st th' eauen Q
31   8. thee] Ed.; there Q
32   8. height] Q (hight)
33   14. when] Q (whē)
34   2. travel] Q (trauaile)
      12. cross] Ed.; losse Q
35   8. thy] Ed.; their Q (twice)
37   7. thy] Ed.; their Q
38   2. breathe] Q (breath)
      2. pour'st] Q (poor'st)
      3. too] Q (to)
39   12. doth] Ed.; dost Q
40   7. thyself] Ed; this selfe Q
43   11. thy] Ed.; their Q
44   13. nought] Ed.; naughts Q
      13. slow] Q (sloe)
45   9. life's] Q (liues)
      12. thy] Ed.; their Q
46   3. thy] Ed.; their Q
      8. thy] Ed.; their Q
      9. 'cide] Ed.; side Q
      13. thy] Ed.; their Q
      14. thy] Ed.; their Q
47   10. Thyself] Q *corr.* (Thy selfe); thy seife Q *uncorr.*
      11. no] Ed.; nor Q
50   6. dully] Ed.; duly Q
51   3. haste] Q (hast)
      10. perfect'st] Ed.; perfects Q

55	1. monuments] Ed; monument Q
	9. enmity] Q (emnity)
56	13. Or] Ed.; As Q
58	7. patience, tame∧ to sufferance,] Ed.; ~∧ ~, ~ ~∧ Q
59	6. hundred] Q (hundreth)
	8. done,] ~. Q
	11. whe'er] Q (where)
61	8. tenor] Q (tenure)
62	13. 'Tis] T'is Q
63	5. traveled] Q (trauaild)
65	12. of] Ed.; or Q
66	5. misplaced] Q (misplast)
	9. tongue] Q (tung)
67	10. veins] Q (vaines)
68	7. second life] scond life Q
69	3. due] Ed.; end Q
	5. Thy] Ed.; Their Q
	14. soil] solye Q
70	1. art] Ed.; are Q
	6. Thy] Ed.; Their Q
	8. unstained] unstayined Q
71	4. vilest] Q (vildest)
73	4. ruined] rn'wd Q
	4. choirs] Q (quiers)
74	10. prey] Q (pray)
75	2. showers] Q (shewers)
76	4, 8. strange? . . . proceed?] *Question marks do not print in one copy of* Q
	7. tell] Ed.; fel Q
77	1. wear] Q (were)
	10. blanks] Ed.; blacks Q
81	14. breathes] Q (breaths)
86	13. filled] Q (fild)
87	9. Thy self] Q
89	11. profane] Q *corr.* (prophane); proface Q *uncorr.*
90	11. shall] Ed.; stall Q
91	9. better] Ed.; bitter Q
92	6. end;] ~, Q

93	6. change.] ~, Q
94	4. cold] Q (could)
98	9. lily's] Q (Lillies)
	11. were] Q (weare)
99	4. dwells∧] ~? Q
	5. dyed] Q (died)
	7. marjoram] Q (marierom)
	9. One] Ed.; Our Q
101	2. dyed] Q (di'd)
102	11. bough] Q (bow)
106	12. skill] Ed.; still Q
110	6. Askance] Q (Asconce)
	10. grind] Q (grin'de)
111	1. with] Ed.; wish Q
112	14. methinks are] Ed; me thinkes y'are Q
113	6. latch] Ed.; lack Q
	13. more, replete] ~∧ ~, Q
	14. mine eye] Ed.; mine Q
116]	Q *corr.*; 119 Q *uncorr.*
116	8. height] Q (higth)
118	10. were∧ not,] ~, ~∧ Q
120	6. you've] Q (y'haue)
121	11. bevel;] ~∧ Q
122	1. Thy] TThy Q
123	12. haste] Q (hast)
125	4. waste] Q (wast)
	7. sweet∧] ~; Q
126	2. sickle∧] ~, Q
	3. show'st] Q (shou'st)
	5. mistress] Q (misteres)
	8. minutes] Ed.; mynuit Q
127	2. were] Q (weare)
	7. bower] Q (boure)
	9. mistress'] Q (Mistersse)
128	11. thy] Ed.; their Q
	11. gait] Q (gate)
	14. thy] Ed.; their Q
129	9. Mad] Ed.; Made Q

10. quest∧ to have,] ~, ~ ~∧ Q

11. proved a] Ed.; proud and Q

12. Before, . . . proposed; behind,] ~∧ . . .
~∧ ~∧ Q

130   2. Coral] Q (Currall)

131   3. heart] Q (hart)

132   6. the east] Q (th'East)

9. mourning] Q (morning)

133   3. Is 't] I'st Q

10. bail] Q (bale)

134   12. lose] Q (loose)

136   6. Ay] Q (I)

137   8. tied] Q (tide)

138   12. to have] Q (t'haue)

140   3. Lest] Q (Least)

5. were] Q (weare)

13. belied] Q (be lyde)

143   12. part:] ~∧ Q

144   2. suggest] Q (sugiest)

5. female] Q (femall)

6. side] *Passionate Pilgrime,* Ed.; sight O

9. fiend] Q (finde)

145   7. doom] Q (dome)

146   2. Pressed with] This ed.; *Booth's conjecture*; My sinfull earth Q

147   12. random] Q (randon)

148   8. men's "no."] mens: no, Q

14. Lest] Q (Least)

149   6. frown'st] Q (froun'st)

6. fawn] Q (faune)

7. lour'st] Q (lowrst)

150   6. deeds∧] deeds, Q *corr.*; deeds; Q *uncorr.*

151   4. Lest] Q (Least)

153   4. cold] Q (could)

14. eyes] Ed.; eye O

154   3. vowed] Q (vou'd)

Venus and Adonis
Textual Notes

The reading of the present text appears to the left of the square bracket. Unless otherwise noted, the reading to the left of the bracket is from **Q**, the First Quarto text (upon which this edition is based). **Q3** is the Third Quarto of 1595; ~ stands in place of a word already quoted before the square bracket; ∧ indicates the omission of a punctuation mark.

Preliminaries 2. *aqua.*] *aqua.* | LONDON | Imprinted by Richard Field, and are to be sold at | the signe of the white Greyhound in | Paules Church-yard. | 1593. Q
Poem 26. precedent] Q (president)
51, 191. hairs] Q (heares)
57. haste] Q (hast)
83. long] Q (lõg)
84. countless] Q (comptlesse)
137. Then . . . then] Q (Thẽ . . . thẽ)
147. hair] Q (heare)
153. strengthless] strẽgthles
167. from] Q (frõ)
186. face;] ~∧ Q
213. Statue] Q (Statüe)
223, 225, 277, 301. Sometimes] Q (Sometime)
231, 239. deer] Q (deare)
259. copse] Q (copp's)
297. strong] Q (strõg)
304. whe'er] Q (where)
308. mind.] ~, Q
362. jail] Q (gaile)
363. alabaster] Q (allablaster)
393. But] Bnt Q
406. dumb] Q (dũbe)
429. mermaid's] Q (marmaides)
432. wounding] Q (woũding)

443. from] Q (frō)
457. marketh.] ~, Q
521. payment] Q (paimēt)
560. handling] Q (hādling)
570. then] Q (thē); woos] Q (woes); when] Q (whē)
583. waste] Q (wast)
607. vain;] ~, Q
638. naught] nanght Q
641. dissemble] Q (dissēble)
642. and] aud Q
658. sometimes] Q (sometime) *twice*
666. them] Q (thē)
678. hounds] Q (hoūds)
680. overshoot] Q (ouer-shut)
685, 687, 689. Sometimes] Q (Sometime)
689. deer] Q (deare)
740. frenzies] frendzies Q
750. sun] Q (sonne)
754. sons] Q (suns)
789. device] Q (deuise)
870, 909, 1029. haste] Q (hast)
899. them leave] Q (thē leaue)
940. random] Q (randon)
966. them] Q (thē)
1005. 'Tis] T'is Q
1031. as] Q3; are Q
1048. confound] Q (confoūd)
1050. from] Q (frō)
1054. drenched] Q (drēcht)
1077. canst] Q (cāst)
1139. low] Q (lo)
1146. dumb] Q (dūbe)
1170. upon] Q (upō)
1176. compares] Q (cōpares)

Lucrece
Textual Notes

The reading of the present text appears to the left of the square bracket. Unless otherwise noted, the reading to the left of the bracket is from **Q**, the First Quarto text (upon which this edition is based). Readings not in **Q** derive from earlier editors of the poem, beginning with Lintott in 1709. These readings are marked **Ed.** No sources are given for emendations of punctuation or for corrections of obvious typographical errors, like turned letters, that produce no known word. *Corr.* means the second or corrected state of the First Quarto; *uncorr.* refers to the first or uncorrected state of the First Quarto; ~ stands in place of a word already quoted before the square bracket; ʌ indicates the omission of a punctuation mark.

Argument 21. treacherously] Q (tretcherouslie)
Poem 13. heaven's] Q (heauēs)
24. morning's] Q *corr.* (mornings); morning Q *uncorr.*
31. apology] Q *uncorr.* (Appologie); Apologies Q *corr.*
50. Collatium] Q *uncorr.;* Colatia Q *corr.;* arrived] Q *corr.* (arriued); ariued Q *uncorr.*
54. When] Q (Whē)
63. When] Q (Whē); fence] Q (fēce)
74. lest] Q (least)
87, 88 *preceded by quotation marks in* Q
95, 331, 530, 1105, 1106, 1786. sometimes] Q (sometime)
124, 516, 1208. life's] Q (liues)
125. himself betakes] Q *uncorr.;* themselues betake Q *corr.*
126. wakes] Q *uncorr.;* wake Q *corr.*
130. abstaining.] ~ʌ Q
133. adjunct] Q (adjūct)
140. bankrout] Q (bāckrout)
147. all together] Q (altogether)
162. upon] Q *uncorr.* (uppon); vppon Q *corr.*
163. sleep] sleeep Q
177. cold] Q (could)

217. strucken] Q (strokē)
321, 552, 650, 1295, 1332, 1668. haste] Q (hast)
346. compass] Q (cōpasse)
396. pearly] Q *corr.* (pearlie); perlie Q *uncorr.;* sweat] Q (swet)
400. golden] Q (goldē)
419. alabaster] Q (alablaster)
434, 462. them] Q (thē)
459. antics] Q (Antiques)
460, 528, 530, 560, 831–32, 853, 867–68, 1109–18, 1125, 1127, 1216, 1687 *preceded by quotation marks in* Q
511. falcons'] Q (Faulcōs)
535. device] Q (devise)
550. from] Q (frō)
555. panteth] Q (pāteth)
560. wear] Q (were)
571. human] Q (humaine)
587. woman's] Q (womās)
599. wound'st] Q (woūdst)
637. from] Q (frō)
718. stands] Q (stāds)
812. quote] Q (cote)
833. themselves . . . them] Q (thēselues . . . thē)
879. 'point'st] Q (poinst)
907. Advice] Q (Advise)
922. inclination∧] ~. Q
999. hands] Q (hāds)
1118. roll] Q (*some copies*); rowle Q (*other copies*)
1119. bounding] Q (boūding)
1127. dumps when] Q (dūps whē)
1129. hair] Q (heare)
1148. men . . . gentle] Q (mē . . . gētle)
1182. by him] Q *corr.;* for him Q *uncorr.*
1229. eyne, enforced∧] ~∧~, Q
1239. then] Q (thē)
1249. remain∧] ~. Q
1252. men can] Q (mē cā)
1260. women] Q (womē)

1263. ensue∧] ~. Q
1271. from] Q (frõ)
1310. tenor] Q (tenure)
1319. fashion] Q (fashiõ)
1321. suspicion] Q (suspiciõ)
1323. them] Q (thẽ)
1329. than] Q (thẽ)
1334. hie] Q (high)
1335. blast] Q *corr.;* blasts Q *uncorr.*
1338. curtsies] Q (cursies)
1345, 1812. silly] Q (seelie)
1350. this pattern of the worn-out age] Q (*some copies:* patterne . . .
   worne-out); the patterne of this worne-out age Q (*other copies*)
1374. lifeless] Q (liuelesse)
1386. far-off] Q (farre of)
1391. paces,] ~. Q
1393. tremble] Q (trẽble)
1395. behold!] ~∧ Q
1452. chaps] Q (chops)
1486. swounds] Q (sounds)
1526. When] Q (Whẽ)
1537. took.] ~∧Q
1544. too,] to∧ Q
1553. round] Q (roũd)
1644, 1851. Rome] Q (Roome)
1662. wreathèd] Ed.; wretched Q
1680. one] Q (on)
1683. foe,] ~. Q
1713. in it] Ed.; it in Q
1728. wounds] Q (woũds)
1729. Life's] Q (Liues)
1833. them] Q (thẽ)
1834. from] Q (frõ)

Shakespeare's Sonnets:
Appendix of
Intertextual Material

Shakespeare's *Sonnets* draw much of their power from literary works to which they allude and with which he could expect his readers to be familiar. This allusiveness makes the *Sonnets* part of a large poetic network and it gives both richness and density to their concise language. This appendix provides some of the passages to which the sonnets may allude, along with a cross-reference to one of the sonnets which may be read in light of the passage.

From Ovid's *Metamorphoses*, trans. Arthur Golding (1567), book 15

(Line numbers correspond to the Golding translation.
Spelling has been modernized.)

A. ll. 198–205 (Compare s. 60)
    Things ebb and flow, and every shape is made to pass away.
    The time itself continually is fleeting like a brook.
    For neither brook nor lightsome time can tarry still. But look
    As every wave drives other forth, and that that comes behind
    Both thrusteth and is thrust itself. Even so the times by kind
    Do fly and follow both at once, and evermore renew.
    For that that was before is left, and straight there doth ensue
    Another that was never erst.

B. ll. 206–7, 221–35 (Compare s. 73)
    We see that after day comes night and darks the sky,
    And after night the lightsome sun succeedeth orderly.
    . . . .
    What? Seest thou not how that the year as representing plain

615

The age of man, departs [i.e., parts] itself in quarters four? First
    bain [supple]
And tender in the spring it is even like a sucking babe.
Then green and void of strength, and lush, and foggy is the blade,
And cheers the husbandman with hope. Then all things
    flourish gay.
The earth with flowers of sundry hue then seemeth for to play,
And virtue small or none to herbs there doth as yet belong.
The year from springtide passing forth to summer, waxeth strong,
Becometh like a lusty youth. For in our life throughout,
There is no time more plentiful, more lusty hot and stout.
Then followeth harvest when the heat of youth grows
    somewhat cold,
Ripe, mild, disposed mean betwixt a young man and an old,
And somewhat sprent [sprinkled] with greyish hair. Then ugly
    winter last
Like age steals on with trembling steps, all bald or overcast
With shirl [rough] thin hair as white as snow.

C. ll. 235–51 (Compare s. 60)

                                  Our bodies also aye
Do alter still from time to time, and never stand at stay.
We shall not be the same we were today or yesterday.
The day hath been we were but seed and only hope of men,
And in our mother's womb we had our dwelling place as then,
Dame Nature put to cunning hand and suffered not that we
Within our mother's strained womb should aye distressed be,
But brought us out to air, and from our prison set us free.
The child newborn lies void of strength. Within a season, though
He waxing four-footed learns like savage beasts to go.
Then somewhat falt'ring, and as yet not firm of foot, he stands
By getting somewhat for to help his sinews in his hands.
From that time growing strong and swift, he passeth forth the
    space
Of youth, and also wearing out his middle age apace,
Through drooping age's steepy path he runneth out his race.
This age doth undermine the strength of former years, and throws
It down.

D. ll. 287–95 (Compare s. 64)

Even so have places oftentimes exchanged their estate.

For I have seen it sea which was substantial ground alate [previously]

Again where sea was, I have seen the same become dry land,

And shells and scales of seafish far have lain from any strand,

And in the tops of mountains high old anchors have been found.

Deep valleys have by watershot [a sudden flood] been made of level ground,

And hills by force of gulling [erosion] oft have into sea been worn.

Hard gravel ground is sometime seen where marris [marsh] was before,

And that that erst did suffer drought becometh standing lakes.

E. ll. 984–95 (Compare s. 55)

Now have I brought a work to end which neither Jove's fierce wrath,

Nor sword, nor fire, nor fretting age with all the force it hath

Are able to abolish quite. Let come that fatal hour

Which (saving of [i.e., except for] this brittle flesh) hath over me no power,

And at his pleasure make an end of mine uncertain time,

Yet shall the better part of me assured be to climb

Aloft above the starry sky. And all the world shall never

Be able for to quench my name. For look how far so ever

The Roman Empire by the right of conquest shall extend,

So far shall all folk read this work. And time without all end

(If poets as by prophecy about the truth may aim)

My life shall everlastingly be lengthened still by fame.

The parable of the talents, Matthew 25.14–30

(Geneva Bible; spelling has been modernized.) Compare s. 4.

14.   For the kingdom of heaven is as a man that going into a strange [i.e., foreign] country called his servants and delivered to them his goods.

15.　And unto one he gave five talents, and to another two, and to another one, to every man after his own ability, and straightway went from home.

16.　Then he that had received the five talents went and occupied with them [i.e., put them out for interest, invested them], and gained other five talents.

17.　Likewise also he that received two, he also gained other two.

18.　But he that received that one went and digged it in the earth and hid his master's money.

19.　But after a long season, the master of those servants came and reckoned [i.e., settled accounts] with them.

20.　Then came he that had received five talents and brought other five talents, saying, "Master, thou deliveredst unto me five talents; behold, I have gained with them other five talents."

21.　Then his master said unto him, "It is well done, good servant and faithful. Thou hast been faithful in little, I will make thee ruler over much; enter in into thy master's joy."

22.　Also he that had received two talents came and said, "Master, thou deliveredst unto me two talents; behold, I have gained two other talents with them."

23.　His master said unto him "It is well done, good servant and faithful. Thou hast been faithful in little, I will make thee ruler over much; enter in into thy master's joy."

24.　Then he which had received the one talent came and said, "Master, I knew that thou wast an hard [i.e., tightfisted, stingy] man which reapest where thou sowedst not, and gatherest where thou strawedst [i.e., strewed, scattered] not.

25.　"I was therefore afraid, and went and hid thy talent in the earth. Behold, thou hast thine own."

26.　And his master answered, and said unto him, "Thou evil servant and slothful, thou knewest that I reap where I sowed not and gather where I strawed not.

27.　"Thou oughtest therefore to have put my money to the exchangers [i.e., money changers] and then at my coming should I have received mine own with vantage [i.e., profit].

28.　"Take, therefore, the talent from him, and give it unto him which hath ten talents.

29.　"For unto every man that hath, it shall be given, and he shall

have abundance; and from him that hath not, even that he hath shall be taken away.
30. "Cast therefore that unprofitable servant into utter darkness; there shall be weeping and gnashing of teeth."

Excerpts from Erasmus's "Encomium Matrimonii," in English translation from Thomas Wilson, *The Arte of Rhetorique* (1553), fols. 21v–34v.

An Epistle to persuade a young gentleman to marriage, devised by Erasmus in the behalf of his friend.

Albeit you are wise enough of yourself through that singular wisdom of yours (most loving cousin) and little needs the advice of others, yet either for that old friendship which hath been betwixt us and continued with our age even from our cradles, or for such your great good turns showed at all times towards me, or else for that fast kindred and alliance which is betwixt us, I thought myself thus much to owe unto you if I would be such a one indeed as you ever have taken me, that is to say a man both friendly and thankful, to tell you freely whatsoever I judged to appertain either to the safeguard or worship of you or any of yours and willingly to warn you of the same. . . . I have felt often your advice in mine own affairs, and I have found it to be as fortunate unto me as it was friendly. Now if you will likewise in your own matters follow my counsel, I trust it shall so come to pass that neither I shall repent me for that I have given you counsel, nor yet you shall forthink yourself, that you have obeyed and followed mine advice. [fol. 21v]

[Erasmus tells of learning from a mutual friend that the young gentleman's mother has died and his sister entered a convent.]

. . . [In] you only remaineth the hope of issue and maintenance of your stock, whereupon your friends with one consent have offered you in marriage a gentlewoman of a good house and much wealth, fair of body, very well brought up, and such a one as loveth you with all her heart. But you (either for your late sorrows which you have in fresh remembrance or else for religion sake) have so purposed to live a single life, that neither can you for love of your stock, neither for desire of issue, nor yet for any entreaty that your friends can make, either by praying or by weeping, be brought to change your mind. [fol. 22]

A. "Or who is he so fond will be the tomb / Of his self love, to stop posterity?" (s. 3.7–8)

What is more right or meet than to give that unto the posterity the which we have received of our ancestors? . . . What is more unthankful than to deny that unto younglings the which (if thou hadst not received of thine elders) thou couldst not have been the man living, able to have denied it unto them? [fol. 22v]

Now again be it that others deserve worthy praise that seek to live a virgin's life, yet it must needs be a great fault in you. Others shall be thought to seek a pureness of life; you shall be counted a parricide or a murderer of your stock: that whereas you may by honest marriage increase your posterity, you suffer it to decay forever through your willful single life. . . . And now it mattereth nothing whether you kill or refuse to save that creature which you only might save and that with ease. [fol. 33v]

B. "Then, beauteous niggard, why dost thou abuse / The bounteous largess given thee to give?" (s. 4.5–6)

We do read that such as are in very deed chaste of their body and live a virgin's life have been praised, but the single life was never praised of itself. Now again the law of Moses accurseth the barrenness of married folk, and we do read that some were excommunicated for the same purpose and banished from the altar. And wherefore, I pray you? Marry, sir, because that they, like unprofitable persons and living only to themselves, did not increase the world with any issue. . . . A city is like to fall in ruin, except there be watchmen to defend it with armor. But assured destruction must here needs follow except men through the benefit of marriage supply issue, the which through mortality do from time to time decay. [fols. 23v–24]

C. "Then how, when nature calls thee to be gone, / What acceptable audit canst thou leave?" (s. 4.11–12)

And the wise founders of all laws [i.e., the Romans] give good reason why such favor was showed to married folk. For what is more blessful than to live ever? Now whereas nature hath denied this, matrimony doth give it by a certain sleight so much as may be. Who doth not desire to be bruited and live through fame among men hereafter? Now there is no building of pillars, no erecting of arches, no blazing of arms, that doth more set forth a man's name than doth the increase of children. [fols. 24v–25]

But what do we with these laws written? This is the law of nature, not written in the tables of brass but firmly printed in our minds, the which law, whosoever doth not obey, he is not worthy to be called a man, much less shall he be counted a citizen. For if to live well (as the Stoics wittily do dispute) is to follow the course of nature, what thing is so agreeing with nature as matrimony? For there is nothing so natural not only unto mankind but also unto all other living creatures as it is for every one of them to keep their own kind from decay and through increase of issue to make the whole kind immortal. The which thing, all men know, can never be done without wedlock and carnal copulation. It were a foul thing that brute beasts should obey the law of nature and men like giants should fight against nature, whose work if we would narrowly look upon, we shall perceive that in all things here upon earth, she would there should be a certain spice of marriage. [fol. 25v]

Hath not God so knit all things together with certain links that one ever seemeth to have need of another? What say you of the sky or firmament that is ever stirring with continual moving? Doth it not play the part of a husband while it puffeth up the earth, the mother of all things, and maketh it fruitful with casting seed (as a man would say) upon it? . . . And to what end are these things spoken? Marry, sir, because we might understand that through marriage, all things are, and do still continue, and without the same all things do decay and come to nought. . . . Thus we see plainly that such a one as hath no mind of marriage seemeth to be no man but rather a stone, an enemy to nature, a rebel to God himself, seeking through his own folly his last end and destruction. [fol. 26]

D. "For where is she so fair whose uneared womb / Disdains the tillage of thy husbandry?" (s. 3.5–6)

Therefore as he is counted no good gardener, that being content with things present, doth diligently prune his old trees and hath no regard either to imp or graft young sets, because the selfsame orchard (though it be never so well trimmed) must needs decay in time, and all the trees die within few years, so he is not to be counted half a diligent citizen that being content with the present multitude hath no regard to increase the number. Therefore there is no one man that ever hath been counted a worthy citizen who hath not labored to get children, and sought to bring them up in godliness. [fols. 26v–27]

Now I pray you, if a man had land that waxed very fat and fertile and suffered the same for lack of manuring forever to wax barren, should he not, or were he not worthy to be punished by the laws, considering it is for the commonweal's behoove, that every man should well and truly husband his own. If that man be punished who little heedeth the maintenance of his tillage, the which although it be never so well manured yet it yieldeth nothing else but wheat, barley, beans, and peas, what punishment is he worthy to suffer that refuseth to plow that land which being tilled yieldeth children? [fol. 29v]

E. "Who lets so fair a house fall to decay, / Which husbandry in honor might uphold . . . ?" (s. 13.9–10)

Now be it that others deserve great praise for their maidenhead, you notwithstanding cannot want great rebuke, seeing it lieth in your hands to keep that house from decay whereof you lineally descended and to continue still the name of your ancestors, who deserve most worthily to be known forever. . . . Will you suffer the hope of all your stock to decay, namely seeing there is none other of your name and stock but yourself alone to continue the posterity? [fol. 28v]

But whereas you . . . are like to have many children hereafter, seeing also you are a man of great lands and revenues by your ancestors, the house whereof you came being both right honorable and right ancient, so that you could not suffer it to perish without your great offense and great harm to the commonweal: again seeing you are of lusty years and very comely for your personage, . . . seeing also your friends desire you, your kinfolk weep to win you, . . . the ashes of your ancestors from their graves make hearty suit unto you, do you yet hold back, do you still mind to live a single life? [fols. 34–34v]

F. "When your sweet issue your sweet form should bear. . . ." (s. 13.8)

What a joy shall this be unto you when your most fair wife shall make you a father, in bringing forth a fair child unto you, where you shall have a pretty little boy running up and down your house, . . . such a one as shall call you dad, with his sweet lisping words. . . . You have them that shall comfort you in your latter days, that shall close up your eyes when God shall call you, that shall bury you and fulfill all things belonging to your funeral, by whom you shall seem to be new born. For so long as they shall live, you shall need never be thought dead yourself. The goods and lands that you have got go not to other heirs than to your own. So that unto such as have fulfilled all things that belong unto man's life, death itself cannot seem bitter. Old age cometh upon us all, will we or nill we, and this way nature provided for us, that we should wax young again in our children. . . . For what man can be grieved that he is old when he seeth his own countenance which he had being a child to appear lively in his son? Death is ordained for all mankind, and yet by this means only nature by her providence mindeth unto us a certain immortality, while she increaseth one thing upon another even as a young graft buddeth out when the old tree is cut down. Neither can he seem to die that, when God calleth him, leaveth a young child behind him. [fol. 31]

G. "Then what could death do if thou shouldst depart, / Leaving thee living in posterity?" (s. 6.11–12)

How many doth the plague destroy, how many do the seas swallow, how many doth battle snatch up? For I will not speak of the daily dying that is in all places. Death taketh her flight everywhere round about, she runneth over them, she catcheth them up, she hasteneth as much as she can possible to destroy all mankind, and now do we so highly commend single life and eschew marriage? [fol. 33]

From Christopher Marlowe, *Hero and Leander*

(Compare s. 4)

Then treasure is abused
When misers keep it; being put to loan,
In time it will return us two for one.
. . . .
Who builds a palace and rams up the gate,
Shall see it ruinous and desolate.
. . . .
Less sins the poor rich man that starves himself
In heaping up a mass of drossy pelf,
Than such as you: his golden earth remains,
Which, after his decease, some other gains;
But this fair gem, sweet in the loss alone,
When you fleet hence, can be bequeathed to none.
. . . .
One is no number; maids are nothing, then,
Without the sweet society of men.
Wilt thou live single still? One shalt thou be,
Though never-singling Hymen couple thee.
. . . .
Base bullion for the stamp's sake we allow;
Even so for men's impression do we you[.]

(234–66)

Henry Constable,
Diana
"Sonnetto decissete"

(Compare s. 99)

My lady's presence makes the roses red,
Because to see her lips they blush for shame.
The lily's leaves, for envy, pale became,
And her white hands in them this envy bred.
The marigold abroad the leaves did spread,
Because the sun's and her power is the same.
The violet of purple color came,
Dyed with the blood she made my heart to shed.
In brief, all flowers from her their virtue take:
From her sweet breath their sweet smells do proceed;
The living heat which her eyebeams do make
Warmeth the ground and quick'neth the seed.
   The rain, wherewith she watereth these flowers,
   Falls from mine eyes, which she dissolves in showers.

Shakespeare's Sonnets: A Modern Perspective

Lynne Magnusson

In the movie *Shakespeare in Love*, it is a conventionally beautiful woman of high social status and at least respectable morality who fires up Will Shakespeare's desire. If the filmmakers were taking their cues for a script about Shakespeare's passions from the *Sonnets*, one might have expected a less orthodox story. Most of the first 126 sonnets—if we can trust that the order in which the 154 sonnets were published in 1609 represents a planned sequence—evoke a poet's highly charged desire for a beautiful young *man* of high status. He is the one praised in Sonnet 18's "Shall I compare thee to a summer's day?," the famous romantic tribute that Will in the movie addresses to his lady. For the sonnet speaker, the fair young man is what grounds his idealizing imagination and his lyrical poetry, the trigger for complex emotions, and the object of sexual desire. The young man's face may be *like* a beautiful woman's, leading the poet to call him "the master mistress of my passion" (s. 20.2), but what is special in this relationship is between men. The reception of the sonnets has been colored by strategies for denying or downplaying this basic situation, allowing readers of scattered anthologized sonnets—like moviegoers—to slip very easily into the unchallenged assumption that the addressee to whom the speaker says "I love you so" (s. 71.6) is a woman like the fair and remote "she" of Petrarchan sonnet convention. Thus, before we come to the necessary qualifications about the sketchiness of the sonnet story, it is important to be explicit about the primary relationship. Shakespeare transforms the conventional sonnet story by making his beloved a "he."

There is also a female lover in the sonnets, the focus of a secondary relationship treated in many of the last twenty-eight sonnets (127–54). But when attention turns to her, it is not to assert the normality of heterosexual romance. Things have gone downhill for the speaker, into an obsessive cycle of longing and loathing. By the conventional standards of the Petrarchan sonnet tradition, the woman

in question lacks beauty and sexual virtue. Regularly referred to by
sonnet readers as the "dark lady," she is described in the famous
anti-Petrarchan poem "My mistress' eyes are nothing like the sun"
(s. 130). It affords her ironic praise by inverting and undermining
unrealistic sonnet compliments. The speaker's passion for the dark
lady, set in contrast to his love for the fair young man, grounds his
discourse in lies and equivocation, triggers out-of-control emotions
and self-loathing, and tangles him in insatiable and shameful lust.
The speaker deploys a playful satiric cleverness in some of these
poems, as if to detach himself from strong emotions, but the savage
self-loathing precipitated by dependence on this woman and even
hints of misogyny break out. The speaker compares the dark lady's
apparently promiscuous sexuality to a "bay where all men ride"
(s. 137.6), and his punning imagination fantasizes a situation with
his "will," or sexual member, only one among others filling her "full
with wills" (s. 136.6). To top it all off, he turns the virtuosity of his
poetic skill to excusing the ultimate degradation of the dark lady's
sexual affair with his own male beloved.

Insofar as the sonnet sequence tells a story of passion, this sketch
sets out some of its basic coordinates. Yet whether the sonnets
are telling any story that bears on Shakespeare's life—or, indeed,
any consistent story with a clear cast of characters at all—is a
contentious issue. Are the sonnets in any sense a record of events,
evoking autobiographical reference or, more generally, particular
sociohistorical contexts? Or are they exquisitely self-contained
poems, to be valued primarily for their artistic play of words? Ad-
mirers of Shakespeare's *Sonnets* have tended to choose one approach or the other, often in an all-or-nothing way. This essay will
argue for a middle course by suggesting how Shakespeare's verbal
artistry is embedded in historical contexts. But let's first look briefly
at the problems with the standoff.

Those seeking Shakespearean life events have cried "eureka"
over identifications of the young man sparked by publisher Thomas
Thorpe's inscription in the 1609 edition to a "Mr. W.H." Some, in-
sisting the initials became somehow reversed, identify the young
man as Henry Wriothesley, earl of Southampton, who was one of
Shakespeare's earliest known patrons; others opt for another

known patron, William Herbert, earl of Pembroke. Still others, adding cues from Shakespeare's wordplay, argue that puns on "will" and "hues" point to a Willie Hughes.[1] Scholars seeking to persuade readers of their various identifications of the mistress with, for example, an Elizabethan lady-in-waiting (Mary Fitton), a female poet (Emilia Lanier), or a London prostitute (Luce Negro), usually isolate the *Sonnets'* somewhat elusive characterization of her in terms of "blackness."[2] With varying interpretive ingenuity, they seek to apply this ideologically loaded descriptor to their candidate's eyes, deeds, hair, character, or complexion.

There are problems with reading the sonnets in this way. To begin with, there is simply too little information about Shakespeare's life on which to build arguments about his personal relationships or their intensity. Furthermore, reading to this end does little to open up the accomplishment of the sonnets: active interpretation of these complex and original poems is sacrificed to a narrow search for evidence. Finally, even if the poems were partly inspired by particular relations and circumstances, these are mediated by the sonnets' interplay with literary traditions and poetic intertexts. Shakespeare's choice of a male beloved is itself a good example, for what it signifies is closely tied to its surprising innovation on Petrarchan convention.

In the other camp, astute critics of lyric poetry such as Helen Vendler and Stephen Booth press readers to attend to the "sonnets as poems," not primarily because information about Shakespeare's life is scarce but because of their conviction about how poetic language works. In Vendler's view, the "true 'actors' in lyric are words," and the event or "drama of any lyric" has to do with innovations in words or "new stylistic arrangements."[3] It is undoubtedly true that the richest pleasures of the individual sonnets are to be gained through active reading. Such a reading process might profitably attend to the overall sonnet structure— to how the shape of the sentences and the trajectory of the thought cohere with or pull against the three quatrains and final couplet of the Shakespearean form. At a more detailed level, the reading might focus on rhetorical figures of speech. Part of the pleasure of a Shakespearean sonnet comes in recognizing its rhetorical play, both where repetitions of words and sounds (e.g., alliteration, assonance) make for rich resonances and where metaphor and wordplay trigger unexpected meanings in words.

Nonetheless, most readers would not accept that words are the only actors. The poems excite curiosity about the speaker's situation, and they powerfully express his emotions and private consciousness. If the lyric refers to or mimes anything outside the realm of words, Vendler claims, it is delimited to "the performance of mind in *solitary* speech." In her view, lyrical poetry typically "strips away most social specification (age, regional location, sex, class, even race)," so that the speaking "I" is "voiceable by anyone."[4] My contention is that to deny the relevance of social context is to misunderstand much of the innovation of Shakespeare's language. These sonnets are not the unaddressed speeches of an anonymous "I." They are utterances in which it matters who is speaking, to whom, and in what situation.

Shakespeare's use of pronouns gives a strong cue that direction of address and situational specifics matter. In other major sonnet sequences of his time, after the first-person pronoun "I," the third-person pronoun (i.e., "she," "her," or "him") occurs with greatest frequency. In Shakespeare, it is the second person of direct address, the "thou" or "you," and these pronouns occur almost as frequently as the speaking "I."[5] Shakespeare's speaker is not analyzing his inner experience in relation to the loved object, the "she" of most other Elizabethan sequences. Instead, the poems work like conversation, even if they get no direct answer. Most Shakespeare sonnets are less the isolated expression of an "I" than a social dialogue, albeit with only one speaker. As with any conversation or phone call overheard, they make a demand on the interpreter to imagine who would say *this* to whom, and in what situation. Speech is a social activity: what one says depends on whom one speaks to and in what context. Shakespeare, a dramatist turning his hand to lyric, innovates by creating the private thought of his speaker out of the materials of socially situated conversation. We as readers cannot come to know this "I" without making an active effort to figure out the context and follow the conversation. The rest of this essay will take a look at the opening movement of the sonnets as a changing "dialogue of one."[6]

Changing the Conversation

While the *Sonnets* as a whole are famous for giving a new intonation to inward feeling and private thought, the focus is not on the speaker's "I" from the outset. The sequence begins with seventeen sonnets often referred to as the procreation group. They advise a beautiful young man to marry and procreate so that his beauty will be replicated and preserved in his children against time's ruinous process of decay: "From fairest creatures we desire increase, / That thereby beauty's rose might never die" (s. 1.1–2). Who would speak this way, and in what situation? It is true that a conventional Petrarchan sonnet lover might use metaphors like "beauty's rose," but this speaker adopts a surprisingly public and authoritative stance. A first cue is the choice of "we" over "I," as if he is speaking for a larger group. In the first line, his vocabulary ("creatures . . . increase") seems to echo God's message in the scriptural creation story, "Be fruitful and multiply" (Genesis 1.22, 28). Nonetheless, the voice that will eventually set up Nature and Time as the reigning forces in the sonnets' worldview sounds more secular than religious, more like a teacher than a preacher. The public role is reinforced in the couplet's directive not to pity a private lover but to "Pity the world" (s. 1.13). This directive raises curiosity about who the addressee can be to be so important that the world should care. Only the addressee's great beauty is given as an explicit reason in Sonnet 1, but soon the vocabulary, even where used metaphorically, comes to associate the addressee with the nobility. His imagined child is spoken of as an "heir" (s. 6.14) and in terms of "succession" (s. 2.12); he is spoken of as if in possession of a "legacy" (s. 4.2) and a "fair . . . house" (s. 13.9); and it is taken for granted he can afford liveried servants (s. 2.3) and the pompous splendor of a "tomb" (s. 3.7).

If the addressee is so important, in a society in which power differences between nobles and commoners were strongly displayed and enforced, how is it that the speaker dares to criticize him? How can he accuse him, even with the indirection of a pun, of being "contracted" (i.e., *pledged* but also *shrunken,* as opposed to *increased*) to his "own bright eyes" (s. 1.5)? In Elizabethan English, power differences are strongly marked in use of pronouns: "you" is the usual address to a social superior, with "thou" tending to denote someone of lesser power or in an intimate relationship that is reciprocal.[7] How, then, is it that the speaker dares to "thou" the addressee throughout the first fifteen sonnets? The answer is in the historically specific social relationship signaled by the details of language: that of humanist poet-educator to youthful highborn patron.

How would an Elizabethan reader recognize this specialized relationship? The procreation group strongly echoes themes and metaphors from a famous letter written in Latin by the humanist educator Erasmus and circulated in English translation in Thomas Wilson's *Art of Rhetoric* as "An Epistle to Persuade a Young Gentleman to Marriage."[8] The letter is the source, for example, for the incredibly unromantic metaphor of plowing—"the tillage of thy husbandry" (s. 3.6)—used of what a man does when he has dutiful sex with a wife for the purpose of procreation.[9] This letter and other educational writings by Erasmus also modeled an interaction script recommended for educators instructing youthful prospective power-holders.[10] The vocation of Shakespeare's speaker is not, of course, tutor but poet. Renaissance poets, however, looked to the educational program of humanism to give an ethical grounding to the poet-patron relationships on which they depended for cash and other kinds of support.

Shakespeare had addressed and dedicated his first two published poems—*Venus and Adonis* and *Lucrece*—to a patron, the earl of Southampton, in an opening epistle that is separated from the artistic composition. With the *Sonnets,* the address to an unnamed patron is assimilated into the composition, given extended voicing in the compliments, advice giving, and boastful offers to the young man of poetic longevity. The speaker sounds like a humanist tutor instructing an aristocratic youth in the duties of his class. Like Erasmus, whose writings illustrate how instructors should use language that is both forceful and familiar to influence their charges, the speaker addresses the patron in ways that half insult and half praise: "Unthrifty loveliness," he calls him, and "Profitless usurer" (s. 4.1, 7). He dares to give him orders, such as "Be not self-willed," and then, like a schoolmaster, balances his reprimands and exhortations with praise and encouragement: "for thou art much too fair / To be death's conquest" (s. 6.13–14). Thus, to make sense of the language in the opening sonnets is not to strip away social specifications. Instead, it involves recognizing the markers of sex, age, class, and vocation in the dialogue script that Shakespeare develops to give initial definition to the primary relationship.

The implied conversation is soon to change. Indeed, Shakespeare constructs the unique love relationship of his sonnets by situating it first as a poet-patron relation and then displacing that relation—that is, changing the conversation. The private "I," withheld until Sonnet 10, begins to make quiet intrusions into the safe and publicly accountable language of instruction. In urging "Make thee another self," the poet repeats his persuasion to "breed," but supplies a new motive: "for love of me" (s. 10.13). The "I" assumes a greater prominence in Sonnets 12 to 15. The speaker is no longer acting as spokesperson for the conventional sexual politics of heterosexual marriage and thereby effacing his own agency. He makes an intoxicating claim to a self-important poetic role: "And, all in war with Time for love of you, / As he takes from you, I engraft you new" (s. 15.13–14). Surprisingly, this emerging "I" also shifts his pronoun of address, at least temporarily, to the more deferential "you" (Sonnets 13, 15, 16, and 17). Why should the addressee now become "you"? I think it is because as the speaker's promise becomes more personal, he cannot hide behind the public role. The dutiful poet-teacher had kept his focus on the other and registered little consciousness of self. But the self-asserting poet-lover is suddenly also self-conscious. To be self-conscious is here to newly recognize what he is, not in himself but in relation to the elite and powerful other. The self-asserting "I" weighs himself in relation to "*your* most high deserts" (s. 17.2; emphasis added), and his status-conscious pronoun choice is an early register of a developing thematic concern with his own self-worth and deserts. If Shakespeare is inventing new language for private self-consciousness, what is fascinating here is how it shows itself in the verbal ballet of "thou" and "you," "we" and "I."

Then, in Sonnet 20, the authoritative script of humanist advice-giving is interrupted, never to be wholly resumed, by a confession—however guarded—of personal involvement, of an intimate love relationship. There has been endless debate about whether this sonnet supports or denies a physically enacted homosexual relationship in the overall sequence. Some readers imagine the debate is only an effect of the other side's intransigence, but it is almost certainly also an effect, at least in part, of the sonnet's language. The confessional speech act is indirect, ambiguous, and deniable—what linguists and politicians call "off-record." The sonnet distances self-revelation by telling a mythical story about how the beloved "master mistress" came to have the kind of beauty and attraction he has. Nature, intending to create a woman,

> as she wrought thee fell a-doting,
> And by addition me of thee defeated
> By adding one thing to my purpose nothing.
> But since she pricked thee out for women's pleasure,
> Mine be thy love, and thy love's use their treasure.
>
> (s. 20.10–14)

Something, we must infer, happens in response to this poem, or else between this poem and the next, for in Sonnets 21 through 32 the discourse and the relationship between the two men have been transformed. For the speaker, the most salient fact is his certainty that "I . . . love and am beloved" (s. 25.13). Now "thou"—pretty clearly here the "thou" of intimacy—replaces the "you" of deference,[11] even though in these poems the overwhelming rapture and the emotional complexity of the speaker's reciprocated affection are heightened and given specific definition by an awareness of status difference. The other's social importance is in large measure what makes the speaker "Unlooked for joy in that I honor most" (s. 25.4). It makes the situation feel all the more miraculous, as though something impossible has nonetheless happened. The speaker, like "an unperfect actor on the stage" (s. 23.1), imagines himself speechless in the face of what he can give in "recompense" for whatever gesture of the beloved has gifted him with love's assurance. He nonetheless knows he has at least one gift to put in the balance—his writing: "O, let my books be then the eloquence / And dumb presagers of my speaking breast" (s. 23.9–10). On the one hand, the recognition of attention from his important friend brings on expressions of unworthiness and self-deprecation: "Duty so great," he imagines, is owed, "which wit so poor as mine / May make seem bare" (s. 26.5–6). On the other hand, the gracious recognition by the important other suggests potential worth in the self-deprecating speaker, putting "apparel on my tattered loving / To show me worthy of thy sweet respect" (s. 26.11–12).

It is important to see that the emotional contours of the speaker's happiness at "falling in love" are not blandly anonymous or universal. Unequal power relations complicate his speech and emotion. The introductory movement of the sonnet sequence has tracked an interruption in one kind of internalized conversation among unequals, the dutiful instruction by a humanist poet of an aristocratic patron. The interruption stages and enables the reader to follow a changed conversation and relationship, still historically specific but now unconventional and intimate. It is a relation for which Shakespeare has invented a new dialogue script, and hence a love relationship that escapes easy stereotyping. Furthermore, the "dialogue of one" in Shakespeare's *Sonnets* is artistically innovative partly because of the exciting way—long before novelists invented the artistic form of stream of consciousness narration—in which it adapts social conversation to put complex inward experience into words. Although the present discussion shows how the words and emotions grew out of their historical moment, they can nevertheless help illuminate the psychological processes of modern-day love relationships. Power imbalances and self-doubt, for example, still affect lovers today, who can recognize in the sonnets variations on their own situations and relational scripts without leveling all differences in such a manner as to colonize the speaker's "I."

I have illustrated a way to read the opening movement of Shakespeare's *Sonnets* that links lyric and history, the linguistic text and social context. Some qualifications are needed before extending this (or any other) interpretive strategy to the overall sequence. The interpretation above treats Sonnets 1 to 32 as a roughly sequential narrative built up out of the speaker's individual speech acts. This takes us back to the question of whether the sonnets can—in any sense— be read as a record of events. The answer is complicated by other unanswered questions. Did Shakespeare authorize the publication in 1609 of his sonnets, many of which must have been written as early as the 1590s? Does their printed order reflect Shakespeare's plan, or could it be indebted to someone else—the publisher Thomas Thorpe, for example? If Shakespeare was writing individual sonnets over the course of many years, later gathered into the 1609 grouping, can we even be sure that the overall sequence has a consistent cast of characters, let alone a developing story line?

Internal evidence certainly casts doubt on any simple assumption that the sonnet order is chronological. Compare, for example, Sonnets 41 and 42 with Sonnets 133 and 134. Both early and late sonnet pairs treat a triangular relationship involving "me," "my sweet'st friend" (s. 133.4), and a mistress. Does the sonnet sequence treat two different triangular relationships separated by a period of time? Or—perhaps more likely—does it return, out of temporal sequence, to the same situation and the same set of characters? Sonnet pairs 57/58 and 153/154 pose a different but related problem as we consider the coherence of the sequence as a whole. Sonnet 58 reads like a rewrite of the situation in 57, with each poem giving vivid expression to the speaker's feeling of slavery at having to wait around until the powerful friend deigns to give him attention. Sonnet 154 replays the mythical anecdote in 153 of Diana's maid stealing Cupid's arrow and creating with its help an ineffective healing bath for diseased lovers like the poet-speaker. Do these twinned sonnets illustrate the Renaissance love of amplification, the art of elegantly varying a single theme? Or did Shakespeare's publisher fail to choose between a draft poem in Shakespeare's manuscript and its revision?

A cautious reader will regard the sonnet order as provisional; but need one go further, as some recent critics have suggested, and discard the overall sequence as contextual moorings for readings of individual sonnets? [12] That is, when we ask key questions—who is speaking? to whom? in what situation?—must we limit evidence to that individual sonnet? To make that argument would, in some cases, come close to reverting to Vendler's anonymous "I" and "thou" stripped of sex, rank, age, and other social specifications, since only about one-fifth of the sonnets specify even the sex of the beloved. But it would, in my view, be the wrong choice, if our aim is to gain insight into the rich psychology of the speaker or the exciting wordplay charging the language. In Sonnet 32, for example, what does Shakespeare's shadow-self mean by calling his own magnificent verse "poor rude lines" or by wittily recommending that his friend resolve: "Theirs for their *style* I'll read, his for his love" (ll. 4, 14; emphasis added)? It is not the false modesty of a great poet. Rather it is the internalized and perhaps inescapable doublespeak of someone living within a hierarchical culture and caught between two measures of self-worth: here, social status and poetic ability. If we are aware, from the context of surrounding sonnets, of the speaker's class consciousness, we will understand that the word choice of this utterance he imagines in his friend's mouth does not simply declare his own verse devoid of poetic style. Consider, for example, how Shakespeare's contemporary, William Cecil, announced his newly awarded peerage: "My *stile* is, Lord of Burghley." [13] In Shakespeare's sonnet, we should be able to hear the speaker's punning dig at his elite friend's snobbish value system: read theirs for their style (i.e., their social titles), mine for my love. It will help us see how the intense emotions arise within a unique relationship and a specific social context. We will better appreciate Shakespeare's poetic language and, through its innovative "dialogue of one" for expressing inward consciousness, something of how he might have felt.

My work on this essay was supported by a grant from the Social Sciences and Humanities Research Council of Canada and benefited from the advice of Barbara A. Mowat, Paul Stevens, and Paul Werstine.

1. Hyder Edward Rollins reviews conjectures up to the date of the New Variorum edition of *The Sonnets* (Philadelphia: J. B. Lippincott, 1944), 2:166–232. Katherine Duncan-Jones reviews recent views and opts for Pembroke in the Arden Third Series, *Shakespeare's Sonnets* (Walton-on-Thames: Thomas Nelson, 1997), pp. 49–69. Donald Foster has argued that the "begetter" of the sonnets referred to as "W.H." is a misprint for Shakespeare's own initials, "W.SH.," in "Master W.H., R.I.P.," *PMLA* 102 (1987): 42–54.

2. See reviews of "dark lady" candidates in Rollins, *The Sonnets*, 2:242–76; Duncan-Jones, *Shakespeare's Sonnets*, pp. 47–55; and S. Schoenbaum, *Shakespeare's Lives*, rev. ed. (Oxford: Clarendon Press, 1991), pp. 493–98.

3. Helen Vendler, *The Art of Shakespeare's Sonnets* (Cambridge, Mass.: Harvard University Press, Belknap Press, 1997), p. 3; for Stephen Booth's similar emphasis on poetic art as multiple verbal patterns, see *An Essay on Shakespeare's Sonnets* (New Haven: Yale University Press, 1969).

4. Vendler, *The Art of Shakespeare's Sonnets*, p. 2.

5. Giorgio Melchiori, *Shakespeare's Dramatic Meditations: An Experiment in Criticism* (Oxford: Clarendon Press, 1976), p. 15.

6. This is John Donne's phrase in his poem "The Ecstasy" (1633), but he uses it with a different sense to refer to the paradox of a communal speech by two persons so closely united as to be one.

7. On further complexities of second-person pronoun variation in early modern English, see Roger Lass, "Phonology and Morphology," in *The Cambridge History of the English Language*, vol. 3, *1476–1776*, ed. Lass (Cambridge: Cambridge University Press, 1999), pp. 56–186, esp. 148–55.

8. Erasmus's letter was first published in 1518 and later circulated widely as an example of epistolary persuasion in *De conscribendis epistolis*. For a modern translation of the latter work, see "On the Writing of Letters," trans. Charles Fantazzi, in vol. 25 of *Collected Works of Erasmus*, ed. J. K. Sowards (Toronto: University of Toronto Press, 1985), pp. 10–254, esp. 129–45. See also Thomas Wilson, *The Art of Rhetoric* (1560), ed. Peter E. Medine (University Park: Pennsylvania State University Press, 1994), pp. 79–100. For excerpts from Erasmus's letter as translated by Wilson, see "Appendix of Intertextual Material," above, pp. 619–24.

9. Compare Wilson, *The Art of Rhetoric*, p. 92.

10. On this interaction script in Erasmus, see Lynne Magnusson, *Shakespeare and Social Dialogue: Dramatic Language and Elizabethan Letters* (Cambridge: Cambridge University Press, 1999), pp. 66–74.

11. This pronominal shift occurs gradually, with no second-person pronoun appearing in ss. 21, 23, or 25, and with s. 24 unusual for alternating between forms of "thou" and "you."

12. See, for example, Heather Dubrow's suggestions for reading strategies that reject the consistency of the standard sonnet story in "'Incertainties now crown themselves assur'd': The Politics of Plotting Shakespeare's Sonnets," *Shakespeare Quarterly* 47 (1996): 291–305; rpt. in *Shakespeare's Sonnets: Critical Essays*, ed. James Schiffer (New York: Garland Publishing, 1999), pp. 113–33.

13. Lord Burghley to Nicholas White, 14 March 1570/1; in Thomas Wright, ed., *Queen Elizabeth and Her Times: A Series of Original Letters* (London: Henry Colburn, 1838), 1:391.

Venus and Adonis and *Lucrece:*
A Modern Perspective

Catherine Belsey

Both of Shakespeare's narrative poems are about nonconsensual sex. In *Lucrece* a man desires a woman who resists his advances, he rapes her, and the consequences are tragic. The gender roles work the other way around in *Venus and Adonis*, but the physiological difference between the sexes prevents any simple reversal of the plot. Instead, Venus makes every effort to seduce the reluctant object of her desire, and the poem is by turns comic, lyrical, and sad. Each event turns out to have consequences beyond the fate of the protagonists. The rape of Lucrece founds the Roman Republic; the unrequited passion of the goddess of love explains the waywardness of all human desire.

Published in 1593 and 1594, when Shakespeare had written no more than a handful of plays, the narrative poems are legitimately seen as a display of the young poet-playwright's talents and literary allegiances. And, contrary to modern expectation, these new versions of stories already familiar to most of their original readers were exceptionally popular in their own period. (Only with the publication of the collected plays in the First Folio of 1623 would the poems, excluded from the collection, begin their relative eclipse for subsequent generations.) But poetic narrative is no longer much to our twenty-first-century taste. Moreover, we have come to think of Shakespeare primarily as a dramatist and only incidentally a poet. Are the poems any more, then, than historical curiosities?

It is not inconsistent with a regard for history to suggest that these texts bring into new focus questions that were obscured by the proprieties of Victorian values. Can women do everything men can? How far are human beings bound by the constraints of sexual difference? Is love the moralizing force our popular romances long to make it? Why do women find rape more damaging than other forms of violence? What is the appropriate response to sexual violation?

Venus and Adonis was published first. Shakespeare's predecessors here clearly include Ovid, the Roman poet of love, who

639

recorded a version of the tale and whose stories of desire continued to influence medieval and early modern Europe. Shakespeare also drew on Marlowe, whose *Hero and Leander* shows how an Ovidian love story in English could be at once sexy, lyrical, and tragic. Even so, there had never before been anything quite like Shakespeare's first narrative poem, where one mood disconcertingly succeeds and displaces another as the goddess of love herself is shown to be capable of frustration.

An earlier generation of critics, anxious to find a handhold in this slippery text, clung to the moment when Adonis pronounces on the antithesis between love and lust. Here at last was a simple and familiar moral:

> "Love comforteth like sunshine after rain,
> But Lust's effect is tempest after sun.
> Love's gentle spring doth always fresh remain;
> Lust's winter comes ere summer half be done.
> Love surfeits not, Lust like a glutton dies.
> Love is all truth, Lust full of forgèd lies."
>
> (799–804)

In this light, the intemperate behavior of Venus could safely be declared reprehensible, though it was not always clear whether the main critical objection was to the sexual harassment of young men or to women who acknowledge the intensity of their desires.

This reading presents its own difficulties, however. In the first place, it makes the chief authority on the love story a figure who gladly affirms his own ignorance of love itself (409), claims that he is too young to respond to sexual advances (524–28), and acknowledges himself "too green" to develop this "old" truism (806). Indeed, Adonis wittily distances himself not only from Venus but also from the tears and tantrums of love itself. He prefers a good night's rest, he says: "my heart longs not to groan / But soundly sleeps while now it sleeps alone" (785–86). We might therefore be inclined to treat his synoptic opposition of love and lust as, at the very least, premature. And in the second place, it is hard to connect such an obvious moral with a work so popular that it had run to twelve editions by the 1620s.

Moreover, moral anxiety about the antics of Venus misses the high comedy of the encounter between the passionate goddess and the pouting boy. As the poem makes clear, the real danger to Adonis is not from the attentions of Venus, who has no tusk to sheath in his soft groin (1115–18). In fact, this, or something like it, is precisely her problem: "Would thou wert as I am and I a man" (369). The goddess of love is accustomed to having her way in her own sphere, and she finds herself baffled by the indifference of Adonis. Much of the narrative concerns her increasingly desperate efforts to elicit his desire. She reasons, coaxes, and threatens, recounts her past triumph over the god of war (97–114), insists on her own beauty (133–44), and offers her body (229–40). If poetic skill alone could generate love, Adonis would surely succumb:

"Bid me discourse, I will enchant thine ear,
Or like a fairy trip upon the green,
Or like a nymph, with long disheveled hair,
Dance on the sands, and yet no footing seen."

(145–48)

This is a goddess who lies, without crushing them, on banks of violets and primroses (125, 151)—early, delicate flowers, like Adonis himself.

Alongside the lyrical Venus, however, a more energetic figure emerges, who urgently maneuvers the young man into position, though still to no avail: "Backward she pushed him as she would be thrust, / And governed him in strength though not in lust" (41–42). She plucks him from his horse, and pulls him to the ground on top of her, but none of this vigorous activity does her any good. Instead, she remains tantalized by a physical proximity that offers no gratification: "He will not manage her, although he mount her" (598; compare 548, 564, 605–7). While Adonis is also intelligible as an object of homoerotic desire for Shakespeare's male readers, the recurring joke about Venus's frustration shows how far the story is from depicting her as a drag queen. On the contrary, when it comes to the heterosexual love that is its theme, *Venus and Adonis* indicates, bodies make all the difference.

Much of the comedy depends on the contrast between a brisk

narrative that moves the action along at speed and a prolix Venus, whose "over-handled theme" (770) can become "tedious," not only to Adonis but also to anyone else who is not in love (841–86). Where the speeches are self-consciously poetic, invoking all the resources of analogy and witty antithesis, the narrative voice often appears artless. A simultaneous element of pathos also depends on the text's capacity to summarize in the most unassuming vocabulary its central paradox: "She's Love, she loves, and yet she is not loved" (610).

Indeed, amid the mock-heroic comedy an elegiac strain is perceptible from the beginning. Venus's description of Adonis as "the field's chief flower" (8) anticipates, for a reader who already knows Ovid's story, the blossom that he is to become. After his death the sadness of Venus is surely unequivocally sympathetic. Now that she has no ulterior motive, no one to convince or seduce, simple sorrow prevails:

"Alas, poor world, what treasure hast thou lost!
What face remains alive that's worth the viewing?
What tongue is music now? What canst thou boast
Of things long since, or anything ensuing?
    The flowers are sweet, their colors fresh and trim,
    But true sweet beauty lived and died with him."

(1075–80)

Abandoning the high style, at this moment Venus could be anyone mourning a dead lover. But the story does not end here. As the goddess of love she also remains, she has the power to characterize the condition she personifies. From now on, Venus declares, love will always be "perverse" (1157), recalcitrant, obtuse, wayward. Lovers will experience the condition as unequal, inconstant, distrustful, sure to end in tears. Love will lead to war (1159), a prophecy Venus herself was to vindicate in another story familiar to early readers, when she gave Helen to Paris and indirectly caused the fall of Troy.

Like so many good fables, then, *Venus and Adonis* recounts a myth of origins: the story explains how love came by its nature. But the poem's conclusion is unexpectedly inconclusive. On the one hand, Venus gently cradles the flower which is all that remains of Adonis; on the other, she names the tragic effects of a fierce imperative that seems remote indeed from the moral antithesis between love and lust he so fluently defined. Love has many modes. In that sense, the stylistic discontinuities of *Venus and Adonis* surely go some way toward enacting the ambiguities that define its theme.

If *Venus and Adonis* displays a degree of indulgence toward the goddess's attempts at seduction, *Lucrece* shows no sympathy whatever with rape. Unwilling to listen to Lucrece's efforts to placate or deter him, gagging her instead with her own nightgown, Tarquin abruptly puts paid to all dialogue. The rape is over in almost no narrative time, but the stark account, in conjunction with imagery so familiar from both the Bible and pastoral poetry that it seems barely metaphoric, leaves in no doubt the brutality of the act and the innocence of the victim:

The wolf hath seized his prey; the poor lamb cries,
   Till, with her own white fleece her voice controlled,
   Entombs her outcry in her lips' sweet fold.

For with the nightly linen that she wears
He pens her piteous clamors in her head,
Cooling his hot face in the chastest tears
That ever modest eyes with sorrow shed.
O, that prone lust should stain so pure a bed!

                                    (677–84)

Not dwelling on the events of the rape itself, the text reserves its detailed attention for the states of mind that precede and follow this moment, just over one-third of the way through the narrative. After the rape Tarquin slinks away. From now on the emphasis will be on the grief of Lucrece and her efforts to decide on an appropriate course of action.

It makes good sense to see the two long narrative poems as linked. In the prefatory letter dedicating *Venus and Adonis* to the earl of Southampton, Shakespeare promises "some graver labor" in due course. The publication of *Lucrece* a year later looks very much like the fulfillment of this undertaking. And despite the antithetical moods of the two works, there is common ground. Both depict the irrepressible force of desire. In each case, the main protagonist is a woman, and the action is seen primarily from her point of view, for better or worse. Once again, *Lucrece* draws on classical sources, in this instance retelling the story of a Roman woman's legendary chastity. And despite its debt to the existing tradition of complaint poems, it too remains unprecedented in the ambitious nature of its project.

Part of the interest of *Lucrece* for a modern reader willing to overcome the unfamiliarity of the complaint form lies in its treatment of rape as an abuse of power, making sexual politics continuous with the politics of the state. Tarquin is driven by the impulse to take possession of what does not belong to him as much as by a passion for beauty. According to Lucrece herself, this constitutes improper behavior for a man who is to be king: good rulers reign by love, not fear (610–11); they do not break the law but embody it, and constitute in the process a model for their subjects (612–16). Unable to deflect Tarquin himself by this account of good government, Lucrece nevertheless resolves to make herself a model for a Rome oppressed by the royal family's misuse of power: "How Tarquin must be used, read it in me" (1195). The men grasp the lesson she teaches them by her death, and go on to overthrow the institution of monarchy itself.

In other words, the rape is shown to have implications at three closely related levels: for Lucrece herself, for her family, and for the state. Her own immediate reaction to the event produces a night of intense grief, spent in a turmoil of sometimes conflicting thoughts, with shame probably uppermost. Although the text has made very clear that she has nothing to reproach herself with, she feels dishonored (1030–36). The "disgrace" is of course "invisible" (827), but it appears to Lucrece that everyone must know what has happened: "Revealing day through every cranny spies / And seems to point her out where she sits weeping" (1086–87). The image of the morning peering and pointing at her through cracks and keyholes draws attention to the way the sense of guilt, however undeserved, makes her feel as if she is under surveillance. Even the servant who comes to take her letter seems to her to be blushing with embarrassment (1338–58). She fears for her good name; people everywhere will tell her story, coupling her guilt with Tarquin's (813–19).

This degree of shame might seem unaccountable, since we know that the rape took place entirely against her will. Lucrece puts that issue to the men she has assembled to carry out her planned revenge:

"What is the quality of my offense,
Being constrained with dreadful circumstance?
May my pure mind with the foul act dispense[?]"

(1702–4)

They are happy to exonerate her on the grounds that "Her body's stain her mind untainted clears" (1710). But Lucrece knows that the implications of rape are more complex than this simple mind-body dualism implies:

. . . with a joyless smile she turns away
The face, that map which deep impression bears
Of hard misfortune, carved in it with tears.

(1711–13)

This smile, however sorrowful, cuts across the distinction between mind and body. A state of consciousness is registered in a physiological event; the expression reveals a mental condition; material tears are the marks of an inward sorrow. In the same way, rape deconstructs the opposition between spirit and flesh: the physical violation affects a speaking being who is neither pure mind nor all body.

Lucrece's shame includes the sense that Tarquin's act has defiled her blood (1029, 1655). In consequence, she is no longer a good wife (1048–50). This is a society where the family constitutes the guarantee of lineage, and the fidelity of a wife ensures the purity of the line. But who can be certain of the fatherhood of her next child? Addressing Collatine in her imagination, she assures him:

"This bastard graff shall never come to growth;
He shall not boast who did thy stock pollute
That thou art doting father of his fruit."

(1062–64)

The dynastic family as the poem presents it is a place above all of possession. The idea of woman as property recurs through the early stages of the narrative: Collatine is happy in the "possession" of a beautiful wife (18); he ought to shelter the jewel he "owns," not boast about it publicly (27–35); indeed, perhaps it was envy of "so rich a thing" that led Tarquin to desire Lucrece as a "prize" (39–42, 279), and so to take her body from its "owner" (413). At the end of the story her father and her husband are still busy disputing which of them has a stronger claim to have owned Lucrece (1793–1806).

The text makes no direct comment on the implications of all this, but it is an outsider, Junius Brutus, who now takes over the initiative, impatient with the competing claims that seem to preoccupy the family. His case is that Roman citizens not only should avenge the "true wife" that Lucrece has shown herself to be but should also cleanse a Rome that is equally "disgraced" by the crimes of the Tarquins (1833). The death of Lucrece is made the occasion to put an end to an autocratic regime: with the expulsion of the Tarquins, Rome becomes a republic.

In retrospect, we can see that the poem foreshadows Junius Brutus's recognition in its account of Sinon. The fall of Troy features indirectly in *Lucrece*, just as it does in *Venus and Adonis*. Looking for a way to pass the dismal time of waiting for Collatine, Lucrece remembers a painting that turns out to expand the domestic sphere, demonstrating the public significance of private wickedness (1478–84). At first it seems that the connection between the picture and Lucrece's situation is the rape of Helen as the cause of the Trojan War. But then her attention is caught by the suffering and bloodshed so minutely depicted, especially the pain of Hecuba, Priam's widow. And finally she lights on the lying Sinon, who pretended to befriend Troy only to release the invading Greek soldiers from the Trojan horse, so causing the sack of the city. Sinon's hypocrisy reminds Lucrece of Tarquin's (1536): at the same time, for the reader it links the domestic narrative with the fall of a regime. Tarquin's crime, we might reflect, betrays not only his friend but Roman values; the tyrannical assertion of his will issues in an intrusion not just into the home and into a woman's body, but also into the good relations that should obtain in a well-ordered community.

In this context, it can hardly be accidental that the rhyme word in the final couplet of this poem about rape and despotism is "consent" (1854). Lucrece, who, despite the patriarchal relations the text records, declares herself mistress of her fate (1069), goes on to inaugurate by her death a new and more equal regime. Like *Venus and Adonis*, then, this "graver labor" is also a myth of origins. But paradoxically, while the lyrical poem depicts the installation of desire's reign of terror, the tragedy of *Lucrece* ushers in a more consensual world.

Shakespeare's Sonnets
Further Reading

Abbreviations: *Ant.* = *Antony and Cleopatra; AWW* = *All's Well That Ends Well; AYL* = *As You Like It; Ham.* = *Hamlet; Lear* = *King Lear; LLL* = *Love's Labor's Lost; Oth.* = *Othello; Rom.* = *Romeo and Juliet; Tro.* = *Troilus and Cressida; TN* = *Twelfth Night*

Booth, Stephen, ed. *Shakespeare's Sonnets, Edited with Analytic Commentary.* New Haven: Yale University Press, 1977.
   Booth provides the text of the 1609 Quarto (Apsley imprint, the Huntington-Bridgewater copy) and his own edited text in parallel, followed by a detailed analytic commentary on each sonnet. What Booth thinks "a Renaissance reader would have thought" in progressing through a sequence felt "as both urgent and wanting" determines both text and commentary. The "pluralistically-committed" glosses reflect Booth's view that the poems are best thought about in terms of "both . . . and" rather than "either . . . or." In an appendix the editor briefly touches on matters relating to authenticity, dating, sources, arrangement, and biographical implications; addressing the question of Shakespeare's sexual preference, Booth observes: "William Shakespeare was almost certainly homosexual, bisexual, or heterosexual. The sonnets provide no evidence on the matter."

Cheney, Patrick. " 'O, Let My Books Be . . . Dumb Presagers': Poetry and Theater in Shakespeare's Sonnets." *Shakespeare Quarterly* 52 (2001): 222–54.
   Cheney counters the commonplace view of Shakespeare as a "playwright and occasional poet." Noting frequent references to Shakespeare's theatrical career and the extensive use of theatrical metaphors and vocabulary (e.g., "show," "mask," "rehearse," "play," "part," "action," "actor," "shadow," "mock," and "dumb"), Cheney finds in the *Sonnets* "an unusual site" for exploring Shakespeare as "inextricably caught" in the rivalry between printed poetry and staged theater for cultural authority in early modern England. Che-

ney's examination of the intersection of poetic and theatrical discourses in several key sonnets (15, 29, 54, 108, 144, and especially 23) leads him to conclude that in these poems Shakespeare—the only prolific professional dramatist of the period to leave behind a sonnet sequence—resurrects and perfects a model of authorship tracing back to the celebrated Ovid, namely, the author as poet-playwright.

De Grazia, Margreta. "The Scandal of Shakespeare's Sonnets." *Shakespeare Survey* 46 (1994): 35–49. [Reprinted in Schiffer, pp. 89–112.]

De Grazia contends that editors and critics have erred in identifying the "scandal" of the *Sonnets* as Shakespeare's "desire for a boy," a desire that, in "upholding [the] social distinctions" essential to a patriarchal society, was really "quite conservative and safe." The real scandal lies in Shakespeare's "gynerastic longings for a black mistress"; these desires are "perverse and menacing, precisely because they threaten to raze the very distinctions his poems to the fair boy strain to preserve." Emphasizing psychosocial rather than psychosexual differences, de Grazia advocates a reclassification of the traditional reading of Shakespeare's "Two loves" that would replace post-eighteenth-century sexual categories of normalcy and abnormalcy with sixteenth-century social categories of hierarchy and anarchy—i.e., "of desired generation and abhorred miscegenation." Recent scholarship on early modern England's contact with Africa and on the cultural representations of that contact encourages an association of the Dark Lady's blackness with racial blackness.

Dubrow, Heather. " 'Incertainties now crown themselves assur'd': The Politics of Plotting Shakespeare's Sonnets." *Shakespeare Quarterly* 47 (1996): 291–305. [Reprinted in Schiffer, pp. 113–33.]

In her revisionist readings of the poems, Dubrow proposes switching the usually assumed addressee to his/her gendered opposite, thereby challenging critical claims based on a "map of misreading" that has characterized scholarship on the *Sonnets* since the end of the eighteenth century—most notably the bipartite division positing a male friend as the focus of the first 126 poems and a

Further Reading 651

woman as the concern of the remaining 28. Also thrown into question is the widely held assumption of a linear plot involving the triangulated desires of Poet, Friend, and Dark Lady. If, for example, Sonnets 18 and 55 are read as addressing the woman, the sequence not only opens up a range of "contestatory images" imparting to her a Cleopatra-like infinite variety but also suggests a period of "idyllic happiness with *her* followed by disillusion." The 1609 Quarto's loose and rather arbitrary arrangement of the poems permits a reader "to construct any number of narratives."

Fineman, Joel. *Shakespeare's Perjured Eye: The Invention of Poetic Subjectivity in the Sonnets.* Berkeley: University of California Press, 1986.

In one of the twentieth century's most influential studies of the *Sonnets*, Fineman argues that "Shakespeare rewrites the poetry of praise by employing (implicitly in the sonnets addressed to the young man, explicitly in the sonnets addressed to the dark lady) in an unprecedentedly serious way the equally antique genre of the mock encomium," in the process inventing "the only kind of subjectivity that survives in the literature successive to the poetry of praise." Within this larger argument Fineman details the visual orientation of Shakespeare's rhetoric in the poet's praise of the young man and then explores how other sonnets in the sequence put into question such a rhetoric and thus how the "eye" is "perjured." Fineman's reading of the poems highlights, among other things, their privileging of their own textuality over visual media of representation. His dazzling critique and its indebtedness to the writings of the French psychoanalyst Jacques Lacan belong very much to the deconstructionist turn in twentieth-century criticism.

Herrnstein, Barbara, ed. *Discussions of Shakespeare's Sonnets.* Boston: D. C. Heath, 1964.

Herrnstein gathers nineteen items spanning the years 1640 to 1960 under the following headings: early commentary (the views of John Benson, George Steevens, Samuel Taylor Coleridge, John Keats, and Henry Hallam), speculation (Leslie Hotson's theory that most of the poems were written by 1589 and F. W. Bateson's retort), interpretation (Edward Hubler's "Shakespeare and the

Unromantic Lady," Patrick Cruttwell's "Shakespeare's Sonnets and the 1590's," G. Wilson Knight's "Time and Eternity," and J. W. Lever's "The Poet in Absence" and "The Poet and His Rivals"), evaluation (negative assessments by John Crowe Ransom and Yvor Winters), and analysis (the Robert Graves/Laura Riding study of original punctuation and spelling in Sonnet 129, William Empson's focus on different types of ambiguity, Arthur Mizener's rebuttal to Ransom's critique of Shakespeare's use of figurative language, and Winifred M. T. Nowottny's discussion of formal elements in ss. 1–6). In the volume's final selection, "The Sonnet as an Action," C. L. Barber claims that the "patterned movement of discourse [i.e., 'determinate rhythm and sound']," not the imagery, is the "main line" of the Shakespearean sonnet.

Hunter, G. K. "The Dramatic Technique of Shakespeare's Sonnets." *Essays in Criticism* 3 (1953): 152–64.

Hunter locates the "peculiar quality" of the poems' excellence in Shakespeare's "bias" toward the dramatic. What distinguishes Shakespeare's treatment of stock themes and use of rhetorical techniques like paradox and simile from that of Spenser, Sidney, Drayton, and Donne is an expressiveness that vividly defines the emotional tension in the "I-Thou" relationship of each sonnet, rendering it immediate, and thereby encouraging the reader to supply "from his imagination a complete dramatic situation." In Shakespeare's hands, "the Petrarchan instruments turn . . . into means of expressing and concentrating the great human emotions, desire, jealousy, fear, hope and despair, and of raising in the reader the dramatic reactions of pity and terror by his implication in the lives and fates of the persons depicted."

Lever, J. W. *The Elizabethan Love Sonnet.* 2nd ed. London: Methuen, 1966. [First published in 1956.]

Following chapters on the Petrarchan model, Wyatt, Surrey, Sidney, Spenser, and the late Elizabethan sonneteers, Lever turns his attention to Shakespeare's reworking of Petrarchan conventions. After a comparatively brief commentary on the sonnets addressed to the Mistress (the "subplot" of the sequence in which satire is the dominant mode), Lever discusses those concerned with the Friend under the following headings: "The Invitation to Marry," "The Poet in Absence," "The Friend's Fault," "The Poet and His Rivals," "The Poet's Error," and "Immortalization." For a full appreciation of Shakespeare's insights into human nature and his attitude toward various kinds of love, the reader needs to be aware of the "dual interpretation" at work in the sequence as a whole. The tension between the love sonnet's Petrarchan origins and a "distinctively English attitude" yields the main dynamic of development that commenced with Wyatt and culminated in Shakespeare.

Magnusson, Lynne. " 'Power to Hurt': Language and Service in Sidney Household Letters and Shakespeare's Sonnets." *ELH* 65 (1998): 799–824. [Incorporated into *Shakespeare and Social Dialogue: Dramatic Language and Elizabethan Letters*, pp. 35–57. Cambridge: Cambridge University Press, 1999.]

Magnusson uses ideas from discourse analysis and linguistic pragmatics, especially "politeness theory," to explore the rhetoric of social exchange in early modern England. Her analysis of the language of servitude in sample household letters of the Sidney family sheds light on how "social relations of power are figured" in several sonnets addressed to the young man, particularly Sonnet 58, which she reads "historically as the outward expression of a subservient social relation developed into the inner speech of the Poet-Servant's complicated desire." Stylistic resemblances between the interlocutory dynamic found in the letters and that in the sonnet—e.g., shared rhetorical strategies of nonpresumption, noncoercion, and self-disparagement on the part of the subordinate—demonstrate that Shakespeare's poetic language "derives something of its peculiar power" from everyday Elizabethan discourse.

Neely, Carol Thomas. "The Structure of English Renaissance Sonnet Sequences." *ELH* 45 (1978): 359–89.

Neely finds in the English Renaissance sonnet sequences a "characteristic overall structure" that is loose and elastic, and hence amenable to refining, reworking, and rearranging over time. This shared structure has several implications: (1) it confirms the indebtedness of the English sequences to those of Dante and Petrarch; (2) it validates the long-questioned standing order of the English sequences; and (3) it helps explain "the perplexing conclusions" of the major ones. The division into two unequal parts is the "primary structuring device" for developing the dichotomy between idealized love and sexual desire at the heart of the sonnet sequence genre. In its movement toward "mutual sexual passion" rather than "solitary sublimation and transcendence," the English sonnet sequence reconstructs rather than reproduces the Italian model.

Roberts, Sasha. "Textual Transmission and the Transformation of Desire: The *Sonnets, A Lover's Complaint,* and *The Passionate Pilgrim.*" In her *Reading Shakespeare's Poems in Early Modern England,* pp. 143–90. London: Palgrave, Macmillan, 2003.

Roberts points out that "perhaps because of their comparative scarcity in print," there are "more recorded transcriptions of Shakespeare's sonnets in manuscript than for any other of his works in the seventeenth century." There are, she writes, "some 24 manuscript copies of the sonnets largely dating from the 1620s and 1630s." Those who copied Shakespeare's sonnets felt free to alter the gender dynamics "so as to construct conventionally heterosexual love poems"; in copying, titles were also added and textual variants introduced. Sonnet 2 is particularly interesting in this context. It was "by far the most popular sonnet for transcription," and, in the context of Caroline collections of amorous verse in which it appeared, it reads "more like a *carpe diem* lyric addressed to a female beloved," a reading "fostered by the addition of the title [in four of the manuscripts] 'To one that would die a maid.'"

Schalkwyk, David. *Speech and Performance in Shakespeare's Sonnets and Plays.* Cambridge: Cambridge University Press, 2002.

Drawing on the work of Ludwig Wittgenstein and J. L. Austin, Schalkwyk reads the *Sonnets* in relation to the Petrarchan discourses in a select group of plays to argue (in contrast to Fineman) that the language of the poems is essentially performative rather than descriptive. Like Magnusson, Schalkwyk argues that their "dialogic art" negotiates power relations between the interior and social worlds of "I" and "You." After an initial examination of the performative of praise (*Sonnets, Ant.*, and *AYL*), the author addresses such issues as embodiment and silencing (*Sonnets, LLL, Rom.*, and *TN*), interiority (*Sonnets, Ham.*, and *Lear*), and transformation (*Sonnets* and *AWW*). In his discussion of proper names and naming events in the *Sonnets, Rom., Tro.*, and *Oth.*, Schalkwyk reopens the autobiographical question, claiming that "it is precisely the peculiar absence of proper names in 'SHAKE-SPEARES SONNETS' that testifies to their autobiographical nature." [Earlier versions of chapters 1 and 2 appeared, respectively, in *Shakespeare Quarterly* 49 (1998): 251–58 ("What May Words Do? The Performative of Praise in Shakespeare's Sonnets") and in 45 (1994): 381–407 (" 'She never told her love': Embodiment, Textuality, and Silence in Shakespeare's Sonnets and Plays").]

Schiffer, James, ed. *Shakespeare's Sonnets: Critical Essays*. New York: Garland Publishing, 1999.

Schiffer's anthology of four reprinted essays and fifteen newly published ones offers a snapshot of critical theories and methodologies dominant in *Sonnets* scholarship of the 1990s. The reprinted essays are those by Peter Stallybrass, Margreta de Grazia, Heather Dubrow, and George T. Wright (see individual entries for annotations). Among the newly commissioned essays are Gordon Braden's revisiting of Shakespeare's Petrarchism; Naomi Miller's examination of the *Sonnets* in the context of early modern codes of maternity; Rebecca Laroche's reconsideration of Oscar Wilde's *The Portrait of Mr. W. H.;* Marvin Hunt's reading of the Dark Lady as "a sign of color"; Joyce Sutphen's discussion of memorializing strategies in the sequence's bipartite structure; Lisa Freinkel's "post-Reformation" reading of the poems' Christian "figurality"; Peter Herman's investigation of the language and imagery of usury in Sonnets 1–20; Bruce Smith's exploration of the sexual politics informing the pronominal interplay among "I," "you," "he," "she," and "we"; and Valerie Traub's examination of sodomy "as simultaneously a construction of and reaction to gender and erotic difference." In his extensive introductory survey of *Sonnets* criticism, Schiffer notes how Fineman's *Shakespeare's Perjured Eye* serves as a "leitmotif" throughout the volume.

Stallybrass, Peter. "Editing as Cultural Formation: The Sexing of Shakespeare's Sonnets." *Modern Language Quarterly* 54 (1993): 91–103. [Reprinted in Schiffer, pp. 75–88.]

In this cultural materialist study, Stallybrass argues that the *Sonnets*, assigned to the margins of the Shakespeare canon prior to Malone's 1780 edition, became in the editions and critical commentary of the nineteenth century a crucial site on which the "sexual identity" of the National Poet "was invented and contested." Out of the "cultural hysteria" prompted by the sexual implications of Malone's "narrative of characterological unity" linking the "I" of the poems to their author came the construction of "Shakespeare" as an interiorized heterosexual, a "back-formation" functioning as a "belated defense against sodomy." Consequently, the unified character of the author we as moderns know as "Shakespeare" is not "punctual"—i.e., is not a product of his own historical time—but rather retroactive, the creation of the nineteenth century's homophobic response to the *Sonnets*.

Willen, Gerald, and Victor B. Reed, eds. *A Casebook on Shakespeare's Sonnets*. New York: Thomas Y. Crowell, 1964.

Willen and Reed offer a newly edited text of the *Sonnets*, accompanied by six full-length essays and eight short explications of individual poems. The focus of the essays by Robert Graves and Laura Riding, L. C. Knights, John Crowe Ransom, Arthur Mizener, Edward Hubler, and G. Wilson Knight is on the poems themselves (their punctuation, structure, figurative language, and symbolism) rather than on "biographical puzzles." In the frequently anthologized "Shakespeare at Sonnets," Ransom faults the poems, with few exceptions, for their lack of logic and coherence, their "great violences" of idiom and syntax, and their "mixed effects." The Hubler piece, "Form and Matter," excerpted from his *The Sense of Shakespeare's Sonnets* (1952), examines Shakespeare's poetic practice to argue that the poet valued matter (the subject) over form (the means by which the subject finds expression); the homely image and the "vignettes of nature" are what we remember. The specific sonnets receiving explication are 57 and 58 (Hilton Landry), 71–74 (Carlisle Moore), 73 (R. M. Lumiansky and Edward Nolan), 129

(Karl F. Thompson and C. W. M. Johnson), 143 (Gordon Ross Smith), and 146 (Albert S. Gerard). The appendices include a bibliography and a series of pedagogic exercises.

Wright, George T. "An Art of Small Differences: Shakespeare's *Sonnets.*" In his *Shakespeare's Metrical Art*, pp. 75–90. Berkeley: University of California Press, 1988.

Wright's focus here is on the contribution of the *Sonnets* to Shakespeare's dramatic verse art. It was in these poems, Wright notes, that "Shakespeare learned, presumably in the early 1590s, after he had written a few plays and the narrative poems, to fashion a reflective verse whose resonances would thereafter be heard in the speeches of his dramatic characters." Wright illustrates the ways in which the metrical art of the *Sonnets* "proceeds by way of small differences, quiet additions or withdrawals of emphasis," making the most "of small differences—of stress, of pattern, of feeling." The phrasing, he shows, is "extremely various," rising "to a height of expressive variation in one line and then [subsiding] in the next," but with the speech-tones "imitated in the sonnets . . . almost always those of quiet, intimate speech." Especially notable is the "softness and musical grace that result from [Shakespeare's] skillful use of pyrrhic feet [i.e., feet composed of two unstressed syllables]." The result is the "essentially quiet register" that characterizes the *Sonnets*.

Wright, George T. "The Silent Speech of Shakespeare's Sonnets." In *Shakespeare and the Twentieth Century: The Selected Proceedings of the International Shakespeare Association World Congress, Los Angeles, 1996*, edited by Jonathan Bate, Jill A. Levenson, and Dieter Mehl, pp. 306–27. Newark: University of Delaware Press; London: Associated University Presses, 1998. [Reprinted in Schiffer, pp. 135–58.]

Noting how we usually read poetry in silence, Wright examines the *Sonnets* as silent meditations, "unvoiced, unsounded, unperformed," in which the phenomenon of silent speech functions as both theme and medium. The "ruminative" tone of the poems makes it easy to "take them to be not really spoken to anyone but as having been produced during 'sessions of sweet silent thought' "

(s. 30). Wright connects this reflective quality, especially strong in the first 126 sonnets, to an emphasis on absence, separation, and silent waiting—themes that distinguish Shakespeare's sonnets from many others. The emergence of an inner voice has important implications for Shakespeare's development as a dramatist and for the development of the later English lyric.

Shakespeare's Poems
Further Reading

Abbreviations: *Venus* = *Venus and Adonis; Pilgrim* = *The Passionate Pilgrim;* "Phoenix" = "The Phoenix and Turtle"

Bashar, Nazife. "Rape in England between 1550 and 1700." In *The Sexual Dynamics of History: Men's Power, Women's Resistance,* edited by London Feminist History Group, pp. 28–42. London: Pluto Press, 1983.

Through a detailed examination of available records, Bashar historicizes rape in England over a period spanning 150 years. Originally understood as the theft of female property belonging to a husband or father, and thus an offense against male ownership, rape was separated from abduction in statutes of 1555 and 1597, when the legal issue slowly and tentatively began to be understood as one of consent. Such statutes notwithstanding, Bashar located only 274 cases of rape in English assize records from the five home counties over the period, and from these there were only 45 guilty verdicts, all of them involving some element of property in the form of virginity. "Whether regarded as a crime against property or a crime against the person, rape was a crime by men against women, and the law as an intrinsic and powerful part of the patriarchy operated for men against women."

Belsey, Catherine. "Love as Trompe-L'Oeil: Taxonomies of Desire in *Venus and Adonis." Shakespeare Quarterly* 46 (1995): 257–76.

Belsey reads *Venus* in light of Jacques Lacan's definition of "trompe-l'oeil" as the promise of a presence that is not delivered. This Lacanian sense of the term as a trick that not only deceives but tantalizes is present in the poem's reference to a painting in which the depiction of grapes is so enticing that birds, deceptively promised oral gratification, find no pleasure for their stomachs (ll. 601–2). Similarly, Venus is drawn to the provocative image of Adonis, whose beauty evokes an unsatisfied longing for his reciprocal desire; holding Adonis in her arms but eliciting no response only intensifies her longing. Because the narrative "prompts in the reader a desire for action that it fails to gratify"—very little actually happens on the level of plot—critics have tried to locate a moral center in Adonis's attempt to distinguish between love and lust (ll. 799–804) that would at least provide meaning on a thematic level. But historically the terms *love* and *lust* were changing in relation to one another, and the poem, especially in its lack of closure, marks this differentiation in the taxonomies of desire as an important "moment in the cultural history of love." *Venus* is itself a literary trompe-l'oeil: "a text of and about desire . . . [that] promises a definitive account of love but at the same time withholds the finality that such a promise might lead us to expect."

Belsey, Catherine. "Tarquin Dispossessed: Expropriation and Consent in *The Rape of Lucrece*." *Shakespeare Quarterly* 52 (2001): 315–35.

Focusing on the instability of the term *rape*, which defines the victim "as at once passive object and resisting subject," Belsey argues that *Lucrece* marks "a moment of early modern cultural redefinition, which is registered in the story of possession and dispossession it recounts." Although the poem does not overtly equivocate in its endorsement of women as property—even at the end, Lucrece's father and husband compete for the right to lament her death based on ownership of her—the tragedy that unfolds depends precisely on "the expropriability of all property." Collatine's treasure is precious precisely because it can be stolen. The poem's image of Tarquin beside himself (ll. 157, 160, 596–97), having lost his faculties and his kingdom in taking possession of Lucrece, underscores the paradox underlying the insecurity of ownership: "the king's son, dissatisfied with what he already possesses, wants what, because it is forbidden, will destroy him and all he possesses." Just as the term *rape* equivocates between the passive and resistant, so does Lucrece's suicide: "the object of violence is simultaneously the subject as agent of her own judicial execution." The effect of the heroine's independently chosen course of action is "a change of regime to one based on consent: *propriety* will no longer be synonymous with *property*." Belsey argues that sexual politics and state politics are interwoven in the poem and finds, in the installation of

the republic resulting from Lucrece's deliberative action, an affir-
mation of a model of state politics that is also based on consent. "If
we read the text as a critique, what it criticizes is a model of both
marriage and government that works to no one's advantage, not the
husband's and not, in the end, the tyrant's."

Berry, Philippa. "Woman, Language, and History in *The Rape of
Lucrece.*" *Shakespeare Survey* 44 (1992): 33–39.
    Berry partially accepts the reading of *Lucrece* as a battle between
men fought over a woman's body (see Kahn and Vickers below), but
she questions the view that Lucrece is never depicted as "posing any
contradiction, any aporia, within patriarchal discourse." Focusing
on the long rhetorical performance from lines 575 to 1722, the author argues that the heroine's private use of a language charged with
"magical, incantatory properties" challenges any interpretation of
Shakespeare's Lucrece as being "simply history's victim"; instead,
she is shown to be an "independent, if somewhat unorthodox (and
confused) historical agent, who uses an Orphic private utterance to
initiate historic change." What comes through her apostrophes to
Night, Time, and Opportunity and her meditation upon a painting
of the fall of Troy is an attempt to replace the loss of a "specifically
feminine 'virtue' with a *virtù*" that can empower her to take control
of her tragic destiny. Berry, however, cautions against overestimat-
ing Lucrece's understanding of her own relationship to language
and history, since her desire for universal justice is at times confus-
edly mingled with concern for her husband's honor, and she herself
underestimates the power of her language of grief to effect historical and political change.

Bowers, A. Robin. "Iconography and Rhetoric in Shakespeare's *Lucrece.*" *Shakespeare Studies* 14 (1981): 1–21.
    In contrast to those who criticize Lucrece for her "typically femi-
nine" rhetorical excesses and what some consider her "moral waywardness," Bowers attempts to show (1) that in keeping with his
literary and artistic contemporaries, Shakespeare develops the legend to demonstrate Lucrece's virtue and (2) that the rhetorical techniques used by both the heroine and narrator consistently
emphasize the violence of rape and Lucrece's resulting mental an-

guish. The aesthetic result of the poem's forensic structure combined with its psychic stress on lamentation is pity for Lucrece's tragic demise, not "scorn for her prolixity or duplicity." Through an "ever-expanding series of debates pitting will against reason, illogic against logic, and despair against hope," *Lucrece* confirms the early modern view of its heroine (found in the poetry and iconography of the time) as an exemplum of chastity, fidelity, and constancy, while at the same time "requiring its readers to tackle the more significant questions of the personal and social implications of rape."

Bromley, Laura G. "Lucrece's Re-Creation." *Shakespeare Quarterly* 34 (1983): 200–211.

For Bromley, Lucrece is not a pawn in the male struggle for possession but a strong woman who directly faces the loss of her personal honor and integrity by declaring "I am the mistress of my fate" (l. 1069). Once the reader accepts as fact what Lucrece and her society, along with Shakespeare and his, accept—namely, that she has indeed been corrupted as a result of Tarquin's violent act—it becomes clear that Lucrece is confronted with a moral dilemma. Underlying the poem is the common Renaissance belief that all things are balanced against their opposites; when Lucrece is raped, she loses her own interior balance. But what the rest of the poem shows are the heroine's attempts to re-create herself in a "wilderness where are no laws" (l. 544). Sensing the past as present in the painting of Troy before her, Lucrece sees herself as part of a historical context and recognizes how "private sin . . . become[s] public plague." Lucrece's suicide—a deliberative act meant to restore order within and outside herself, thus satisfying both personal and societal demands—should be read as "positive, constructive, and self-creative."

Bullough, Geoffrey, ed. *Narrative and Dramatic Sources of Shakespeare*, vol. 1, pp. 161–76 (*Venus*) and 179–99 (*Lucrece*). 1957. Reprint, London: Routledge and Kegan Paul; New York: Columbia University Press, 1975.

Bullough discusses *Venus* and *Lucrece* as companion pieces describing, respectively, "desire unaccomplished against reluctance" and "desire accomplished by force." Ovid was the primary source for both: the *Metamorphoses* as translated by Arthur Golding (1567) for *Venus*, and the *Fasti* for *Lucrece*. Bullough reprints excerpts from Ovid's tales of Venus and Adonis (10.585–651, 826–63), the amorous water nymph Salmacis and the unresponsive Hermaphroditus (4.347–481), and the self-absorbed Narcissus (3.427–542, 635–42). Shakespeare used the hostility of Hermaphroditus and Narcissus to female charms in his discussion of Adonis because the poem "was conceived as a study in the coyness of masculine adolescence [and] the frenzy of female longing." Along with portions of Ovid's *Fasti* in its original Latin (2.721–852), supplemented by a 1640 translation, Bullough includes parts of "The Second Novell" of *The Pallace of Pleasure* by William Painter (1566) as a translation of a definite source, Livy's *Historia* (chapters 57–60), and a portion of *The Legende of Good Women* by Geoffrey Chaucer (ll. 1680–1885) as a probable source. Shakespeare expanded Ovid's brief account of Lucrece "by filling out the outline of the Roman's sophisticated simplicity into long disquisitions on the physical and emotional states of the main figures." The two Ovidian poems, in which Shakespeare "transformed Roman style and matter with . . . rich if tedious eloquence, were not only a springboard to his imagination but gave him topics, myths and allusions" to which he would often return.

Cheney, Patrick. *Shakespeare, National Poet-Playwright.* Cambridge: Cambridge University Press, 2004.

The volume includes separate chapters on *Venus, Lucrece, Pilgrim,* and "Phoenix." (Chapter 7 reprints the essay annotated on p. 649 in the Further Reading section for the *Sonnets.*) Because Shakespeare was known among his contemporaries as both a poet and a man of the theater, it is possible to trace in his work an intertextual line of descent that positions him as the national poet-playwright, successor not only to Marlowe but also to Spenser. In *Venus,* the form of desire depicted by Ovid and Marlowe prevails over Spenserian chastity; *Lucrece* marks a shift from pastoral in the direction of epic, while at the same time calling into question the celebration of empire that marks the epics of Virgil and Spenser. These two poems—but *Lucrece* more so—are "imbued with the discourse of both the theatre and the print shop," and both concern the issue of authorship itself. The poems, a corpus in their own right, together with the plays that they complement, "record a sustained conversation not merely on theatre but also on the art of poetry. . . . By listening in on this conversation, we can become attuned to a particular Shakespearean language of authorship that we might not have known existed."

Donaldson, Ian. "'A Theme for Disputation': Shakespeare's *Lucrece.*" In *The Rapes of Lucretia: A Myth and Its Transformations,* pp. 40–56. Oxford: Clarendon Press, 1982.

In this book-length study of the story of the rape of Lucretia from Ovid to Giraudoux, Donaldson devotes the third chapter to Shakespeare's poem, which he finds, despite "many local subtleties and felicities," ultimately incoherent as it wavers between the conflicting ethics of ancient Rome and those of Christianity in addressing the dilemma of a "dishonored" woman. For all the psychological insight Shakespeare introduces into the story—no other version is more attentive to the mental processes of the two central characters—one is left with the sense that moral issues are "talked around, but seldom through." Whereas in Ovid and Livy there is a stress on the superiority of deeds to words, in Shakespeare Tarquin's decision to rape Lucrece and her decision to kill herself are logically and morally indefensible because they seem to be undertaken only to end the interminable process of debate. In the end, disputations are neither concluded nor finely poised in their inconclusiveness. Atypically, Shakespeare "does not take moral repossession of the older story, confidently charging it with new depth and intricacy."

Dubrow, Heather. *Shakespeare and Domestic Loss: Forms of Deprivation, Mourning, and Recuperation.* Cambridge: Cambridge University Press, 1999.

This reexamination of several of Shakespeare's texts, including *Lucrece* (pp. 45–61), centers on their engagement with forms of deprivation that threatened domestic security in early modern England: namely, the loss of goods through burglary, the loss of one's dwelling place, and the loss of parents when a child is still relatively young. Loss pervades *Lucrece* in that the heroine loses her chastity and her life; Tarquin, his integrity; and Collatine and Lucretius, their wife and daughter, respectively. But it is the losses resulting from burglary that are the most significant. In making this claim, Dubrow intends not to minimize Lucrece's suffering but rather to put the rape in a new perspective that illuminates "the assignment of guilt and responsibility[,] . . . a problem with many implications for the workings of male subjectivity and other questions about gender." Dubrow's focus leads her to conclude that Shakespeare's poem emphasizes not only the wife's duty to protect the threatened dwelling place but also her incapacity to do so under some circumstances; significantly, it holds Collatine culpable for failing to guard and protect the home and all it holds. The figurative language in lines 834–40 and 848–49 presents "the nexus of intrusion, robbery, and contamination that recurs in the actual rape."

Dubrow, Heather. " 'Upon Misprision Growing': *Venus and Adonis*" and " 'Full of Forged Lies': *The Rape of Lucrece.*" In *Captive Victors: Shakespeare's Narrative Poems and Sonnets*, pp. 21–79, 80–168. Ithaca: Cornell University Press, 1987.

In the first two chapters of this study, the author focuses on *Venus* and *Lucrece*, poems that are often misread and more often left unread, largely because of their elaborate rhetorical ornamentation, often seen as an impediment to characterization. The author admits that not all of the poems' rhetorical devices are skillfully used and that Shakespeare does not, as he does elsewhere in the canon, vary meter to show nuances of emotion and personality. Nevertheless, she contends that it is precisely through the extensive use of rhetorical figures that Shakespeare "unlocks, anatomizes, and variously condemns and admires the hearts of his protagonists," producing in the poems a "subtle exploration of human emotion, a coherent analysis of human character." Following Fineman (see below), Dubrow explores how *Lucrece*, a poem about rape, is fittingly structured around synœciosis (the conjoining of contraries to form an expanded oxymoron), a figure "grounded in conflict and contradiction" and hence evocative of tension. In *Venus*, the author focuses on the goddess's "predilection for conditionals," which reflects the other ways "she attempts to reshape and manipulate experience." Dubrow advocates reading the two narrative poems in connection with the *Sonnets* (the subject of her final chapter titled "Conceit Deceitful"), because all three works are deeply concerned with character and the ways in which people respond to flux. In raising similar questions about love, power, powerlessness, and the use and abuse of language, *Venus, Lucrece,* and the *Sonnets* reveal "the multiple and indissoluble links between the art of rhetoric and the art of living." In none of them do rhetorical figures "upstage human ones."

Ellrodt, Robert. "An Anatomy of *The Phoenix and the Turtle." Shakespeare Survey* 15 (1962): 99–110.

In order to demonstrate Shakespeare's original treatment of the phoenix theme, Ellrodt examines the poem's symbolism and philosophical assumptions in light of both earlier critical interpretations and Renaissance adaptations of the phoenix myth from Petrarch to Donne. Shakespeare's originality lies in focusing attention on the birds not as individuals but as universals, their union (in contrast to Donne) being solely spiritual; using imprecision and ambiguity to underscore a sense of mystery; and withholding any assurance or even hint of survival in a world beyond, for nothing is born of Shakespeare's mutual flame. In fact, the lyric's painful sense that "Truth may seem, but cannot be" for "Love and constancy is dead" (ll. 62, 22) is strikingly similar to the mood of *Hamlet.* What the poem celebrates is not true lovers and beautiful creatures but the abstractions "Love and Constancy, Truth and Beauty, straining after the highest intensity," in which lies the perfection of all art.

Empson, William. "The Phoenix and the Turtle." *Essays in Criticism* 16 (1966): 147–53.

Calling the poem "exquisite but baffling," Empson touches on biographical matters surrounding the two men most concerned with *Love's Martyr,* the book in which Shakespeare's poem appears: Sir John Salusbury, whose knighthood *Love's Martyr* celebrates, and Robert Chester, the main contributor to the volume. Empson argues for an earlier compositional date than 1601, the date of publication. In contrast to Ellrodt (see above), Empson proposes 1598 or early 1599, which would place the poem's genesis around the time of *Henry V* rather than *Hamlet.* Reading "Phoenix," Shakespeare's "only consistent use of the Metaphysical style," in the context of the other contributions sheds light on his puzzling praise of the mythical bird for extinguishing its breed through "married chastity," the theme of the entire volume.

Enterline, Lynn. " 'Poor Instruments' and Unspeakable Events in the *Rape of Lucrece.*" In *The Rhetoric of the Body from Ovid to Shakespeare*, pp. 152–98. Cambridge: Cambridge University Press, 2000.

Enterline's examination of the complex, often violent, connections between body and voice in narrative, lyric, and dramatic works by Ovid, Petrarch, Marston, and Shakespeare focuses on the trope of the female voice in Ovid's *Metamorphoses* and on early modern attempts to "ventriloquize" women's voices that are indebted to Ovid. In the chapter on *Lucrece*, she connects "the problems haunting Lucrece's voice with the poem's representation of authorship" and claims that in order to examine the consequences of Petrarchan rhetoric, Shakespeare "stages a return to Ovid's text that differs profoundly" from Marston's *Metamorphosis of Pigmalions Image*, which is discussed in an earlier chapter, and even from the Lucrece story as found in Ovid's *Fasti.* Unlike Marston's mute statue, not only does Lucrece cry out at length before and after Tarquin's crime, but she does so in a number of Ovidian voices, including those of Orpheus, Philomela, and Hecuba. It was as if Shakespeare did not find Ovid's Lucrece Ovidian enough and rewrote her voice "in the vein of the poet." Using Shakespeare's language of musical instruments and of the borrowed tongue, Enterline analyzes the unraveling of voice, authorial agency, and gender "identity" in the poem's various Ovidian figures. While the narrative may produce a sense that we know what we mean by the words *man/woman, male voice/female voice,* and *male desire/female desire,* its "figural language of imitation and ventriloquism continue to disturb that seemingly self-evident knowledge."

Fineman, Joel. "Shakespeare's Will: The Temporality of Rape." *Representations,* no. 20 (Fall 1987): 25–76. Reprinted in *The Subjectivity Effect in Western Literary Tradition: Essays toward the Release of Shakespeare's Will,* pp. 165–221. Cambridge, Mass.: MIT Press, 1991.

Fineman gives *Lucrece* an extremely close and detailed reading that takes as its springboard the poem's dedication to Southampton in which Shakespeare writes, "The love I dedicate to your Lordship is without end; whereof this pamphlet without beginning is but a superfluous moiety." The poem, starting *in medias res,* may be said to be "without beginning"; and the systematic completeness between the extremes of "without beginning" and "without end" hints at the rhetorical device around which the poem is structured and which the author explores in terms of erotic movements of crossing and folding: synœciosis (the union of contraries to form a paradoxical truth), first glimpsed in line 8 ("Haply that name of 'chaste' unhapp'ly set"). The image of a liquid portion overflowing—the meaning of *superfluity*—"is quite central to [*Lucrece*], figuring not only the rape but also its motivation and consequences." As he does elsewhere, Fineman probes the interaction between the "contingent personality" of Shakespeare and the literary phenomenon of "Shakespearean characterology"—i.e., the relation between "the personal and the . . . person who creates literary personae." By making "such a vivid issue of the relation between "Will" and "writing," *Lucrece* "provides a clear-cut illustration of the way the impression of psychologistic person in Shakespeare's texts characteristically effects and is effected by the mark of Shakespeare's person." For an annotation of the author's related study of the *Sonnets,* see p. 651 in the present volume.

Kahn, Coppélia. *"Lucrece:* The Sexual Politics of Subjectivity." In *Rape and Representation,* edited by Lynn A. Higgins and Brenda R. Silver, pp. 141–59. New York: Columbia University Press, 1991. (Incorporated in Kahn's *Roman Shakespeare: Warriors, Wounds, and Women* [London: Routledge, 1997], pp. 27–45.)

Kahn considers "the representation of male and female subjectivities within a feminist problematic of rape, by looking closely at the language of power and the power of language" found in the discourse of Lucrece and Tarquin. While his rape of Lucrece violates Roman law, Tarquin's shaking his sword at her is "congruent with the Roman martial ethos." The brutality of his stifling of Lucrece's cries during the attack notwithstanding, that act itself reinforces the dominant tendency of a patriarchal culture in concealing, sealing off, and muffling women's speech. Lucrece's resistance— couched in appeals to religion, social hierarchy, male friendship, marriage, and the law—in effect cancels itself out, "because it is inscribed within the same structures of power as the rape is." Kahn concedes that rape gives Lucrece a voice, but it is the voice of a victim. Even her suicide, in which she uses the same blade that Tarquin had used against her, sanctions the militaristic ethos and male rivalry that led to the rape in the first place. Like the story upon which it is based, "one of the founding myths of patriarchy," the poem is thoroughly and relentlessly grounded in a "stridently patriarchal ideology": Shakespeare pities Lucrece for her "feminine weakness" and praises her for her "quasi-masculine" strength in dying like a Roman. Referring to her earlier essay (annotated below) in which she cited three stanzas of authorial comment in the narrator's voice as evincing "Shakespeare's sensitive understanding of the social constraints that force Lucrece into a tragic role" (ll. 1240–60), Kahn now claims that Shakespeare's understanding of such constraints is itself "constrained by the basic assumption underlying the entire passage: that women are 'naturally' the weaker of the species." For Kahn's subsequent refinement of her position on Lucrece's agency, see her "Publishing Shame: *The Rape of Lucrece*" in *A Companion to Shakespeare's Works*, vol. 4, edited by Richard Dutton and Jean E. Howard (Oxford: Basil Blackwell, 2003), pp. 259–74.

Kahn, Coppélia. "The Rape in Shakespeare's *Lucrece*." *Shakespeare Studies* 9 (1976): 45–72.

In this foundational feminist reading of the poem as a competition between two men for possession of a woman—and hence insistently concerned with the relationship between sex and power—Kahn contends that *Lucrece* "must be understood in a psycho-social context which takes account of sex roles and cultural attitudes toward sexuality." Observing that Shakespeare found in his Latin sources a story that mirrored the patriarchal system in England, Kahn locates the poem's central metaphor in the stain repeatedly attached to Lucrece, the "perfect patriarchal woman," with no sense of herself as an independent moral being apart from her role in marriage. Because the assumption of marital guardianship of a woman made her chastity a component of her husband's honor, Lucrece judges herself guilty of a crime against Collatine. Deprived of being a truly chaste wife to him, her raison d'être, and seeing herself as a paradigm of female chastity for all ages, Lucrece can regain her social and personal identity as a chaste wife only by dying, a sacrifice that, on a larger scale, ensures the survival of marriage as the strongest bulwark against lust. Shakespeare's sensitive understanding of the social constraints that force Lucrece into this tragic role is made explicit in three stanzas of narrative comment (ll. 1240–60). In conformity with the dictates of patriarchal ideology, Lucrece suffers for a crime she did not commit.

Kolin, Philip C., ed. *Venus and Adonis: Critical Essays*. New York: Garland, 1997.

This collection gathers together a great deal of material spanning the years 1774–1997. Along with an extract from Dubrow's *Captive Victors* and Belsey's full essay (both annotated above), Kolin excerpts chapters from Douglas Bush's *Mythology and the Renaissance Tradition in English Poetry* (rev. ed., 1963) and S. Clark Hulse's *Metamorphic Verse: The Elizabethan Minor Epic* (1981). Other reprinted pieces include commentaries by Gervinus, Coleridge, and Sidney Lee; Rufus Putney, "Venus Agonistes" (1953); A. C. Hamilton, "Venus and Adonis" (1961); Christopher Butler and Alastair Fowler, "Time-Beguiling Sport: Number Symbolism in Shakespeare's *Venus and Adonis*" (1964); Coppélia Kahn, "Self and Eros in *Venus and Adonis*" (1976); W. R. Streitberger, "Ideal Conduct in *Venus and Adonis*" (1978); and Nona Fienberg, "Thematics of Value in *Venus and Adonis*" (1989). The volume also contains eight new essays: João Froes, "Shakespeare's Venus and the Venus of Classical Mythology"; Patrick Murphy, "Wriothesley's Resistance: Wardship Practices and Ovidian Narrative in Shakespeare's *Venus and Adonis*"; M. L. Stapleton, "Venus as Praeceptor: The *Ars Amatoria* in *Venus and Adonis*"; Richard Halpern, " 'Pining their maws': Female Readers and the Erotic Ontology of the Text in Shakespeare's *Venus and Adonis*"; Robert P. Merrix, " 'Lo, in this hollow cradle take thy rest': Sexual Conflict and Resolution in *Venus and Adonis*"; James Schiffer, "Shakespeare's *Venus and Adonis*: A Lacanian Tragicomedy of Desire"; Joseph Wortis, "*Venus and Adonis*: An Early Account of Sexual Harassment"; and Georgianna Ziegler, "Picturing Venus and Adonis: Shakespeare and the Artists." Kolin's introduction provides an overview of criticism and theatrical reception; reviews of the poem in performance round out the volume.

Lindheim, Nancy. "The Shakespearean *Venus and Adonis.*" *Shakespeare Quarterly* 37 (1986): 190–203.

While not a great poem, *Venus* is still fully Shakespearean and merits attention as a pivotal work in the poet-playwright's technical and intellectual development. An Elizabethan Ovidian poem that would take into account love's darker side, salacious wit, and possibility of pain required of the poet new techniques involving shifts of tone, perspective, and sympathy. The first part of the essay emphasizes Shakespeare's conceptual maturity in describing love's emotional complexity, most obvious in the depiction of Venus not as "Love" in the abstract but "in the contradictory way [love] is experienced," i.e., as both comic and pathetic; the second part focuses on technique, the author singling out the mastery of tonal shift that occurs with Adonis's death. In a way not apparent in the stage works preceding *Venus,* Shakespeare deftly "integrates comedy with tragedy, parody with straight representation, all the while manipulating our response to Venus so that by the time she comes to fear and then know Adonis's death, Shakespeare has moved us from ridicule to sympathy." The paradox at the heart of *Venus* inheres in its being "a comic poem with a tragic action."

Orgel, Stephen, and Sean Keilen, eds. *Shakespeare's Poems.* Shakespeare: The Critical Complex Series. New York: Garland, 1999.

In addition to Colin Burrow's introduction titled "Life and Work in Shakespeare's Poems" and eleven essays on the *Sonnets,* this anthology includes six previously published studies of *Venus* and *Lucrece:* William Empson, "The Narrative Poems" (1966); Catherine Belsey, "Love as Trompe-L'Oeil: Taxonomies of Desire in *Venus and Adonis*" (1995), annotated above; Katharine Eisaman Maus, "Taking Tropes Seriously: Language and Violence in Shakespeare's *Rape of Lucrece*" (1986); Jane O. Newman, " 'And Let Mild Women to Him Lose Their Mildness': Philomela, Female Violence, and Shakespeare's *Rape of Lucrece*" (1994); Richard A. Lanham, "The Politics of *Lucrece*" (1980); and Nancy Vickers, "This Heraldry in Lucrece'

Face" (1985)—an essay different from though related to that annotated below. Among the items dealing with the *Sonnets* are those by
de Grazia, Dubrow, Fineman, and Stallybrass annotated in the separate Further Reading section on the *Sonnets* (see p. 649). Taken as
a whole, the essays in the Orgel–Keilen collection present Shakespeare's poetry as "the work of a poet fully conversant with the lyric
and epic tradition, and one with a unique lyric and narrative sensibility." The poems should not be considered "adjunct" to the plays.

Vickers, Nancy. " 'The Blazon of Sweet Beauty's Best': Shakespeare's
Lucrece." In *Shakespeare and the Question of Theory,* edited by Patri-
cia Parker and Geoffrey H. Hartman, pp. 95–115. London: Methuen,
1985.

    In this influential feminist essay on *Lucrece,* Vickers merges the
two traditions of the blazon—the conventional heraldic description
of a shield and the conventional poetic description of an object
praised or blamed by a rhetorician-poet—to explore the limits and
insufficiencies of a descriptive rhetoric that, especially when used
by a man in praising a woman, reduces her to an exquisite but
"troubling . . . totality [of] . . . fragmentary and reified parts." She
argues that in *Lucrece,* "occasion, rhetoric, and result are all in-
formed by, and thus inscribe, a battle between men that is first figuratively and then literally fought on the fields of woman's
'celebrated' body." Metaphors commonly read as signifying heterosexual battle emerge here from a male rivalry that positions "a third
(female) term in a median space from which it is initially used and
finally eliminated." Although the narrative begins and ends with
two men competing over a displayed Lucrece, Vickers focuses on
the first part of the poem, where Collatine's lavish description of his
wife's beauty (implicitly self-praise in owning such a creature) sets
in motion the rape by Tarquin. Reading Lucrece in terms of the blazon not only reveals the rhetorical strategies generated by descriptive occasions but also "underlines the potential consequences of
being female matter for male oratory." Rape is the price Lucrece
must pay for having her beauty blazoned.

Shakespeare's Sonnets
Index of First Lines

Index of Illustrations

677